THE ENTREPRENEURIAL CITY

GEOGRAPHIES OF POLITICS, REGIME AND REPRESENTATION

Edited by

TIM HALL

*Cheltenham and Gloucester College
of Higher Education*

PHIL HUBBARD

University of Coventry

JOHN WILEY & SONS

CHICHESTER • NEW YORK • WEINHEIM • BRISBANE • SINGAPORE • TORONTO

Other Wiley Editorial Offices

John Wiley & Sons, Inc., 605 Third Avenue,
New York, NY 10158-0012, USA

WILEY-VCH Verlag GmbH, Pappelallee 3,
D-69469 Weinheim, Germany

Jacaranda Wiley Ltd, 33 Park Road, Milton,
Queensland 4064, Australia

John Wiley & Sons (Asia) Pte Ltd, 2 Clementi Loop #02-01,
Jin Xing Distripark, Singapore 129809

John Wiley & Sons (Canada) Ltd, 22 Worcester Road,
Rexdale, Ontario M9W 1L1, Canada

British Library Cataloguing in Publication Data

A catalogue record for this book is available from the British Library

ISBN 0-471-97707-1

Typeset in 10/12pt Garamond from authors' disks
by Mayhew Typesetting, Rhayader, Powys
Printed and bound in Great Britain by Biddles Ltd, Guildford and King's Lynn

This book is printed on acid-free paper responsibly manufactured from sustainable forestry,
for which at least two trees are planted for each one used for paper production.

THE
ENTREPRENEURIAL
CITY

CONTENTS

1 The Entrepreneurial City and the 'New Urban Politics'   1
  Phil Hubbard and Tim Hall

   PART I   SELLING THE ENTREPRENEURIAL CITY

   Introduction   27
   Tim Hall

2 Place Marketing: A Historical Comparison of Britain and North
  America   31
  Stephen V. Ward

3 Urban Crises/Urban Representations: Selling the City in Difficult
  Times   55
  John Rennie Short and Yeong-Hyun Kim

4 The Narrative of Enterprise and the Enterprise of Narrative: Place
  Marketing and the Entrepreneurial City   77
  Bob Jessop

   PART II   ENTREPRENEURIAL GOVERNANCE, POLICY AND PRACTICE

   Introduction   103
   Tim Hall

5 On Losing the Local in Responding to Urban Decline: The
  Honeysuckle Redevelopment, New South Wales   107
  Pauline M. McGuirk, Hilary P.M. Winchester and Kevin M. Dunn

6 Pro-growth Local Economic Development Strategies: Civic Promotion
  and Local Needs in Britain's Second City, 1981–1996   129
  Patrick Loftman and Brendan Nevin

7 Suburban Entrepreneurialism: Redevelopment Regimes and Co-
  ordinating Metropolitan Development in Southern California   149
  Amer Althubaity and Andrew E.G. Jonas

8   From Socialism to Post-Fordism: The Local State and Economic
    Policies in Eastern Germany   173
    Tassilo Herrschel

        PART III   REPRESENTATION, CULTURE AND IDENTITIES

    Introduction   199
    Phil Hubbard

9   A Game of Appearance: Public Art and Urban Development –
    Complicity or Sustainability?   203
    Malcolm Miles

10 Popular Culture, Cultural Intermediaries and Urban Regeneration 225
    Justin O'Connor

11 Writing the New Barcelona   241
    Donald McNeill

        PART IV   POLITICS, REGIMES AND REGULATION

    Introduction   255
    Phil Hubbard

12 Entrepreneurs are Made, Not Born: Learning and Urban Regimes in
    the Production of Entrepreneurial Cities   259
    Joe Painter

13 Questions of Scale in the Entrepreneurial City   275
    Andrew Wood

14 Economic Uncertainty, Inter-Urban Competition and the Efficacy of
    Entrepreneurialism   285
    Helga Leitner and Eric Sheppard

15 Afterword: Mappings of the Entrepreneurial City   309
    Tim Hall and Phil Hubbard

List of Contributors   321
List of Figures   323
List of Tables   324
Acknowledgements   325
Bibliography   327
Index   363

1

THE ENTREPRENEURIAL CITY AND THE 'NEW URBAN POLITICS'

PHIL HUBBARD AND TIM HALL

INTRODUCTION: NEW TYPES OF CITIES?

During the 1980s and 1990s a number of writers have been sketching the contours of a new kind of Western city. This post-industrial, post-modern metropolis is depicted as being dramatically different from its predecessor, with its revitalised city centre of gleaming offices, high-tech transport nodes and secure, privatised shopping malls surrounded by a veritable archipelago of élite enclaves, fragmented neighbourhoods and 'edge' cities (Soja, 1989; Knox, 1991; Zukin, 1991). Neat models of urban structure, many of which could be traced back to the pioneering work of the Chicago school of the 1930s, have thus come to appear as increasingly anachronistic within this seemingly ageographic city as spectacular new urban forms – out-of-town retail parks, waterfront developments, heritage centres and so on – change the nature of urban spatiality. But beneath the glitz and glitter, many of these very same writers are seeking to draw attention to the fact that the city is increasingly carceral, dividing and separating populations like never before along class, race and sexual lines. The leitmotif of a polarised city is therefore inevitably employed to describe a situation whereby new gentrified spaces are found only a few hundred metres from some of the most deprived areas of inner-city decay, characterised by chronic dependency, poverty and frequent social unrest. It is thus the contradictory nature of these emerging city forms that provides much of the fascination for urban theorists; never before has the city attracted and repelled in such obvious ways, as a futuristic vision of a visually enticing city of dreams becomes entwined with a post-apocalyptic scenario of urban unrest, deprivation and despair.

In parallel with the appreciation that the contemporary Western city looks and feels different from its predecessors, urban theorists and researchers are concurrently seeking to draw attention to the fact that these changes are being accompanied by shifts in the ways in which cities are being run. In this sense, it has frequently been asserted that Western cities are now being managed, organised and governed in different ways, leading some to proclaim the emergence of a 'new urban politics' (Cox and Mair, 1988; Kirlin and Marshall, 1988). In essence, it appears that this new urban politics is distinguished from the 'old' by virtue of the ways in which the policies pursued by local governments are being steered away from the traditional activities associated with the city state. This reorientation of urban government is characterised by a shift from the local provision of welfare and services to more outward-orientated policies designed to foster and encourage local growth and economic development. Furthermore, these policies are supported and financed by a diverse array of new agencies and institutions, as public agencies struggle to promote economic growth at the local level on their own terms. Such co-operation with the private sector has seen local government imbued with characteristics once distinctive to businesses – risk-taking, inventiveness, promotion and profit motivation – leading many commentators to refer to the emergence of *entrepreneurial* cities (Mollenkopf, 1983; Judd and Ready, 1986; Gottdiener, 1987; Harvey, 1989b).

The notion of entrepreneurialism, which evocatively captures the sense in which cities are being run in a more businesslike manner, is now a widely cited concept, regularly employed in the rhetoric of local politicians and public administrators who increasingly posit the adoption of an entrepreneurial stance as the key to creating conditions conducive to capital accumulation within a city's boundaries. Such discourses of entrepreneurship thus argue that the only way that cities can compete in an increasingly unpredictable and globalised economy is by pursuing specific proactive strategies designed to secure competitive advantages over their perceived competitors, stressing that:

> If key local economic and political actors . . . can get their acts together . . . and if urban management focuses on economic regeneration rather than on the 'welfare' issues that have unfortunately preoccupied policy makers in recent decades, a new era of urban economic development may be anticipated (Lovering, 1995, 110).

Jessop (1996) thus suggests that entrepreneurial governance has become the dominant response to urban problems because of the very popularity and plausibility of this discourse, which appears particularly attractive to those cities caught in a seeming downward spiral of deindustrialisation and decline. Hence the notion of entrepreneurialism permeates the flood of glossy pamphlets and literature extolling the virtues of Western cities as they seek to convince others (as well as themselves) that they are major players in the entrepreneurial game.

Similarly, the notion of urban entrepreneurialism currently enjoys wide currency among academics, especially in urban geography, where the examination of urban politics and local socialisation forms a logical outgrowth of the localities studies which came to prominence in the 1980s (e.g. Cooke, 1989). Abundant interest in the emergence of entrepreneurial forms of urban politics has been displayed by planners, sociologists and cultural theorists, particularly as the reassertion of space in social theory has heightened awareness of the ways in which locality-specific factors mediate more general processes of economic and social change (Soja, 1989). Surprisingly though, there are fewer contributions to the debates surrounding urban entrepreneurialism by political scientists than the casual observer would initially suppose, with Hoggart (1991) suggesting that the examination of local governance has always occupied a rather subordinate position within political science. None the less, the breadth of interest in urban entrepreneurialism is considerable, and has resulted in much healthy cross-fertilisation of ideas and concepts across both national and disciplinary divides. There is of course a danger here in that the notion of entrepreneurialism is used in a number of different and potentially conflicting manners by different individuals and groups, becoming a classic example of what Sayer (1992) has described as a 'chaotic concept', an abstraction that ultimately obscures more than it reveals. Clearly, the notion of entrepreneurialism is of little use as a theoretical, conceptual or pedagogical tool if we are unable to define with any meaningful precision exactly what we are talking about.

This book is therefore an attempt to draw together some of the burgeoning cross-disciplinary literature on urban entrepreneurialism in an attempt to provide an introduction to the central debates surrounding the entrepreneurial city, mapping the myriad ways in which new modes of governance are implicated in the economic, social and cultural transformation of Western cities. That such a synthesis has, to date, not really been attempted indicates that much of the writing on new forms of urban politics rests on theoretically and conceptually impoverished grounds. What is lacking is any consensual understanding of how entrepreneurialism differs from previous forms of urban governance and local growth alliance or how it relates to the broader dynamics of advanced capitalism. Yet there is clearly no shortage of studies charting the emergence of entrepreneurial cities throughout the Western world, documenting the uptake of so-called entrepreneurial policies and the agencies and institutions that have implemented them. Indeed, for those wishing to assemble 'facts and figures' about the different forms of city governance and associated urban policies emerging across a variety of Western nations, there are a wealth of texts available (e.g. Judd and Parkinson, 1990a; Goetz and Clarke, 1993; Rothblatt and Sancton, 1993). Similarly, there are numerous comparative texts which examine the inter-city variations in political culture and forms of governance within specific nations (e.g. in a British context, see Cooke, 1989, Imrie and Thomas, 1993a and Bailey, Barker and McDonald, 1995). Yet other texts have provided richly detailed accounts of the transformation of specific cities, and although these have not always contextualised their empirical observations in terms of debates about the nature of urban governance, the interested reader will find much of value in the numerous monographs on prototypical entrepreneurial cities such as Atlanta (e.g. Stone, 1989; Rutheiser, 1996), Los Angeles (Soja, 1989; Davis,

1990), New York (Zukin, 1982; Mollenkopf and Castells, 1991) and London (Fainstein, 1994).

Therefore, rather than attempting to develop an exhaustive overview or typology of different forms of entrepreneurial policy, this volume sets out to achieve what initially appears a more modest task; to provide an introduction to the debates surrounding entrepreneurial governance. In the remainder of this chapter, an attempt will be made to provide an overview of some of these issues in an attempt to clarify what is meant by urban entrepreneurialism. In doing so, it will be stressed that the debates on the nature of the entre-preneurial city raise questions which are of a more general importance for researchers of urban and regional studies, touching as they do on central geographical themes of scale, territory, community and identity. Conversely, it will be acknowledged that many writers on entrepreneurialism remain blissfully ignorant of such debates, with much of the writing on the entre-preneurial city, despite its avowed sophistication, exhibiting crucial silences, potentially glossing over some fundamental questions about the ways in which culture and capital are intimately intermeshed in new forms of urban spatiality. These are omissions that hopefully the contributions to this book may go some way to redressing, though clearly, it will become apparent that there are a number of fundamental questions that still remain unanswered.

CHANGING URBAN POLITICS, CHANGING URBAN POLICIES: THE CITY AS ENTREPRENEURIAL

While there are some major differences in the interpretations which leading authors make of the emergence of new forms of urban governance, there appears to be a broad agreement that urban entrepreneurialism is essentially characterised by the proactive promotion of local economic development by local government in alliance with other private sector agencies:

> The new entrepreneurialism has as its centrepiece the notion of public–private partnership in which a traditional local boosterism is integrated with the use of local governmental powers to try and attract external sources of funding, new direct investments or new employment sources (Harvey, 1989b: 7).

Therefore, it seems that urban entrepreneurialism can be defined through two basic characteristics; firstly, a political prioritisation of pro-growth local econ-omic development and, secondly, an associated organisational and institutional shift from urban government to urban *governance*. It is worth examining each of these characteristics in further detail, to consider why writers on the contemporary Western city have sought to distinguish contemporary forms of urban politics from their predecessors.

Urban politics and the promotion of pro-growth local
economic development

The majority of accounts of urban entrepreneurialism begin by drawing attention to the increased involvement of the local state in the proactive encouragement of economic development. In this sense, entrepreneurialism has been described as distinctive political *culture* primarily concerned with improving the prosperity of the city and its ability to create jobs and investment (Graham, 1995). The objectives of entrepreneurial policies are thus described as inherently growth-oriented: creating jobs, expanding the local tax base, fostering small firm growth and (crucially) attracting new forms of investment. While the latter goal of attracting new forms of business is seen as of fundamental importance, improving the local embeddedness of existing firms may also be a key intention of entrepreneurial governance. This does not imply that local ownership of firms is crucial, or that the promotion of small businesses is a necessary step to improving local economic control, but that firms which foster strong links with specific cities can play a key role in local socialisation processes. The aim of such policies is thus to promote the comparative advantages of the city relative to other cities which may be competing for similar forms of investment.

This notion of urban entrepreneurialism as being a new kind of local economic policy is at the heart of the new urban politics, and it is in this manner that it is most frequently understood by local politicians and policy-makers. The metaphor of the city as a 'growth machine' (Logan and Molotch, 1987), marshalling its resources in the pursuit of economic growth, has thus been utilised by many commentators seeking to document the way in which the local state has undergone a conceptual reorientation as it strives to promote capital accumulation within its boundaries. This reorientation of the local state, and the adoption of pro-growth policies, was initially noted in the previously affluent industrial cities of mature Western developed nations where 'Rust Belt' industries such as steel, vehicle manufacturing, textiles and chemicals rationalised in the face of foreign competition and new corporate strategies following the oil-based recession of the mid-1970s. Consequently, the cities of Glasgow, Liverpool, Cleveland, Detroit, Milan and Marseilles have frequently been cited as the archetypal entrepreneurial cities (Peterson, 1981; Hall, 1988; Vicari and Molotch, 1990). Given the widespread disinvestment that occurred in these cities, it is commonly argued that their elected governors were left with little choice but to compete for investment in an attempt to reverse their economic fortunes. Subsequently, however, it has been possible to discern the adoption of entrepreneurial strategies among more buoyant cities which possess a high proportion of their workforce in propulsive sectors of the economy – for example, craft industries, high-technology industries, offices and financial services. Hence 'Sunbelt cities' such as Montpellier or Seville, as well as more affluent towns in the south-west of England (Bristol,

Swindon and Cheltenham), have embarked on specific policies designed to promote particular forms of local economic development (DiGaetano and Klemanski, 1993; Bassett, 1996). Even the most successful 'world cities' (e.g. London, Tokyo, New York) appear to have adopted facets of entrepreneurial policy, promoting their status as the command centres of the global economy through a combination of environmental enhancement, property development and cultural boosterism (Brownill, 1993; Fainstein, 1994; Markusen and Gwiasda, 1994).

The current ubiquity of such entrepreneurial policies throughout the advanced capitalist world is now indisputable, and it is possible to conclude that an entrepreneurial attitude has infiltrated even the most recalcitrant and 'conservative' urban regions. According to Eisenschitz and Gough (1993), what appears to have been crucial in encouraging this proliferation of entrepreneurial policies is that they apparently offer something for all local governments, irrespective of political ideology. To the left, the entrepreneurial approach promises a way of asserting local co-operation, promoting the identity of place and strengthening municipal pride; for the right, it can be seen to support ideas of neo-liberalism, promotion of enterprise and belief in the virtues of the private sector. In either case, the promise of improvements in overall social welfare by bringing the local population into sync with the demands of a globalised capitalist economy has been a crucial impetus to the adoption of entrepreneurial governance (Jessop, 1996). Although the term is much misused, and often crudely interpreted, there is no doubt that the concept of globalisation, together with an associated rhetoric of 'think global, act local', has played a major role in promoting an entrepreneurial attitude among city governors. In short, the idea of the internationalisation of economic activity, the increased geographical mobility of production and investment, and the rising power of transnational corporations appears to have instilled an edgy insecurity at all levels of the urban hierarchy, with urban governors and representatives feeling obliged to adopt suitable policies to attract capital investment given their perception of an increasingly competitive global economy.

Although there may be some crucial differences between cities in terms of the pro-growth economic development strategies they adopt, there are often remarkable similarities in the key elements of such policies, leading many to talk of a 'generic' entrepreneurial model of governance reliant on specific boosterist policies. Centrally, it is apparent that most city governments are allocating increasingly high budgets for the advertising and promotion of the city as a favourable environment for business and leisure as 'market-place' politics become predominant (Savitch and Kantor, 1995). Almost every city now has its requisite series of promotional pamphlets, posters and other cultural products communicating selective images of the city as an attractive, hospitable and vibrant *international* city in which to live and work (Barke and Harrop, 1994). What is also increasingly evident is that this marketing of place seldom restricts itself to extolling the existing virtues of the city, but seeks to redefine and reimage the city, weaving specific place 'myths' designed to erase the negative iconography of dereliction, decline and labour militancy associated with the industrial city (see Watson, 1991; Barke and Harrop, 1994; Dunn, McGuirk and Winchester, 1995; Short and Kim, Chapter 3 this volume). This conscious manipulation and promotion of city imagery, evocatively termed 'imagineering' by the pioneers of the Disney theme parks, has been subject to considerable cynicism from academics who point out the ways in which city identities are sanitised, commodified and distorted in accordance with the perceived demands of the global market-place (see especially Kearns and Philo, 1993; Gold and Ward, 1994).

Changing the image of a locality is thus seen as a central component of entrepreneurial governance, and, as such, it is perhaps best to consider the entrepreneurial city as an imaginary city, constituted through a plethora of images and representations. Indeed, given the pervasive nature of place marketing, it might be argued that it no longer makes much sense to distinguish between the 'myths' and 'realities' of the city, as the images of the city incorporated in the promotional brochures, adverts, guidebooks and videos come to define the essence of the city as much as the city itself. None the less, in the midst of the 1980s property boom, the large-scale physical redevelopment of the city itself took centre stage in this process of enhancing the city's image (Graham, 1995; Hubbard, 1995). In their desire to stress their internationality, no aspiring entrepreneurial city was seen as complete without its requisite designer spaces and scenographic enclaves (Crilley, 1993b). This has been particularly evident in the construction of numerous prestige developments, variously described as 'flagships' or 'megaprojects', which have aimed to emulate the perceived success of the rejuvenation of Baltimore's inner harbour in the 1960s (Bianchini, Dawson and Evans, 1992; Berry and Huxley, 1992; Olds, 1995). Heavily promoted as part of the boosterist politics pursued in Baltimore, these designer spaces became enshrined as a readily identifiable symbol of the 'renaissance' city (Falk, 1986). Similarly, the names of these monumental spaces quickly become associated with the cities in which they are located: London's Canary Wharf, Barcelona's Olympic Marina, Paris's La Defense, Vancouver's Pacific Place, New York's Battery Park, Atlanta's Peachtree Center, Sydney's Darling Harbour and so on.

These hypermediated developments, composed of a formulaic mix of commercial, residential, leisure and industrial uses, have been described as 'analogous' cities because of the way they accommodate office workers, tourists and conference visitors in an ageographic hermetic space uncontaminated by traditional street life (Boddy, 1992). Hence, these spectacular, large-scale urban settings have attracted considerable attention in the literature on the entrepreneurial city, but the importance of less sizeable urban spaces should not be ignored. Less substantial, but often highly publicised, assemblages of public art and civic statuary have also been fabricated as the entrepreneurial urban landscape is made increasingly liminal and playful, blurring the distinctions between entertainment, information and advertising (Hall, 1992; Miles 1997; and Chapter 9 this volume). Together with mega-events such as World Expos, City of Culture celebrations, and, perhaps most significantly, the Olympic Games (where even the bidding process has become a major marshalling point for the urban boosterism and civic peacockery), this transformation of the fabric of the entrepreneurial city has been interpreted as a fundamental means by which city governors have attempted to provide previously industrial cities with a new identity geared to the needs of a globalised economy, and to secure a new economic role for the locale (Short et al, 1993).

In this light, the *cultural* transformation of previously productive cities into 'spectacular' cities of (and for) consumption, populated by a harmonious and cosmopolitan citizenry, has been hypothesised as perhaps the most important element of entrepreneurial forms of local politics. As Harvey (1994) argues, competition between places to attract inward investment of any type has become sharper as community after community falls over itself to offer more and more inducements for 'capital to come to town'. This entrepreneurial transformation of place identity is thus seen as an essential means by which cities can attract business, enhancing their position in the allegedly more competitive era of inter-urban competition. As a component of local economic development, cultural regeneration is thus designed to assert the unique identity of the city and stress its comparative advantages, with the afore-mentioned mega-projects and mega-events providing a locus for the anticipated investment (Page, 1995). Yet while the conscious manipulation of city image is principally designed to make the city more attractive to *external* investors, it has also been argued that it plays an *internal* role in galvanising local support and fostering civic pride, potentially gathering widespread support for entrepreneurial policies. As Rutheiser (1996) suggests, entrepreneurial urban policies can 'bedazzle and bamboozle the multitudes', potentially distracting from the social and economic problems that may persist in the city despite the espousal of a growth-oriented outlook. As such, the manipulation of city images, cultures and experiences has become probably the most important part of the political armoury of urban governors and their coalition partners in the entrepreneurial era. It is the nature of these political partnerships and coalitions that we turn to next.

New urban politics, new institutional arrangements: from government to governance

From the above description, it should be apparent that the type of policies being pursued by city governments in the so-called era of entrepreneurialism represent a relatively novel combination of boosterist strategies and policies designed to promote growth. Closely associated with this new type of urban policy is the expansion of local political action to involve not merely the local state but also a wide number of private and semi-private actors (Leitner, 1990;

Graham, 1995). Inevitably, the type of speculative projects and initiatives that form the cornerstone of entrepreneurial policy are underwritten by the private rather than the public sector. Hence, while there might be some important differences in the aims and objectives of entrepreneurial policies at the local level, it is certainly the case that the *rapprochement* between political and business communities, as manifest in a bewildering array of partnerships, networks and development corporations, is making it harder to detect the boundaries between the private and public sectors. This convergence of private sector (typically business and property) interests and the public sector has inevitably undermined the class-based politics of old, particularly the voting power of the working-class constituency, and resulted in a heightened control of the polity by new bourgeoisie and property interests, consisting almost exclusively of business*men* (Savage and Warde, 1993; Peck, 1995).

In seeking to understand the proliferation of public–private partnerships in urban areas, many researchers have drawn on the theoretical insights of regime theory (e.g. DiGaetano and Klemanski, 1993; Bailey et al, 1995). From the perspective of regime theory, the ability of the city government to shape urban futures and development needs to be understood in terms of the social production and control of governance. Such ideas were initially sketched out by Clarence Stone in his studies of the local state in the United States, where he defined an urban regime as an informal arrangement 'by which public bodies and private interests function together in order to be able to make and carry out governing decisions' (Stone, 1987: 6). Central to this perspective is the notion that regimes do not need to exert total power over the city's population to act effectively (i.e. whether through the ballot box or other means), but rather that they merely need the power to act. From the perspective of regime theory, the crucial question in urban politics is not 'who governs?' but 'who has the capacity to act and why?' (Leitner, 1990). The formation of coalitions or partnerships is thus seen as one of the principal means by which governors achieve this capacity to act. By stressing that regimes can potentially consist of a multiplicity of diverse interest groups, Stone sought to propose a valuable corrective to the idea that urban politics is dominated by monolithic interest groups who gain leverage only by virtue of their electoral power.

Researchers who have sought to understand entrepreneurial governance from this regime perspective have thus generated some crucial insights into the constitution of urban coalitions, which consist of loose or informal partnerships of a multiplicity of interest groups who function together to make and carry out sometimes very specific governing decisions (see Leitner, 1990; Harding, 1992; Lawless, 1994). However, while urban regimes or coalitions can potentially consist of very diverse interest groups, the main players in such regimes (besides the local authority or city government itself) are typically property interests, rentiers, utility groups, universities, business groups, trade unions and the local media (Carley, 1991; Thomas, 1994; Imrie, Thomas and Marshall,

1995). The regime approach thus adopts what has been termed an elite pluralist position that recognises that access to local politics is uneven, so that certain groups enjoy more favourable terms (Peck, 1995). Such groups typically represent a limited range of interests and have very partisan interests in the type of projects and redevelopment carried out in the name of local economic development. Despite this fact, the ability of a coalition to implement policy depends on its seeming ability to act in the interests of the majority of the urban population. Borrowing from Gramsci's (1971) notion of cultural and political hegemony, researchers have begun to examine how these regimes succeed in mobilising popular support, to determine how this élite constellation that speaks for the city comes into being (Judd and Parkinson, 1990a). Clearly, the notion of consensus is, to some extent at least, forged around the seeming commitment of these coalitions or regimes to 'value-free' development and growth, which, despite the obvious benefits to particular sections of the community, is claimed to be in the interests of all.

A regime perspective thus draws attention to the ways in which elected public officials (often with limited resources at their disposal) purposefully co-operate with the private sector to produce the capacity to govern. Inevitably, the range, stability and formality of these coalitions vary considerably, and rely on a tacit understanding of the objectives of the coalition as well as the means needed to achieve those ends. Many coalitions are deliberately ephemeral in nature, formed around the idea of realising visible policy results within a limited time-span, while inevitably looking to increase the prosperity of the city by attracting investment and spending (Mollenkopf, 1983). As a result, a substantial proportion of public–private partnerships are organised to develop very specific initiatives or proposals, such as mega-events or mega-projects. The short-lived Olympic bid partnership in Manchester is one such example, where local business and property interests co-operated with local politicians in an attempt to attract the Olympics for 1996 (Robson, 1989). Likewise, the Glasgow Action group, formed by influential business representatives, met between 1986 and 1990 with the specific goal of promoting the city internationally (Boyle and Hughes, 1995). The ephemeral nature of many coalitions tends to result in a piecemeal approach to urban development that lacks strategic foresight or long-term planning. On the other hand, there have also been numerous examples of local alliances and partnerships characterised by relative longevity. Such coalitions appear to be based on a clear understanding of the objectives of the coalitions, a strong leadership capacity and (often) the presence of a visionary individual prepared to act as the figurehead for the regime (see Chapter 12).

Research into the nature of entrepreneurial governance has also highlighted international differences in the nature of urban regimes, and particularly illustrated the dangers in (uncritically) importing formulations made in a North American context to the other nations (Boyle, 1995; Boyle and Hughes, 1995). In North America, the formation of urban 'growth coalitions' has been evident for a number of years (Logan and Molotch, 1987), with the regeneration of Detroit, Toronto, Vancouver and especially Baltimore in the 1960s and 1970s frequently cited as 'successful' examples of the way in which state and market could co-operate. This notion of cities as growth machines was not only seized upon widely by politicians, but also by a number of academics who sought to document the rise of similar growth coalitions in Europe and Australasia (e.g. Lloyd and Newlands, 1988; Bassett and Harloe, 1990; Harding, 1992; Goetz and Clarke, 1993). Yet in the USA, city governments *had* to recruit business leaders as coalition partners because of the inherent fiscal weakness of the local state. Subsequently, key figures in the business community have frequently played the co-ordinating role in North American growth coalitions, with rentiers, landlords and utility companies often crucial players (Mollenkopf, 1983). In European cities, however, which often possess stronger forms of urban government, the key, co-ordinating role in many of the resulting urban regimes is usually taken by the local authorities themselves (Harding, 1991; Hubbard, 1995), essentially because of their local expertise, a preponderance of bureaucratic professionals and a superior financial position relative to their US counterparts. In these cases, the local state has not been 'captured' by coalitions of private capital, but continues to take ultimate responsibility for local economic development (Meegan, 1993).

Therefore, although the rhetoric surrounding the incorporation of business interests into entrepreneurial governance has often posited the 'maverick entrepreneur' as the driving force behind such initiatives, Peck (1995) has suggested that the reality has proved much more mundane, with local business leaders co-opted into local politics through their individual incorporation on to the boards of new non-elected local agencies (local enterprise councils, locally managed trusts, development corporations, training partnerships, etc.). In this way, it might be argued that the forging of a new urban entrepreneurialism at the local level is much less about 'rolling back' the frontiers of the state than a restructuring of the local state apparatus in the interests of the central state (Tickell and Peck, 1992). The selective incorporation of business interests into urban regimes has thus been interpreted as representing an attempt by *central* government to redefine both the institutional form and policies of the local (welfare) state (Imrie, Thomas and Marshall, 1995). In this sense, despite the seeming prominence of local business representatives in the new urban politics, it is clear that the 'voice' of the business community is still carefully circumscribed by both central and local government, with the power often attributed to the private sector in urban coalitions frequently more apparent than real.

What is thus evident about the changing nature of urban politics in the entrepreneurial era is that although the private sector is becoming more and more involved in the evolution and implementation of policy, the type of partnerships which underpin entrepreneurial strategies are more varied than the original US thesis of the 'growth coalition' suggested. What is also evident is that such regimes of interest are potentially fragile, and that coalition partners frequently become disillusioned, marginalised or redundant as the aims of the regime change or the promised rewards of entrepreneurialism fail to materialise. The collapse of the worldwide property market in the early 1990s, for example, had deleterious results for many regimes who had based their activities on the development of mega-projects; the financial problems of the London Docklands Development Corporation following the collapse of property developers Olympia and York provides an all too obvious example of this (Brownill, 1993; Harvey, 1994). Even in the USA, where many cities have relatively strong regimes under the leadership of charismatic business leaders, coalitions of interest often find themselves at odds as the varied demands of different interest groups become increasingly irreconcilable in times of fiscal or political stress. Such tensions can prove particularly acute when the issue of race is high on the agenda, and many have alluded to the ways that uneasy truces between 'white money and black power' can break down as either side tries to set the agenda (Wilson, 1996; Fainstein and Fainstein, 1996). According to Rutheiser (1996), this was the case in Atlanta, where a relatively durable local élite found itself increasingly divided as it discussed how the Centennial Olympics ought to be used to benefit the city's population.

CONCEPTUALISING THE ENTREPRENEURIAL CITY: DEBATES AND CONTROVERSIES

Notwithstanding the documented differences in regime composition and longevity at the local level, as well as the varied nomenclature employed by researchers in different countries, there does appear to be general agreement that the whole terrain of urban politics appears to have been shifted with the emergence of urban entrepreneurialism. This new form of city governance, reliant on co-operation with the private sector and the speculative mobilisation of local resources to promote growth, has certainly ushered in a new way of thinking and writing about city politics. As noted above, there is much literature noting the rise of urban regimes throughout the advanced capitalist world, reviewing the proactive strategies designed to stimulate the local economy and charting the associated transformation of city images and landscapes. But despite this weight of empirical literature, we should also note that the theoretical conceptualisation of much of this material remains weak. Without wishing to denigrate many of the fastidiously detailed studies of entrepreneurial politics in Western cities, there is clearly a large repository of material in existence which has failed to adequately relate to ongoing debates about the nature of contemporary urbanisation. Specifically, there appear to be many questions which remain unanswered about the importance of entre- preneurial governance relative to changing relations of culture and capital in Western cities. Perhaps more fundamentally, there also appears to be a paucity of studies which have hypothesised as to the likely long-term consequences of entrepreneurialism for those living in affected cities. What is essentially being argued here is that, given the centrality of urban governance in shaping the character of place, there is little point in studying urban political transition in isolation from broader social, cultural and economic trends. In this respect, a number of important questions about entrepreneurialism demand particular clarification and investigation, as highlighted below.

The shift to entrepreneurialism: exploring the differences

In the final analysis what characterises the 'new urban politics' as distinctive is the way in which urban entrepreneurialism is perceived to be fundamentally different from the other forms of city governance which have preceded it. In writing of entrepreneurialism as a new mode of politics, many writers seek to stress the shift that has occurred away from a concern with broad-based welfare and social policies (the provision of welfare, services and collective consumption) to the adoption of a more outward-oriented stance designed to foster and encourage local development and economic growth. The assertion that this amounts to a fundamental and deeply significant change in the nature of urban governance is supported with reference to the widely cited 'dual theory of the state' (Saunders, 1981, 1986). This theory hypothesised that state governance plays a dual role within a capitalist mode of production – firstly to ensure effective production (i.e. capital accumulation) and secondly to main-tain adequate levels of consumption (i.e. the reproduction and socialisation of labour). Drawing on an analysis of the British state, Saunders argued that such tasks were characteristically split between the national and local level, with:

> a corporate state located at national and regional levels of government . . . producing investment policies designed to support capital accumulation in the monopoly sector of the economy and a competitive sector located principally at the local level of government and producing social consumption in response to popular pressures but within an overall context of political and economic restraint (Saunders, 1981: 45).

Saunders' model was never intended as a definitive account of the hierarchical arrangement of political structures, and it certainly reduces the multitude of political institutions and organisations to an empirically unsustainable local–national dualism, yet many commentators regard it as a potentially useful schema for exploring the spatial specificity of state governance within a capitalist mode of production (Hoggart, 1991). Clearly, as urban governments adopt more proactive growth strategies, the division of 'responsibility' for different facets of social and economic regulation between local and central state is undeniably being recast.

Urban entrepreneurialism thus appears to undermine 'traditional' ideas that the politics of production is normally controlled at the level of the nation state. On this basis, it could be argued that urban entrepreneurialism is a distinctive mode of governance, based on a local politics of growth rather than a politics of income redistribution. What is clearly missing here is any consideration of the extent to which urban governments can pursue both objectives in tandem or whether both modes can coexist. Indeed, an objective assessment of the extent of this transition is difficult, if not impossible, given that many commentators take for granted that local governance prior to the early 1970s was dominated by managerial politics, to the extent that this has attained the level of an assumed axiomatic truth among writers on the entrepreneurial city (Carley, 1991; DiGaetano and Klemanski, 1993), and has led to the perpetuation of a dualistic conception of managerial and entrepreneurial forms of urban governance. However, while city governors are undeniably adopting a more proactive stance and spending more on local economic policies than ever before, this expenditure rarely rivals that on education and welfare services, suggesting that there has not been a wholesale abandonment of managerial policies, and that there are important continuities between the two modes which are often depicted as polar opposites.

As Savitch and Kantor (1995) have forcibly argued, the perpetuation of a dualistic model of managerialism and entrepreneurialism thus overshadows the way in which most city governments adopt an amalgam of managerial (socially progressive) and entrepreneurial (growth-centred) policies. Furthermore, such ideas also serve to mask the fact that city governments, to a lesser or greater extent, have always pursued entrepreneurial strategies and played a crucial role in local economic development (see Chapter 2). Indeed, perhaps the clearest expressions of boosterist sentiments came in the late nineteenth century, especially in the USA, where city governors obsessively sought to extol the virtues of frontier towns through the promotion of a series of elaborate and often fanciful place myths. Similar processes of place invention and promotion, dating back to pre-colonial times, have also been uncovered in Australian cities (see Dunn, McGuirk and Winchester, 1995). Additionally, it is important to note that such attempts at civic boosterism by the local state were frequently in alliance with the private sector. Writing of the territorially bound 'class alliances' which have historically characterised many cities and regions, Harvey (1985a) has argued that urban governors have always been the most important actors in such alliances by virtue of their authority and ability to create local coherence through institutions of law, governance and political participation. In this sense, the role of the local state in actively promoting conditions favourable to capital accumulation within its territorial boundaries should not be considered exclusively as a recent phenomenon – rather, it might be suggested that entrepreneurial forms of governance are merely the latest in a long line of political strategies which have attempted to create conditions conducive to the economic success of the city. We are not arguing

here that there has not been an important shift in the nature of urban governance; clearly, as the chapters in this book document, there have been some
major changes in the way cities are governed, and the way that the political
process operating in cities impinges on the lives of urban populations. Rather,
we simply wish to stress that there are dangers in accepting the idea that
entrepreneurial governance is distinct from other modes of governance in all
respects.

Explaining the changes in urban governance

Whether or not it is accepted that the new urban politics is so different from
the old (and this clearly needs to be clarified), it is generally agreed that the
emergence of the entrepreneurial city has something to do with broader shifts
in the nature of the capitalist economy (Fitzgerald, Ely and Cox, 1990). In this
respect, most theories of the transition to entrepreneurial governance are
clearly rooted in the political economy approach. Starting from the assumption
that the aim of state intervention is to create conditions that ensure the reproduction of the economy and society, specifically by mediating the production–
consumption nexus, it has been argued that changes in urban governance are
inherently intended to resolve local tensions between capital and labour. In
this respect, the fundamental transition that has occurred in the nature of (late)
capitalism has been a theorised shift from a Fordist to a post-Fordist mode of
accumulation. The exact nature of this transition need not trouble us here, and
its defining features have been sufficiently documented elsewhere to make a
detailed recapitulation here unnecessary (see Harvey, 1989a; Amin and Thrift,
1992). In essence, though, this transition is hypothesised to have resulted from
a breakdown in the profitability of Fordist mass production, typified by the
production of standardised goods in vertically integrated production units. This
mode of accumulation, executed by a technologically harnessed workforce,
was underpinned by a heavy regulatory framework, dependent upon the
careful maintenance of the labour/capital relationship through the Keynesian
'welfare state'. With the crisis of Fordism, bought on by a combination of
organisational and technical limitations, and the subsequent shift to flexible
modes of accumulation, this established mode of political regulation is perceived to have been modified as the polity seeks to adapt to new forms of
economic and social relationship. It is this adaptation to new forms of production and consumption that has thus been most frequently hypothesised as
shaping the 'new politics of place' (Swyngedouw, 1989) and the transition to
entrepreneurial forms of city politics is clearly one part of this (see Chapter 14).

Thus, although there is general agreement that the rise of urban entrepreneurialism is intimately connected with a transition to new types of capital
accumulation, the precise importance of entrepreneurial governance in mediating the production/consumption nexus is much less clear. What is evident,
however, is that the reorientation of the local state cannot be understood in

isolation, but needs to be examined against a wider context of global economic and regulatory restructurations. Probably the most thorough exploration of such ideas has been by David Harvey (1987, 1989b, 1993), as part of his ongoing consideration of the role of urban processes in the historical development of capitalism. By placing contemporary urban politics into broad spatial and temporal contexts, he has sought to draw attention to the role of urban politics in resolving the contradictions resulting as time–space compression and the reorganisation of investment threaten local distinction and people's identity with place. In doing so, Harvey appears to suggest that post-Fordism has actually heightened the salience of territorial politics as place becomes more, rather than less, important, even though space is of diminishing importance as a boundary to exchange and capital mobility. In terms of effecting the transition to advanced capitalism, Harvey thus postulates that entrepreneurial politics play a role in perpetuating unequal development while reproducing local social relations which are more conducive to flexible modes of accumulation. In this sense, Harvey makes the point that the new urban politics and the aspirations of urban regimes should be seen not so much as a reaction to global forces, but rather as a trigger to new forms of competitive capitalism (and as Lovering, 1995, contends, potentially contribute to their own problems).

Notwithstanding Harvey's careful elucidation of the role of entrepreneurialism in relation to geographical–historical materialism, it appears that the literature on the new urban politics overwhelmingly exhibits a crude conception of the ways that urban politics is implicated in broader shifts in the nature of globalised capitalism. Reiterating many of the well-rehearsed arguments emanating from the globalisation literature, discourses surrounding the entrepreneurial city fallaciously stress the way that localities are individual, contingent and particular, while the global is abstract, social and general (Senbenberger, 1993). This dichotomous view of local and global implies that cities are 'fixed', waiting for 'mobile' capital and waves of economic change to ebb over them, disregarding the potential autonomy of cities or their potential to actually shape global circuits of capital (Robson, 1989). This is exemplified in Massey's (1984) oft-cited geological analogy, in which the way layers of global investment impinge on the locality is seen to be dependent on locally contingent factors such as industrial relations or political culture. Cox (1993) has picked up on this unconvincing articulation of local–global relations, suggesting that such theorisations seriously overgeneralise the mobility of capital at different scales, ignoring the fact that much capital is fixed (in the form of productive facilities and built environment) while human resources (local governments and workers) are inherently mobile. In the face of the lack of empirical evidence for the hypermobility of capital (though see Soja, 1989), Cox goes on to argue that it is the possibility, rather than the actuality, of hypermobile investment capital, that is providing the impetus to entrepreneurial government. Clearly, a more sophisticated conceptualisation of local/global relations is necessary by both academics and policy-makers alike, one which pays serious attention to issues of the local dependence of capital at a variety of scales.

In this sense, adherents of regulation theory have sought to propose a more holistic interpretation of the role of urban politics in relation to the international circulation and accumulation of capital which appears to offer a more promising avenue for theorising the entrepreneurial city (see Chapter 13). Deriving from the work of French Marxists in the 1970s, regulation theories have been adopted in a number of different ways by urban geographers and political theorists, to the extent that it no longer makes sense to talk of a single regulation theory, but rather of a generic regulationist approach. Despite this fact, which has led to some fundamental misconceptions about the approach (Dunford, 1990), the essence of such a perspective is a belief that the capitalist system is underpinned by evolving forms of regulation which are used to attenuate against the potential crises and contradictions which threaten to topple the system at any given time (Aglietta, 1979). According to this perspective, the role of the state within processes of social and economic regulation is to facilitate the transition of the economy in the interest of capital accumulation while absorbing the social costs of this transition. The idea here is that political processes are not so much reactive to global forces (as the rhetoric of entre-preneurs often stresses) but that these policies are part and parcel of a more pervasive reorganisation of the regulatory framework that controls global capitalism.

Many researchers are beginning to use the concepts and terminology of regulation approaches to interpret changes in urban governance, considering the local state as both a product and an agent of regulation (e.g. Mayer, 1991; Painter, 1991; Goodwin, 1993; Peck, 1995). Far from being unwittingly caught up in wider changes, such accounts depict the local state as playing an active (if not always deliberate) role in forging new social, economic and cultural relations at both the local and global level (Saunders and Stone, 1987). This point has also been made by Harvey (1985a) in his discussion of regional class alliances, where he suggests that the state plays a key role in legitimating specific regimes of accumulation at different spatial scales, and that the processes at work under capitalism would create modes of social regulation conducive to its continual reproduction if they did not already exist. In a manner that is clearly compatible with Harvey's ideas, regulationists view the changing nature of urban politics as merely one aspect of the shift in social regulation associated with the transition to new regimes of accumulation, albeit a crucial aspect. This does beg the question, however, as to whether current modes of social regulation (which are taken to include entrepreneurial forms of governance) merely represent a transitory period of crisis, or whether they mark the advent of a fundamentally different (but inherently stable) post-Fordist mode of regulation. In short, we need to ask whether the strategies, policies and mechanisms associated with entrepreneurial governance are capable of gener-ating sufficient *regulatory capacity* to promote successful capital accumulation while successfully resolving local tensions between capital and labour. It is in this regard that thorough assessments of the impacts of entrepreneurial governance are necessary to speculate as to the sustainability of this political paradigm.

Whose city? The consequences of the politics of growth

Although there have been a plethora of studies of the adoption of entre-preneurial policies, a clear lacuna in the literature is any real consideration of the impacts of these policies. In this respect, while studies of the politics of the entrepreneurial city have drawn attention to the unequal distribution of power inherent in regime politics, particularly focusing on the exclusion of groups defined by virtue of their 'other' race, gender and sexuality (see Keith and Pile, 1994; Brown, 1995; Fainstein and Fainstein, 1996), geographers have been remarkably reticent in identifying the social benefits and disbenefits resulting from the espousal of a politics of growth (though see Wollmann et al, 1994). Instead, debates about the effectiveness of entrepreneurial policies in regenerating the city and improving the living conditions of its citizens are dominated by the hollow rhetoric of politicians and policy-makers (Leitner and Garner, 1993). Despite the perceived success of Baltimore and Detroit in securing the revitalisation of their downtowns through prestige development, anecdotal evidence is beginning to suggest that entrepreneurial strategies are attracting little new inward investment or having any discernible impact on job creation (Barnekov, Boyle and Roch, 1988). In fact, many of the image-enhancing schemes which have been promoted as profit-making have turned out to be loss-making. As Harvey (1989b) points out, with all cities competing in the same global marketing game, there are bound to be winners and losers. As he contends, just how many successful marinas, convention centres or heritage centres can there be? This was vividly illustrated in the case of Sheffield's 1991 Student Games, which burdened the local population with a large long-term debt repayment to be met from council taxes (Goodwin, 1993; Lawless, 1994). Atlanta's Omni Centre, a mixed sports, office and hotel complex, similarly received massive state funding, but proved to be one of the biggest real estate disasters in history (Rutheiser, 1996). Such examples are by no means isolated, and reinforce the point that the policies pursued by the regimes are inherently speculative, with the volatility of the property market exposing how fragile the basis of entrepreneurial policies can often prove (Imrie and Thomas, 1993a; Turok, 1992).

Therefore, although entrepreneurial policies can do many things, and can benefit local elites, it appears that they inevitably tend to subjugate the overall interests of the community in the interests of capital accumulation with competition with other cities for economic growth assuming primacy over distributional issues. Hence, even when such speculative policies do succeed in attracting investment, within the 'successful' cities, there will be many communities that continue to find themselves disadvantaged. It is these negative impacts of entrepreneurial policies within cities that have exercised most commentators. Logan and Molotch (1987) have baldly stated that as entrepreneurial strategies generally favour development and growth over the redistribution of wealth and opportunity, the result can only be a net transfer of wealth from the less well-off to urban élites. Similarly, Harvey (1989b) has suggested that entrepreneurial policies constitute a subsidy for the affluent at the cost of welfare for the poor. On the other hand, few are prepared to suggest that such policies have no trickle-down benefits whatsoever, and Fitzgerald, Ely and Cox (1990) claim that in many cases indirect jobs are often created for the poorest urban groups. Yet, according to one of the rare independent studies which has attempted to assess the distributive impacts of entrepreneurial strategies, while Birmingham City Council succeeded in creating a limited number of jobs through its prestige development programme, these were primarily poorly paid or part-time positions in service sector employment (see Chapter 6). Furthermore, spending on these entrepreneurial policies was seen to detract from welfare and education expenditure, with dire results for the least well-off in the city. This phenomenon has also been noted in a number of US cities, where entrepreneurial strategies have (controversially) been implicated in the creation of a new urban 'underclass' (Hambleton, 1991; Galster, 1992), resulting in the so-called 'dual' city (Mollenkopf and Castells, 1991).

The failure of urban entrepreneurialism to alleviate the social and economic problems of many cities, and in particular its neglect of issues of social equity in favour of the prosperity of certain élite groups, has therefore been argued to have exacerbated social and territorial disparities in the city. Recently, Goodwin (1995) has argued that the sharp social polarisations in London are evidence of the failure of entrepreneurial governance to ensure adequate regulatory capacity at the local level, implying that the current mode of entrepreneurial regulation will ultimately prove unsustainable (see also Peck and Tickell, 1995b). Yet in the short term, the question is whether entrepreneurial policies are producing a new urban geography steeped in the ideals of economic growth rather than the principles of social justice. Certainly, the ideals of neo-liberal economics which underlie entrepreneurial strategy consider that the free market is as efficient and as just as state intervention in delivering goods and services to citizens. Yet the evidence to date suggests this is not the case, and that without accompanying socially progressive policies (Savitch and Kantor, 1995) there is little reason to suppose that the benefits of entrepreneurial policy will be fairly distributed.

In this light, Susan Smith (1994) argues that rather than simply investigating the impacts of entrepreneurialism at the abstract level, the changing govern-ance of the city demands a re-engagement with questions of social justice, and a consideration of whether entrepreneurial strategies produce a fair and defendable distribution of benefits and burdens in society. The difficulty, of course, arises when it is realised that there are as many views as to what constitutes fairness as there are people, ranging from utilitarian liberalism to social egalitarianism (S. Smith, 1994). In an era where the relativist thinking characteristic of post-modernism tends to preclude the establishment of universal rules or principles of social justice it is perhaps not surprising that geographers have shied away from such issues. However, although it might be easy for researchers to be entranced by the hype and the spectacle of the hyper-real entrepreneurial city, Leitner (1990) has argued that there remains a pressing need for assessments of the 'real' costs and benefits of entrepreneurial policy among different geographical areas and social groups in the city. Although there are many difficulties in making *ex post* analyses of the efficacy of such policies (for example, over what time-span are the benefits of such policies supposed to trickle down to the poorest in the city?), such analyses would appear to be crucial in evolving appropriately inclusive and democratic entrepreneurial policies, noting that the form of such policies will, of course, need to be adapted for local circumstances.

The place of entrepreneurial politics: examining local difference

A further area in which the current literature on the entrepreneurial city might be considered to be lacking is in its failure to adequately consider local variations in entrepreneurial policies. This claim might seem somewhat surprising given the wealth of studies which address variations in the organisation of urban regimes and policies in different ciities. However, it is clear that many researchers have neglected to focus on one of the most important aspects of urban governance, that is to say, the way in which their composition, orientation and objectives vary according to local cultural, social and political characteristics. As Stoker and Mossberger (1994) point out, the adoption of a regime perspective necessarily requires an in-depth analysis of the constitution of these coalitions at the local scale, with particular attention being given to their aims and achievements in relation to the local context, which refers to:

> The distinctive internal characteristics of the city, its site characteristics, (and) also its particular situation as expressed through its relations with other locations. Therefore the local context is taken to include both the locality-specific social, economic and political structures and relations, the cultural traditions that the city has inherited, and its changing position within the wider national and international political economy (Leitner, 1990: 153).

Often then, despite a seeming preoccupation with emphasising local difference, many researchers seem to overlook some of the fundamental characteristics of the city in their desire to draw generalisations about the adoption of a stereotypical growth coalition model. This often results in an atemporal and ageographic account of urban politics which fails to relate the trajectory of entrepreneurial governance to (often deeply embedded) 'local structures of feeling' (Williams, 1965; P. Jackson, 1991).

The essential point being made here is that researchers seldom look at the lived culture of entrepreneurial cities or at the changing textures and rhythms of everyday life as they are affected by (and, of course, affect) entrepreneurial governance:

> One crux in local political cultures is the sense of belonging to a locality; people must identify with the sentiments that its core values imply. Part and parcel of such feelings is the belief that these values are worthy. Such assessments emerge from internal circumstances (e.g. a belief amongst the populace that growth brings jobs for them) . . . (or) from area residents' impressions of where their locality stands in the national space economy (Hoggart, 1991: 184).

This task of exploring the manner in which entrepreneurial cities are experienced and understood by local populations, and the ways in which this differs from the hyperbole of the city boosters, has as yet received little attention. This reflects a limited engagement of researchers in this area of study with Lefebvre's (1974) idea that it is essential to bridge the gap between representations and experiences of space. Although some have been critical of this omission (Ley and Mills, 1993; Jackson, 1993; Savage and Warde, 1993), until recently there was little indication of any real move beyond this position. However, there have been some more recent studies which have begun to offer some promise in this direction by focusing on the ways in which the transformation of city identity under entrepreneurial governance is consumed and, in some cases, rejected by local populations.

What is evident from such studies is that local populations, or at least, parts of those populations, do not always accede to selling of the city or the policies espoused by the élite coalition (Goodwin, 1993). However, opposition to entrepreneurial policy is often carefully circumscribed by the state, and it is only rarely that it coalesces into effective campaigns of protest (termed by Berry and Huxley, 1992, as 'anti-growth coalitions'). Thus, although very visible protests against entrepreneurial policies have been found in some cities (e.g. anti-Docklands protests in London – Brownill, 1993; Rose, 1992), it is generally the case that opposition remains latent. Hence it is necessary for researchers to develop a more sensitive and critical awareness of how such policies are received at the grass-roots level, and to display a nuanced understanding of the cultural politics of identity as they are played out in different contexts. For example, Taylor, Evans and Fraser (1996) used focus group discussions with local community groups to give a fascinating insight into the anxieties and aspirations of people living in Manchester and Sheffield, two contrasting entrepreneurial cities, and showed how the local images of the city were very much at odds with those promoted by the place marketers. Similarly, Hubbard (1996b) utilised psychological techniques to explore interpretations of Birmingham's entrepreneurial landscape, concluding that people's appreciation of this particular cultural product played a major role in legitimating the transition to new forms of governance.

What is being argued here is that any understanding of the scope, role and impacts of entrepreneurialism in city governance demands a heightened awareness of local culture. In this sense, we are arguing that to understand the evolution, maintenance or even abandonment of entrepreneurial policy, there is a need to appreciate how such policies are supported or disrupted by cultures, both élite and popular. This stresses that culture should not be seen as marginal to economic and political processes (i.e. as a superstructure supporting an economic base), but as an active part of the political arena. As such, culture is contested and negotiated between different groups, and it is within this cultural struggle that urban regimes seek to shape the direction and form of their policies.

THE SCOPE OF THIS BOOK

At the beginning of this chapter an attempt was made to define urban entrepreneurialism in terms of shifts in political action and culture, though subsequently it has become apparent that a consideration of the new urban politics encompasses far more than an examination of the local state. Urban entrepreneurialism, it has been contended, has ushered in a whole range of changes in the ways that cities operate at all levels, changes that can only really be comprehended with reference to the changing processes of urbanisation operating in an era of late or disorganised capitalism. As such, entrepreneurial governance is taken as being part and parcel of the broader changes which have transformed Western cities, being centrally implicated in the creation of new urban spaces, economies and cultures. Thus, this is a book that defies easy categorisation, and if the following chapters blur the boundaries between economic, cultural and political geography, then this merely confirms the growing realisation among urban theorists that the political economy of the city and its cultural politics are intimately intermeshed.

The various chapters that follow develop many of the issues which have been identified in the preceding discussion, and while each chapter is intended to stand alone, the chapters fall naturally into a number of separate sections addressing these issues. In Part I, a chapter by Jessop reiterates and develops many of the ideas about entrepreneurialism constituting a distinctive political paradigm, with its discursive identification as an innovative and proactive form of governance resulting in its widespread uptake. The importance of marketing the city as entrepreneurial is similarly seized upon by Ward and Short and Kim, with the former developing the idea that place marketing is not necessarily a new phenomenon. In Part II, examples from three continents are used to demonstrate the ubiquity of entrepreneurial policy, as well as the very real differences in the form and consequences of these policies as they are played out at the local level. Chapters by McGuirk, Winchester and Dunn, Loftman and Nevin, Althubaity and Jonas, and Herrschel thus provide concrete examples of the nature of the pro-growth local policies for economic development being pursued in different contexts, while delivering some important general lessons about their failure to deliver benefits for all. Part III considers the specific importance of local cultural identity in entrepreneurial policy and the ways local culture is harnessed for both external and internal benefit. O'Connor's chapter on Manchester focuses on the key intermediaries in this marketing process, noting how they walk a tightrope between the commodification and enhancement of identity. The contribution of cultural products to the image of the city is also tackled in Miles's chapter on the role of public art in urban redevelopment. Finally in Part III, McNeill addresses the issue of how researchers represent the often diffuse and intangible structures of feeling that constitute the entrepreneurial city, taking the example of Barcelona's Olympic developments. In Part IV, 'Politics, regimes and regulation', Wood begins by thinking about the conceptual tools which researchers have used to interpret the rise of the entrepreneurial city, namely regime and regulation theory. In doing so, he begins to address the crucial issue of scale, an issue that is picked up in Painter's chapter on the way local entrepreneurs are emerging in an apparently global era. Leitner and Sheppard's chapter similarly seeks to expand this point by considering the way entrepreneurialism is encouraging the uneven production of space and the formation of a new urban order with often devastating effects for marginalised urban populations. Finally, in the conclusion, we attempt to pull some of these ideas together, giving special and particular attention to the ways in which the breadth of empirical and theoretical material generated by discussions on the entrepreneurial city may be applied by policy-makers as they seek to come to terms with new economic, social and political realities.

PART I

SELLING THE ENTREPRENEURIAL CITY

INTRODUCTION

TIM HALL

There can be little doubt that one of the most obvious manifestations of entrepreneurialism among city governments has been the attention devoted to the transformation, or at least enhancement, of the image of the city. This has begun to draw considerable attention from academics from geography and cognate disciplines in the social sciences (see the collection of essays in Kearns and Philo, 1993, and Gold and Ward, 1994) as well as from disciplines such as tourism, leisure and heritage management and urban planning (see Ashworth and Voogd, 1990; Page, 1995). This attention has opened up a number of critical perspectives on the process of 'selling cities', perspectives that are reflected and expanded upon by the three chapters in this section.

Academics have been generally critical of the increased attention paid to place promotion by cities. This is so for a number of reasons. Increased attention to place promotion necessarily involves increased investment by local authorities. Although one of the things that has bedevilled research into place promotion has been a lack of reliable data, it is clear that both the number of cities involved in place promotion and the range of methods and media employed to sell cities have increased since the 1970s (Barke and Harrop, 1994: 97). However, despite this Holcomb (1994), drawing on various surveys of place promotion by American cities in the late 1980s (Guskind, 1987; Bailey, 1989; Ward, 1989), argues that cities are still 'undersold' compared to most commercial products. Bailey (1989: 4) cites the example of economic development advertising in US media totalling $46 million annually compared to an annual total of around $100m. for Miller Lite Beer. Similarly selling cities is done largely by members of local authority departments without specialist advertising training (Holcomb, 1994). Consequently Holcomb (1994: 121) can conclude that 'the marketing of cities tends to be generic and repetitive'.

Place promotion is unlikely to diminish in importance in the near future. It is likely, therefore, to increase in sophistication, necessitating further investment from local authorities into the creative and technological aspects of city marketing if the circle of repetition is to be broken. This process is likely to continue in parallel to the reduction in government funding to local authorities (Goodwin, 1992). The trade-off facing local authorities between expenditure on place promotion as part of economic development programmes and more basic welfare spending is likely to become increasingly acute in the future.

Much academic criticism of place promotion stems from the supposed dualism of image and reality implicated by projects of place promotion (see Burgess and Wood, 1988; Watson, 1991). Most severely place promotion and projects of economic development of which it is an integral part, have been labelled the 'carnival mask' of late capitalist urbanisation (Harvey, 1988: 35), the argument being that while such images create the impression of regeneration and vibrancy within cities, they do nothing to address the underlying problems that necessitated regeneration programmes in the first place (Harvey, 1988).

This propagation of image by cities necessitates a process of social exclusion in the imagination of new urban identities. Because the audiences for place promotion are predominantly white and wealthy, the people who populate the imagined cities of place promotion are similarly white and wealthy. This mirrors the material polarisation of populations within entrepreneurial cities.

Another area of criticism from academics is that place promotion involves the appropriation and sanitisation of contested place and social histories and identities, reconstructing them around notions of what constitutes an 'official' urban image. Where place promotion does pay attention to 'alternative' or otherwise marginalised histories and identities it does so through reducing the complexity and contest inherent in their formation and negotiation to a few stereotypical slogans or saleable, appealing images. The Oliver Twist-like child smiling from the front of the leaflet advertising the heritage quarter or 'living' museum has already become a cliché. Similarly ethnic minorities are transformed into providers of a 'lively street life' and complex, contested identities drawing on industry, memory, community and resistance become 'a proud tradition of manufacturing'. This is not to suggest an idealisation of these earlier histories and identities, many for example are clearly masculinist and problematic in other ways, but rather to highlight their unproblematic (re)presentation through narratives of place promotion.

Further, place promotion is both an obvious manifestation and contributory cause of the heightened inter-urban competition associated with entrepreneurialism. The iniquitous intra-urban and wasteful inter-urban consequences of this are well known (Harvey, 1988; see also Chapters 6 and 14).

While the essays collected in this section clearly reflect these concerns they also seek to extend these critiques by demonstrating the ways in which the process of place promotion has become integral to the process of urbanisation in the late twentieth century, something conventional accounts of urban geography have been slow to pick up on. As image assumes ever greater importance in the post-industrial economy it is becoming increasingly apparent that the actual shaping and production of urban landscapes are reflecting the imperatives of the necessity for cities to present positive images of themselves to the outside world. Similarly, programmes of economic development are becoming driven more and more by image-enhancing initiatives. Politically urban governance is becoming constituted to a greater extent around the narratives of entrepreneurialism envisioned by, among other things, place promotion.

To understand this it is important to appreciate the differences between the processes of selling and marketing when applied to the case of cities. Selling is a process whereby advertising is determined by the product being sold: the consumer is persuaded that they want or need what one has to sell. Marketing, however, is a process whereby advertising determines, or at least shapes, the product for sale: what one has to sell is shaped by some idea of what the consumer wants (Bailey, 1989: 3; Fretter, 1993: 165; Holcomb, 1993, 1994). The distinction between 'selling the city' and 'marketing the city' is crucial in understanding the relationship of place promotion to urbanisation. It would be true to say that cities, as they have become increasingly entre-preneurial, have become increasingly shaped by the necessity to project a positive image of themselves. There is probably no greater advert for cities than their own landscape (Crilley, 1993a). Marketing cities, therefore, has become a process synonymous with and fundamental to the urban geography of entrepreneurial cities.

> [Marketing] is the principal driving force in urban economic development in the 1980s and will continue to be so in the next decade. . . The logic that more jobs make a city better is giving way to the realisation that making a city better attracts more jobs (Bailey, 1989: 3).

> Place marketing has thus become much more than merely selling the area to attract mobile companies or tourists. It can now be viewed as a fundamental part of guiding the development of places in a desired fashion (Fretter, 1993: 165).

The three chapters in this section each reflect and emphasise this theme. Ward, taking a historical view, not only charts the shift from selling to marketing cities, but, drawing on a range of examples from the UK, USA and Canada, illustrates the extent to which both of these processes have been integral to urbanisation in these countries. In doing so he demonstrates that entre-preneurialism is not simply a characteristic of the late twentieth century, but rather, has been embedded, in some form or another, in urban systems for some time. Short and Kim, looking at place promotion in US cities and focusing on two 'stories', illustrate just how fundamental place promotion has become, not just for the images and landscapes of these cities, but also for their economic development. Indeed as the two stories show, the relationship between image and economic development is reciprocal, Memphis's economy now defining it as 'America's distribution centre'. Finally, Jessop demonstrates how the narrativity of place promotion specifically and entrepreneurialism more generally is fundamental to the constitution of entrepreneurialism within cities in a number of ways.

Traditionally place promotion has been afforded little room in accounts of urban geography, economy and development. Hopefully the case of the entrepreneurial city highlighted by the chapters collected in this section will serve to address this omission.

2

PLACE MARKETING: A HISTORICAL COMPARISON OF BRITAIN AND NORTH AMERICA

STEPHEN V. WARD

INTRODUCTION: TWO TALES OF TWO CITIES

In 1983 local authorities in two British cities, both of them suffering acutely from the effects of deindustrialisation, unemployment, poverty and deprivation, both solidly Labour-controlled, launched notable advertising campaigns about themselves. Much the better known of the two was 'Glasgow's Miles Better', an image-boosting campaign that was directly inspired by the earlier 'I ♥ New York' campaign of 1977 (Figure 2.1) (Struthers, 1986: 8–11; Keating, 1988: 174; Boyle, 1990: 121–3). The jocular double meaning of its slogan (miles better/smiles better) and the visual interest created by the substitution of the O in Glasgow for Mr Happy from the Mr Men cartoon series conveyed a spirit of jaunty optimism.

Over the next few years the message was disseminated by virtually all known techniques of advertising and public relations (Jack, 1984). There were advertisements in the colour supplements, and international business magazines, posters on the London Underground and the sides of its red double decker buses. Videos documenting how Glasgow really was 'miles better' won prizes at the New York International Film and Television Festival in three successive years, 1983–85. There were multilingual car bumper stickers by the million and 'miles better' tee-shirts. HMS *Glasgow* carried the campaign around the world. Meanwhile in City Chambers a former crime reporter (who had done more than his fair share to blacken the city's reputation with stories of the razor gangs of the Gorbals and the East End) now sent forth a stream of good news to substantiate the promoted message. By 1986 celebrities from Margaret Thatcher to the actor Robbie Coltrane were queuing up to link their names to what had already become Scotland's biggest ever marketing campaign (Struthers, 1986).

The other campaign, launched by the London Borough of Hackney (Hackney LBC, 1983), experienced a very different fate (Figure 2.2). In a general sense this effort grew from the same underlying problems. Spurred by the publication of deprivation indices based on the 1981 Census of Population that showed it consistently in the worst position of all the metropolitan areas in England and Wales (though not, interestingly, Scotland, which did not feature in the analysis),

FIGURE 2.1 Glasgow's Miles Better was the first major example of American-style municipal entrepreneurialism. Source: Struthers Advertising/Copyright Promotions (Mr Happy figure copyright Mrs Roger Hargreaves)

it too looked to its external image. Yet the campaign it launched, aimed mainly at media and political opinion-formers, could not have been more different from that of Glasgow. Its theme slogan, 'Hackney: Britain's Poorest Borough', made no attempt to look on the bright side. The optimism of Mr Happy was replaced by grim bullet points itemising and quantifying the borough's distress.

Soon these same points were appearing in the press and TV documentaries. The irony was that Glasgow actually outdid or ran Hackney close on many of those deprivation indicators. It could, with a clear conscience, have used much the same slogan itself. A few voices in the Scottish city called for just that and saw Mr Happy as 'insultingly patronising' to the many deprived Glasgwegians (Barnett, 1991: 168). Yet this was not a majority view (Wishart, 1991: 44) and today, Glasgow's city leaders can have little cause to regret their first major foray into the world of image promotion. In contrast to the regular recycling of elements from Glasgow's Miles Better in subsequent advertising (Mr Happy as

FIGURE 2.2   The London Borough of Hackney's 1983 image campaign shunned the jaunty optimism of 'Glasgow's Miles Better', emphasising instead the notion of city as victim. Source: London Borough of Hackney, lent by Peter Edwards

artist in the 1996 Festival of Visual Arts for example), 'Hackney: Britain's Poorest Borough' has largely been forgotten.

The new entrepreneurialism and its antecedents

This sharp contrast between the image campaigns of two declining city areas in 1983 serves to highlight that particular year as a defining moment, marking the final emergence of a fully fledged tradition of promotional city marketing in Britain. The essential message of Hackney's unsuccessful campaign was backward looking. It was predicated on the notion of city as a victim and relied on shaming the central state into providing resources to alleviate its distress. It looked back to a period when considerations of local need and welfare were, alone, primary determinants of central allocation of public funds. By 1983, however, welfarism, if not quite dead, was no longer enough. The economic changes of the 1970s and the political changes of the 1980s together called forth a new urban policy narrative. Rather than whining about their misfortune the new *Zeitgeist* of Thatcherism wanted to find an entrepreneurial spirit, of declining cities being prepared to pick themselves up, dust themselves off and start all over again.

Glasgow was the first really convincing British example of this new policy narrative. In its campaign and related initiatives to develop its cultural and service infrastructure, to shift it decisively from a centre of production to one of consumption, it took on the role of entrepreneurial 'comeback' city. This phenomenon was already identifiable in the USA. Boston, Baltimore, New York, Cleveland and other American cities had already begun to project this story about themselves, with varying degrees of justification.

Yet the adoption of this entrepreneurial narrative of urban success marked less of a break with established US urban policy traditions. The idea of boosterist city marketing was deeply entrenched as a part of the North American agenda for the city, forming an integral part of the whole process of settlement and urbanisation. The growth of federal initiatives from the New Deal to the 1970s had certainly pushed local boosterism into the background, especially in Canada. But the US tradition in particular never died; the memory was always recoverable.

There was a sharp contrast here with Britain, where such boosterism and inter-urban competition to capture economic activity had never been so widespread or integral to the urban system. From the first, urban public policy in industrial cities such as Glasgow was rather less concerned with engendering economic growth than with coping with its consequences. This is not to say that there were no British precedents for the kind of entrepreneurial boosterism which has become universal since 1983. The point is that they had relatively little effect on the urban main stream. They were largely confined to particular urban subsystems or, if they spread more widely, to short periods of unusual economic stress.

THE MAIN EPISODES OF PLACE MARKETING

This essential contrast between the USA and Britain, to a large extent perhaps between North America and Europe, forms the subject of this chapter. Thus I review and document briefly the main historical episodes of place marketing in the two countries and then draw together the findings, using the patterns of spatial differences and similarities to highlight the key variables in the process. In that respect, this historical review will contribute to understanding contemporary practice.

Selling the frontier

Logically, we might expect there to be some form of place marketing associated with every freely conducted act of land settlement. Yet, if it did take place, relatively little evidence survives in Britain. We do not know, for example, by what mechanisms the Saxon brigands who attacked the declining Romano-British settlements led the way for the waves of English settlement that followed (e.g. Stenton, 1947; Whitelock, 1972). If Britain was 'marketed' by the exaggerated tales of these marauders, we know nothing of it. Such a conclusion seems to hold true for all long-settled lands, including much of Europe. We gain occasional glimpses of conscious strategies to attract settlers to the less settled corners of the continent. In the sixteenth and seventeenth centuries, for example, the Swedish crown offered tax incentives to Finnish peasants who settled in the Varmland region. But such evidence is exceptional in a European context.

North America was, of course, very different. From the times of the first European contacts there seems to be evidence of the importance of some form of place marketing. Initially this was primitive in the extreme. But gradually it assumed characteristics that we would recognise as similar to modern forms of place marketing. By the eighteenth century place marketing efforts would proceed from official proclamations, inviting the settlement of particular tracts of land (for example that issued by the Governor of Georgia in 1773). These official statements would give details of incentives, convey an optimistic impression of the area and play down difficulties. There were also other unofficial publications, often produced commercially, that described the new lands in glowing terms.

It was not, however, until the 1840s that more intense and truly modern forms of place marketing appeared. These coincided with the development of regular steamship communication between Europe and North America and the development of railroads that progressively opened up more of the West for settlement. In 1849 a major settlement marketing campaign was begun by the state of Michigan. Wisconsin and Iowa followed soon after. The decision, in 1852, to make a huge federal land grant to encourage the building of the Illinois Central Railroad (ICRR), moved the business of area marketing into a much more intensive mode (Figure 2.3) (Gates, 1934).

As the first of the land grant railroads, the ICRR became a pioneer also of place marketing. In 1854 it began to produce promotional publications and issue huge volumes of newspaper and public advertising. Its agents also did much to encourage and advise intending settlers in Europe and in other parts of America. These efforts to dispose of its vast public endowment of land continued over the following decades. By then, though, its lead had been followed as the land grant became the typical mechanism for securing railroad construction. The Civil War also emasculated the strong Southern opposition to westward settlement, allowing the 1862 Homestead Act to be passed. This, together with other legislation, encouraged further marketing efforts by state governments, by railroads and by a wide variety of private agencies (Quiett, 1934; Dumke, 1944; Fitte, 1966; Wishart, 1987). Canadian experience followed that in the USA, as the railways were developed on the land grant principle and homesteading legislation, based directly on the US legislation, was passed in 1872.

Town promotion and early city boosterism

With agricultural colonisation went another form of place marketing, the promotion of towns. Again, in long-settled Britain, where the development of

IN THE GARDEN STATE OF THE WEST.

THE ILLINOIS CENTRAL RAILROAD CO., HAVE FOR SALE
1,200,000 ACRES OF RICH FARMING LANDS,
In Tracts of Forty Acres and upward on Long Credit and at Low Prices.

THE attention of the enterprising and industrious portion of the community is directed to the following statements and liberal inducements offered them by the

ILLINOIS CENTRAL RAILROAD COMPANY.
which, as they will perceive, will enable them, by proper energy, perseverance and industry, to provide comfortable homes for themselves and families, with, comparatively speaking, very little capital.

LANDS OF ILLINOIS.
No State in the Valley of the Mississippi offers so great an inducement to the settler as the State of Illinois, There is no portion of the world where all the conditions of climate and soil so admirably combine to produce those two great staples, Corn and Wheat, as the Prairies of Illinois.

EASTERN AND SOUTHERN MARKETS.
These lands are contiguous to a railroad 700 miles in length, which connects with other roads and navigable lakes and rivers, thus affording an unbroken communication with the Eastern and Southern markets.

RAILROAD SYSTEM OF ILLINOIS.
Over $100,000,000 of private capital have been expended on the railroad system of Illinois. Inasmuch as part of the income from several of these works, go to diminish the State expenses ; the taxes are light, and must consequently every day decrease,

THE STATE DEBT.
The State debt is only $10,106,308 14, and within the last three years has been reduced $2,969,746 80, and we may reasonably expect that in ten years it will become extinct.

PRESENT POPULATION.
The State is rapidly filling up with population ; 868,025 persons having been added since 1850, making the present population 1,723,663, a ratio of 102 per cent. in ten years.

AGRICULTURAL PRODUCTS.
The Agricultural Products of Illinois are greater than those of any other State. The products sent out during the past year exceeded 1,500,000 tons. The wheat crop of 1860 approaches 35,000,000 bushels, while the corn crop yields not less than 140,000,000 bushels.

FERTILITY OF THE SOIL.
Nowhere can the industrious farmer secure such immediate results for his labor as upon these prairie soils, they being composed of a deep rich loam, the fertility of which is unsurpassed by any on the globe.

TO ACTUAL CULTIVATORS.
Since 1854 the Company have sold 1,300,000 acres. They sell only to actual cultivators, and every contract contains an agreement to cultivate. The road has been constructed through these lands at an expense of $30,000,000. In 1850 the population of forty-nine counties, through which it passes, was only 335,598 ; since which 479,293 have been added ; making the whole population 814,891, a gain of 143 per cent.

EVIDENCES OF PROSPERITY.
As an evidence of the thrift of the people, it may be stated that 600,000 tons of freight, including 8,600,000 bushels of grain, and 250,000 barrels of flour were forwarded over the line last year.

PRICES AND TERMS OF PAYMENT.
The prices of these lands vary from $6 to $25 per acre, according to location, quality, &c. First class farming lands sell for about $10 to $12 per acre ; and the relative expense of subduing prairie land as compared with wood land is in the ratio of 1 to 10 in favor of the former. The terms of sale for the bulk of these lands will be

ONE YEAR'S INTEREST IN ADVANCE,
at six per cent per annum, and six interest notes at six per cent., payable respectively in one, two, three, four, five and six years from date of sale ; and four notes for principal, payable in four, five, six and seven years from date of sale ; the contract stipulating that one-tenth of the tract purchased shall be fenced and cultivated, each and every year, for five years from date of sale, so that at the end of five years one-half shall be fenced and under cultivation.

TWENTY PER CENT. WILL BE DEDUCTED
from the valuation for cash, except the same should be at six dollars per acre, when the cash price will be five dollars

Pamphlets descriptive of the lands, soil, climate, productions, prices, and terms of payment, can be had on application to

J. W. FOSTER, Land Commissioner,
CHICAGO, ILLINOIS

For the name of the Towns, Villages and Cities situated upon the Illinois Central Railroad, see pages 188, 189 and 190 Appleton's Railway Guide.

most towns long preceded the appearance of printed mass media, there is little surviving evidence of this type of place marketing (there were a few exceptions, as a small number of additional settlements were inserted, but I will deal with these below). Once again, however, it was a type of activity that was very common in North America.

One of the major imperatives was the disposal of town lots either by railroads or land companies. Railroads were in a particularly strong position because they controlled one of the factors most important for a town's long-term success: transportation. Many towns were directly promoted as commercial ventures by railroads (something which was strongly discouraged in Britain by the legislation governing railways). Others were more completely speculative creations, or already existed before the railroads, as mining settlements. In such contexts the railroad was essential to guarantee future success, so much so that railroads were able to exact subsidies from towns in return for serving them (McKelvey, 1963). Even future major cities such as Los Angeles or Denver had to pay heavily to secure rail links (Quiett, 1934; Dumke, 1944). The pattern was even more intense in Canada, where miniscule Winnipeg, for example, eclipsed its then larger neighbours, buying its prairie gateway position with railway subsidies (Morris, 1989). Even Montreal and Toronto, already pre-eminent in their provinces, had to pay heavily to maintain their dominance (Bloomfield, 1983). Yet such practices were quite unknown in Britain, where the railway companies had largely to negotiate their way into an already well-established urban and regional system.

Similarly the characteristic North American place rivalry to secure the various additional trappings of urban credibility, such as state universities, prisons, even asylums for the insane, or to become county towns, was barely visible in Britain (Gates, 1934; McKelvey, 1963). Only occasionally did the reorganisations of British local government in the late nineteenth century raise the question of location. In almost all cases the location of Britain's county towns was a foregone conclusion, resolved centuries earlier and often enshrined in the very names of places.

The intense sense of place competition which was manifest at a very early stage in much US urbanisation, especially in the Mid- and Far West, found expression in a variety of promotional publicity. A characteristic form was the promotional map, showing town lots for sale, produced by land or railroad companies (Reps, 1965). Later, as the town itself began to develop its own booster institutions, such organisations would themselves issue publicity material. In North America then, place marketing was an integral part of the settling of the land and the creation of the first urban places over much of the continent. It also played a key role in the initial establishing of dominance

---

FIGURE 2.3 The Illinois Central Railroad was one of the pioneers of place marketing, as shown in this example from the 1860s. Source: Author's collection

within the emergent urban hierarchy. This inter-place competition was expressed in many ways. Culture, architecture and urban improvement became important weapons in the assertion of major city status, used to considerable effect by centres throughout the West in the late nineteenth and twentieth centuries. As Wilson has shown, the ideals of the city beautiful became a powerful weapon in the boosterist armoury (Wilson, 1989). Meanwhile boosterist publicity was used to market ambitious towns and cities, not only in the West, but also in the post-bellum South. Henry Grady's vision of a 'New South', based on industry and urban growth, was expressed in a welter of promotional brochures, led by Atlanta (Cobb, 1984; Russell, 1988; Rutheiser, 1996).

In Britain, entirely new town promotions were extraordinarily rare. After the seventeenth century only a small number of significant new urban places emerged. Chief among these were the seaside resorts and the residential suburbs, extremely important exceptions that I will discuss more fully below. Of the rest, Middlesbrough, Barrow-in-Furness and Ashton-under-Lyne were the only important industrial towns to be created in the eighteenth and nine-teenth centuries (Briggs, 1963; Darby, 1973). Such place marketing to promote new urban places was, then, a very limited theme in British urbanisation in the eighteenth and nineteenth centuries.

So too was the kind of boosterism associated with the establishment of the urban hierarchy, the process by which what Boorstin (1965) has aptly termed 'upstart cities' struggled to make themselves more important than their neigh-bours. Historical geographers and others have often been uncertain as to whether to stress continuity or discontinuity in the British urban hierarchy (e.g. Carter and Lewis, 1990). By comparison with the USA, however, it is the remarkable stability of the British urban system that is most striking. By 1700 London was already dominant, and the pattern of the principal English pro-vincial cities, the regional capitals, was already apparent. Some older centres, such as Norwich and Exeter, were certainly becoming less significant, but there was no sudden transformation, certainly not in the nineteenth century.

By 1840 the British urban rank size hierarchy looked remarkably similar, with the exceptions already noted, to the pattern of 1960. It was not simply that the city and town size relationships remained fairly stable through a period of great population growth. So too did the underlying functional relationships between places. Each major provincial city became a regional 'command centre' for particular industrial activities. Each was surrounded by a constel-lation of smaller towns which were its dependent production centres. At the head of the whole system was London, dominant and unchallenged in administration, banking and trade.

Against such a background, there was less impetus for the kind of com-petitive boosterism that was so typical of North America, especially in the emergent West or the 'New South'. Accordingly Britain saw little of the explicit rhetoric of place marketing. There were no American-style promotional brochures and the political agenda of Britain's cities in the nineteenth century was more concerned with cleaning up the mess that industrialisation and growth had brought, rather than seeking to stimulate further growth. It was essentially concerned with the social reproductive rather than the economic productive functions of cities (Morris, 1989).

Selling the resort

The principal exception came in the new seaside resorts which had begun to appear in Britain by the early eighteenth century. Most unusually for Britain, many of them were actually substantially new settlements (Walton, 1983). They became much more numerous and important following the development of the railways. These allowed widening sections of the populations of the industrial towns and cities to enjoy them, for day excursions and longer holidays. By the later nineteenth and early twentieth centuries resorts were among the most rapidly growing towns in Britain.

Their success depended on drawing attention to themselves and it was in this setting that large-scale place marketing first appeared in Britain. Both the railway companies and, increasingly, the resorts themselves played an important part in doing this. There was extensive competition between railway companies, eager to promote their particular resorts and secure the increased traffic receipts which resulted. The towns themselves were also actively drawn into this sense of place competition. Unusually for Britain, the resorts were an extremely unstable part of the British urban system, with rapid changes in the rank size hierarchy among the resorts within only a few decades. It was, then, not surprising that the first British town to secure local powers to permit municipal advertising was also its first truly mass resort, Blackpool, in 1879 (Figure 2.4) (Ward, 1988). Emulation by other resorts initially proved difficult because of central resistance to powers for competitive advertising (improbably enough, Parliament claimed not to have noticed the relevant clause in Blackpool's local bill). Many resorts formed voluntary publicity associations, but eventually, in 1921, all resort municipalities secured advertising powers.

Meanwhile very similar things were happening in North America. From about the same period, US resorts began to be actively promoted by a combination of railroad and more local efforts. Here then was one instance, at least, where British and North American experiences were broadly similar. There were more similarities than differences in how Atlantic City and Blackpool, for example, were promoted and marketed (Funnell, 1975). Yet important differences still remained. Atlantic City was less typical of American resorts than was Blackpool of British resorts. This was because in Britain the seaside town was the most typical manifestation of the resort phenomenon, compared to more inland resorts, often smaller, in the USA and Canada.

Thus relatively fewer American resorts developed into sizeable towns on the British pattern. Local government and local business networks would therefore be rather more modest than in the average British seaside resort. This was

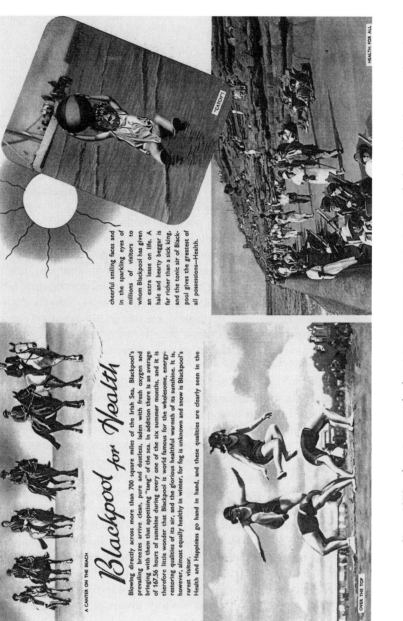

A CANTER ON THE BEACH

Blackpool for Health

Blowing directly across more than 700 square miles of the Irish Sea, Blackpool's prevailing breezes arrive clean, pure and dustless, laden with fresh oxygen and bringing with them that appetising "tang" of the sea. In addition there is an average of 167.56 hours of sunshine during every one of the six summer months, and it is therefore little wonder that Blackpool is world famous for the wholesome, energy-restoring qualities of its air, and the glorious healthful warmth of its sunshine. It is, however, almost equally healthy in winter, for fog is unknown and snow is Blackpool's rarest visitor.

Health and Happiness go hand in hand, and these qualities are clearly seen in the cheerful smiling faces and in the sparkling eyes of millions of visitors to whom Blackpool has given an extra lease on life. A hale and hearty beggar is far richer than a sick king, and the tonic air of Blackpool gives the greatest of all possessions—Health.

OVER THE TOP

HEALTH FOR ALL

FIGURE 2.4 Since 1879, when it secured advertising powers unique in Britain, Blackpool has dominated in the selling of the seaside. This example dates from the 1930s. Source: Author's collection

perhaps one reason why the railroads were able to play an even more important role in their marketing, compared to Britain. Many western mountain resorts, for example, had been directly promoted by railroad companies and continued to be so into the twentieth century (Runte, 1991, 1992, 1994). And many American resorts, including Atlantic City, had railroad involvement in the original ownership and development of land. This was something which was illegal in Britain so that only occasional instances can be found (for example at Cleethorpes in Lincolnshire) (Biddle, 1990).

The notion that advertising should be conducted by the municipality seems to have been particularly highly developed in Britain (though it was also apparent in Canada). The kinds of business groupings that were important in promoting Atlantic City (or indeed many other non-resort cities in the USA) rarely seem to have operated as effectively in Britain. Local publicity associations operated by local business interests usually experienced funding problems. Yet the broad point, that the British did market their resorts with at least as much vigour as did the Americans, is an important one.

Selling the suburb

Another facet of British place marketing involved the residential suburbs which began to proliferate in the later nineteenth century. Like the resorts, these were, unusually for Britain, 'upstart' places, increasingly created *de novo*. Unlike the resorts, however, the British approach to marketing the suburbs seems to have owed a lot to American experiences (Jackson, 1985). Mass marketing of suburban places in the USA seems to date from the late 1870s/ 1880s. In this, as in much else on the urban scene at that time, Chicago appears as the centre of innovation. During these decades the city was rapidly growing, more so than any other large city in the world, and extending outwards along railroads and street-car lines. And more than many other cities, the development of its suburban residential areas was in the hands of specu-lators (Daunton, 1990). The more co-operative building and loan associations that were common in older cities like Philadelphia or Baltimore, or even some smaller Midwestern cities such as Milwaukee, were unknown in Chicago.

This mix of factors encouraged more extensive suburban marketing in Chicago than anywhere else in the 1880s. The unrivalled master of this process was the biggest of all the US developers catering for the mass market, S.E. Gross, from whose offices came great volumes of suburban promotional advertising of a sophistication never before experienced (Berger, 1992; Clark and Ashley, 1992). One of the characteristic features of the speculative devel-opment process was the close links with improvements in transit, especially the street-car lines. Developers like Gross commonly had links with transit operators, either by part-ownership of street-car lines or mutual agreements. In turn, the street-car lines were extended out into open country well beyond the built fringe of the city, particularly after electrification. Flat fares, irrespective of distance, were typical of American practice. The prospect of a share in real estate development profits was a key factor in these strategies. In turn, the improvements in electric street traction forced the main steam railroads into defensive action, promoting suburban living along their own lines to stimulate their flagging suburban traffic.

These approaches, which were well established throughout US cities by the early twentieth century, began to spread to Britain along with electric traction. Much of the early electric transport technology applied in British cities was American, and there was a minor invasion of American transit capitalists, managers and engineers about the turn of the century (Barker and Robbins, 1963, 1974). Most prominent was Charles Tyson Yerkes, the former Chicago transit magnate, who took over the stalled London tube system and brought it to fruition in the early twentieth century. Yerkes and his associates also brought US ideas about transit-encouraged suburban development, ensuring that the proposed lines began to be extended out into the green fields. Happily for them, they were also able to participate in the resultant local building boom.

The problem was, however, that general British conditions even in the early twentieth century were less conducive to mass suburbanisation than they had been as early as the 1880s in the USA (Harris and Hamnett, 1987). Real incomes were lower in British cities and brick houses in Britain were more expensive to produce compared to US timber construction. The development industry in Britain still operated on a small scale. Moreover, there was not yet a mass demand for home ownership, as opposed to renting, something that was crucially important in suburban marketing. Accordingly the suburban boom happened on a much smaller scale than the US promoters expected. The new London tubes undermined the traffic of the existing steam railways, though without themselves making worthwhile profits. It was also more difficult in Britain to offset operating losses with land development profits, because of the legal limitations on the involvement of railways in the land market.

Thus it was that the large-scale marketing of the suburbs in Britain grew out of the financial insecurities of suburban rail operators, including the London Underground (Jackson, A.A., 1986, 1991). They had either invested heavily and failed to gain a commensurate return, or were facing heavy falls in pre-existing traffic. The years from about 1905 saw a proliferation of suburban marketing initiatives from mainline railway companies and London's newly electrified tube, District and Metropolitan Railways. The latter, which had powers, unique in Britain, to allow it to become involved in land development, soon became the most active of the suburban railway promoters.

These initiatives continued in the rather more auspicious circumstances of the interwar years, when Britain experienced a huge housing boom even through the worst years of the world depression (Gold and Gold, 1990, 1994). Around London the Underground, the Southern Railway and the Metropolitan, with its famous Metro-Land campaign, set the pace in the 1920s. By the 1930s,

Leave the smoke of the valley—

for the sunshine of the hills

ON

LAINGS

SHOOTERS HILL ESTATE

Adjoins Golf Course and Park.   Close to Schools.   Gravel Subsoil.

This delightful Estate is built at the top of Shooters Hill commanding beautiful views and receiving the sea breezes as they drift up the Thames Valley. Every house has 3 or 4 bedrooms, 2 large reception rooms, fitted labour saving kitchen, tiled bathroom, 4 large bay windows and ample garden space. Each house is soundly constructed and architect designed. The Estate is laid out with tree-lined roads and delightful lawns and shrubberies a truly desirable place to live in.

MANY ADVANCES THROUGH WOOLWICH BOROUGH COUNCIL

£780 TO £1155

FREEHOLD

From 2l/2 Weekly Rates 6/I

Write for FREE Illustrated Booklet K.I.

LAINGS SHREWSBURY PARK ESTATE, SHREWSBURY LANE or PLUM LANE, SHOOTERS HiLL, S.E.18
or Phone: WOOLWICH 1495

From Charing Cross to Woolwich Arsenal Station (Southern Electric). Bus Nos. 53, 53a, 54, 153 and 289a to end of Plum Lane, or Trams 44 and 46from Well Hall Station, or bus No. 21a to Shrewsbury Lane, Shooters Hill.

FIGURE 2.5   By the 1930s, British developers had become the major sellers of suburbs, in the manner of the famous Chicago developer of the late nineteenth century, S.E. Gross. Source: John Laing Archives

private housebuilding was occurring at a higher level than ever before or since. The house development industry was by then showing more signs of concentration into fewer, and larger firms, such as New Ideal Homesteads, John Laing, Taylor Woodrow, and Wates, who were operating powerful estate marketing machines. Meanwhile, the pump being well primed, most railways were diminishing their suburban marketing efforts. The main exception was the Southern, whose interwar electrification far outstripped those of any other railway, extending its commuter net throughout the southern home counties. Overall though, the balance of suburban marketing activities in Britain had finally shifted. The main London residential developers were, by 1930, doing what S.E. Gross had begun half a century earlier (Figure 2.5). They also learned very quickly over the following decade, in some ways overtaking the depressed US housing development industry in marketing expertise.

Selling the industrial town

Differences in timing notwithstanding, the two cases of resort and suburban marketing show important similarities between British and North American

experiences. There was also some tendency to convergence in the way industrial towns and cities marketed themselves. Here though the convergence
between British and US experiences was incomplete. The essence of the North
American pattern was that marketing and promotion were pursued more
vigorously in areas of peripheral industrialisation. We have seen how boosterism was integral to the selling and settlement of the West. In most respects,
though, it was the southern USA and Canada which showed the most aggressive
approaches to industrial promotion, effectively buying industries with various
kinds of local subsidies (Ward, 1994). As we have seen, for many areas this
practice had begun with the railroads as towns and cities paid subsidies to
guarantee the tracks would serve them. In Canada this also began to be applied
on a large scale to industry in the 1870s (Bloomfield, 1983). Huge amounts of
money were paid in local cash bonuses, interest-free loans, tax exemptions, free
gifts of various kinds and other incentives (Ward, 1991). The practice gradually
became subject to provincial controls, earlier in the west than in Ontario or
Quebec. It was not until the 1920s that effective controls were introduced and
certain local powers to give tax exemptions continued until 1962.

The southern USA started later into the buying of industries as part of an
industrial promotion strategy (Cobb, 1993). After the Civil War there had been
much windy rhetoric, voiced most persistently by the Atlanta journalist, Henry
Grady, about the creation of a 'New South', based on industry and urbanisation
rather than agriculture and plantation (Figure 2.6). Beyond advertising,
however, relatively little was done to implement this vision, at least outside
Atlanta, until the 1920s. The boll-weevil and the depression between them
killed off any residual notions of the South as an agrarian Utopia and triggered
one of the most aggressive strategies ever seen anywhere, to market places for
industrial development. Local subsidies of dubious legality were common-
place. In 1936 Mississippi finally found an enduring and legally acceptable
basis for local subsidies under the so-called BAWI (Balance Agriculture With
Industry) Programme. This allowed tax-free municipal bonds to be used to
finance new industrial development.

In Britain, serious attempts to market industrial towns came very late (Ward,
1990). The first such programme was launched in 1899 by the Bedfordshire
town of Luton, already internationally renowned for the making of straw hats.
Its feared overdependence on one industry which was becoming increasingly
vulnerable to international competition caused its leaders to seek new
industries. Compared to contemporary US and Canadian experience, however,
it was a puny effort with miniscule funding. Yet its apparent success quickly
encouraged other British towns to emulate Luton's initiative and several
pressed for municipal advertising powers. Even more consistently than for the
resorts, such municipal pleading foundered on the rocks of central government
opposition.

The interwar period and the effects of depression on many industrial towns
in the older coalfield areas intensified local concerns about the need to

INVENTORY YOUR TERRITORIES, TOO

PEOPLE are important to business, to *you*, not in terms of How Many, but How Much. Per se it is not important that the incorporated area of Atlanta includes three hundred thousand or more people. Nor that the overnight circle encompasses eighteen million.

What these millions are able to buy is the important fact.

It has been estimated that an $8,000 income in Atlanta is the equivalent of a $12,000 income elsewhere,—for the Atlanta dollar buys a higher standard of living than elsewhere. In other words, the margin is greater for comforts, for luxuries—for the things you sell.

And this year you who sell luxuries and semi-luxuries will need more than ever to search out fields where your kind of goods can be bought.

This is inventory time. Make a careful analysis of your major territories. Find out the *true* purchasing power in each, the sales you are making in each, the sales you *should* be making in each.

The South is a vital market. Its purchasing power has trebled in the past ten years. It has far outrun the ability of statisticians to record the growth that is taking place. Yet you are apt to find your Southern volume under your expectations—unless you are operating from a branch in the South.

Modern marketing conditions have made it necessary to put a branch in each major market. Your trade expects "overnight" delivery—and your Southern trade looks to Atlanta, because fifteen main railroad lines reach most quickly to the whole rich territory and because America's outstanding concerns, already here, have created the habit.

Branch offices in Atlanta have a way of growing into branch factories. Improved distribution facilities increase volume, to the point where a branch factory becomes practical. Fundamental economies in the Atlanta Industrial Area make it an unusually desirable location, with efficient labor, plentiful raw materials, low taxes, low-cost power, low ground rents, low building costs, equable climate and many other factors all helping to lower production cost and increase profits.

Can we help you make your inventory of the South? The Atlanta Industrial Bureau is organized for the job. It is ready to go out and develop a first hand study especially for you without charge or obligation, and in the strictest confidence. The work will be started at once if you will write,

> **1929**
> Prosperity
> assures Big
> Southern
> Business in
> **1930**

INDUSTRIAL BUREAU, CHAMBER OF COMMERCE
Chamber of Commerce Building

Send for this Booklet! It contains the fundamental facts about Atlanta as a location for your Southern branch

ATLANTA

Industrial Headquarters of the South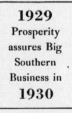

FIGURE 2.6 In 1926, the Forward Atlanta movement set new standards in industrial promotion. This shows one of many advertisements produced in the late 1920s. Source: Atlanta Public Library

stimulate new industries. The traditional caution of the Local Government Board and its interwar successor, the Ministry of Health, over the encouragement of municipal competition was overtaken by the concerns of a more powerful central ministry. Thus the Board of Trade became a convert to the cause of local promotional initiative, largely because it was unwilling to countenance the alternative strategy of decisive central intervention. By the late 1930s, in the wake of the (extremely weak) advertising powers granted under the Local Authorities (Publicity) Act 1931, and various, usually ambiguous, municipal powers to develop and market factories, there was something of a flowering of industrial promotion in Britain (Fogarty, 1947). At that time very similar approaches, resting on advertising and factory or site provision, were evident in Britain, Canada and the US South.

In Britain, and to a lesser extent Canada, the localised approach was short-lived. The Second World War brought to Britain what the 1930s depression alone had not: decisive central government controls over the granting of subsidies for industrial location, under the guise of regional policies. This nationally orchestrated distribution of industry policy was actively pursued until the 1970s, dampening down the more localised efforts at industrial promotion. Canada also began to shift in this same direction, more so from the 1960s (Rea, 1985). The USA also showed similar tendencies but the efforts of higher governments never managed (or indeed seriously sought) to supplant local boosterism. The South, for example, evolved a distinctive promotional approach that linked state and municipal governments, creating one of the most aggressive and sustained episodes of place marketing ever seen (Cobb, 1993).

Selling the post-industrial city

Yet the most widespread form of place marketing is that dominant today. As I showed at the outset, the time-lag in the international diffusion of the current manifestation of urban entrepreneurialism has been much shorter than ever before. As always, the USA has been the principal source of place-marketing ideas, but the economic and political changes of the last quarter of the twentieth century have universalised them.

The main economic changes which have underpinned this latest episode of city marketing have been those associated with deindustrialisation. Between 1977 and 1993, the USA lost roughly 2 million – about a tenth – of its manufacturing jobs. Britain was even more severely affected, losing 3.6 million – 45% – between 1974 and 1994 (Ward, 1998). The brunt of this decline fell on the older industrial cities. In the USA these were concentrated in the north-eastern states. In Britain, by contrast, nowhere was immune, though northern and midland England, Scotland and Wales generally suffered more. Yet the urban effects of a structural decline in British industry more severe than in the USA were mitigated by a much stronger British tradition of central support for local government finances (Kirwan, 1986). As we have seen, Hackney's ill-starred 1983 campaign tried to appeal to this tradition of central support, even though it was already beginning to break down. Nor was the real local tax base of most British cities quite so weak as the older US cities. Few were as tightly locked as their American equivalents into boundaries that excluded more prosperous suburban districts. The erosion of service employment that reinforced the deindustrialisation of US cities was also much less pronounced in Britain. British planning policies, especially tight green-belt policies, and lower car ownership for many years limited the decentralisation of major retailing and office employment and thus protected traditional central areas.

Overall, therefore, we can see the earlier emergence of post-industrial marketing in the USA as more than just a consequence of the long North American tradition of city boosterism. Despite Britain's more serious under-lying structural economic problems, there were specific institutional and spatial processes which concentrated and exacerbated the effects of structural decline in American city cores (Wolman and Goldsmith, 1992). Unlike British cities, economic decline was quickly reflected in a fiscal crisis of city government. Thus New York narrowly avoided bankruptcy in 1975 (Kotler, Haider and Rein, 1993). Cleveland was forced to default on debt repayments three years later. There have been many others. It was this comparative absence of any financial cushioning, allied with a tradition of greater local autonomy than in Britain, which projected US cities into the forefront of the latest phase of boosterism (Bailey, 1989). If they did not swim, they sank.

Meanwhile in Britain, the greater willingness of the Thatcher government to move down the American road, particularly by cutting central financial support for local government and loosening the planning policies that had traditionally limited the decentralisation of retailing and office employment, encouraged increasingly similar responses. So too did the more explicit attempts to foster urban entrepreneurialism evident in the creation of the urban development corporations (UDCs) from 1981 (Imrie and Thomas, 1993a). Along with the municipal pioneers such as Glasgow, the UDCs set a new style in the early-middle 1980s, a style in which economic promotion and marketing were far more important than had been usual in elective local authorities. Yet, by the end of the decade, the new entrepreneurialism and city marketing had become accepted by all local governments. Unlike any previous British episode of place marketing, it pervaded the whole of the British urban system.

The content of marketing strategies has also been derived largely from the USA (Ward, 1997). I have noted, for example, how New York inspired Glasgow's advertising campaign. As wider representations of the post-industrial city, Boston and Baltimore were particularly potent exemplars throughout Britain and Europe (Lyall, 1982; Harvey, 1989b; O'Connor, T.H., 1993). If New York had set the pace for city boosting image campaigns it was Boston and Baltimore which led in defining the nature of the post-industrial city as a centre for consumption. It was their harbour-front developments, festival marketplaces, aquaria, conference facilities, museums, galleries and much else that created the marketing image of the reinvented, post-industrial city. It was also their development of strong traditions of public–private partnership in regeneration which defined what appeared, to British eyes, to be the secret of success (Figure 2.7).

Ironically these older eastern cities are places with less of a tradition of aggressive boosterism than other US cities. Their geographical positions and, in the case of Boston, its seminal historic role in the US urban system, have meant that they were rather different from the upstart cities of the West, or the post-bellum cities of the South, trying to reinvent themselves. But today they are, literally, post-industrial cities which have lost (and are losing) their traditional sources of employment. More importantly, they are perceived as being successful in dealing with those problems (Wolman, Ford and Hill, 1994).

British and, indeed, most other Western attempts at marketing the post-industrial city have largely followed the same basic formula. The pursuit of the tourist market has been a central theme. Much marketing effort has been devoted to developing the big cities as tourist destinations (Law, 1993). Liverpool, for example, has undertaken major renewal of its historic docks to draw visitors to its 'Vintage Port' (Parkinson and Bianchini, 1993). The development of conference and exhibition business has also become very important, most obviously in Birmingham, 'Europe's Meeting Place' (Duffy, 1995; Hubbard, 1996a). In approaching these projects, the US concept of the partnership or growth coalition of business and public authority has also been much invoked, though rarely replicated (Judd and Parkinson, 1990b). The involvement of private interests in development initiatives has become essential (Healey et al, 1992). Private leadership in regeneration has, however, been more apparent than real.

There are, then, some significant differences in the detailed character of city marketing. On the whole, British (and Canadian) initiatives tend to betray more obviously the hand of government agencies than their US equivalents. Yet the broad point is of a remarkable pervasive form of place marketing, spread rapidly and more completely than any earlier episodes.

CONCLUSION

Place marketing has, then, been an integral part of the history of urbanisation in North America, unlike Britain. British episodes of place marketing have been altogether more limited. Until very recently, what might be termed 'routine' boosterism, on the American pattern, has not been apparent. British experiences have paralleled American experiences only when there has been very active place competition among new types of settlement (resorts and suburbs) or when there has been major economic change threatening the main livelihood of places (industrial towns in periods of depression and post-industrial cities). This last form seems, however, to have produced a degree of

Where you can catch a few rays.

Spend a picture-perfect afternoon.

And get to know some crusty characters.

*B*ALTIMORE IS A CITY OF HISTORY, CULTURE AND CHARM. A VIBRANT METROPOLIS WITH SMALL-TOWN CHARACTER. BUT MORE IMPORTANTLY, BALTIMORE IS A CITY OF ACTIVITY, WHERE EXCITING THINGS HAPPEN EVERY DAY. HERE, YOU WILL FIND ATTRACTIONS LIKE THE NATIONAL AQUARIUM, HARBORPLACE AND THE MARYLAND SCIENCE CENTER. THE B&O RAILROAD MUSEUM AND RENOWNED INSTITUTIONS OF FINE ART. FORT MCHENRY AND ORIOLE PARK AT CAMDEN YARDS. SPECTACULAR SHOPPING AND SUPERB CHESAPEAKE BAY CUISINE. ALL CLOSE TO DOWNTOWN.

BALTIMORE IS ALSO EASILY ACCESSIBLE FROM VIRTUALLY ANYWHERE BY AIR, TRAIN OR HIGHWAY. PLUS, WE OFFER A FULL RANGE OF MODERATE-TO-DELUXE HOTEL ACCOMMODATIONS. SO WHETHER YOU ARE TRAVELING ALONE OR WITH THE ENTIRE FAMILY, YOU CAN BE SURE WE'LL PROVIDE THE EXACT LEVEL OF COMFORT AND VALUE YOU NEED. THERE'S SO MUCH TO SEE AND DO HERE -- AND SO MANY NEW THINGS UNDERWAY. WE INVITE YOU TO EXPERIENCE THE ENERGY, THE ENTHUSIASM, THE UNIQUE SPIRIT OF BALTIMORE. YOU'LL SEE WHY WE SAY THE EXCITEMENT IS STILL BUILDING.

Baltimore
Area Convention and Visitors Association
100 Light Street • 12th Floor • Baltimore, Maryland 21202

FOR MORE INFORMATION, CALL TOLL-FREE 1-800-282-6632 OR LOCALLY 410-837-4636.

FIGURE 2.7   Baltimore was one of the US leaders of post-industrial reinvention, its experiences much studied by other cities throughout North America and Europe. This 1996 tourist advertisement sums up much of its image appeal. Source: Baltimore Area Convention and Visitors Association

congruence in place marketing between Britain and North America that has not hitherto been experienced.

On the basis of this discussion I want to draw out five of the key variables shaping the nature and incidence of place marketing in North America and Britain.

Place as commodity

The historical episodes I have examined invariably show that more effort is likely to be expended marketing a place if there is something tangible associated with that place that can be directly exchanged for money. In most cases, land is the most tangible place-related commodity. It is notable that in both Britain and North America place marketing has been most vigorous where sales of real estate are involved. Thus the selling of the frontier and early town promotion were essentially concerned with the commodification of land. The suburbs too were sold, at least by developers and building societies, as forms of real property. It is also apparent that regeneration agencies concerned with property development, such as the UDCs, have been to the forefront in the selling of post-industrial cities. Although land is the most prominent place commodity, it is certainly not the only one. There were other directly marketable commodities represented by place. To transport operators, it was the ticket sales which provided the incentive to sell the resorts and the suburbs. And to the tourist industry it was obviously the sale of tourism services which provided the direct incentive to market the resorts.

Settlement history

Such intrinsic characteristics help explain why the incidence and marketing of tourist places or suburbs have tended to be a fairly universal phenomenon. Yet they leave much unexplained about the specificity of particular national or regional experiences. The historical process of settlement within particular countries or groups of countries is therefore an important variable. Thus North America was very rapidly settled at a time when capitalism and market systems were highly developed and facilities for mass transportation were allowing long-distance migration. The comparable phase of Britain's, and indeed Europe's, settlement was more gradual, with much primary colonisation of the land predating capitalism, the creation of a market economy and facilities for mass movement over large distances.

Place competition

Linked with the previous point, much place marketing has normally been associated with locations where capital and/or people have been either scarce or very mobile. In turn, this has engendered a strong sense of competition between places for these highly mobile factors of production. This competition was inherent in the prominence of place marketing in North America as the urban frontier moved westward (and where the competition was not merely between cities but also between these cities and the rural farmlands). Something of the same competition for people was also apparent in Canada. Meanwhile the South sought to industrialise by attracting external capital.

Conversely, Britain's nineteenth-century industrial and urban growth was characterised by an abundance of capital and an absence of place marketing. Britain's growing cities did not have to win external or mobile capital, nor did they have to draw migrants from any further than the surrounding countryside to sustain their growth. As I have noted, the upshot was relatively stable regionalised urban industrial systems that survived for well over a century. Accordingly, the energies of chambers of commerce in British cities were more productively devoted to the exploitation of the economic niche their city nestled comfortably within, rather than the restless search to win new sources of wealth that characterised US and Canadian boosters.

In recent years, however, the universality of post-industrial place marketing has followed directly from an exodus of capital from older cities everywhere. Even Britain's stable urban industrial system and the most stable parts of the US system, the older port cities of the east, have decayed. Capital everywhere has become far more mobile. Few places now enjoy the luxury of indigenous local capitalists, loyal to their urban regions in the manner of British (or New England) industrialisation. Every city now competes to win the highly mobile spending of tourists or the investment funds of major firms.

Local government autonomy

In addition to structural variations in economic circumstances, place marketing has also varied significantly with differences in the attitudes and actions of governments and other institutions. To the extent that place marketing rested on municipal action, therefore, the degree of local government autonomy has been extremely important. In North America the extent of this has always been greater than in Britain. Central government asserted progressively stronger control over British local government from 1835. By the late nineteenth century it was already granting financial assistance to local revenue, something which increased hugely after 1914. In contrast, North American municipalities have remained far more dependent on local finances than in Britain. They have also had access to a wider range of potential sources of local revenue. Both these have underpinned the greater autonomy of US city governments. Thus it has always been much easier to mount local marketing and economic development policies in the USA than in Britain.

There is, by contrast, abundant evidence of the way central government in Britain has sought to curb local place competition orchestrated by municipalities. For the Local Government Board and its successors, municipal advertising and other promotional endeavours funded from local taxation were seen as immoral. At times, the desire to encourage local entrepreneurialism, particularly in the 1930s and the 1980s, partially overcame this traditional moral imperative. But it remains more deeply rooted in Britain's unitary state than the US federal system. Canadian experiences incorporate something of both traditions though, until the 1920s at least, its towns and cities enjoyed great freedom of action.

The varying character of non-governmental promotional agencies

Another important contrast has been that between non-governmental agencies in Britain and North America. As we have seen, North American railroad companies were also effectively land and development companies. This endowed them with an interest in place development that went beyond the priority merely to maximise traffic. In Britain, such additional involvements were normally illegal and consequently much rarer. It is significant that the only major British exception to this rule, London's Metropolitan Railway, also mounted one of Britain's most famous and sustained place-marketing campaigns. Nor were these the only differences. Chambers of commerce have also tended to be much weaker in Britain than in the USA (or other western European countries). Thus while the chambers of commerce of many US cities were (and often still are) the premier promotional bodies in their cities, this has very rarely been the case in Britain. By default the role has often fallen to municipal authorities even though, as I have noted, their roles have been heavily circumscribed by central government.

These five broad variables begin, then, to suggest some of the major sources of the different historical experiences of place marketing in Britain and North America. The combination of variables which reflect structure and agency goes a long way to explanation. But there is always more. Broader circumstances which may influence the likelihood of place-marketing activity do not automatically ensure it or determine its character. To complete the explanation of any particular episode of place marketing we would also need to look at the specifically local circumstances which underlay the desire to grow and compete, or to regenerate and reinvent. The famous marketing efforts of, for example, Blackpool, Atlanta or Glasgow, were only partly conditioned by the broader parameters of structure and institutions. To understand them fully we must understand the nature of local leadership and the way in which wider local consent to boosterist promotion was secured. Why, to put it more simply, were some places, outwardly similar to many others, more 'growth-minded' or committed to reinventing themselves than others?

This chapter has sought to extend the usual time frame of comprehending place marketing and, by extension, urban entrepreneurialism. In doing this it has highlighted those variables which operate systematically, underpinning and shaping the general character of the key episodes of place marketing. By implication, at least, I have argued against the purely local or idiosyncratic approach to understanding place marketing. Yet such factors, if not sufficient in themselves, remain important and are certainly necessary for any satisfactory understanding.

Space does not permit a full development of case studies to demonstrate this point. I can, though, briefly refer back to the more famous of the two examples from the 1980s with which I started this chapter. Thus we can explain much about 'Glasgow's Miles Better' in terms of the acute structural decline of the west-central Scotland economy and the unusually favourable shifts in wider government thinking (certainly compared to England) evident in the Scottish Office and related bodies such as the Scottish Development Agency. But these alone did not guarantee the campaign. It was the local political realignment of the deeply entrenched Glasgow Labour group towards 'market realism', much earlier than elsewhere, and the quite extraordinary individual roles of Provost Michael Kelly and advertising executive, John Struthers, which ensured that 'Miles Better' actually happened (Struthers, 1986; Keating, 1988). The example also shows that examining the narrative that lies behind place-marketing campaigns, even such genuinely inspired efforts as Glasgow's, can be much more revealing than concentrating only on the place narrative they seek to promote.

ACKNOWLEDGEMENT

I owe the idea for the Glasgow/Hackney comparison to my colleague, Peter Edwards.

3

URBAN CRISES/URBAN REPRESENTATIONS: SELLING THE CITY IN DIFFICULT TIMES

JOHN RENNIE SHORT AND YEONG-HYUN KIM

INTRODUCTION

Cities are represented in a variety of ways: street maps, coats of arms, sports teams, slogans, spectacles and built form. In a previous paper we have argued that there has been a crisis of urban representation as cities compete in the world of global, mobile capital and a rapidly changing space economy (Short, 1998). The rapid transformation of this space economy, especially the global shift of manufacturing, the dispersal of control and service functions and the shrinkage in the space–time networks, has presented a set of new challenges and opportunities to cities around the world. The predominant forms of urban representation now revolve around the marketing of the city.

Cities are marketing (selling, promoting, advertising) themselves to create and change their image with the intended goal of attracting business, tourists and residents. Although urban marketing has been practised since the age of colonial expansion (Ward, 1990, 1994; Ward and Gold, 1994) in recent years it has undoubtedly increased in importance and intensity as cities around the world compete in a crowded global market.

Marketing the city has been discussed by various commentators with two broad approaches apparent; first, there is a body of work that ties urban marketing to a deeper political economy (Logan and Molotch, 1987; Harvey, 1989b; Kearns and Philo, 1993); second, there are studies which focus on the range and success of various marketing strategies (Ashworth and Voogd, 1990; Kotler, Haider and Rein, 1993; Gold and Ward, 1994). The approaches are not mutually exclusive, and many writers use both, often in the same work, but there are differences of orientation: the former emphasises the transformation in urban governance and the involvement of business coalition in local economic development, the latter focuses on the detailed processes and strategies of urban marketing. In this chapter we use both approaches. We position the phenomena of urban marketing in the context of the changing space economy of contemporary capitalism, the resultant crisis of urban representation and the transformation in urban governance towards entrepreneurialism. We then provide detailed case studies of two US cities and of magazine advertisements of US cities. This concentration on the USA is deliberate. It is a national urban system where place promotion has been an integral and important part of urban development, growth and decline (see Chapter 2). The selling of cities has played a very important part in the evolution of urban USA.

URBAN CRISES

The context in which we can position the growth of urban marketing is the increased competition between cities around the world. We can characterise the general story thus: throughout much of the nineteenth century and most of the twentieth there was a relatively crude division of labour; manufacturing production was undertaken in the industrial cities of the capitalist core economies while command functions were concentrated in the large cities, especially the world cities. In the past 30 years there have been major changes in manufacturing production. Technological developments, leading to the deskilling of labour and the decreasing size of transport costs, have allowed manufacturing production to be undertaken around the world. Location is now driven more by labour costs than the need to be close to markets or pools of skilled labour. The net effect is the relocation of manufacturing, a global shift that has seen the decline of older manufacturing cities in the capitalist core economies and the growth of cities in the newly industrialising countries.

New footloose industries have also arisen, especially in the high-tech sectors, which have very different locational requirements from the older metal-bashing industries. They are more concerned with access to information than closeness to a coalfield or sources of power. These brain-driven, knowledge industries have a high degree of locational flexibility. Service and command functions can, because of technological changes such as email, video-conferencing, cheaper telephone and fax rates, also be located away from the previously dominant cities. While there is still the pull of personal contact and inertia the push of rising costs has allowed the relocation of functions previously tied to the very large cities.

In total, there is a greater locational flexibility in the contemporary economy. This has been reinforced by the growing pool of mobile capital, as witnessed in the growing number of tourists, conventions and rotating spectacles such as the Olympic Games. There is a growing pool of money that can be attracted with the right mix of incentives and attributes, to particular cities. The perceived mobility of capital, as well as the actual mobility of capital, part of a general trend that sees impermanence and change rather than permanence and stability, is an important factor. The threat or potential of hypermobility of capital, as much as the actual mobility of capital, promotes entrepreneurialism in contemporary city government.

These profound changes have led to a new urban order where jobs and investment move quickly and often around the world, from city to city, up and down the urban hierarchy. In this chaotic geography cities need to position and reposition themselves. There is a crisis of urban representation as old images are cast aside and new images are presented for the new urban order.

The profound economic changes have also left an imprint of changes in urban governance. A substantial number of studies have focused theoretically and empirically on the transformation in urban governance from the welfare-state model towards an economic-development model in the European and North American context. The list of terms popularly used in the literature might be helpful for understanding this transformation: city as a growth machine (Molotch, 1976; Logan and Molotch, 1987); urban entrepreneurialism (Harvey, 1989b; Leitner, 1990); the post-Keynesian state (Gaffikin and Warf, 1993); urban regimes (Stone, 1989; Harding, 1994); city challenge (Lewis, 1994); flagship development (Smyth, 1994). Other terms include urban boosterism, urban corporatism, urban privatism, growth coalition and public–private partnership. Although the focus and methods of these studies vary, there is a widespread agreement that the background of the shift in urban governance is the growing competition between cities for local economic growth. Globalisation of markets, production, technology and finance, global economic restructuring, post-Keynesian urban policy (Thatcherism and Reaganomics), and the high mobility of capital have comprised a broader context of the increased competition between cities. US cities, in particular, have suffered due to the loss of federal funds in the post-federal period. To cope with this tough situation, city governments have been attempting to solve fiscal problems by chasing local economic development. Rather than diagnosing their problems from a systemic perspective many cities see raising capital as the solution to their problems (Kotler, Haider and Rein, 1993).

In this sense, almost all city governments have come to promote growth aggressively on a scope unimaginable just a decade ago. Haider (1992) calls this situation 'place wars' in the 1990s. Severe competition to attract and retain business forces city governments to introduce a range of policy initiatives, such as enterprise zones, urban development corporations, urban subsidies and public–private partnerships (Gaffikin and Warf, 1993). These programmes are intended to make the city more attractive to investors.

Many scholars have asked who are the main beneficiaries of this shift. There are competing interpretations. One, most often represented by Peterson (1981), argues that the growth of cities is to the benefit of all residents because any development project has only positive consequences for the city overall. Contrary to this argument, a group of scholars point out that local economic growth does not necessarily promote the public good. Logan and Molotch (1987) identify a politically motivated local élite as the main actor and bene-ficiary of local economic growth. The authors argue that place entrepreneurs, because of their attachment to land ('local dependence' in Cox and Mair, 1988), strongly encourage local growth for their own gains. In their attempts to promote the economic growth of the city place entrepreneurs organise the growth (business) coalitions that involve and mobilise local governments to intensify land uses for their private gain of many sorts. Peck (1995) critically calls them 'movers and shakers', Lowe (1993) uses the term 'local hero', and along the same line Schneider and Teske (1993) refer to them as 'progrowth entrepreneurs' (see also Chapter 12). Their business interests are established as political phenomena and subsequently institutionalised (Peck and Tickell, 1995a). Logan and Molotch (1987: 62) remark, 'once organized, they stay organized'.

The institutionalisation of business interests of regional entrepreneurs has been encouraged by the ideology and policies of post-Keynesian administrations (Lowe, 1993). Their 'growth ethic' – growth is good – is used to eliminate any alternative visions of the purpose of local government or the meaning of community (Logan and Molotch, 1987), and thus civic pride on the growth and loyalty cut across class lines (Cox and Mair, 1988). The coalition draws on local histories, culture and images to underpin its activities. Peck and Tickell (1995a) summarise the contribution of growth coalition, first, to the subordination of welfarist goals to the overriding imperatives of local competitiveness and growth; second, to an acceleration in place-based competition for both public and private investment; and third, to the formation of a new layer of business–political actors at the local level.

Detailed case studies and specific review articles can provide a more nuanced picture (see Hall and Hubbard, 1996), but in general terms, city government has become less concerned to control or regulate local business and rather more concerned to promote local economic growth; and marketing the city has become an important and growing force in contemporary urban economic development.

MARKETING THE CITY

Reflecting on the current processes of economic restructuring and the accompanying rise of the new urban entrepreneurialism, Paddison (1993: 340) says, 'the concept of the marketing of cities has gained increasing attention as a means of enhancing their competitiveness'. He also identifies a series of different, but related, objectives of marketing the city: raising the competitiveness, attracting inward investment, improving its image and the well-being of its population. These objectives have been repeated in many other studies on the marketing of cities. According to Kotler, Haider and Rein (1993), the targets of city marketing are business firms, industrial plants, corporate and divisional headquarters, investment capital, sports teams, tourists, conventioneers, residents, and so on, all of which promise increased employment, income, trade, investment and growth. The authors argue that strategic, aggressive place marketing is the most adaptive and productive approach to the problems of cities. They even affirm that cities that fail to market themselves successfully face the risk of economic stagnation and decline.

Urban researchers as well as city marketeers no longer view cities merely as settings for business activity. Instead, cities have become commodified, packaged, advertised and marketed much as any other product in a capitalist society (Goodwin, 1993). This city marketing process consists of several phases. Haider (1992) suggests five activities: analysing marketing opportunities, researching and selecting target markets, designing marketing strategies, planning marketing programmes, and organising and implementing the market effort. Ashworth and Voogd (1990) provide a broader context: analysis of market, formulation of goals and strategies, determination of geographical marketing mix, and elaboration and evaluation. Kotler, Haider and Rein (1993) focus more on setting attractive incentives and promoting the city's values and image so that potential users are fully aware of the city's distinctive advantages. Of these diverse elements of marketing, this chapter pays strict attention to imaging activities that make cities more attractive.

Obviously image is a critical factor in how buyers buy in the market. Thus people's attitude and actions towards a city are highly conditioned by their beliefs about it, and influenced by depictions and descriptions of it (Fleming and Roth, 1991). The primary goal of the city marketeer is, Holcomb (1993: 133) says, 'to construct a new image of the city to replace either vague or negative images previously held by current or potential residents, investors and visitors'. The improved image of the city can be acquired by an energetic marketing campaign as well as economic growth (reality) (Holcomb 1993: 135). The presence of two sources in the improvement of city image implies the gap between image and reality. Barke and Harrop (1994) note that images may exist independently of the apparent facts of objective reality through image making in place promotion. Holcomb (1994) compares image (re)making by the city marketeer to cosmetic 'make-overs'. Thus, image marketing is the most frequently employed approach to city marketing (Haider, 1992: 131), particularly for traditionally industrial cities whose economies are either declining or stagnant (Watson, 1991; Barke and Harrop, 1994).

In the early 1990s Canon ran a very successful advertising campaign with the slogan 'Image is Everything'. With reference to the marketing of cities, the slogan was only half-right, but also half-wrong. It was half-right in that as we increasingly move in a world of signs, symbols and images, our world is image-rich and sign-saturated, it is important for cities to present a positive image. There is almost a desperate attempt to give the city an image – to do otherwise would be to drown in the limbo of imagelessness. Much of city marketing is a frantic attempt to avoid such a fate. But image is only half the story. For sustained economic development, the brute facts of comparative advantage come into play. While image may be important in getting a city recognised, it does not guarantee economic success (see Wolman, Ford and Hill, 1994).

There are remarkable similarities in the images projected by cities. Most cities, Holcomb (1994: 115) shows, are trying to create and project an image reflecting a vibrant, growing place with accessible locations, reconstructed city center, and sunny business climate. She continues to say that the parts of many US cities which have been redeveloped in the last two decades present the visitor with a striking uniformity of appearance and feeling. Other common features in the promotional texts are appealing quality of life and cultural promotions such as fairs, festivals and sporting events (Ward, 1994: 58). Burgess (1982) notes the growing significance of quality of life in image making in her survey of the effects of environmental images on the locational decision of executives. Post-modern architecture (Crilley, 1993a) and high-tech industries (Watson, 1991; Holcomb, 1993, 1994; Barke and Harrop, 1994) have also been photographically portrayed in splendid clarity by declining industrial cities to attain a revitalised image.

Projecting similar images between different cities is criticised for the lack of originality in image marketing (Burgess, 1982). According to Holcomb (1994) there are still very few firms specialising in place marketing and the selling of cities is still in its infancy. Images portrayed by cities tend to be developed by the city's marketing consultancy contracted by the chamber of commerce, economic development association, the visitors bureau, etc. Thus, common images mentioned above may be termed the 'official image' of the city (Goss, 1993). Focusing on the printed pictorial images of Australia found in published government propaganda, Ryan (1990) investigates which Australian landscapes have been incorporated into the national stereotype, and which have not. In the same token, Sadler (1993) argues that city marketing operations involve the construction or selective tailoring of particular images of the city. Each city selects and authorises particular favourable images. There is a gap in the literature as well as our understanding; the transformation in urban governance is discussed under the heading 'business agenda' (Peck and Tickell, 1995a) and the politics of local economic development (Cox and Mair, 1988, 1989) but the authorisation of particular image, the politics of image making, is, as yet, rarely studied.

There is one item which is particularly desirable to many American cities that are looking for new attractions to add and new images to marketise: a professional sports team. According to Kotler, Haider and Rein (1993: 44), a professional sports team is a powerful image-generating machine and an economic anchor for a city. Molotch (1976: 315) points to the support for a professional sports team's carrying the locality name as one of boosterism supported by government funds. The athletic teams are, he says, 'an extra-ordinary mechanism for instilling a spirit of civic jingoism regarding the progress of the locality'. Many cities have made considerable efforts to build a new sports stadium with the intent of attracting a professional sports team that would provide them with big-city status, a vital and youthful image, and a tremendous vehicle for economic development (Zelenko, 1992; Wulf, 1995). Kotler, Haider and Rein (1993: 39) call these efforts the 'stadium-mania' of American cities. The city of Nashville, for example, built a $120 million arena for a National Hockey League team and a $292 million stadium for a National Football League franchise, the (former) Houston Oilers.

MAGAZINE ADVERTISEMENTS OF US CITIES

According to Williams (1980) advertising is a magic system reinforcing particular ideologies and a route through which dominant class images can be constructed, reinforced and replicated. Through an intense focus on commercial advertising and its ideological role, Wernick (1991) places advertising within the cultural formation of late capitalism, 'pan-promotionalism'. Burgess and Wood (1988) report the enormous impacts of city advertising on small firms' relocating decision in the Enterprise Zone of London Docklands. Fleming and Roth (1991) analyse how advertisers use the images of place to create an appealing context for marketing a product or a service.

Advertising has traditionally been the main component of local economic development strategies (Ward, 1990; Haider, 1992). After setting attractive incentives and selecting desirable images cities carry on an advertising campaign to convey these messages to their target audience. There are a variety of advertising packages used by cities: city guides, glossy brochures, fact sheets, xerox of industrial commercial information, and advertisements in journals (Burgess, 1982). In this chapter we chose magazine advertising conducted by city governments in order to interpret and analyse a detailed process of city marketing. Many cities advertise themselves in major business or travel journals in which their target audience have easy access. We collected 34 cities' advertisements from the following periodicals, *Advertising Age, Business Week, Financial World, Forbes, Fortune, Historic Preservation, National Geographic Traveler, New Choices for Retirement Living* for the period 1994–95. Some of these adverts are major texts; the page count for advertising supplements for Boston, Kansas City, Milwaukee, Philadelphia and Rochester regularly exceeded 20 pages. We focused on the slogans and images signified by each city.

As an eye-catching device, the slogan is one of the simplest and most effective means to implant ideas and to aid in name recognition (Burgess, 1982: 5). A list of city slogans is given in Table 3.1. Two themes are apparently noticeable in the advertising literature: business (economic benefits) and quality of life. We can see a lot of positioning words such as America's (world's) ____; first ____; heart of ____; gateway to ____ (Figure 3.1). Positioning is the act of designing a place's image and value offered so that one's customers understand and appreciate what the place stands for in relation to its competitors (Haider, 1992: 131). Many cities use the term 'business' in their slogans to show that they are good for business. Cities with spectacular natural settings or historical heritage or entertainment facilities, often try to illustrate their advantages to tourists and residents by means of metaphors like sun, sea, adventure, magic and history (Figure 3.2).

TABLE 3.1 Slogans of city advertising

Category	City	Slogan
Business	Atlanta, GA	Strategically located for global business
	Baltimore, MD	More service, more choices
	Boston, MA	Progress through partnerships; America's working city
	Chicago, IL	At the heart of everything
	Dallas, TX	The city of choice for business
	Fairfax, VA	The 21st century's first destination
	Findlay, OH	Hot spot for business development
	Jacksonville, FL	The expansion city on Florida's first coast
	Kansas City, MO	America's smart city
	Los Angeles, CA	Capital of the future; Together we're the best
	Miami, FL	The birth of the new Miami
	Memphis, TN	America's distribution center; The new gateway to the world
	Milwaukee, WI	The city that works for your business
	New York, NY	The business city that never sleeps
	Norfolk, VA	Where business is a pleasure
	Oak Ridge, TN	When it comes to technology . . . Oak Ridge means business!
	Philadelphia, PA	The real Philadelphia story; All roads lead to Philadelphia
	Pittsburgh, PA	America's future city; A model of post-industrial economic renaissance
	Phoenix, AZ	Moving business in the right direction; The best of the best
	Rochester, NY	The world's image center
	San Jose, CA	Capital of Silicon Valley
	Troy, OH	A great location for your company
Quality of life	Atlantic City, NJ	America's favorite playground
	Battlement Mesa, CO	Where every day is picture-perfect
	Denver, CO	A cultural and environment adventure
	Fisher Island, FL	Unlike any community in the world
	Hampton, VA	From the sea to the stars
	Lexington, KY	The gateway that's not far away
	Lincoln City, OR	Here, the sights see you too
	Louisville, KY	Your kind of place
	Nashville, TN	Music city
	Omaha, NE	Wild creatures loose in city
	Orlando, FL	Sun and fun; You never outgrow it
	Salisbury, NC	Where the past is still present
	San Antonio, TX	Something to remember
	Santa Fe, NM	Where traditions live on
	Saratoga, NY	Discover the magic!
	St Augustine, FL	Your place in history

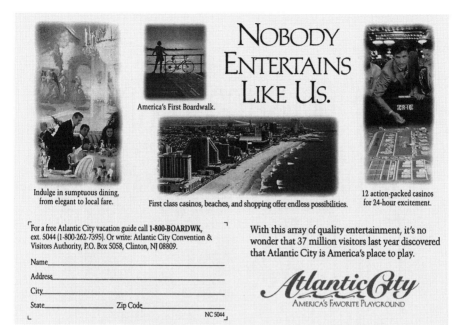

FIGURE 3.1 Atlantic City: America's favourite playground. Source: *New Choices for Retirement Living*, April 1995

Table 3.2 lists a set of common images or standard repertoires projected in 34 cities' advertisements. Cities marshal a long list of good incentives and images in their ads. To attract and retain business cities advertise that they possess a pro-business political climate, ideal workforce, high-technology industries and research institutes, solid infrastructure and healthy local economy (Figure 3.3). Locational advantage is also a big pride of cities located in the central time zone or near bigger cities. Not only cities in the coastal area of the Sunbelt but almost all cities include information on tourism in the advertisements.

Many studies on marketing the city note an increased attention to quality of life matters, including healthier, greener environment and cultural, recreational facilities (Burgess, 1982; Goss, 1993). This demonstrates that quality of life has become an important element in the more recent phase of advertising activities. Ward (1994: 58) coins the term 'cultural promotion' to describe cities' appeals to the quality of life. He says this bolsters more than just tourism, because it can be used intentionally to enhance and demonstrate the attractiveness of cities as locations for higher-level economic activities like conferences and exhibitions. One such example of a financial success of 'cultural tourism' ('urban tourism' in Law, 1992) was the exhibit of Claude Monet's paintings at the Art Institute of Chicago, which ran from 22 July to 26 November 1995, and generated $389 million in economic benefits for the city and a $5 million profit for the museum (*USA Today*, 1995).

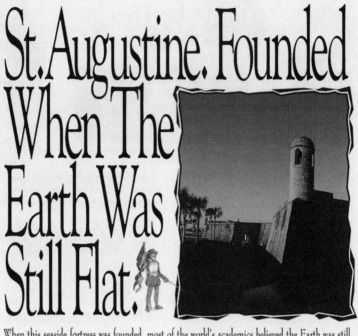

When this seaside fortress was founded, most of the world's academics believed the Earth was still flat. Sure, Columbus sold his story to the queen. Society, however, thought he'd gone over the edge. Pedro Menendez de Aviles didn't care. He was busy laying claim to a breathtaking stretch of beach in The New World. Soon it was booming with activity. And cannons. Today, St. Augustine's architecture, cobblestone streets and mighty fortresses still reflect an age of discovery. And of disbelief. Eventually, the world came around. We hope you will, too.

YOUR PLACE IN HISTORY.

For information on St. Augustine, or St. Augustine Beach on Anastasia Island call 800-OLD CITY (800-653-2489). Or write to St. Augustine Tourism, 88 Riberia Street, St. Augustine, Florida 32084. Funded by St. Johns County Tourist Development Council.

FIGURE 3.2 St. Augustine: your place in history. Source: *Historic Preservation*, May/ June 1995

TABLE 3.2 Major repertoires in city advertisements*

	Category	Content
Business (economic benefits)	Pro-business political climate (public/private partnership)	Business-assistance programmes Sound fiscal policies Industry-specific taxes and incentives
	Ideal workforce	Young, educated, skilled, hard-working labour force Concentrations of educational institutions Sound work ethic Successful labour/management relations
	High-technology (the advent of the twenty-first century)	High-tech industry/university partnership Concentration of high-tech industries
	Solid infrastructure	Transportation (highway, international airport) Telecommunications (fibre optics network) Local gas and electricity
	Healthy local economy	Economic stability or fast economic growth Upswing trend in job creation Higher proportion of future's industries
	Central location	Central time zone Proximity to large markets (population) Border cities or coast cities
Quality of life	High quality of life	Affluent natural amenities (beach, lake, fall, mountain, clean air, etc.) Mild weather (sun, warm climate) Health services (world class hospitals) Low cost of living; wide range of housing options Friendliness
	Distinct life-style advantages	High quality of cultural and recreational activities (museum, opera, symphony orchestra, theatre, art centre, festivals, fairs, professional sports teams, golf course) Historical heritage

* Based on 37 cities mentioned in Table 3.1.

Most advertisements use an impressive listing of (inter)nationally known companies based in local areas. It is one rhetorical device through which advertisers seek to give credibility to their discourse by referring to their previous successes (Gold, 1994: 30). The quotations of the opinion of independent surveys on the city are also one of the popular features in the ads. For example, Kansas City boasts of its No. 1 ranking workforce in the USA by *Fortune* magazine based on skills and availability (*Business Week*, 1994). Fairfax County mentions that last year *City and State* magazine proclaimed the

FIGURE 3.3 Kansas City: a place where it all works together – workforce, technology, value and location. Source: *Business Week*, 26 December 1994

county the best financially managed county in the nation (*Financial World*, 1994). The testimonial of senior executives of local companies who express their satisfaction with the city is a popular strategy to show how wonderfully the city will work for your business. They also imply that your business can get more economic benefits in their city than in any other. Photo-imagery, including fabulous pictures, is one of the major elements in the advertisements. These pictures capture images of great natural beauty, post-modern architecture, high-tech equipment (Figure 3.4), gorgeous night scenes of downtown, rich historical and recreational places, festivals, and photos of governors and CEOs of major local companies.

There are common features in the design of the advertisements. This is because of the similarity in the projected images between cities and also because of the preferences of the dominant advertising agencies specialising in place marketing such as Leslie Singer Design which has designed the majority of city advertisements printed in *Forbes*. Despite the similarities, however, there are also numerous examples in magazine advertisements of efforts to distinguish a city from others. To make their cities widely recognised, advertisers create specific symbols or metaphors: Boston's local research institutes with impeccable reputations; Chicago as a world class financial centre; Fairfax's and Oak Ridge's high-tech; Memphis's distribution advantages; Rochester as a world image centre; Atlantic City's year-round entertainment; Nashville's music; Jacksonville's and Orlando's pro-sports teams (Figure 3.5); and St Augustine's historic heritage. They each claim that its particular individual advantage is globally or nationally recognised. There are contradictory trends of homogenisation (similarity) versus distinctiveness (uniqueness) in urban images projected in advertisements.

In summary, we can identify a number of themes which run through city marketing in magazine adverts, as well as other outlets. The two principal ones are the city as a place for profitable business and the city as a good place to live: there are subthemes; the world city, the green city, the fun city, the culture city, the pluralist city and the post-industrial city. All of these can be seen in the marketing of cities in the USA and around the world. The subthemes condense complex imagery into simple slogans, easily understood images and accessible selling points (Short, 1996b: 428–32).

TWO STORIES OF MARKETING THE CITY

There has clearly been renewed interest in the marketing of cities. However, there are few examples of detailed case studies in the USA with the exception of Holcomb (1993, 1994), Kotler, Haider and Rein (1993), Short et al (1993) and a few studies on New York's Battery Park City (Fainstein, 1991; Crilley, 1993a). In this chapter we will illustrate two cities' marketing stories: Memphis and Milwaukee. The former is perhaps the best example of successful marketing programmes creating and confirming its image with very customised market

Where will all the smart roads and smart cars get their intelligence?

By the early 21st century, your car will be equipped with an electronic map that will navigate you through traffic. A computerized voice will direct you as you drive. Electronic road signs will warn you of traffic congestion and suggest alternate routes. Traffic signals will automatically adjust to the ebb and flow of cars.

This is no passing fancy. The technology is already here. And much of it is coming from companies located in Fairfax County.

The network of satellites, sensors, onboard computers and guidance systems that will make intelligent highways and vehicles work are by-products of technologies that these companies developed for the national defense.

Further, the policies that will be used to deploy this technology are being developed at Fairfax County's George Mason University.

Smart ideas like smart cars and smart roads are why smart companies move to Fairfax County.

If you want to compete in the 21st century, it's the best route you can take.

> Please send me more information on the business advantages of Fairfax County.
>
> Name_____
> Title _____
> Company _____
> Address _____
> City_____ State_____
> Zip_____ Phone_____
>
> Fairfax County Economic Development Authority
> 8300 Boone Boulevard, Suite 450, Vienna, Virginia 22182
> Telephone 703-790-0600, Fax 703-893-1269

Fairfax County, Virginia. The 21st Century Is Here.

For additional information, circle no. 13 on the Reader Response Card.

FIGURE 3.4 Fairfax County: the twenty-first century is here. Source: *Forbes*, 9 May 1994

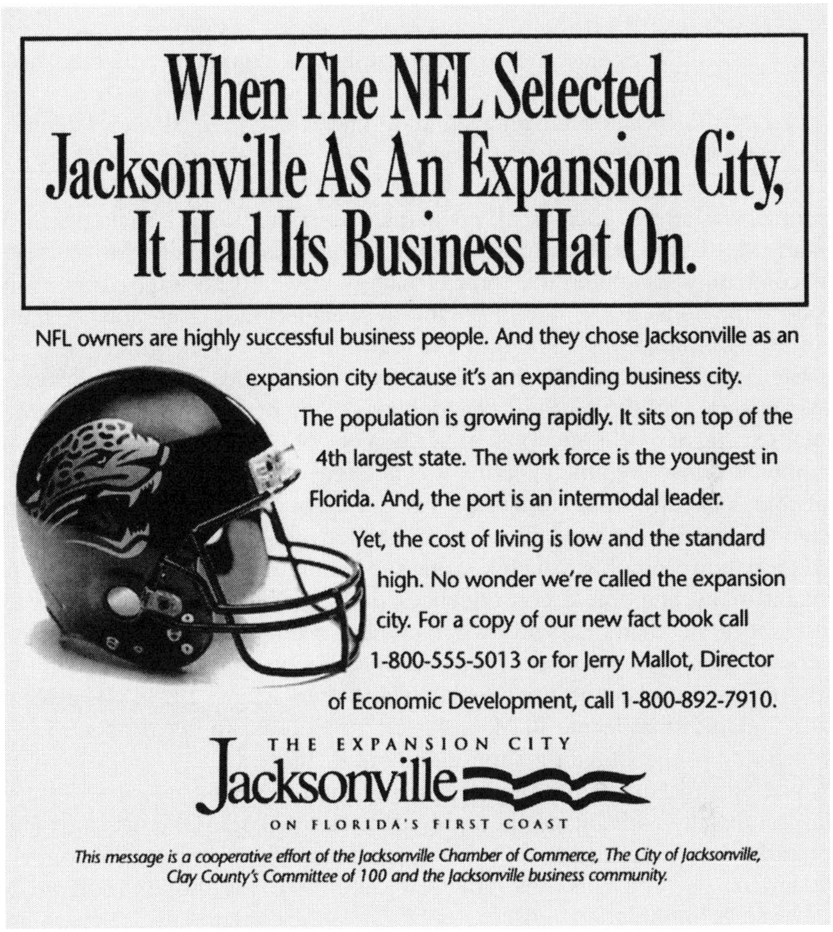

When The NFL Selected Jacksonville As An Expansion City, It Had Its Business Hat On.

NFL owners are highly successful business people. And they chose Jacksonville as an expansion city because it's an expanding business city.

The population is growing rapidly. It sits on top of the 4th largest state. The work force is the youngest in Florida. And, the port is an intermodal leader.

Yet, the cost of living is low and the standard high. No wonder we're called the expansion city. For a copy of our new fact book call 1-800-555-5013 or for Jerry Mallot, Director of Economic Development, call 1-800-892-7910.

THE EXPANSION CITY

Jacksonville

ON FLORIDA'S FIRST COAST

This message is a cooperative effort of the Jacksonville Chamber of Commerce, The City of Jacksonville, Clay County's Committee of 100 and the Jacksonville business community.

FIGURE 3.5 Jacksonville: an NFL city and expanding business city. Source: *Forbes*, 23 October 1995

appeals. Compared to Memphis's success, Milwaukee is still putting a large amount of effort to replace its negative publicity with that of a vibrant image showing a growing local economy.

Memphis: America's distribution centre

Memphis has all the natural assets needed for a distribution centre. Its location on the Mississippi River and in the central time zone, and its well-connected highway and railroad systems indicate that the city meets certain preliminary conditions as a distribution centre. Only one additional thing was needed, a nationwide advertising campaign to illustrate Memphis's comparative advantages. In 1981 the Memphis Area Chamber of Commerce, ad agency Walker & Associates and the existing distribution community teamed up to launch the campaign, using magazines and direct mail to spread the word of the city's distribution advantages; they first created the slogan, 'Memphis: America's Distribution Center' (Salomon, 1995). The campaign paid for distribution success stories in many magazine ads placed in various business and distribution journals. Local truck companies used the bumper sticker with the slogan on all their trailers. More recently, direct mail marketing to *Fortune*'s 500 companies has taken the form of battery-powered messages announcing 'Good Vibrations from Memphis' and a weather radio offering 'A Sunny Forecast from Memphis' (Salomon 1995: 14).

That Federal Express (FedEx) is headquartered in Memphis has played a major role in establishing the city's identity as America's distribution centre. A senior executive of the Memphis Area Chamber of Commerce said FedEx gave Memphis's slogan credibility. FedEx was headquartered in Memphis in 1973. At that time, local airport authorities provided a lot of attractions to the company, including warehouse and office space (McConville, 1993). FedEx's phenomenal growth in Memphis, which became the community's largest employer, has brought many favourable consequences to Memphis. David W. Cooley, the president of the chamber, said, 'We even have a thing called "Memphis-based pricing", where you get a better price from FedEx by being based in Memphis, and you can ship later in the evening' (*Financial World*, 1993: 51). It means that companies that locate in Memphis do so in order to get products out to the majority of the USA in a shorter amount of time.

Three advertisements for Memphis were found in periodicals. Two of them focus on the city's advantages in distribution (Figure 3.6). Along the same lines, the third ad emphasises the city's first international direct air route: Memphis to Amsterdam. The city calls itself 'The New Gateway to the World'. Here we can see how Memphis's advertising, public relations, economic development solicitation and general civic identity all swirl around the city's advantages in distribution.

The chamber claims that its marketing programmes are responsible for at least 60% of the 103 000 jobs created since 1985 and plans to keep Memphis's national marketing programme in place for the next 10 years (Salomon, 1995). It expects a total economic impact in excess of $25 billion on the local economy during that period. As we have seen, Memphis's success story is very clear. It has called itself America's distribution centre for over a decade, supported distribution facilities to companies, especially FedEx, and then attracted scores of companies.

Milwaukee: a shining star in the Rust Belt

Milwaukee cannot ignore a declining image that most industrial cities have suffered from since the 1970s. Its economy has been hit hard by the devaluing

FROM MEMPHIS, YOU CAN RUN DISTRIBUTION RINGS AROUND YOUR NORTH AMERICAN COMPETITION.

CHICAGO

TORONTO

MEMPHIS

ATLANTA

DALLAS

MONTERREY

For additional information, circle no. 35 on the Reader Response Card.

Because you can distribute to the U.S., Canada and Mexico faster and cheaper from Memphis • centrally located between the industrial centers of Toronto and Monterrey, and just miles from the U.S. population center • a massive transportation and distribution network in place, including the international hub of Federal Express • a committed partnership of business and government that cuts red tape • a lower cost of operation • a life-style that lets you work more efficiently, live more enjoyably. So ring in a new, prosperous era. In Memphis.

Ring Chris Clifton, CED at 1-800-238-1200 for complete details. Or write him at: Economic Development Division, Memphis Area Chamber of Commerce, P.O. Box 224, Memphis, TN 38101.

FOR FAST FACTS
1-800-636-3299 Ext. 400
MEMPHIS
America's Distribution Center

FIGURE 3.6 Memphis: America's distribution centre. Source: *Financial World*, 10 October 1995

processes of manufacturing during the past decades. Milwaukee has suffered from a considerable number of manufacturing plant closings, job loss and decaying downtown. *Blue Collar Goodbyes* (Doro, 1992), a collection of poems, is an example of writings that describe devastating consequences of plant closings to communities and workers in Milwaukee.

Milwaukee's current local economic development and city marketing have been greatly driven by its mayor, John Norquist, elected in 1988. He has been described as one of America's three boldest mayors (Eggers, 1993); the brave marketeer of Milwaukee (*The Economist*, 1995); and a disciple of the new urbanism (Auer, 1995). A magazine advertisement of Milwaukee (*Forbes*, 19.12.94; Figure 3.7) cites Norquist's vision for the city's future, 'Milwaukee should be a private-sector city and a free-market city.' Public–private partnership is his weapon of choice, including the construction of Wisconsin Center in the battle to reinvigorate the city's downtown business district. He gave up completely the city's welfare-state tradition, stating that high taxes and a welfare system had been associated with high crime, family breakdown and neighbourhood decay (Eggers, 1993: 70).

In conjunction with many revitalising efforts, the city authorities decided to launch the magazine advertisement campaign to convey the message of success in ridding itself of its Rust Belt image and attracting business, tourists and residents. 'The City That Works for Your Business' is used as its marketing slogan. Two big advertising supplements that were found in *Advertising Age* (20.6.95) and *Forbes* display the city's continuing economic growth, strong demographics and numerous business assistance programmes. These advertisements also illustrate that Milwaukee's economy is growing and its unemployment level is lower than the national average. The city compares its figures of population decline with those of other Midwest metropolitan areas in order to assert its better situation. Milwaukee's other attractions to potential residents and tourists are local-based professional sports teams, Bucks (basketball) and Brewers (baseball), lakefront festivals (Summerfest and various ethnic festivals), and Lake Michigan as the destination of family vacations. In this sense Milwaukee's efforts to transform its declining image to a post-industrial image with a vibrant economy and high quality of life, are very similar to the marketing programmes of other manufacturing cities like Cleveland and Philadelphia (Holcomb, 1993).

WRITING THE CITY

It is sometimes useful to see the city as text, that is constantly being written, reconstructed and deconstructed (see Chapter 11). The city as text metaphor also raises the notion of authorship and what is left out as well as what is written. When the city is reimagined, reconstructed and represented (and marketing the city is an attempt to both reimagine and represent the city) it

FIGURE 3.7 Milwaukee: a shining star in the Rustbelt. Source: *Forbes*, 19 December 1994

bears the mark of power and authority. The dominant images presented in city marketing schemes are not innocent of social authority and political power. The city is written from a particular perspective for a particular audience. The text has its silences. These include the notion of the city as a place of redistributional social policies. Images of social justice are rarely presented; the just city never appears as one of the subthemes in the city as a good place to live. The poor are rarely discussed and never presented. The dominant images represent conflict-free cities, where pluralism leads to a variety of ethnic restaurants rather than competition for scarce resources, where the good life is neither marred nor affected by the presence of the poor and marginalised. The dominant city image is both produced and consumed in the boardroom by the rich and the powerful. The poor are excluded, marginalised and ignored. The good city is not the fair city, the just city or the equal city, and this is particularly pronounced in the USA where social redistributional policies have less appeal than they do in Europe. The images presented of US cities stress individual consumption rather than collective welfare, private attainment rather than social justice and the city as private pleasure rather than of collective good. The consequences of this are still being explored, and this is an important theme returned to in later chapters.

CONCLUSION

In this chapter we have discussed city marketing in the USA. The rise of the new urban entrepreneurialism and the increasing involvement of business coalitions in local politics constitute the framework of urban marketing in the USA. In the magazine advertisements of cities we have noticed the manipulation of place imagery as well as common features that cities try to advertise. The marketing campaign stories of Memphis and Milwaukee provided an introduction to cities' efforts to promote local economic growth by reimaging the city.

A number of questions remain. First, how can we assess the effectiveness of urban marketing? There is a real need for some assessment of the effectiveness of these campaigns. Barke and Harrop (1994) cite an officer's sceptical view, 'We do it because everyone else does it.' They comment that many cities are not really aware of any significant direct gain to their localities from their promotional activities. City governments and chambers of commerce will always take the most favourable interpretation and thus there is a need for a systematic measurement of the effectiveness of these campaigns. Second, the chapter raised but did not fully address the issue of the redistributional consequences of these reimagings of the city. To what extent is the notion of fair, just cities being marginalised in the attempt to compete in the place wars? Third, there is a connection between changes in the space economy and marketing that goes both ways. We have argued that these marketing campaigns have been conducted because of changes in the space economy. But to what extent can marketing campaigns bring about shifts in the space economy? The three questions are related. They pose the difficult issue of measuring the effects and consequences of city marketing. This is an important topic that deserves careful consideration and further work.

4

THE NARRATIVE OF ENTERPRISE AND THE ENTERPRISE OF NARRATIVE: PLACE MARKETING AND THE ENTREPRENEURIAL CITY

BOB JESSOP[1]

INTRODUCTION

In a recent survey of trends in a wide range of European cities, Parkinson and Harding argue that 'the years to 2000 will be an age of entrepreneurial cities' (1995: 66).[2] This trend continues a general movement over the last decade 'towards greater entrepreneurialism, more intense inter-urban competition and the conscious promotion of place-specific development strategies' (1995: 67). Moreover, as these authors suggest, this involves more than an objective trend in urban economic development policy; for being an 'entrepreneurial city' has also become a central element in many cities' self-imaging and/or place-marketing activities. This is well illustrated by the reworking of the thematic of the 'entrepreneurial city' as a key feature of urban discourses connected with the 'enterprise culture' in Britain, North America, and the antipodean outposts of neo-liberalism. Nor is this thematic restricted to neo-liberal discourses: entrepreneurial city strategies can also be linked with neo-corporatist, neo-statist, or even community-based modes of governance. But it is usually conceded that the eventual success of all such strategies will still depend on market forces.

Thus, after the defeat of left-wing 'municipal socialist' strategies opposed to Thatcherism in Britain, a new economic consensus has emerged at local and regional level. This emphasises cities' need to promote economic and extra-economic conditions for sustainable endogenous development; and/or to market themselves as being 'business-friendly' as well as committed to working with the private sector. In both regards there is a strong emphasis on the role of partnerships (operating on various levels of social organisation,[3] in and across different functional domains, and on different spatial scales) in the active promotion and support of these policies. This approach is now part of the mainstream (or 'centrist') understanding of local economic development strategy in Britain (Eisenschitz and Gough, 1993); and it is likely to survive the transition to New Labour (if only because of continued financial constraints on government spending). Moreover, despite some obvious and necessary local variations, these initiatives typically share an 'entrepreneurial' concern to innovate through 'new combinations' of economic and/or extra-economic factors to further urban and regional competitiveness. Similar trends are found beyond Britain in Europe and elsewhere; and, while especially evident, perhaps, for cities and regions, they are also advocated for nations and supranational blocs (e.g. Przeworski, 1986; Eisinger, 1988; Fosler, 1988; Harvey, 1989a; Stewart and Stoker, 1989; Stöhr, 1989, 1990; Leitner, 1990; Preteceille, 1990; Hirsch, Esser and Fach, 1991; Gaffikin and Warf, 1993; Keating, 1993; Ettlinger, 1994; Mayer, 1994b; Storper and Scott, 1995).

The frequently alleged novelty of such narratives and policies is, of course, at odds with the historical record. For, as the editors of this volume have noted elsewhere, 'city governments, to a less or greater extent, have always pursued entrepreneurial strategies and played a crucial role in local economic development' (Hall and Hubbard, 1996: 155). There are, none the less, real discontinuities with the immediately preceding phase, in some British cities, of municipal socialism; and, indeed, with the more common municipal welfarism that developed here over the postwar period. Such discontinuities can be discerned not just in cities' currently preferred economic policies but also in the discourses and self-images associated with them. In this sense, then, we can still ask, firstly, why local economic development policies have recently been reoriented (at least in part) to promote local innovation and other supply-side conditions favouring business enterprise; and, secondly, why these entre-preneurial strategies have come to be explicitly narrated as 'entrepreneurial' in character.

We should also consider how these changing narratives and economic functions are related. Among possible links, three merit attention here. First, there is a complex, multidimensional crisis of cities as forms of socio-economic, civil and political organisation: this has prompted debates over new ways to manage cities and deal with their many and varied problems. In this context, specific problems rooted in uneven economic development within and across nations and a more general financial crisis affecting all governments are especially important in the resurgence of the 'entrepreneurial city' as it attempts to address (endogenous) urban development with limited resources. This does not mean, of course, that such economic changes and constraints alone explain the rise of the entrepreneurial city. Instead they are more appropriately seen as setting the context within which debates and struggles over the future of particular cities and/or the 'city' in general occur. Second, these general urban crisis tendencies have been aggravated by the changing status of the national state at home and abroad, which is often linked to overly exaggerated claims about the crisis of the national state. This changing status is reflected in recent reorientation of its economic and social roles, encapsulated in such notions as 'competition state' (Cerny, 1989) or 'Schumpeterian work-fare state' (Jessop, 1993). These changes have in turn made cities and their hinterlands more significant as nodes and vectors in organising economic, political and social life than they were during the period of Atlantic Fordism. They have also highlighted the importance of cities' differential capacities to reflect on and secure the conditions for economic dynamism (cf. Storper, 1997). And, third, major changes in prevailing modalities of competition in an increasingly 'globally integrated' but still multi-scalar, unevenly developing, and tangled economy are modifying both the forms and interrelations of inter-urban as well as international competition. All three sets of factors have contributed to important shifts in the role of cities as subjects, sites and stakes in economic restructuring and systemic (or structural) competitiveness.[4]

It is in this context that the present chapter tries to define the nature of 'entrepreneurial cities' and identify the various ways in which cities can be (said to be) entrepreneurial. I take my theoretical lead here from the work of Schumpeter, an emblematic thinker for contemporary capitalism, who defined entrepreneurship as the creation of opportunities for surplus profit through 'new combinations' or innovation (Schumpeter, 1934; see below). This provides the basis for distinguishing between entrepreneurship oriented towards strong competition and that oriented towards weak competition. This distinction in turn derives from Cox's work (1995). Thus, whereas strong competition refers to potentially positive-sum attempts to improve the overall (structural) competitiveness of a locality through innovation, weak competition refers to essentially zero-sum attempts to secure the reallocation of existing resources at the expense of other localities. Cox adds that, whereas weak competition is socially disembedding, strong competition involves the territorialisation of economic activity (1995: 218). Combining these closely related approaches leads me to claim that, despite the increasingly common rhetoric and narrative of 'entrepreneurialism', there are few cities which genuinely qualify for this title in the strong sense. For there are few cities which are systematically oriented to securing sustainable dynamic competitive advantages through continuing economic, political and social innovations that are intended to enhance productivity and other conditions of structural and systemic competitiveness. And even those that do have such an orientation tend to fail for various reasons to ensure continued capital accumulation. Weaker forms of competition are usually more concerned with modifications in formal and substantive regulatory, facilitative or supportive measures[5] aimed at capturing mobile investment (a deregulatory race to the bottom) as well as simple image-building measures with the same purpose (boosterism). Cities engaged in such weak entrepreneurialism are even more likely to fail in the longer term because of the ease with which such activities can be copied.

In developing these claims I initially address the issue of entrepreneurship in relatively abstract theoretical terms. I then illustrate some of these arguments by distinguishing four (by no means exhaustive) types of relatively weak entrepreneurial economic strategy (often closely linked to place-marketing narratives and activities) which typify much of what has passed for economic development strategies in a Britain dominated from the early 1980s by a neo-liberal accumulation strategy at the national level – with little sign at the time of writing that matters will change under 'New Labour'. These strategies are primarily concerned with securing economic growth by finding the most suitable forms of insertion of local economic (and often, indeed, micro-economic) spaces into the broader spatial division of labour. In presenting these strategies I am not suggesting that they are the only strategies currently being pursued in Britain nor, even more importantly, that they exhaust the range of weak or strong entrepreneurial strategies that could be pursued in more neo-corporatist, neo-statist or associationalist contexts. My concluding remarks once again turn to more abstract and general considerations on the limits of economic strategies, entrepreneurial or otherwise.

NARRATIVES OF ENTERPRISE: COMPETITIVENESS AND ENTREPRENEURIAL CITIES

The distinctive feature of 'competition states' at national or European level and of 'entrepreneurial cities' at urban and regional level is their manifest function of – or, at least, their declared self-image as proactively engaged in – pro-moting the capacities of their respective economic spaces in the face of intensified competition in the global economy. This is often linked in turn to changes in forms of government and governance. Thus Parkinson and Harding have described the entrepreneurial city as 'one where key interest groups in the public, private and voluntary sectors develop a commitment to realising a broadly consensual vision of urban development, devise appropriate structures for implementing this vision and mobilise both local and non-local resources to pursue it' (1995: 66–7). Elsewhere Harding has defined the content of these entrepreneurial policies as involving growing concern with:

> the state of the local economy; the fortunes of locally-based businesses; the potential for attracting new companies and/or promoting growth within indigenous firms; the promotion of job-creation and training measures in response to growing urban unemployment; the modernisa-tion of the infrastructures and assets of urban regions (communications, cultural institutions, higher educational strengths and capacities) to attract investment and visitors and support existing economic activities; and the need to limit further suburbanisation, retain population (particularly middle-to-upper income families) and workplaces and create compact, livable cities (Harding, 1995: 27).

This raises the interesting and important question why the response to the above-mentioned economic and fiscal crisis of cities and regions should take the form of what I have described above as *entrepreneurial measures narrated in entrepreneurial terms*. Two issues are posed here: policies and discourses. For, whatever the objective economic and political conditions prompting such policies might be, the development of the latter is always mediated through changing understandings of competitiveness as linked to emerging discourses about the 'competition state', the 'entrepreneurial city' and, most recently, the 'learning region'.

Competitiveness

Economic competitiveness is an essentially contested, inherently relational and politically controversial concept. There are many ways to define it, many modalities of competition and many sites of competition. The key question for present purposes, however, is whether nations and cities can be 'units' and/or 'subjects' of competition. A secondary question, assuming for the moment a positive answer, is whether the conditions of success for a city or nation are analogous to those for a single firm (on nations, Porter, 1990 and Warr, 1994; on cities, see also Porter, 1995; Storper, 1997). Can nations and cities achieve competitiveness in similar ways to firms and, if not, can (or do) they pursue economic competitiveness in the same way as each other? It is only if cities are meaningful units of competition which can also pursue competitive strategies that we can speak of their actually becoming 'entrepreneurial' actors as opposed to merely representing themselves as such through entrepreneurial narratives. Otherwise, they can at best be seen as spatialised configurations of institutions and practices that offer more or less favourable conditions for individual firms (or alliances and/or networks of firms) to compete in a more or less entrepreneurial manner. The manner in which this occurs will vary, of course, with the changing nature and forms of competition.

Two general points need making about competition, competitive advantage and entrepreneurialism before we consider their particular relevance to cities. First, there are many types of competitive advantage and different bases of each.[6] One useful distinction is that between static comparative and dynamic competitive advantages. While the former refer to superior so-called 'natural'[7] factor endowments as compared to those of potential trading partners, the latter are somewhat more obviously socially created and can also be socially transformed.[8] If competitiveness is understood purely in terms of comparative advantages, what matters is the overall efficiency of resource allocation, especially in producing traded goods and services. This approach is often said to be most relevant to nations, regions or cities that are currently producing primary products and standardised manufactured goods. But such factor-based advantages are usually hard to sustain – especially given the standardisation of many technologies and capital goods (permitting their relatively quick and easy adoption if the necessary finance and skills are available), the mobility of international capital (reflected in access to mobile money capital as well as productive capital's search for lower production costs), and the shift of comparative advantages over the product cycle (which puts increasing emphasis on production costs as markets mature) (cf. Warr, 1994). This suggests longer-term competitiveness would be better based on developing and maintaining dynamic competitive advantages. This holds not only for firms but also for industrial or central business districts, cities, regions, nations and any other spaces able to create spatialised competitive advantages. The more broadly these are understood (including the social context of enterprise), the more one can talk of structural or systemic competitiveness (on structural competitiveness, see Chesnais, 1986; and, on systemic competitiveness, Messner, 1996; Esser et al, 1996).

Using this distinction, it is clear that not all so-called 'entrepreneurial cities' are concerned with the same forms of competitiveness. In some cases policy innovations involve little more than attempts to secure largely static comparative advantages by attracting inward investment from mobile capital at the expense of other places through such measures as tax breaks, subsidies and regulatory undercutting and/or simple, civic boosterist image-building. In other cases, cities and regions introduce economic, political and social innovations to enhance productivity and other conditions affecting the structural and/or systemic competitiveness of both local and mobile capital. This would be reinforced to the extent that they possess a socially dense, 'institutionally thick' space for economic reflexivity and the flexible pooling of risks and uncertainties in an increasingly turbulent national, regional and global environment (cf. Storper, 1997; Veltz, 1996). [1]

The entrepreneurial function

The concept of entrepreneurship is applicable, in principle at least, to any field of activity where innovation generates benefits which are appropriable – at least temporarily – by the innovating agent. This helps to explain the concept's current popularity in political and policy analysis. Moreover, as commodification and market mechanisms are extended to more spheres of social activity, the scope for economic entrepreneurialism proper is also expanded. It is the economic entrepreneurialism of cities that concerns us here.

In the economic sphere, entrepreneurship is a function that can be exercised at any moment in the overall circuit of capital and/or the articulation of these moments. But it must be distinguished from the routine reproduction or regularisation of the circuit: it always involves some form of innovation or 'new combination'. Likewise, although exercising an entrepreneurial function typically involves taking uncertainty (since innovation means venturing into the unknown), it is far from identical with economic speculation or economic risk-taking in general.[9] Indeed Schumpeter claims that the entrepreneur as such is never a risk-bearer: for the economic risks involved are a function of capital not entrepreneurship (Schumpeter, 1934: 137).[10] For the distinctive function of the entrepreneur is *innovation* rather than technical *invention* (however original this may be), the routine *management* of capitalist activities, or the bearing of risk. Entrepreneurship in its strict, strong or Schumpeterian sense involves the devising and realisation of new ways of doing things to generate above-average profits (i.e. 'rents' or, in Marxist terminology as applied to production, relative surplus value) in the course of capitalist competition. Moreover, although it is common to equate the entrepreneur with the individual business dynamo, the function(s) of entrepreneurship can be exercised through various types of agency. Indeed its forms will vary with the nature of combinations, the forms of competition and the objects of entrepreneurial governance. Finally, we should note that, like all economic activities, entrepreneurship is socially embedded. Thus individual entrepreneurs are commonly socially embedded in networks of interpersonal relations (even where their gift or capacity for innovation is linked to marginality from the wider society); entrepreneurial firms or organisations are institutionally embedded; and an entrepreneurial society is embedded in complex web of institutional orders (and life worlds) which sustain structural competitiveness and provide an enterprise culture. Entrepreneurial cities in the strong sense are likely to combine all three forms of embeddedness.

Schumpeter listed several ways in which entrepreneurial innovation can occur:

> (1) The introduction of a new good – that is one with which consumers are not yet familiar – or a new quality of a good. (2) The introduction of a new method of production, that is one not yet tested by experience in the branch of manufacture concerned, which need by no means be founded upon a discovery scientifically new, and can also exist in a new way of handling a commodity commercially. (3) The opening of a new market, that is a market into which the particular branch of manufacture of the country in question has not previously entered, whether or not this market has existed before. (4) The conquest of a new source of supply of raw materials or half-manufactured goods, again irrespective of whether this source already exists or whether it has first to be created. (5) The carrying out of the new organisation of any industry, like the creation of a monopoly position (for example through trustification) or the breaking up of a monopoly position (Lim, 1990: 215, summarising Schumpeter, 1934: 129–35).

Although the phrasing of Schumpeter's list of 'new combinations' bears the imprint of commercial and industrial capitalism, nothing limits it to these fields. It can clearly be applied to innovations in other fields, such as new forms of finance; and it also embraces the specifically spatial and/or temporal dimensions of commercial, industrial, financial or other forms of economic activity. It is worth emphasising the potential scope of a Schumpeterian analysis because of the increased significance of services, the increased importance of space and time in dynamic competitive advantages, and the more general redefinition of the 'economic sphere'. Regarding the last of these three tendencies, we can note that discourses of structural or systemic competitiveness now claim that such a capacity depends not only on an extensive range of economic factors (as one might readily suspect) but also on the valorisation of a wide range of extra-economic institutions and relations. Indeed Pierre Veltz has recently suggested, against orthodox economics, that the 'extra-economic' is [now] at the heart of the 'real economy' (1996: 16). This feature of contemporary capitalism is reflected in the growth of new technologies based on more complex national and regional systems of innovation, in the paradigm shift from Fordism with its emphasis on productivity growth rooted in economies of scale to post-Fordism with its emphasis on mobilising social as well as economic sources of flexibility and entrepreneurialism, and in more general efforts to penetrate the micro-social level in the interests of valorisation. Such changes have major implications for local and regional governments at local and regional levels in so far as supply-side policies are supposedly more effectively handled on these scales than at the national level; and for governance in so far as public–private partnerships are more effective than traditional legislative, bureaucratic and administrative techniques. It is in this context that we can try to locate the rise of urban entrepreneurial policies narrated in entrepreneurial terms.

Urban entrepreneurship

There are obvious analogies between Schumpeter's list of economic innovations and the activities associated with urban entrepreneurship. Moreover, just as his original list comprised analytically distinct but empirically overlapping or interdependent activities, the same holds for the entrepreneurial city and its undertakings. Attention should also be paid to the increasing interdependence between innovation and marketing in these areas: issues of image, representation, narrative and discourse arise in all five fields of urban innovation. These fields comprise:[11]

1. The introduction of new types of urban place or space for living, working, producing, servicing, consuming, etc. Examples include multicultural cities, cities organised around integrated transport and sustainable development, and cross-border regional hubs or gateways.
2. New methods of space or place production to create location-specific advantages for producing goods/services or other urban activities. Examples include new physical, social and cybernetic infrastructures, promoting agglomeration economies, technopoles, regulatory undercutting, reskilling.
3. Opening new markets – whether by place marketing specific cities in new areas and/or modifying the spatial division of consumption through

enhancing the quality of life for residents, commuters or visitors (e.g. culture, entertainment, spectacles, new cityscapes, gay quarters, gentrification).

4. Finding new sources of supply to enhance competitive advantages. Examples include new sources or patterns of immigration, changing the cultural mix of cities, finding new sources of funding from the central state (or, in the EU, European funds), or reskilling the workforce.

5. Refiguring or redefining the urban hierarchy and/or altering the place of a given city within it. Examples include the development of a world or global city position, regional gateways, cross-border regions, and 'virtual regions' based on interregional co-operation among non-contiguous spaces.

In each regard we can see that urban entrepreneurialism contains the element of uncertainty that many see as the very essence of entrepreneurial activity. In this sense 'it is speculative in execution and design and therefore dogged by all the difficulties and dangers which attach to speculative as opposed to rationally planned and coordinated development' (Harvey, 1989b: 7). This may be a further reason why cities are becoming more entrepreneurial. For the nature of risk and uncertainty is changing and some theorists argue that we now live in a 'risk society' (Beck, 1992). Without directly responding or referring to this latter argument, Storper's more recent analysis of the 'reflexive city' claims that uncertainty and risk are changing in a period when market forces and the extra-economic environment for economic actors are becoming more turbulent, more influenced by the strategic calculation of other actors, and more open to influence on a wide range of spatial scales. This puts a premium on forms of urban organisation which enable economic actors to share risks and to cope with uncertainty through dense social and institutional networks (Storper, 1997; cf. Veltz, 1996).

Whether in regard to firms or cities, there is a typical economic dynamic to entrepreneurial activities. As an integral element in competition, they are inseparable from its attendant risks and uncertainties. Although a successful innovation will initially generate surplus profits (or 'rents'), these tend to decline and eventually disappear as the innovation is either adopted (or superseded) as 'best practice' by other competitors and/or as less efficient competitors (are forced to) leave the market. Unless an effective (practical or legal) monopoly position can be established, this will tend to return profits to normal levels.[12] Moreover, once an innovation is generalised, the cost of production and the search for new markets begins to matter, changing the balance of competitive advantages within the product cycle. While this emphasis on costs leads to the competing away of initial advantages, it also prepares the ground for the next wave of innovation and entrepreneurship – either by the initial pioneers or perhaps latecomers who are able to exploit their competitive position in a later stage of the product cycle to build a resource base for subsequent innovations. Making due allowance for obvious differences in the product and its associated cycle, this dynamic is seen in inter-urban competition. The capacity of global cities to remain at the top of both world and national hierarchies is linked to their ability to remain at the forefront of economic and institutional innovation. But inter-urban competition can also lead to displacement of competitive advantages across cities lower down the hierarchy. Some cities begin apparently irreversible decline as they are outmanœuvred by innovations in other established or emerging cities; this is especially likely where their initial superiority in the hierarchy was based on static comparative advantage. At the same time, of course, imitation and speculation can also lead to overproduction both within individual growth centres and in general through diffusion. This is the 'crowding' phenomenon noted by Schumpeter (1934: 131–2). It is currently reflected in the 'serial production of world trade centres, waterfront developments, post-modern shopping malls, etc.' (Harvey, 1989b: 10). In general, as Krätke's work on the changing urban hierarchy in Europe suggests, the trajectories of cities in the 'snakes-and-ladders' game of inter-urban competition are closely related to (a) the quality and richness of control capacities, finance and service functions; and (b) specialisation in innovative or traditional industrial production structures. The capacity to remain at the top of the hierarchy or to move up it depends on cities' capacities and strategies for acquiring complex strategic activities and/or promoting innovative production (Krätke, 1995: 136–42). All of this points to the importance for inter-urban competition of entrepreneurial capacities.

ENTREPRENEURIAL CITIES?

This said, there are both theoretical and practical dangers in accepting uncritically the narratives and/or discourses of the 'entrepreneurial city'. Theoretically, we run the risk of treating the city unproblematically as a subject capable of action. Even if this risk is avoided, however, there are clear dangers in trivialising urban entrepreneurial activities by reducing them to all manner of routine activities which are directly economic or at least economically relevant; and/or in mistaking a city's self-image and place marketing as entrepreneurial for the presence of strong entrepreneurial activities. Thus some cities may simply be administering or managing an existing business-friendly climate efficiently rather than actually engaged in innovation. That this may be sufficient to maintain capital accumulation does not mean that the city concerned is entrepreneurial. Likewise, some cities may be engaged in nothing more than routine place marketing. Furthermore, on a practical level, there is a risk that most cities believe they can succeed in the entrepreneurial race and/or can successfully pursue policies that have worked elsewhere. If every city is entrepreneurial in a 'me-tooist' way, however, any resulting particular competitive advantages may well prove ephemeral. This is especially risky for accounts of entrepreneurship which ignore the complex contextual conditions making for success and emphasise instead the 'animal spirits' of gifted individuals or equally inspired corporations. So let us first consider how the idea of entrepreneurship could apply to cities.

Although early work tended to see entrepreneurs as heroic individuals (which would exclude cities from exercising their functions), it has long been accepted that entrepreneurship can also be exercised collectively. This holds not only for organisations such as firms (whether acting alone, in strategic alliances or in networks) but also for institutional complexes such as the state. This led Schumpeter to argue that the function of heroic individual entrepreneurs was losing its social significance as innovation became more routinised and met less resistance (1943: 132). Prima facie, this suggests that cities could, perhaps, become socially more significant in this regard. From a structural viewpoint, an 'entrepreneurial city' would be one which is so institutionally and organisationally equipped that it offers a privileged strategic space for innovation. From a strategic viewpoint, it would be one that has achieved the capacity to act entrepreneurially. It may then itself directly act as an economic entrepreneur, targeting one or more of the above-mentioned facets of the urban 'product'; and it may also actively promote various institutional and/or organisational conditions favourable to more general economic entrepreneurship on the part of other forces. Finally, from a purely discursive viewpoint, a city may present itself as 'entrepreneurial' in structural and/or strategic terms – without necessarily meeting the relevant conditions.

The possibility of localities becoming subjects is crucial to the second and third of these possible forms of entrepreneurial city. This is an issue that is hotly debated by various urban geographers. There is a real danger of equating cities merely with the city's political leaders and other notables or, alternatively, with a specific growth or grant coalition. Indeed, Harvey warns against language which makes it seem as if 'cities' can be active agents when, in his words, they are mere things. He calls instead for analyses of urbanisation 'as a spatially grounded social process in which a wide range of different actors with quite different objectives and agendas interact through a particular configuration of interlocking spatial practices' (Harvey, 1989b: 5). Conversely, Cox and Mair are more than happy to discuss preconditions for localities to become subjects. They suggest that:

> If people interpret localised social structures in explicitly territorial terms, come to view their interests and identities as 'local', and then act upon that view by mobilising locally defined organisations to further their interests in a manner that would not be possible were they to act separately, then it seems eminently reasonable to talk about 'locality as agent' (Cox and Mair, 1991: 198).

Clearly, these requirements would also apply (without thereby exhausting all the necessary conditions) to cities' capacities to mobilise diverse social forces and organisational (meta-)capacities in pursuit of entrepreneurial projects. Among the key elements to be considered here are: the discursive constitution of the identities and modes of calculation which justify claims about an 'imagined community of entrepreneurial interest' and its associated collective project, the various actors (not necessarily local or locally dependent) who are mobilised behind the entrepreneurial strategy, the various interpersonal and (inter-)organisational mechanisms through which such forces are mobilised and given coherence, and the manner in which these mechanisms are embedded in broader social arrangements so that the capacities of the city (or localised social structure) are in some sense collective and thus irreducible to those of individual actors resident or active therein (on the last of these points, see Cox and Mair, 1991: 204). At stake here are the forms in which cities can and do 'add value' in the (capitalist) economic process by providing a complex of localised and specific economic and extra-economic assets which are socially regularised and socially constructed (cf. Storper, 1997: 17–19).

In structural terms, this requires us to look at the spatialised complex of institutions, norms, conventions, networks, organisations, procedures and modes of economic and social calculation that sustain entrepreneurship. In strategic terms, one should look well beyond city dignitaries to assess the involvement of a wide range of actors behind a collective project and the institutional factors that help to consolidate their support. These actors can include branches of the local and/or central state, quangos and hived-off state agencies, political parties, firms, consultancies, trade associations, chambers of commerce, employers' organisations, business round tables, trade unions, trades councils, citizens' and community groups, voluntary sector organisations, public–private partnerships, local educational and religious institutions, new social movements. How solid such projects are will depend on their interpersonal, interorganisational, and institutional embeddedness (hence the existence not only of partnerships but networks of partnerships structured both horizontally and vertically) as well as their feasibility in the light of existing structural constraints and horizons of action.

Among such projects one can include measures to support entrepreneurs (e.g. venture capital, subsidies, business parks, technology transfer mechanisms and technical assistance, investment in knowledge production through public R&D or locally oriented R&D consortia, industry service centres, local and regional development funds, public procurement policies, and so forth). Also relevant are policies that aim to increase the overall supply of entrepreneurs, to develop enterprise skills/competencies in under-represented sectors (such as ethnic minorities or women), or to promote new forms of enterprise (such as co-operative or community venture programmes). More generally one might say that such policies should favour 'approaches that are (a) context-sensitive, i.e., concerned with the embeddedness of industrial practices in specific contexts and regions, (b) production-systems-oriented rather than firm-oriented, and (c) directed towards the ongoing adjustment capacities of regional economies, rather than once-and-for-all implementation of so-called best practices' (Storper and Scott, 1995: 513). The last of these categories can be extended to include organisational and institutional features that promote a place-specific enterprise culture and society, with creative, flexible and enterprising citizens (Cho, 1996; Rosa, 1992; Storper and Scott, 1995: 509–17).

Turning back to the structural aspects of the 'entrepreneurial city', there are two dimensions worth exploring. These comprise, first, institutions and structures that directly support entrepreneurs, existing or potential; and, second, institutions and structures that sustain an entrepreneurial climate. An interesting but difficult question in this regard is how far a general climate conducive to entrepreneurship can be attributed to the form of the city itself as opposed to other localised factors, e.g. the presence of well-integrated industrial clusters (Porter, 1990), flexible industrial districts (Third Italy), regional systems of innovation, and so forth. It is hard to separate the effects of an entrepreneurial space/place from the effects of specific entrepreneurial city strategies since structure and strategy interact and co-evolve.

One way to resolve this analytical difficulty in distinguishing between what Lipietz (1994a) terms a 'space-in-itself' and a 'space-for-itself' would be to explore the extent to which there is a clear accumulation strategy formulated for the city and its region and to which this strategy has become hegemonic. Thus Lipietz suggests that, for a space-in-itself to become a space-for-itself, a hegemonic bloc and a state are necessary. When these two conditions are organically linked, he continues, one can talk of a 'regional armature'. This is 'a space-for-itself where the dominant classes of the hegemonic bloc mobilize ideological and political apparatuses enabling the appropriate regulation at this level [of spatial organization] of some aspect or another of the socioeconomic conflict' (Lipietz, 1994a: 27). This notion can clearly be extended to include more than issues of 'reproduction-regulation' to include the pursuit of entrepreneurial policies oriented to (permanent) innovation in inter-urban competition. In this context political forces must mobilise not only ideological and political apparatuses but also forms of organisational intelligence and mechanisms for collective learning (Willke, 1992, 1997; Storper, 1997). Thus, to the extent that the city can be considered as an agent in this regard, one should be able to identify its strategic role (and not merely structurally selective bias) in organising the conditions for competitive advantages. Entrepreneurial urban policies would be a means to the end of 'adaptive technological and organizational learning in territorial context' (Storper and Scott, 1995: 513). They would be especially oriented to the meta-problem of the co-variation, co-selection and co-retention of such policies to produce both a 'structured coherence' at local level and dynamic complementarity with other levels (cf. Willke, 1992, 1997). The development of such meta-capacities would depend on the supply of relevant knowledge and organisational intelligence rather than capital; on shaping the institutional context in which firms operate rather than providing subsidies; on organising place-specific advantages rather than an abstract space of flows; and on the (re-)territorialization of activities rather than their emancipation from spatial and temporal constraints. In this way dynamic competitive advantages can be targeted rather than static comparative advantages with the attendant risk of a race to the bottom.

CHANGING SPACES OF COMPETITIVENESS?

The crisis of national economies and the declining capacity of national states to manage national economies as if they were closed has expanded the space for cities and regions to engage in territorial competition. Indeed, it sometimes seems that cities are replacing firms as 'national champions'. This may well be linked to the 'relativisation of scale' linked with the current dialectic logic of globalisation and regionalisation. This signifies that, in contrast to the privileging of the national economy and national state in the period of Atlantic Fordism, no spatial scale is currently privileged. Instead there is a more complex nesting and weaving of different spatial scales due to the complex rearticulation of different spatial scales (Amin and Robins, 1990; Collinge, 1996).[13] This creates complex and changing opportunities for cities to organise territory as a place for production and for fixing capital in place and to organise the city as a space of flows to capture surpluses from the movement of capital and labour (cf. Hall and Hubbard, 1996: 160).

Reflecting this dialectic of place and space, views on the mechanisms of inter-urban competition differ. Thus Porter (1995) argues that the logic of competition at the regional and urban levels does not differ in principle from that operating at the level of the nation state. Indeed, he has applied his 'diamond' model to the competitive advantages of the inner city and identified various ways in which its public and private sectors can promote competitiveness by responding positively to the logic of market forces. Boisot goes even further. Using the concept of 'culture space', he proposes a much more mercantilist account of territorial competition than Porter and claims far greater room for local industrial policy (Boisot, 1993). Even the celebrated management consultant who advocates a 'borderless world', Kenichi Ohmae, suggests that there is scope for regional economies and city states in an era of globalisation. He argues that what defines regional economies 'is not the location of their political borders but the fact that they are the right size and scale to be the true, natural business units in today's global economy. Theirs are the borders – and the connections – that matter in a borderless world' (Ohmae, 1995: 5). On all three readings from quite different perspectives, real competition does seem possible among cities.

The basis of competitive strategies in this regard is always and necessarily an 'imagined' economy.[14] The constitution of an economy involves its discursive construction as a distinctive object (of analysis, regulation, governance, conquest or other practices) with definite boundaries, economic and extra-economic conditions of existence, typical economic agents and extra-economic stakeholders and an overall dynamic. The struggles to constitute specific economies as subjects, sites and stakes of competition typically involve manipulation of power and knowledge in order to establish recognition of their boundaries and geometries. The formulation of economic development strategies in this context depends on the dual distinction between: (i) the local economy and the extra-local or supra-local economic context; and (ii) the local economy and the extra-economic local environment (of community, family, polity, and so forth) (see Jessop, 1997a). How these distinctions are drawn varies with prevailing images of the economy, modes of competition and cities' place therein.

In this context, the current consensus on the need for 'entrepreneurial' cities is a product of convergent public narratives about the nature of key economic and political changes affecting postwar Europe and North America – narratives which have been persuasively (but not necessarily intentionally) combined to consolidate a limited but widely accepted set of diagnoses and prescriptions for the economic and political difficulties now confronting nations, regions and cities and their respective populations. Thus we find selective narrations of past events and forces which generate a distinctive account of current economic, social and political problems – the resolution of which is now deemed to require decisive changes in the purposes, organisation and delivery of economic strategies focused on the urban and/or regional levels and infused with some kind of entrepreneurial spirit. The entrepreneurial city or region has been constructed through the intersection of diverse economic, political and socio-cultural narratives which seek to give meaning to current problems by construing them in terms of past failures and future possibilities. These narratives are often linked to complementary discourses that are mobilised to contextualise these changes and reinforce calls for action.

The persuasiveness of this sort of entrepreneurial strategy is closely linked in turn to the parallel discursive constitution of specific sites of economic activity as 'natural' (commonsensical, taken-for-granted) units of economic management, regulation or governance. In the postwar boom years the tendency was for this site to be seen as the national economy; more recently views of 'naturalness' have bifurcated in the direction of global and local economies – subsequently synthesised in some strategic contexts (especially by firms and places seeking to attract them) in the idea of 'glocalisation'. In this context cities (and their hinterlands) are increasingly regarded as natural sites for economic innovation and entrepreneurship. Moreover, with the increasing interest in dynamic competitive advantages and the bases of structural and/or systemic competitiveness, the extra-economic dimensions of cities have also come to be increasingly significant in urban entrepreneurial strategies. So-called 'natural' economic factor endowments become less important (despite the continuing path-dependent aspects of the positioning of places in urban hierarchies); and socially constructed, socially regularised and socially embedded factors have become more important for inter-urban competitiveness. Entrepreneurial city strategies must therefore not only position urban place and space in the economic sphere but also in extra-economic spheres.

FOUR TYPES OF ECONOMIC STRATEGY

This section seeks to illustrate in a brief (and necessarily partial) manner some of the preceding arguments. It focuses on some of the weaker forms of urban entrepreneurial strategy – which are, in fact, far more typical than the strong competitive strategies or milieux which characterise the leading cities in urban hierarchies – and the extent to which they are an essential part of narratives of enterprise and place marketing in the current period. In this sense they are the strategies of the 'ordinary city' (Amin and Graham, 1997) rather than the one-sidedly presented and atypical exemplars of hyped-up trends. The typology derives largely from observation of the British case in the 1980s and 1990s and clearly needs to be extended to incorporate other periods in Britain as well as other countries in the European Union, let alone elsewhere. The four strategies to be discussed differ in at least three respects: their respective concepts and discourses of competitiveness, the spatial horizons over which they are meant to operate, and their association with different local contexts and positions in prevailing urban hierarchies. What they share is the key role of local authorities in their overall framing and promulgation. In this sense, for all the talk of the crisis of the state (at whatever level), public authorities still appear to have a major role in organising entrepreneurial policies for the city (including inner cities and metropolitan regions) and narrating such policies in entrepreneurial terms.

Within the current mainstream local economic development consensus in Britain (Eisenschitz and Gough, 1993), there is still scope for the strategies pursued by local authorities, economic development agencies and public–private partnerships to reflect local strategic contexts. Indeed, subject to overall compliance with the top-down imposition of a neo-liberal orientation and its attendant fisco-financial constraints, this was one of the explicit goals of the continual redesign of the local economic strategy apparatus under the Thatcher and Major governments. Thus local authority involvement in economic development is now as much about shaping the overall context within which partnerships (whether local, regional, translocal or transregional) can be forged, as it is about developing specific strategies and initiatives (a role which is increasingly devolved to individual firms, consultancies, private associations or public–private partnerships). Local authorities appear to be increasingly required to engage in a process of near permanent institutional and organisational innovation in order to maintain the possibility (however remote) of sustained economic growth. In this sense, even if they do not act directly as economic entrepreneurs (as sponsors of property-led development, tourist spectacles, etc.), cities must promote an entrepreneurial environment on a range of scales which might help to sustain local growth and make the best of any opportunities to promote entrepreneurship and/or market their places/ spaces. In this latter regard four main strategies can be identified.

The search for growth: local–regional–national

An increasingly common strategy is for cities and regions to pursue some form of 'structured complementarity' by building favourable linkages to the wider economy. This is typically reflected discursively in attempts 'to position places centrally on "stages" of various spatial scales: regional, national, international, global' (Hall and Hubbard, 1996: 163–4). On a practical level, it typically involves promoting local economic development by exploiting growth dynamics at progressively ascending spatial scales from the local through the regional and national to the supranational. However, it may also involve uncoupling the local economy (at least temporarily) from the wider economy, either to protect it from the negative impact of wider economic processes or to bypass more immediately encompassing scales to seek closer integration with processes on other scales (such as the EU).

Economic strategy documents from district, metropolitan and county authorities from the 1980s and 1990s suggest this is the conventional view of the basic conditions for local economic development in mainland Britain. Specific locales and growth foci must be positively co-ordinated in the local economy; the local economy in turn must be favourably linked to subregional economic spaces; subregional economic spaces with regional modes of growth; and so forth. To this end, local economies must first be identified. This involves their discursive construction as a spatially specific object of economic regulation and/or governance; and the definition of potential complementarities within the 'local economy' and across local growth foci then becomes a basis for exploiting external dynamics. Local economic development projects and their associated accumulation strategies must then be inserted within, and draw growth potential from, subregional and regional growth opportunities wherever they exist.

The search for growth: transnational local alliances

For some regions, however, improved communications and infrastructural linkages with Europe have also facilitated a certain bypassing of the national state[15] and the corresponding need for a complementary mode of insertion within a national accumulation strategy. Strategies based upon constructing metropolitan growth regimes in a neo-liberal context have proved hard to realise and, as the possibilities of bypassing the national state have begun to reveal themselves, a series of compensating or buttressing economic development strategies have recently emerged. These strategies are connected to the tendential 'hollowing-out of the national state' and its associated 'relativization of scale' (Collinge, 1996). The development of a Single European Market and improved communication links to the Continent have prompted greater involvement of British local authorities in translocal and transregional linkages (Benington, 1994; Benington and Harvey, 1994; Cappellin, 1992; Maillot, 1990; Sinclair and Page, 1993). They are designed to maximise the European lobbying power of authorities with (what they perceive to be) common territorial interests and/or identities; and, at the same time, they are often favoured by an emergent European state as it seeks to promote a Europe of the regions in which the power of national states may be reduced. These partnerships, initiatives, networks and lobbying agencies demonstrate the range of alternative resources for economic development which can be deployed by local authorities seeking access to European economic dynamics by consciously bypassing the national state. None the less it remains to see how significant is their real impact on economic development and rank in the emerging European city hierarchy as opposed to their role in place marketing. One side-effect has been far greater transnational policy transfer.

The search for growth: the resource procurement model

Resource procurement characterises economic development in many inner metropolitan authorities (cf. Malpass, 1994; Martin, 1995: 207–8; Randall, 1995). This is an understandable response to a lack of land for property development schemes, large areas of urban deprivation and poor housing, a weak fiscal base, and political and institutional fragmentation which makes co-ordinated growth strategies more difficult. In addition to the traditional source of 'procurable assets' in the central state, local authorities can now access European Union funds, especially Structural Funds. The problem of metropolitan and regional fragmentation emerges here too, however, because the EU often requires regional submissions. This advantages those member states (unlike Britain) with regional tiers of government and/or regional development agencies. Where both exist, as in Scotland and Wales, bids for European funding seem more successful. In England, where both are lacking, energetic lobbying has occurred to get the EC/EU to extend the eligibility criteria for European regional development funding – in particular to include partnerships between local authorities (Benington, 1994: 29).

Successful bids under a resource procurement strategy typically come with strings attached. This constrains the range of economic initiatives that can be pursued and threatens the coherence of an overall economic development plan (Hay, 1994). Thus urban authorities appear to face an unenviable choice: opting for ideological integrity and maximum autonomy regarding disposition of limited (and diminishing) resources or plumping for compromise and limited autonomy over a significant resource base. However, since the EU monitors expenditure less closely than the Department of Trade and Industry or the Department of the Environment, there are probably fewer strings tied to EU funding – and even these often have a juster, less neo-liberal bias. An additional problem is, of course, that 'prestige economic development' initiatives may have little resonance or benefit for inner-city residents (see Chapter 6). This can threaten the legitimacy and electability of Labour-controlled inner metropolitan areas whose economic development strategies tend to result in jobs for commuters and entertainment for the suburban middle class.

Place marketing: local regulatory undercutting and international 'beauty contests'

Place marketing has become more central to cities, with increasing budgets set aside for image construction and advertising (Hall and Hubbard, 1996: 161). Sometimes this involves little more than a search for electoral and political legitimacy by identifying local notables with flagship projects. But such boosterism can also play a role in developing economic confidence and/or attracting inward investment from within or beyond national borders. Indeed Wilson considers such city marketing the most common form of economic development strategy. This often takes the form of reimaging or reinventing the city by emphasising the uniqueness of local traditions, local heritage, local ethnic or cultural differences, etc. in a sanitised, marketable way (Wilson, 1995: 648). This can lead to the paradoxical result, however, that local identity scripts often have a uniform appearance (Cox and Mair, 1991).

One target group for such place marketing is mobile international capital. In this sense the strategy may bypass not only the national, but also the European, state; and focus on attracting North American, East Asian and other foreign direct investment. This is particularly common in the North-east and West Midlands but occurs throughout Britain. Among many 'success' stories are the attraction of Nissan to Washington near Sunderland, Toyota to Derby, Samsung to Cleveland, and most recently Siemens to the Hadrian Business Park overlooking the Swan Hunter shipbuilding yard on North Tyneside. These companies are attracted by the prospect of assembling products within the otherwise relatively protected Single European Market (Bachtler and Clement, 1991; Collis and Noon, 1994), and by the absence of significant degrees of labour-market regulation found elsewhere in Europe – reflected in correspondingly 'competitive' labour costs (Sadler, 1992: 129).

Local authorities and local partnerships are often aided and abetted in this regard by the central state. High-profile projects in particular tend to be highly dependent upon national assistance through regional financial incentives such as Regional Selective Assistance, infrastructure investment, and so forth (Sadler, 1992). Local authority strategy often involves local 'context-shaping', i.e. attempts to restructure key local relationships to attract FDI to a given site. In this regard local economies tend to compete in terms of their comparative labour-market deregulation, sacrificing workers' rights in return for the prospect of potential local reductions in (the rate of growth of) unemployment.

Such regulatory undercutting is a counter-productive strategy for generating jobs in areas of economic decline but one that is none the less favoured by European integration and, until recently, Tory opposition to the Social Chapter (which appears in key respects to be maintained even under New Labour with its rather neo-liberal reading of workfare).

CONCLUSIONS

There is no quick and easy recipe for a successful entrepreneurial city. Most urban entrepreneurial projects (which involve little more than property-led regeneration) fail, being prone to speculative boom and bust. The scope for successful mobility is largely limited to cities in the middle of the urban hierarchy, with dominant cities exploiting their past success and low-ranking cities mostly trapped at the bottom. In any entrepreneurial race, moreover, there are necessarily losers as well as winners. Even middle-ranking European cities with a well-developed entrepreneurial orientation (such as Dublin or Barcelona) may not succeed if there are few opportunities for economic expansion. Indeed, centre–periphery relations and urban hierarchies seem remarkably stable in this regard with the possibilities of movement being largely confined to intermediate regions and depending on patient, long-term strategies (Krätke, 1995; Parkinson and Harding, 1995; Steinle, 1992).[16]

In addition, entrepreneurial strategies are subject to at least four sets of constraints: first, there are the growth dynamics and resulting structural contradictions at the heart of any capitalist economy; second, there are the strategic dilemmas which not only beset any choice of entrepreneurial strategy but also extend to the need to balance entrepreneurial goals and economic growth more generally against other desiderata (social inclusion, democratic participation, accountability, etc.) which are often excluded from economic calculation; third, given the multiplicity of relevant scales of economic activity and the absence of any one dominant level as compared to the Atlantic Fordist period, issues arise about how best to articulate the urban level with other scales of innovation to increase the chances of successful projects; and, fourth, there are limits associated with the insertion of entrepreneurial activities into the broader structures and activities of the state.

Among the many structural contradictions of capitalism, two are especially significant for local economic strategies: first, that between productive capital as mobile capital in flow and as concrete capital in the process of valorisation; and, second, that between wages as a cost of production and as a source of demand. The first involves dilemmas around producing place and capturing flows in space. 'Strong competition' typically involves a search for ways to overcome this dilemma by linking the two processes so that (re-)territorialisation tendencies dominate over those of deterritorialisation. But 'soft competition' is more concerned with the search to capture mobile factors of production and is therefore more prone to promote a 'zero-sum' competition between cities, switching mobile investments around in Ricardian competition without expanding them. The second contradiction creates dilemmas around regulatory undercutting in the attempt to reduce wage costs regarded as a national (and increasingly international) cost of production and the attempt to create endogenous demand within the urban economy so that it is less dependent on an uncertain export demand. Both contradictions illustrate a more general feature of entrepreneurialism, especially in its neo-liberal form. For it is far from socially neutral in its implications. It typically transfers resources and power: from localities to firms, from local collective consumption to investment, and from immobile to mobile firms (cf. Harvey, 1989b). Even when it is embedded in more neo-statist or neo-corporatist contexts, however, entrepreneurialism encounters difficulties. For as entrepreneurial activities become more successful, the more this entrenches the need for permanent innovation. This is the basis for recent claims about the dynamism of the global city, the informational city, or the 'reflexive city'.

Secondly, the strategic dilemmas affecting urban entrepreneurial policies include: striking a balance between co-operation and competition (both in and among cities); between imitation (of existing best practice) and innovation (the search for new and better practices); and between measures to secure the survival of individual firms and to maximise the overall vitality of an economic space.[17]

Thirdly, issues of scale also pose dilemmas. For the multi-tiered governance of entrepreneurial policies has contrasting horizontal and vertical aspects: while there is heterarchic (self-organising) co-operation on any given level, there is a greater tendency for hierarchy to be retained in the co-ordination of governance across tiers. As Collinge and Hall note, 'relations within the state system *between* tiers are hierarchical, and largely political, administrative or fiscal in character; networks between tiers therefore reflect these characteristics. Relations *within* tiers, however, are horizontal and co-operative – or increasingly – competitive, and networks are therefore constrained by the balance between these two' (1995: 20). This creates contradictory pressures. Sometimes competition at lower levels may need to be suspended to secure higher-level resources from the state (e.g. in bidding for Single Regeneration Budget funding within microeconomic spaces or for EU funding for broader-based urban, regional, or translocal projects) or from mobile international capital (e.g. by offering a single union policy, co-operation between private and public sectors, or between urban and county authorities). But sometimes cities may engage in political and institutional collaboration in the search for common solutions to common problems (cf. Harding, 1995: 55).

Fourthly, urban entrepreneurship is limited by the contingent insertion of its particular organisations, institutions and activities into the state system more generally – a system which is itself tending to become more multi-tiered, decentred and complex but within which the national state retains a key intermediating role. Urban entrepreneurship depends on a range of flanking and supporting measures of both a material and symbolic nature taken by the state; on complementary temporal horizons; on the avoidance of unnecessary duplication or counteraction by other co-ordination mechanisms. Moreover, although various entrepreneurial mechanisms may acquire specific techno-economic, political and/or ideological functions, the local state and, even more, the central state typically monitor their effects on state capacities to secure social cohesion in divided societies. The state keeps to itself the right to open, close, juggle and rearticulate urban governance arrangements not only in terms of particular functions but also in terms of their implications for partisan and overall political advantage. This may explain why entrepreneurial urban and regional development is often not as significant as entrepreneurial narratives might suggest: it is hard for governments to break with inherited commitments to territorial fairness and national equity and to live with the redistributional effects of entrepreneurialism (cf. Harding, 1995: 44).

Finally, I want to end by noting that there could be alternatives to the dominant pattern of capitalist entrepreneurialism in cities. These would involve promoting the enterprise society rather than a bourgeois enterprise culture; the focus would be on personal and community enabling and empowerment rather than private enterprise and private profit; and on the learning region rather than the entrepreneurial city. If enterprise involves new combinations, then perhaps it is time to emphasise innovation that maximises human capacities rather than private profit.

NOTES

1. This chapter derives from research funded by the Economic and Social Research Council in its Local Governance Programme, Research Grant L311253032. I wrote it while Hallsworth Fellow in the School of Geography at Manchester University. I am grateful to Adam Holden, Martin Jones, Jamie Peck, Steve Quilley and Adam Tickell for discussion at Manchester; and to Alan Harding for inspiration in other contexts. The final part of the chapter draw extensively on joint work with Colin Hay. The usual disclaimers apply.
2. The present chapter complements a paper more directly focused on narrative aspects of the 'entrepreneurial city' (Jessop, 1997b). The latter explores: the reimaging of local economies and states through discourses about the 'entrepreneurial city'; the implications of this reimaging for the redesign of urban governance; links between these changes and the complex spatial rearticulation of the 'global economy' and an emerging primacy of geo-economics over geopolitics; and the general context of these interconnected urban changes.
3. I have in mind here interpersonal networking, interorganisational negotiation and co-ordination, and inter-systemic partnerships bringing together representatives of different but interdependent institutional orders. See Jessop (1997c).
4. For a discussion of the 1980s concept of structural competitiveness and its dimensions, see Jessop, Nielsen and Pedersen (1993); and, on the more recent concept of systemic competitiveness, see Esser et al (1996) and Messner (1996).
5. These terms are defined in Jessop (1982: 245–55).
6. Different theories of international competitiveness are often linked to different

typologies and disputes about the bases of competitive advantage. But different types of advantage may also prove complementary in practice.

7. The Ricardian discourse with which this concept is linked tends to treat factors as 'natural' which are in fact heavily dependent on broader social conditions: an abundance of cheap wage-labour is only the most obvious such example.

8. 'The classical theory of comparative advantage rested on some seriously simplified assumptions: international market prices were assumed to be known and stable; there was no uncertainty about the prices that would be obtained for export products, or paid for imports; there was no learning-by-doing; technology was known; constant returns to scale prevailed; resources were all fully employed; and the characteristics of commodities were fixed and known to everyone' (Warr, 1994: 4).

9. For example, in his famous article on the shift from urban managerialism to urban entrepreneurialism, Harvey tends to equate entrepreneurship and speculation (Harvey, 1989b). Routine risk-taking in property speculation is better understood as a form of deal-making rather than entrepreneurship in a Schumpeterian sense.

10. This suggests that, when private capital enters into partnership with the state (at whatever level) and the latter bears a significant share of the economic risks, the state is acting as a capitalist as much as (if not more than) an entrepreneur. Much of what passes today as the actions of the so-called entrepreneurial city is risk-bearing for private capital. As Harvey notes, a key feature of risk absorption in the current period of capital accumulation is the major role of the local (as opposed to national) public sector in this regard. Thus the present phase of urban entre-preneurialism is distinct from earlier phases of civic boosterism in which private capital seemed generally much less risk averse (1989b: 7).

11. Notwithstanding the comment in note 9 above, the following list is inspired in part by Harvey (1989b: 9–10).

12. Indeed, if there is an excess of speculative imitation, the resulting oversupply could reduce profits below normal levels.

13. Hall and Hubbard argue that the discourse of the entrepreneurial city reflects this in so far as it stresses the individual, contingent and particular character of locality, whereas the global is seen as abstract, social and general (1996: 160). This may well be true as a description of discourses; but it is misleading as a description of global processes in all their unstructured and unstructurable complexity.

14. The real economy is so unstructured and complex in its operation that it cannot be an object of management, governance or guidance.

15. But there is no escape for cities as opposed to firms from its regulation; nor from the institutional and political constraints it imposes.

16. Thus Rubinstein notes in his study of individual entrepreneurs in the nineteenth century, it was important for them to be in the right place at the right time. For 'both degrees of entrepreneurial success and the areas or fields in which entre-preneurial success are most likely to occur are virtually predetermined by the underlying structure of that society' (1983: 21, emphasis in original).

17. Hence the paradox that 'the short life cycle of many high-technology firms may be helpful for sustaining the long-term innovative capability of an ecosystem such as Silicon Valley. In addition to maintaining the stream of new firms, which in turn provide employment opportunities and create new products and services, ephemeral firms increase the variety of experiments – and, when acquired, they can help rejuvenate other entities or become reconfigured in the form of new entities' (Bahrami and Evans, 1995: 85).

PART II

ENTREPRENEURIAL GOVERNANCE, POLICY AND PRACTICE

INTRODUCTION

TIM HALL

This book is in part an attempt to address some of the inadequacies that have characterised the debates and theorisation of the entrepreneurial city. Two of the most fundamental of these inadequacies are: a failure to acknowledge the important variations which exist in entrepreneurial policies between cities and the factors which underpin these differences, and a failure to assess the impacts of entrepreneurial governance physically, on urban landscapes, socially, economically and environmentally. These themes are addressed directly in the chapters collected in this section and by a number of others throughout the book (see, for example, Chapters 9 and 14).

There has been a tendency to paint the recent entrepreneurialism of urban governments as a universal response to a universally similar set of problems. Neither conception is true or adequate. The four chapters in this section comprise a series of case studies drawn from three continents. They focus on the differing circumstances surrounding the transition to entrepreneurialism in the urban governments of Newcastle, New South Wales, Australia; Birmingham, UK; various cities in southern California and six cities in eastern Germany. A clear strength of this section lies in the contrasts they mark out between the entrepreneurial response in these cities, a clear reflection of the contexts within which they evolved. These contributions highlight that 'localness' is too important a dimension to overlook in the study of the emergence of entrepreneurialism in cities across the world. A close reading of these chapters together reveals that the nature and trajectories of urban entrepreneurialism are contingent upon a number of locally specific factors. The two most significant dimensions revealed by the cases discussed here are the local political and governmental context and the local urban context.

While urban entrepreneurialism is primarily a characteristic of a late-capitalist regulatory framework, the nature of this political context is locally mediated and dependent upon the combination and interaction of a number of factors. Primary among these factors are the questions of what levels of government are implicated in shifts towards urban entrepreneurialism and to what extent each level is afforded autonomy. In each of the four cases here the trajectories of the centre–local relationship differ significantly, for example in the number of levels of government encompassed by this relationship and in the extent and type of power and autonomy afforded to each. The cases discussed in this section encompass three variations of this relationship. In the British case (Chapter 6) Birmingham can be regarded as typical of many British former manufacturing cities in that the coincidence of deindustrialisation and the attack on the power, autonomy and finances of local government are typically credited with forcing these urban governments to adopt entrepreneurial, 'pro-growth' responses to their problems. However, this is not to deny the very different histories of entrepreneurial urban development in these cities. For example, the degree to which entrepreneurial strategies were 'forced' upon cities by their circumstances varied with, among other things, their histories of an entrepreneurial (often referred to as 'bold') political culture and associated developments and the presence of powerful and charismatic public officials in these cities. The Australian case (Chapter 5) and the southern Californian case (Chapter 7) highlight the particularities of entrepreneurialism developing under federal systems of government. The Australian case highlights the way in which the history of entrepreneurial urban government and the specific development of one project in Newcastle, New South Wales, was shaped in part by its position at the juncture of three levels of government: federal, state and local. By contrast, the southern Californian case highlights how the trajectory of entrepreneurialism there was shaped by the context of Californian state legislature, particularly the result of Proposition 13 undermining property tax as the major local revenue source since the late 1970s. Finally Herrschel discusses the cases of six cities in eastern Germany whose entrepreneurialism stemmed from the fundamental, 'overnight' political transformation of regimes in eastern Europe and how the trajectories of individual cities' development were contingent upon a series of local factors and their relationship with the more far-reaching and broader political changes affecting their region. Clearly then local instances of entrepreneurialism are intermeshed with broader political geographies. However, it would be a mistake to imagine that locally entrepreneurialism is determined by broader political change. Rather it should be stressed that the relationship is reciprocal. This nexus is discussed in all four cases.

The influence of powerful, usually charismatic individuals over the course of entrepreneurial developments and wider policy is a widely recognised yet arguably under-researched area. There are a number of instances where powerful public officials have driven through strongly entrepreneurial, and in the context of their cities, radical policies and initiatives. These have frequently been instrumental in a sea change in the political culture of these cities and a significant reshaping of their skylines. Often significant aspects of urban entrepreneurialism, for example the manufacture of consensus and clinching private sector support, have depended to a large extent on the force of personality of powerful public officials, their promotion of an image of strong civic leadership and their relationship with influential local bodies such as newspapers and television companies. Classic examples of this include the Premier of British Columbia during the 1980s who described himself as the 'father' of

Vancouver's Expo 86 (Ley and Olds, 1988) and the mayor of Baltimore from 1971 to 1986, William Schaefer's influence over the physical refashioning of the city (Hula, 1990). Although instances of these are explicitly discussed in only two of the cases here similar instances are unlikely to be absent from the other two cases or from cases of entrepreneurialism generally. In the case of Birmingham (Chapter 6) a radical shift in the stance of the city council to their programme of prestige project urban development followed the replacement of the leader of the city council with someone with a very different set of spending priorities.

The latter two cases discussed in this section also illustrate how the local urban context is an important influence on the production of entrepreneurialism. The six cities discussed by Herrschel deliberately include cities of contrasting size and consequently of different position in the urban hierarchy. This, as Herrschel demonstrates, is an important local mediator of the general shift towards entrepreneurialism in the region. Similarly Althubaity and Jonas, in discussing suburban, rather than the more usually discussed, centre-city entrepreneurialism, demonstrate the particular form of entrepreneurialism under these circumstances.

Finally, but certainly not least, it is worth mentioning how funding arrangements have influenced the production of urban entrepreneurialism. Entrepreneurial strategies, regimes and initiatives come together to secure an enormous array of funding types from an equally diverse range of sources. Clearly, differences in the entrepreneurial response reflect this. Contrast, for example, the ways in which cities have approached Olympic bids with their approaches to funding from the Single Regeneration Budget. Analysis must take account of the influence of the funding source and type over regime formation and the associated entrepreneurial strategies and developments. Returning to the comments made at the beginning of this introduction, the conditions and circumstances within which entrepreneurialism is produced are far from universal, similarly the entrepreneurialisms so produced vary, reflecting this. All four cases discussed in this section make instructive comparisons in this regard.

Although the production of urban entrepreneurialism appears to be, in part at least, locally contingent, the outcomes appear to be so to a much lesser degree. It is interesting to compare Herrschel's discussion about a post-Fordist homogeneity coming to replace that associated with socialism, with McGuirk, Winchester and Dunn's discussion of how the Honeysuckle redevelopment is likely to contribute to, to borrow John Rennie Short's (1989) term, a new international 'blandscape'. The tensions stemming from locally specific mediations of the broad shift towards entrepreneurialism in city governments around the world, and the tendency towards generic, repetitive outcomes run throughout, and are illustrated by the four chapters in this section.

The exploration of the material, as well as the symbolic, geographies of entrepreneurial cities has been, and continues to be, a major task facing urban geographers and others from cognate disciplines in the social sciences. Again the four cases included here are instructive in this regard. The cities shaped by entrepreneurial urban polices, and significantly those parts of the city which are excluded from this 'new' urbanism, involve significant redrawing of the geographies of social, economic and environmental disadvantage. The four cases discussed in this section add to our knowledge of the outcomes of entrepreneurialism for different sections of the urban populations. Again, this is a theme that runs throughout, and is highlighted by, many of the contributions to this volume.

5

ON LOSING THE LOCAL IN RESPONDING TO URBAN DECLINE: THE HONEYSUCKLE REDEVELOPMENT, NEW SOUTH WALES

PAULINE M. MᶜGUIRK, HILARY P.M. WINCHESTER AND KEVIN M. DUNN

INTRODUCTION

The adoption of the 'new urban politics' (Cox, 1993) as a means of dealing with urban decline through entrepreneurialism engenders a range of threats to the local. These threats have not been fully explored in the new urban politics literature partly because, in looking at 'the entrepreneurial city', it has conceptualised the relations between the global and the local in an unproblematic manner (Hall and Hubbard, 1996). This chapter addresses global–local relations by examining how entrepreneurialism has been used to deal with urban decline in inner Newcastle, New South Wales (NSW). We look at the importance of the discourse of globalisation in encouraging entrepreneurialism at all levels of government, as espoused by the political ideology of neoliberalism. In addition, we emphasise the potential for the local to be lost as a result of the mutually reinforcing discourses of globalisation and entrepreneurialism. We question the capacity of local communities and discordant voices to influence the course of local development, and problematise the representation of local identity in entrepreneurial schemes.

In this case study, we examine the redevelopment of the 45 ha Honeysuckle site under the auspices of a development corporation imposed by the state government of NSW. This site, formerly the publicly owned Honeysuckle goods yard, stretches along a continuous 3 km of Newcastle harbour (Figure 5.1). Here, the Honeysuckle Development Corporation (HDC) is implementing a Masterplan prepared to guide redevelopment over the next 20 years, presenting 'one of the greatest opportunities for urban renewal and revitalisation in Australia' (Hunter Economic Development Council (HEDC) n.d.: 12). The advent of the HDC has gone hand in hand with the adoption of entrepreneurial methods of local governance in Newcastle and with the linking of the Honeysuckle project into a major federally funded programme of urban reform – the Better Cities (BC) programme. The BC programme is a federal

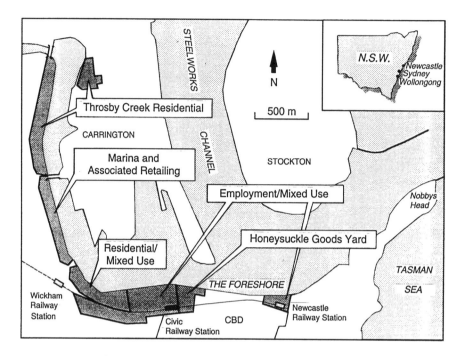

FIGURE 5.1 The Honeysuckle redevelopment site with proposed development precincts. Source: Authors' collection

government response to the pressure to adapt Australian cities and their management to the rigours of global competition. The local, regional, national and global scales are intimately related in this example of the entrepreneurial city. So here we deal with questions about how the local and the global interact, and investigate the implications of entrepreneurial urban governance for the local.

THE ENTREPRENEURIAL STATE AND THE ENTREPRENEURIAL CITY

The emergence of the entrepreneurial state at federal, state and local levels is now well documented (Eisinger, 1988; Deakin and Edwards, 1993; Gaffikin and Warf, 1993). In particular, the regulationist school has argued that an entrepreneurial state has evolved as a mode of governance suited to the regulatory tasks of government in the era of global capitalism (Esser and Hirsch, 1994; Jessop, 1996). The politics of the Keynesian welfare state has been replaced by those of the Schumpeterian workfare state (Jessop, 1994). Under this regime, government policy and practice aim to achieve (i) an economy characterised by private sector dominated innovation and competition and (ii) a body of social policy geared towards encouraging flexibility. This form of the state is associated with neo-liberalism and its fundamental philosophy of minimising state intervention in the operation of market forces (Pickvance and Preteceille, 1991). The political and administrative reorientations involved in this transition span the multi-scaled contexts in which emerging urban and regional policies are set. These reorientations have had major implications for (i) the role and power balance of national and subnational government, (ii) the relationship between state and capital and (iii) the relationship between places resulting from heightened place competition.

Central-local relations

The impacts of entrepreneurialism in government have reverberated through inter-government relations and involved contradictory impulses of increased centralisation and greater responsibilities for subnational governments (Pickvance and Preteceille, 1991). While the nation-state is undergoing continual redefinition of its role within global capitalism (Pooley, 1991; Probert, 1994) the impact of glocalisation on inter-government roles and relations has been a reorganisation of the internal division of responsibility (Swyngedouw, 1992). In Australia, the politics of the entrepreneurial state is evident in the dominance of economistic policy orientation at a federal level, in the institutional structure of federal–state financial relations and as the dominant political discourse (Pusey, 1991; Winter and Brook, 1993; Evatt Foundation, 1996). These politics have had implications for the responsibilities of subnational government and for how urban development is managed.

Matters of urban and regional development in Australia have traditionally been the concern of state and local government. Nevertheless federal government's interest in such matters revived in the early 1990s and a centralist but entrepreneurial approach to urban policy has emerged (Alexander, 1994). Recent enquiries into regional decline reflected this in their recommendations of self-sufficiency which obviated central state responsibility by making regions market and plan for their own development (Kelty, 1993; McKinsey and Company, 1994; Standing Committee on State Development, 1994). Similar shifts have occurred at the local level as the politics of urban government have been caught up in these broad changes. Despite the severely constrained nature of local government power in Australia, there have been significant changes in the style and content of urban politics (Goodwin, Duncan and Halford, 1993; Stilwell, 1993). State and local governments have been engulfed in the shift towards an entrepreneurial culture. Both have assumed new roles and are taking on new functions involving partnerships, involvement in development projects, and marketing cities and regions to prospective investors. These functions often require new institutional arrangements, new sources of revenue and new links with the business community. This represents a qualitatively different relationship between the state and capital.

State–capital relations

In the urban arena, adopting the politics of entrepreneurialism has involved incorporating the private sector directly into decision-making about urban development through a variety of means including informal growth coalitions, partnerships and urban development corporations such as at Honeysuckle (Squires, 1991; McGuirk, 1994). This involves a growing emphasis on economic outcomes as the basis of decision-making. Urban entrepreneurialism embraces institutional mechanisms such as public–private partnerships which allow a focus on economic growth with a minimum of obstacles. Such obstacles often include planning regulations, public participation and social equity considerations. The entrepreneurial state thus requires that government institutions be more attuned to the direct interests of capital, incorporating an emphasis on efficiency above equity, and wealth creation above redistribution (Gaffikin and Warf, 1993). This strengthens the voice of the private sector in public decision-making forums by conferring public status upon it as the voice of consensus (Peck, 1995).

Place competition

Global shifts in the nature, scale and organisation of production have had uneven local impacts which are clearly visible in the economic, social and built environments of the urban and regional landscape (Massey, 1984; Squires, 1991). These new economic geographies both contribute to, and are created by, the new urban politics of local entrepreneurialism and are further cultivated by the hegemonic discourse of globalisation. The importance of inter-urban competition has been accentuated by the global reach of contemporary capitalism (Markusen, 1987; Cox and Mair, 1988; Scott and Storper, 1990; Paddison, 1993). Each location needs to offer a favourable set of production, regulatory and reproduction conditions couched in a perceptible 'go-ahead' attitude among local institutions. These prerequisites are a product of the growing mobility of capital and of the discourse of globalisation which bestows on capital a kind of fickle hypermobility which constructs it as capable of shifting location with great ease (Cox and Mair, 1988). In such a climate, the pressure to create a local enterprise culture has imbued state action with the logic of the market-place. Entrepreneurial local governance then becomes part of the competitive advantage of cities (Anderson, 1990). Both the instability experienced as cities jostle for position in the fluid global pattern of production and consumption, and the nature of central–local relations escalate place competition. The pressure to compete for new forms of investment (Paddison, 1993), combined with the dominant advice that entrepreneurialism is the only appropriate reaction to this need, lies behind the proliferation of urban redevelopment schemes similar to Honeysuckle. In that sense entrepreneurialism is both an effect, and a contributory cause, of the discourse of globalisation (Painter and Goodwin, 1995).

Entrepreneurial schemes are, none the less, a critical part of cities' attempts to secure themselves a place in the fluid urban hierarchy of the contemporary space economy. For those cities like Newcastle, with a strong industrial heritage which is deeply ingrained in local social relations and embedded in its physical form, entrepreneurialism entails three general forms of restructuring:

1. A physical restructuring of the redundant fabric of the city, remaining from its industrial legacy. The emerging new landscape must be capable of accommodating an anticipated shift in the economic base of the city towards a new consumption-based economy (Harvey, 1989b; Short et al, 1993).
2. A symbolic restructuring in which the location's image is reparcelled to create a newly fabricated cultural landscape (Roberts and Schein, 1993; Dunn, McGuirk and Winchester, 1995). This new and more 'upbeat' image can then be incorporated in the city's marketing drives.
3. An institutional restructuring in which the local business climate is presented as part of the location's competitive advantage.

The institutional restructuring that is an integral part of the transition of urban politics means that the concept of 'local government' is better described and discussed as 'local governance'. This incorporates the range of interests, both private sector and community based, that are involved in managing, servicing and regulating the local urban area – the urban regime (Cochrane, 1993; Hay, 1995). Emerging new institutional forms that are characteristic of entrepreneurial city governance include:

1. Central government initiatives, often with statutory authority, instituted in a local context, e.g. Newcastle's Honeysuckle Development Corporation (HDC).
2. Local public or quasi-public development agencies, often with statutory powers, carrying out local economic development activity, e.g. the Hunter Economic Development Council (HEDC).
3. Newly formed organisations or alliances of local business élites that may or may not co-ordinate their activities with the local authority, e.g. Newcastle's City Centre Committee.

The combined task of these institutions of local governance is to create investment-ready production sites equipped with all the requisite social and physical infrastructure, and a favourable business climate (Cox, 1993). In Newcastle, the actively entrepreneurial HDC has been the chief co-ordinator of this multidimensional reformulation.

NEWCASTLE AS AN AUSTRALIAN PROBLEM REGION

The Newcastle region is one of only two major Australian regions with a traditional reliance on a heavy industry complex. Coal, steel, textiles and shipbuilding have been its industrial backbone and have had a profound impact on the economy, landscape and external perception of the region. The industrial base of the economy is reflected in the industrial landscapes which encircle the centre of the city itself. This spatial sectoral concentration has undergone massive contraction in the last 20 years. Important changes in the manufacturing base occurred with the rationalisation of the shipbuilding industry in the 1970s and 1980s, the steel industry in the early 1980s, and coal from the mid-1980s. These changes, resulting partially from the integration of the Australian with the global economy (Fagan and Webber, 1994), left the locality struggling to respond to the local and regional impacts of global economic change. Change in the structure of the regional economy is reflected by the decline in manufacturing employment from 24.6% in 1976 to 13.8% in 1991 (Industry Commission, 1993: 33). A major consequence of industrial decline has been a substantial increase in unemployment, currently at 9.4%, placing the region considerably above the NSW rate of 7.4% (Australian Bureau of Statistics, 1996). In particular, there is a concentration of unemployment, deprivation and disadvantage in the inner urban areas of Newcastle surrounding the Honeysuckle site. By the late 1980s the city faced a crisis in terms of both its regional manufacturing base and its industrial identity. Much of the industrial infrastructure had become obsolete, the urban landscape derelict and polluted, and the image of the industrial city had become negative rather than powerful and positive (Dunn, McGuirk and Winchester, 1995). The rhetoric of 'crisis' also became the dominant discourse as these events of rationalisation and growing unemployment unfolded (Metcalfe and Bern, 1994). Newcastle and the Hunter came to be seen as a problem region within the Australian and NSW economy. As such, it became a prime laboratory for the application of entrepreneurial strategies for regeneration and morphological change.

Many industrial cities have attempted reindustrialisation in specific economic sectors such as high-tech industries or the development of new sites of consumption at a waterfront or harbour-side location (Hoyle, Pinder and Hussain, 1988; Watson, 1991). The reindustrialisation focus for the Newcastle regional economy is relatively unusual in that it does not propose new high-tech industries but relies on updating existing industry and making it more competitive (HEDC, 1991:3). In addition to the focus on revived, globally competitive industry is a focus on developing the Newcastle region for tourism and recreation (Calkin and Associates, 1996).

The major focus for new economic growth in Newcastle city itself is distinct from the HEDC's growth focus for the Hunter region. For the city, the focus is on tourism and recreation, a theme which is predominant in the marketing of the city (Dunn, McGuirk and Winchester, 1995). Much of this push towards tourism and recreation is spatially concentrated in the city centre, close to beaches and the waterfront. Transformation to a new tourism/recreation focus is no small task. The central city of Newcastle has been undergoing population decline for a number of decades which has had a deleterious effect on the commercial viability of the centre. It was recently outstripped as the prime centre for retail sales by Charlestown Square, a major suburban shopping complex, while its capture of retail sales almost halved in the decade between 1979–80 and 1991–92 (Hirst Consulting Services, 1995). The city has also suffered from falling within the shadow of the Sydney metropolitan region. Investment, financial and development interests have rarely viewed it as a regional city in its own right, so its role as a regional centre for retail, financial and professional business services is underdeveloped (NCC, 1988; HEDC, 1991; City Centre Committee, 1993). The legacy of industrial pollution and a declining manufacturing base (peculiarly situated in the heart of the city), the dearth of investment in new developments and the lack of quality hotel accommodation have all militated against spontaneous, market-led reinvestment. These problems of urban morphology are a particular disincentive to the investment being sought in service provision and consumption-centred activities.

NEWCASTLE'S SHIFT TO ENTREPRENEURIALISM: THE HONEYSUCKLE REDEVELOPMENT

The wide-ranging problems of Newcastle and its regional economy have prompted a range of federal, state and local government and private sector responses. A significant part of the strategies adopted to cope with decline has been the use of an entrepreneurial approach to create development opportunities to rescue the crisis-ridden city centre. A wide range of locally produced strategies and policies (NCC, 1988, 1992; HEDC, 1991; City Centre Committee, 1993) stress the importance of creating business opportunities, and of developing promotion and management strategies for city recovery in a comprehensive strategy of rejuvenation. Local development policies are liberally scattered with entrepreneurial references to the need to create a positive climate for investment, develop a high profile for the CBD and encourage council involvement in development ventures in order to raise the city's competitive status. Also suggested are a range of entrepreneurial incentives such as refunding development application fees to successful developers, rate 'holidays', and 'fast-tracking' development applications. The widespread acceptance of these mechanisms reflects the adoption of the 'new urban politics' of boosterism and direct private sector support. This also reflects Newcastle's jostling for position in the new global–local interplay brought about by the changing economic and political circumstances at both the global and local scales.

The HDC is the clearest symbol of Newcastle's adoption of entrepreneurialism. It is also the mechanism through which the physical, symbolic and institutional transformations of Newcastle will be achieved. In 1986, the Newcastle City Council (NCC) sponsored a series of 'Partners in Progress' workshops in which it took the advice of local business interests on how the city might be revitalised. Together, the council and local business interests identified the unused Honeysuckle goods yard as the single most important development site in the city. It was visualised as a potential catalyst to trigger a broader rejuvenation of the whole central city area while addressing the problematic industrial image of Newcastle. In 1988, as a first step in trans-forming the morphological imprint of the industrial past, a 15 ha area of industrial wasteland along the foreshore was redeveloped in an intergovern-mental project to celebrate the Bicentenary of European settlement in Australia. The site, which abuts directly on to the Honeysuckle site, was metamorphosed from railway marshalling yards, old wharves and a former power station to a landscaped park and foreshore promenade. The park is adjoined by restored heritage buildings of the harbour master's house and Customs House. The foreshore promenade running along the waterfront incorporates the Queen's Wharf restaurant, entertainment and bar complex, which has been referred to as the 'jewel in the crown' of the foreshore (BOMA, 1993: 20). The contrast with previous land uses and the images of industrial decline at this site is stark.

The NSW state government then established the Honeysuckle Development Advisory Board in 1990. It produced a development strategy to encourage opportunities for 'employment, residential, entertainment, recreational and cultural activities (at Honeysuckle) whilst maximising returns to the local and regional community and optimising returns to government' (Zullo, 1991:19). In the current climate of Australia's federal–state government financial relations, state governments are ever more keen to capture mobile investment and to maximise returns from publicly owned lands (Winter and Brook, 1993). The outcome of the board's deliberations was the Honeysuckle Masterplan which provided a blueprint for the site's redevelopment over the next 20 years. This Masterplan has been whole-heartedly embraced by property interests as the means to create 'a vibrant new heart for an expanding self-confident city' (BOMA, 1993: 14). It was lauded as offering 'unsurpassed opportunities to build a new part of the inner city of Newcastle . . . [and] provides Newcastle with a clear vision of opportunities' (Property Services Group, n.d.: 12).

The Honeysuckle site has been divided into a series of precincts aimed to guide private sector investment according to the principles of the Masterplan (Figure 5.2). Approximately half of the site is reserved for residential use and public open space and is targeted to house up to 5000 people in a mixture of private and public housing. Office, commercial and mixed use spaces are aimed to accommodate a workforce of 5000–8000 people. Other planned facilities highlight the service/recreation emphasis: two hotels, a recreational and commercial marina, and a range of retail space including outdoor markets, crafts, food halls, restaurants and speciality retailing. Heritage buildings within the site are to be restored and are currently planned to be used as a 'cultural

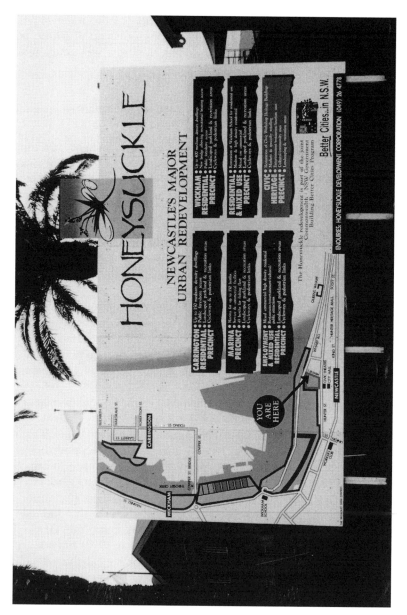

FIGURE 5.2 Billboard advertising the HDC's development precincts. Source: Authors' collection

facility' comprising artists' workshops. The success of the redevelopment is believed to rely on its successful integration with a consolidated CBD, supporting a renewed residential population and employment opportunities. This requires both a symbolic and material reconstruction of the inner city as a place to live and in which to invest. Both of these are critical to the commodification of place and its active marketing in order to attract mobile investment (Harvey, 1989b).

THE MULTI-SCALED IMPLEMENTATION OF ENTREPRENEURIALISM

The Masterplan incorporates two major phases of development that can be associated with the public and private sectors respectively: (i) the provisional work which will use public funds in an elaborate site preparation exercise and (ii) the redevelopment proper which, if realised as anticipated, will be carried out by the private sector in response to the development opportunities created at the site. Both elements are to be co-ordinated by the HDC which was established in 1992 as the management body for the Honeysuckle project. Through it, the city's physical and institutional frameworks are to be refashioned so as to attract the new investment which will complete inner Newcastle's anticipated material and symbolic transformation.

The HDC has the broad role of creating the appropriate climate for private sector investment and joint public/private sector redevelopment of the project area. The powers vested in the HDC, which is answerable to the NSW Minister for Planning, illustrate the transition towards urban entrepreneurialism and reflect the growth of the entrepreneurial state at other levels of government. It operates at the cusp of federal, state and local government and so reflects the impact of changing inter-government relations associated with neo-liberal politics. It is a state government initiative, instituted in a local context, whose operations are largely funded by the federal government. The HDC was established in the aftermath of the federal government's stepping up of its microeconomic reform agenda as part of its ongoing reaction to the material impacts and the discursive construction of globalisation (Galligan, Lim and Lovegrove, 1993; McGuirk, 1997). This has created the opportunity for the Honeysuckle redevelopment to become associated with the federal BC programme which will provide much of the funding for the HDC's site preparation activities. The BC programme, launched in 1992, provided over A$800m. in support of demonstration projects involving all three levels of government which would improve the efficiency, equity and sustainability of Australian cities while promoting best practice in urban management strategies. The programme complements the attention being paid to the role of federal–state relations in achieving microeconomic reform to improve Australia's competitive position in the international economy (Hilmer, 1993; Filmer and Dao, 1994). The Honeysuckle site is one of four demonstration projects in NSW at which development schemes are to be carried out. The HDC is being funded as part of this programme to the tune of approximately $70m. along with another $100m. of state and local government funding.

To date, more than $50.4m. has been spent in the HDC area (HDC, 1995). Almost all of this has been spent on physical works which are transforming the material legacy of Honeysuckle's industrial role: site clearing, landscaping, land reclamation, streetscaping and the restoration of heritage buildings. Existing industry and port activity is being consolidated, while abandoned sites are being cleared and groomed for redevelopment, setting the stage for private investment. These site preparation activities have been accompanied by a vigorous marketing campaign presenting Newcastle as a forward-looking city with a go-ahead attitude and plentiful opportunity for profitable, trouble-free investment. As yet no major new investment has been captured though it is estimated that $120m. has been generated in the regional economy as a result of the multiplier effect of HDC spending (Hunter Valley Research Foundation, 1995).

CRITIQUE OF NOVOCASTRIAN ENTREPRENEURIALISM: LOSING THE LOCAL

The forms of urban policy and practice emerging from this transition to entrepreneurialism highlight a range of questions about local concerns. In examining Honeysuckle, we concentrate on two of the major implications of entrepreneurialism for the local. Firstly, we look at the consequences of presenting the city as a uniformly active and monolithic agent in redevelopment for expressing discordant voices. Secondly, we examine the power of the discourse of globalisation, espoused by neo-liberalism, as the climate in which entrepreneurial politics have taken hold at all levels of the state. That discourse is heavily responsible for channelling local responses to the new global–local interplay of the contemporary global space economy.

Responsiveness to local equity concerns

The mechanisms adopted as part of the entrepreneurial culture typically involve extra-local agents, in this case state and federal government, and greater attention to private sector concerns. These extra-local political and economic regimes have concentrated on dealing with unblocking constraints to private investment whereby the emphasis is shifted towards meeting the needs of the private sector. In the race to lift such constraints, local conditions and needs can be eclipsed as extra-local agents, in combination with local pro-growth business interests and sought-after private sector investors, are able to outweigh the needs of local communities (Anderson 1990; Leitner, 1990; Wolman and Goldsmith, 1992). This has implications for the redistribution of resources within the community.

The fact that entrepreneurial urban governance relies on private sector investment as a growth mechanism enables the threat to local concerns to become real. Success at Honeysuckle is predicated upon convincing the private sector to take advantage of a pro-business environment and of publicly subsidised infrastructure. At the same time, the shifting balance of responsibility and revenue between federal and state government in Australia has ensured that the state government must optimise long-term returns through the sale of government land. The NSW state government is expected to invest approximately $100m. in the Honeysuckle scheme. The aim is to recoup at least $74m. of this through land sales (*Newcastle Herald*, 1992d: 3). Faced by the harsh realities of stringent state government budgets and a preoccupation with public debt (Evatt Foundation, 1996), adequate returns from Honeysuckle are a necessity. Within this financial and political framework, the priorities of economic growth and investment returns are accorded primacy over social issues of distributional equity. The ability of the social objectives of the redevelopment to withstand being dominated by economic needs will be severely tested. This is particularly the case given the pressure to evaluate incoming investment on the basis of the attractiveness of the investment rather than its applicability to locally defined needs. Currently, the distribution of benefits resulting from the material reconstruction of Newcastle's inner area relies heavily on a 'trickle down' mechanism. Great faith is placed on the impact of a multiplier effect on job creation. Yet there has been scant attention paid to how the local skills base and employment needs, resulting from the city's industrial legacy, might be adapted to suit anticipated employment generated in the services and administration, festival shopping areas, entertainment and leisure complexes of Honeysuckle. Current experience suggests that such schemes have widened disparities in wealth and income distribution. New jobs may indeed be created. However, these are jobs that serve a new workforce rather than dealing with the sizeable remnant workforce of Newcastle's industrial economy.

Another equity concern revolves around the question of affordable housing which is a key priority of the rhetoric of the HDC and the BC programme. Inner Newcastle's current housing profile is weak. In the rental market, 38% of households pay more than 30% of their income on rent and median household income is $9000 less than the national median (Travis McEwen ••• et al, 1993). In recognition of this, $12.5m. of a BC housing strategy funding is being used to provide affordable rental housing for low-income earners (Travis McEwen et al, 1993). However, BC funds are not to be used to assist with the current public housing programme despite a waiting list of 3000 in the Newcastle local government area. Nor will the provision of housing for owner-occupation be tampered with. The housing strategy considers that subsidising affordable owner-occupied housing is 'inappropriate' (Travis McEwen et al, 1993: 24). Instead it is suggested that the private housing market will respond to incentives which trade concessions on development standards in return for the provision of more affordable housing.

Even if affordable owner-occupied housing eventuates, there is no mechanism to ensure that it remains affordable once exposed to market operations. Housing authorities in Newcastle have no means of mitigating the impacts of Honeysuckle's anticipated success on rental property prices (Winchester, 1991). The investment potential of housing in neighbourhoods surrounding Honeysuckle has been avidly seized upon by local real estate agents (e.g. *Newcastle Times*, 1994: 12) and the rateable values of residential properties in these contiguous neighbourhoods have increased by up to 84% since 1991 compared to an increase of just 31% across the whole local government area (Elton and Associates, 1996). The market appears to be priming itself for a major period of gentrification and it is acknowledged that rising property values will impact upon the low-income population (Elton and Associates, 1996; Rofe, 1996).

Existing site works at Honeysuckle have resulted in the displacement of a range of services aimed at a considerable homeless population who traditionally called its old wharves and derelict buildings 'home' (Winchester and Costello, 1995). The commencement of gentrification in the immediate environs of Honeysuckle will result in the displacement of Newcastle's most highly disadvantaged population who are concentrated in the surrounding neighbourhoods of Carrington, Wickham and Tighes Hill (Winchester, 1991). The uneven distributional outcomes of what benefits do trickle down from Honeysuckle are glossed over in the rhetoric of the HDC's promotional literature. Ideals of social equity are obscured by the distributional outcomes of development under entrepreneurialism which offer benefits particularly to commercial interests including real estate agents (Leitner and Garner, 1993; Short et al, 1993). Such development has specifically catered to the demands of these interests in order to ensure their crucial involvement in redevelopment. The 'equity versus efficiency' issue here is a primary example of how presenting the city as a uniform and willing recipient of redevelopment ignores the range of conflicting interests and contested agendas involved in any redevelopment project. The myth of trickle down is utilised to suppress the question of whose interests are being pursued in the redevelopment. Local issues about the nature of employment, the impacts on housing affordability, the silencing of marginal voices and social groups are all subdued by the impulse of entrepreneurialism and its neo-liberal faith in the maxim that 'a rising tide lifts all boats'.

Local accountability

Newcastle's perceived need to fight for investment through an entrepreneurial approach is writ large in the assumptions under which the HDC operates. These assumptions expose how the need to present a united front to would-be investors is constructed. As one of the consultants who produced the Masterplan put it:

Honeysuckle will not happen if the people of Newcastle place stringent conditions on its development. You must compete with other more prestigious cities nationally and internationally for investment. To be blunt, if you regard Newcastle as being on par with say Sydney or Brisbane, you are kidding yourself. . . . [I]n order to attract investment to Newcastle . . . we have to accept that we must provide an easier, more accommodative investment environment with clearly defined planning objectives. By easier I mean easier than *anywhere else*. I would even go so far as to say that the political process should be taken out of the approval mechanism. Get all your objectives sorted out now. Provide a blueprint for investment and then hand the approval process over to an executive body, with no political interference. . . . We don't have a public purse for this project so somewhere you have to allow someone to make some money. Don't fight them in this process, if you do the site will lie in ruin for years to come. (Cullen, 1991: 59–62).

These aims are pursued through an extra-local body that is ultimately answerable to the state government and to its non-elected (and entirely male) board, drawn from the local business and industrial sectors. Community groups do not have representation on the board, though there is a Community Consultation Committee which serves the purpose of information diffusion. Limited public accountability is an integral part of a development corporation strategy to facilitate and speed up investment and, indeed, the charge of lacking public accountability has regularly been laid against local entrepreneurial schemes (Mayer, 1992; Eisenschitz and Gough, 1996). The HDC's programme of community consultation regularly gauges community feeling towards the project but public consultation channels are one-way and are kept open at the discretion of the board. Complaints have been made by public representatives regarding the adequacy and partial nature of public involvement to date (Sutton, 1991; Stephenson, 1993). Meanwhile, favoured private interests are incorporated into the body governing the course of redevelopment. The extent of public consultation on any issue is dependent upon the compatibility of community sentiment with commercial feasibility, and upon whether the rhetoric of consensus is maintained. The fact that the HDC is funded from extra-local sources beyond local tax revenues affords additional insulation by distancing budgetary decisions from local considerations (Hula, 1990).

The redistribution of inter-government revenue and responsibility under neo-liberalism has meant that cities and regions cannot rely on national economic growth for increased revenue (Winter and Brook, 1993). Local or regional growth is now a priority in order to ensure greater funding at this level. This has encouraged local entrepreneurialism and changed the relationship between localities and higher levels of government. In Newcastle, the debate surrounding the removal of the rail link between Civic Station and

Newcastle provided a useful exposition of accountability. It also brought into focus the broader issue of the conflictual relations between spheres of government which entrepreneurialism generates. Currently, the Sydney to Newcastle rail line terminates at Newcastle station, adjacent to the foreshore. The line runs linearly between the foreshore and the city's peculiarly elongated CBD (Figure 5.1). The state government and the HDC viewed the existing line as a major barrier to public access to the foreshore area, hence to potential investors and to state government's chances of recouping its costs in this project. The Masterplan proposed to cut the rail line at Civic Station, 1 km west of the current terminus where an elaborate new rail and bus interchange was proposed. This would allow for undisrupted pedestrian and vehicular access to Honeysuckle and for the sale and redevelopment of the state-owned land released by removing the rail line. The state government was insistent that the rail link be cut despite federal ambivalence on the issue and marked local opposition expressed in, among other things, a petition of 18 000 signatures (Sutton, 1991; *Newcastle Herald*, 1994a: 1). A lengthy and acrimonious debate was triggered with NCC and community groups aligned against the position taken by the HDC along with local business representatives. The dispute became thoroughly embroiled in party politics as Newcastle's Labor public representatives opposed the Liberal state government's position on the rail. The Premier of NSW berated local Labor Party representatives for their 'blinkered thinking', which was 'threatening the potential of the excellent Honeysuckle proposal' (*Newcastle Herald*, 1992a: 8). Federal government's position was ambivalent as its priority was simply to get the programme established and showing progress. However, it stipulated that no BC funding was to be spent on removing the line.

In June 1992, as a way of forcing the hand of local interests, the state government dropped the Honeysuckle project from the four being put forward from NSW to attract BC funding. The state government argued that it would not accept the BC funding for the Honeysuckle if the federal government attached conditions to how those funds could be spent. Nevertheless, revealing the agenda more accurately, the NSW Minister for Planning warned that Honeysuckle would have no hope of being reinstated to the BC list if guarantees were not forthcoming that city council and local Labor politicians would unconditionally accept the proposal to terminate the rail line at Civic Station. An emergency council meeting, which excluded the media, was held to discuss the ultimatum. The motion, passed by council with a 9 to 2 majority, acknowledged that council recognised:

> A divergence of view by some members of the community, but believes the overwhelmingly positive impacts on employment and investment in Newcastle are such that the (State) Government can be assured of council's unconditional acceptance of the Government's right to determine the future of the Newcastle Civic railway line. (Council) acknowledges that

it is the State Government's view that the termination of the rail line is a key part of the Honeysuckle project. (*Newcastle Herald*, 1992c: 4)

The overriding impact of economic pragmatism is clearly visible in the council's eventual acceptance of state government's position. One local councillor noted, 'there's no clear indications [*sic*] that if we (agree to the ultimatum) we will get the money. But what is an absolute certainty is that if we don't agree to it we don't get anything' (*Newcastle Herald*, 1992b: 1). Local politics were successfully subsumed within the need for the city to be presented as a monolithic agent in the redevelopment. With the city's economic fortunes being seen to ride on a single development strategy centred around Honeysuckle, city council's power to represent the conflicting views of its constituents was deflated.

Once the motion was accepted, the major obstacle to funding had been removed in state government eyes, as had the major barrier to recouping costs. The Honeysuckle project was reinstated in August 1992 and BC funding was guaranteed. State government was able to convert its apparent stand against federal attempts to place conditions upon BC funding into an ultimatum to undermine local opposition. Upon the community's acceptance that the rail line be cut, the state conveniently retreated from its stand on non-interference, accepting BC funds with conditions attached. State government could rely upon the self-legitimising force of getting visible 'cranes on the skyline' to justify overruling local opposition (Leitner, 1990). The views of the informal local growth machine of state government, its agent the HDC, and the local business élite became hegemonic.

Discordant voices have continued to be excluded from the dominant discourse of local development. The then NSW Premier John Fahey referred to the whole debate about the rail line as 'silly local politics' (*Newcastle Herald*, 1992e: 1) deriding the validity of public objection and asserting the primacy of broader regional and economic considerations. A telephone survey conducted by the *Newcastle Herald* which found that 67% of respondents did not want the rail line to be cut was dismissed by the HDC as 'irrelevant' (*Newcastle Herald*, 1994c: 1), despite their heavy use of telephone surveys as a means of gauging public opinion on their operations. Furthermore, a leaked memo from the HDC's General Manager to its board members revealed that the release of the Lower Hunter Integrated Transport Study was delayed because it failed to suggest a 'politically saleable' alternative mode of transport to be utilised once the rail line had been removed. It was seen to threaten the public image of the HDC and cause the 'inevitable public brawl' (*Newcastle Herald*, 1994b: 1). The memo suggested delaying the release of the report until it could be 'fine-tuned' to the point where it could be accepted by the Newcastle community. Thus the appearance of consensus would reign, reflecting the élitist localism of entre-preneurial government (Winter and Brook, 1993; Peck and Tickell, 1994). Local community groups and their political representatives have been disempowered both by the representation of the local interest by the pro-growth agenda and by the enforced politics of consensus. The growing influence of market priorities and the need to facilitate investment have shifted the balance of power away from local government and community opinion and exposed its already weak position. Local resistance capitulated in the face of a construction of Newcastle as a monolithic entity desperately in need of reinvestment to re-establish itself in a new global economy.[1]

MANUFACTURING CONSENT: COLONISING THE LOCAL

The pressures of place competition combined with the mechanisms of entre-preneurialism respectively encourage and enable the presentation of the city agenda as uniformly pro-growth. There is strong pressure for places to be marketed as singularly active and monolithic agents in seeking redevelopment. This representation equates city interests with the pro-growth agendas of the regime of local governance (Hall and Hubbard, 1996). Despite the difficulty of identifying a unified business voice (Charlesworth and Cochrane, 1994; Peck, 1995) the public status awarded to private sector interests confers on them a powerful voice in defining the local development agenda. This is then presented in public forums as the legitimate voice of 'the people' (Eisenschitz and Gough, 1993). Somewhat inevitably, development is equated with progress and the benefits of such progress, it is assumed, will be reaped for 'the community' and by the entire community (Harvey, 1989b; Hall and Hubbard, 1996). So internal cleavages are glossed over or suspended. The locality and the course of its development are depoliticised, contradictory interests are elided and 'community' is used as a unitary concept with a collective consciousness whose support gives legitimacy to the development agenda (Charlesworth and Cochrane, 1994; Cox, 1995; Peck, 1995). Community resistance is only mar-ginally accommodated due to the pressure to reach consensus and to promote that consensus as a selling point for the locality (Leitner and Garner, 1993; Imrie, Thomas and Marshall, 1995). The politics of growth construct a powerful image in which local internal divisions and differences, the often conflicting agendas of varying interests within the business sector, within the local community, and between community and business interests are subsumed by the pressure to present the locality as a competitive business environment. Conflict over the course and outcomes of urban entrepreneurialism can threaten that image. As Newcastle's experience reveals, the monolithic presentation of local sites as ready and willing to provide amenable conditions for private investment conceals a reality fraught with conflict. The redefinitions of roles and relation-ships associated with entrepreneurialism has exposed the scope for clashes both within the locality and of local priorities with state and national agendas (Fox-Przeworski, 1986; Bovaird, 1992). It has also provided the mechanism with which to quash these conflicting concerns.

The monolithic representation of the local raises concerns particularly about the ability of entrepreneurial forms of local governance to respond to locally specific interests should they depart from the pro-growth agenda. This is symptomatic of the reconstitution of the relationship between community and state at the local level (Hall and Hubbard, 1996). Moreover it raises concerns about the ability of local governance to address concerns of social equity given the cost-recouping emphasis and reliance on the private sector that is a defining feature of Newcastle's entrepreneurialism.

THE DISCURSIVE SETTING OF ENTREPRENEURIALISM

The local practice and outcomes of entrepreneurialism result not just from the material outcomes of institutional, economic, political and social processes but of discourses as well (Painter and Goodwin, 1995). In Newcastle, local institutions have been restructured to pursue priorities imposed from the macro-political level. This has rendered them increasingly vulnerable to the discourse of globalisation which positions the local as being at the mercy of external, uncontrolled and mythologised global forces (Howitt, 1993; Fagan and Le Heron, 1994). The BC programme which has driven the progress of the HDC is explicitly positioned within and propagates this discourse. The programme is a major constituent of federal government's push to make Australia ready for global competition (Neilson and Spiller, 1992).

Losing the local in a globalising discourse

The globalisation discourse positions the local as being capable only of reacting to the impulses of globalisation and to their local and regional manifestations rather than as a formative and constitutive part of global processes (McGuirk, 1997). The power of this discourse has overriden the concept of the place dependence and local embeddedness of capital investment. Despite deregulation-induced mobility and the internationalised nature of economic interaction, capital is place-dependent at *some* scale and capital mobility is bounded at *some* scale (Storper, 1992; Cox, 1995). However, its potential mobility, and the need to be globally competitive to attract and/or keep investment, rather than its actual mobility is evoked at every level of governance to produce an entrepreneurial response (Cox, 1993). This 'response' affords no role to the local as a formative element in constituting some aspects of the global. The international trend towards entrepreneurial modes of governance is reinforced by these reactions, legitimising those methods as the most effective response to threats posed by global economic change and growing competition between individual localities. The 'local' response springing from such positioning is decidedly 'unlocal', it is in fact repeated almost universally, reflecting the global context and discourse in which it is positioned (Peck and Tickell, 1994). The relationship between locality and capital engendered within entrepreneurial urban governance (Cox, 1995) and the common development thrust of many entrepreneurial schemes threatens the subjugation of local concerns and local identity.

Economic sustainability

The attractiveness of entrepreneurial enticements to local investment is much reduced by the availability of similar incentives at numerous other locations, nationally and internationally (Eisenschitz and Gough, 1993). Similarly if the mix of flagship developments resulting from state-sponsored redevelopment schemes produced standardised landscapes of standardised land-use mixes, this too cancels out the benefits of place marketing based on these developments. The HDC's Masterplan and the images promoted by the HDC are similar to those of Sydney's The Rocks, San Francisco's Fisherman's Wharf and Boston's Faneuil Markets. Sketches and models abound of a leafy, sunny complex of shops and festival markets with strolling shoppers, well-cliented restaurants, marinas bursting with activity and bobbing boats, and adapted heritage buildings bustling with life as artists' workshops. These images are quite typical of a multitude of waterfront developments internationally (Hoyle, Pinder and Hussain, 1988).

In any case, there are questions over the ability of the Hunter region to sustain a redevelopment of the magnitude suggested in the Honeysuckle Masterplan. Honeysuckle's success is hinged upon reversing the ongoing decline of the central area while targeting new, perhaps international, sources of investment and altering the region's industry-dominated occupational structure and decentralising tendencies. There is sparse evidence of such schemes' success in building sustainable urban regeneration, or of creating (rather than relocating) suitable employment (Foley, 1992; Gaffikin and Warf, 1993). Employment losses in the Hunter region due to industry rationalisations have not been magically replaced by a boom in services and other white-collar employment. In the likely absence of an expanding productive base in the region, it is questionable whether the Honeysuckle redevelopment can sustain the proposed employment expansion in the services and retail sectors (O'Neill, 1991). The retail–recreation complex proposed for Honeysuckle requires a larger resident inner-city population, or visitors, with a high level of disposable income. Presently Newcastle has neither. Nor has it ever successfully attracted sustained investment in commercial property (Ross, 1991). It is a regional city rather than a cosmopolitan metropolis. Even its status as a regional base is broadly questioned by the HEDC, the City Council and the City Centre Committee (NCC, 1988; HEDC, 1991; City Centre Committee, 1993). The redevelopment potential is currently sustained by a blind faith in market forces. It is assumed that, once property is available for development, financial and business services will take advantage of the opportunities. The prospects for this are not overly hopeful. The federal government's transformation of the

Custom House into office accommodation at a key site bridging Honeysuckle and the CBD was unable to secure a tenant and was converted for use as a cafe and function centre. In addition, the planned redevelopment of the council-owned site on the city's main street was scaled down from a proposed $55m. to a $9m. development due to a lack of expected demand for new office space (*Newcastle Herald*, 1995: 3). Newcastle's offering of 'more of the same' and the sinking of enormous funds in order to pitch the city into the global arena seem misguided.

Local identity, made up of the convict heritage, working-class roots and industrial legacy, is all being glossed over in the attempt to present the city as a slick retail and recreation location (Dunn, McGuirk and Winchester, 1995). Only those aspects of its heritage that are considered internationally saleable are celebrated and marketed. The wisdom of attempting redevelopment in a manner that is already being done, and done more successfully at other locations, is dubious. This is particularly the case when it necessitates sacrificing the uniqueness of what the local economy and culture could offer in order to reproduce a post-modern 'blandscape' (Short, 1989). The new marketed 'local' identity is indistinguishable from a mass of other similar waterfront/leisure places, and offers little that is unique to Newcastle in an era when place is considered to have a resurging importance. Attracting investment increasingly requires distinguishing the social, physical and cultural character of places as investment sites (Clarke, 1993; Harvey, 1993). However, the globally oriented entrepreneurialism and the nature of redevelopment proposed at Honeysuckle have the potential to emaciate local identity and to replace it with repetitious mass-produced images. This could pose serious threats to the economic viability of the redevelopment.

The approach of governance and the manner in which funding is being applied are conditioned by positioning the local within the discourse of globalisation. This raises questions about whether more genuinely local initiatives to nurture local business, mobilise indigenous resources and develop local skills bases would ultimately be a more successful option (Eisenschitz and Gough, 1993). The international consumption investment sought would bring development which is 'in', not 'of', the locality. This would have little local embeddedness thereby maximising local vulnerability and minimising local empowerment.

CONCLUSION

While the Honeysuckle redevelopment undoubtedly has had positive outcomes, the unproblematic adoption of entrepreneurial approaches to achieve local revitalisation is fraught with difficulty associated with the subsumption of the local and the uncritical embrace of the discourse of globalisation. This discourse assumes that local fortunes are determined by trends of globalising capitalism and that localities must become globally competitive and capable of holding their own as economic actors in the international economy. The power of this discourse overwhelms other options for local economic redevelopment and throws Newcastle into a round of place-competitive strategies in which it must attempt to outclass numerous other locations – some of which are undoubtedly better equipped than Newcastle is to attract the type of investment sought. This allows private sector interests to play one location off against another in demanding concessions and heightens the pressure to supress local contestation as part of a competitive strategy (Sadler, 1993). Place competition, within these discursive parameters, is ultimately regressive and destructive and threatening to local social equity.

Particular attention must be paid to inter-government relations as the state takes on an increasing range of entrepreneurial practices under the guiding political paradigm of neo-liberalism. The ascendancy of market 'realism' or economic pragmatism is reflected in how inter-government roles and relationships have changed and in the growth of entrepreneurial approaches at all levels. Although new tasks have been taken on by local government, this has not meant that local political power has increased. Local redevelopment at Newcastle has been orchestrated by federal and state governments and imposed on relatively weak structures of local governance where local government is simply one player among many (Clarke and Steward, 1994; Charlesworth and Cochrane, 1994). Newcastle's entrepreneurialism thus follows the discourse of globalisation adopted by central government. One crucial outcome of this has been the suppression of local discord and contestation because of the need for a politics of consensus that emerges from this discourse. Entrepreneurial authorities such as the HDC are thus willing to undertake public relations and information diffusion exercises such as pamphlet distributions or telephone polls. These exercises have useful legitimising roles. They are less willing, however, to undertake more consultative or participative exercises which encourage the expression of dissenting or marginal voices which may raise issues of local social equity.

The relationship between state and capital under entrepreneurialism in Newcastle revolves around reliance on the private sector to undertake the physical redevelopment to transform the Honeysuckle into a post-industrial consumption complex. This reiterates the vulnerability of local development authorities to the demands of private sector interests and to market fluctuation (Barnekov and Rich, 1989; Turok, 1992). Caught within the logic of the complementary discourses of entrepreneurialism and globalisation, localities are increasingly vulnerable to the demands of capital, constructed as hypermobile. The threat that other places which better maximise their competitive advantage will capture investment is used to justify a range of economistic decisions and empowers certain interests above others. The balance of power here between the state and multinational capital, between the different tiers of the state and between the local and the global, has been altered by the emergence of entrepreneurial ideology within urban governance. It is altered in a way that disempowers the local, relegates local equity concerns, threatens local identity and local distinctiveness. This examination of the Honeysuckle redevelopment in inner Newcastle illustrates how the complementary assumptions of the globalisation and entrepreneurial discourses, both outcomes of neo-liberal political ideology, encourage place competition, threaten the eradication of local identity, and undermine any hope of pursuing social equity through redevelopment.

NOTE

1. As a result of the Labor Party's victory in the state elections of 1995, plans to remove the rail link were shelved. The balance of interests shifted once again with the landslide victory of the Liberal Party in the federal election of 1996. However, it remains to be seen whether a major change in the region's political complexion will alter the course of Newcastle's entrepreneurialism significantly.

6

PRO-GROWTH LOCAL ECONOMIC DEVELOPMENT STRATEGIES: CIVIC PROMOTION AND LOCAL NEEDS IN BRITAIN'S SECOND CITY, 1981–1996

PATRICK LOFTMAN AND BRENDAN NEVIN

INTRODUCTION

During the 1980s urban local authorities in Britain, and within developed capitalist nations generally, have increasingly adopted policies aimed at promoting local economic growth and attracting inward investment and jobs. Key elements of such pro-growth local economic development strategies have included the development of high-profile prestige property projects and investment in city place promotion or boosterist activities, geared at enhancing the economic position of a city in relation to other urban centres (Harvey, 1988; Bianchini, Dawson and Evans, 1992; Loftman and Nevin, 1995, 1996). As the chapters in this volume suggest, this shift in city government policy priorities is a reflection of a broader transition in the nature and role of local government away from a managerial approach (focused mainly on the provision of services for city residents and a concern for welfare-related issues) towards entrepreneurial approaches, which instead focus on inter-city competition; speculative development projects and promotional initiatives; and emphasising private sector interests in the formulation and implementation of public policies (Harvey, 1989b). The impact of this transition in the role of local government is most evident in the establishment of an elaborate array of public–private partnerships at the local level, which often entail a transfer of public policy-making and implementation away from local authorities.

In the context of the global restructuring of industry in the 1970s and 1980s, the increased internationalisation of economic activity (evidenced in the increased geographical mobility of investment and production) and the intensification of inter-urban competition for investment and jobs, it is argued that declining cities unwilling to adopt entrepreneurial policies focused on encouraging economic growth, are contributing to their own economic demise (Kotler, Haider and Rein, 1993; Fainstein, 1994). These global pressures on

British city governments have been compounded by a shift in national urban policy (during the 1980s) away from a concern with welfare-related issues towards economic ones, a shift encouraged by tight central government restrictions on the powers and resources of local government and the espousal of urban regeneration approaches adapted from the United States (Loftman and Nevin, 1996). In the context of these trends, it is argued that city leaders have been compelled to restructure the physical fabric of the city order to maintain or improve the position of their city in the global economic hierarchy. Thus, pro-growth local economic development policies may represent the only practical course of action to local governments to achieve economic prosperity within their jurisdictions (Fainstein, 1994).

This chapter examines Birmingham City Council's adoption of pro-growth local economic development strategies in the 1980s and early 1990s which explicitly attempted to revive Birmingham's flagging economic fortunes and place the city firmly on 'the international map'. Since the Victorian era, the City of Birmingham gained a reputation for forward-thinking local government and dynamism, with one commentator stating that 'Birmingham is regularly described as the most dynamic city in the world today; if any city is more dynamic, Heaven help it' (Bird, 1979: 15). Furthermore, Birmingham's bold pro-growth local economic development strategy during the 1980s has been described as 'a "textbook" example of the way in which traditional urban geographies are being rapidly restructured and repackaged in an attempt to rejuvenate the local economy' (Hubbard, 1996b: 1450). A key element of Birmingham City Council's regeneration strategy in the 1980s was the focus of local government activity and investment on the physical restructuring of Birmingham's city centre (particularly the development of prestige property projects) and the projection of a new city image via aggressive civic boosterism initiatives.

This chapter, in examining Birmingham's approach, first sets out the local political and economic context to Birmingham City Council's regeneration policies implemented since the 1980s. This is then followed by a review of the city council's adoption of a pro-growth (entrepreneurial) local economic development strategy under the Labour Party leadership of Sir Richard Knowles (between 1984 and 1994). This review of the Knowles era focuses on the following themes: the city council's formulation of a 'vision' for the 'new' Birmingham; the implementation mechanisms devised to secure the new vision for Birmingham; the claimed economic impact of Birmingham's pro-growth strategy; and the distributional consequences of its implementation. The chapter concludes by examining the recent shift in Birmingham City Council's policy priorities, following the election of Theresa Stewart as leader of the city council in 1994, resulting in a reprioritisation of the council's strategic goals – giving greater emphasis to the delivery of 'basic' local authority services, such as education, over entrepreneurial pro-growth policies.

BIRMINGHAM PRE-1980: LOCAL POLITICAL AND ECONOMIC CONTEXT

A tradition of civic leadership and political pragmatism

Birmingham, located in the heart of England's industrial West Midlands region, is Britain's second largest city with a population of just under 1 million people. As such, it is generally considered to be the nation's leading provincial city and is often referred to, albeit contentiously, as Britain's 'second city'. Reflecting the scale of the city itself, Birmingham City Council is the most powerful metropolitan district local authority in England, with an annual gross revenue expenditure of £1.8 billion, employing over 37 000 people, and owning approximately 30% of the city's land area. The City of Birmingham's political and economic history, dating back to the late nineteenth century, provides the foundations of many of the pro-growth local economic development policies implemented by the local authority in the 1980s and 1990s (Birmingham City Council, 1989a; Shaylor, 1990). This was noted by the city council itself in 1989 (its centenary year as a city): 'Birmingham's history is dominated by two themes – its emergence as a great industrial city and a tradition of civic achievement unequalled by any other British city. These themes continue to dominate the city today' (Birmingham City Council, 1989b: 4).

Over the past century Birmingham has acquired a reputation for strong and active municipal leadership, entrepreneurship and pragmatic party politics, which has largely emanated from the city council's active and leading role in expanding and redeveloping the physical structure of the city (Cherry, 1994). The city council has a long-standing tradition of powerful elected leaders and chief officers and an ability for political parties (regardless of political control of the council) to work together in the interests of Birmingham and to collaborate with the private sector (Sutcliffe and Smith, 1974; Deakin and Edwards, 1993; Cherry, 1994). Deakin and Edwards argue that 'the persistence of this climate of co-operation sets Birmingham apart from other English major cities, in particular because it is politically bipartisan' (1993: 132). In addition, Birmingham is referred to as a city with a 'history and confidence of being first, biggest and best' (Fretter, 1993: 166).

The city council's motto, 'Forward' has been dramatically reflected in its pioneering approach to local government and its implementation of grand civic construction schemes since the Victorian era (Birmingham City Council, 1989a). Birmingham's municipal tradition of enterprise and civic leadership can be traced back to the 1870s when the city, under the mayorship of Joseph Chamberlain, was widely acknowledged for its dynamic and achievement-orientated council:

In the 1870s and early 1880s Birmingham gained an international reputation as being the best governed city in the world. Civic pride was the driving force of the new civic philosophy, known at the time and since as 'the civic gospel'. Birmingham was regarded as experimental, adventurous and diverse. This set a tradition in Birmingham of leadership in municipal enterprise (Bishop's Council for the Diocese of Birmingham, 1988: 10).

Chamberlain's achievements as mayor (between 1873 and 1876) in securing the redevelopment of Birmingham's city-centre slums to create a new planned commercial and retail area, the construction of bold city centre civic developments (including two railway stations, an art gallery, a reference library and the current council house), ensured that Birmingham 'acquired not just national but international prestige in municipal governance' (Cherry, 1994: 81). Furthermore, Cherry argues that the Chamberlain era established a 'tradition of municipal service which was effectively preserved into the 20th century among Birmingham's business and professional strata' (1994: 81).

During the twentieth century civic leaders in Birmingham have sought to continue the legacy of Chamberlain by expanding the services of the council into managing utilities (such as water and gas), an airport and even its own municipal bank. In particular, between the 1950s and 1960s, despite frequent changes in the political control of the local authority, a cross-party consensus on inner-city problems enabled the city council (and its powerful chief city engineer and surveyor, Herbert Manzoni) to undertake a massive inner-city slum clearance programme; construct Birmingham's infamous Inner Ring Road project; plan the development of the city's current Central Reference Library (the largest in Europe); and facilitate construction of the Bull Ring shopping centre scheme (Sutcliffe and Smith, 1974; Birmingham City Council, 1989a; Cherry, 1994).

The demise of Birmingham's economic base

Throughout most of the nineteenth and twentieth century the local economy of Birmingham and the West Midlands conurbation was based on manufacturing industry. During the postwar period up to the 1970s, Birmingham and the West Midlands enjoyed unparalleled economic prosperity. This economic success was based on a relatively small number of manufacturing industries (in particular, motor vehicle manufacture and engineering) with unemployment in the West Midlands county rarely exceeding 1% between 1948 and 1966 (Spencer et al, 1986). However, the overdependence of Birmingham and its region on manufacturing, and, moreover, on a relatively small number of manufacturing firms, made the local economy vulnerable to structural changes in the national and global economy particularly during periods of recession (Birmingham City Council, 1985; Spencer et al, 1986).

The West Midlands region was adversely affected by national and global economic change in the 1970s, and within a decade was transformed from being one of the nation's most economically prosperous regions to a low-wage, low-productivity economy suffering chronic levels of unemployment. Whereas, in 1971, the West Midlands was the second highest ranked region in Great Britain in terms of GDP (gross domestic product) per capita, by 1983 it had fallen to the second lowest ranked region. Unemployment within the West Midlands region rose faster than in any other region across the country between 1974 and 1984 – increasing from 2 to 15%, with the region's unemployment rate ranked fourth highest among European Community regions in 1981 (Birmingham City Council, 1985).

Birmingham's local economy was particularly hard hit by the restructuring of the regional manufacturing base (Spencer et al, 1986; Bryson, Daniels and Henry, 1996). Between 1971 and 1987 Birmingham lost 191 000 jobs, amounting to 29% of total employment in the city. The city's manufacturing base was particularly devastated, losing 149 000 jobs over the same period. This loss represented 46% of total manufacturing employment in Birmingham between 1971 and 1987 (Champion and Townsend, 1990). According to the city council, non-local economic factors (largely structural changes at the national and international levels) accounted for a 7% fall in total employment within Birmingham between 1971 and 1983, but an alarming 32% fall in city manufacturing jobs over the same period (Birmingham City Council, 1985). The collapse of Birmingham's manufacturing base, however, was not mitigated by expansion in service sector employment in the city, which provided only meagre growth (an increase of 9000 jobs) between 1971 and 1987 (Birmingham City Council, 1992a). The local impact of Birmingham's economic decline in the 1970s and 1980s was further compounded by changes in patterns of commuting. Between 1961 and 1981, the proportion of Birmingham jobs held by city residents declined from 82 to 69% (a fall of 203 000 jobs) (Birmingham City Council, 1985). In particular, the impact of commuting patterns was concentrated within Birmingham city centre, with the number of non-Birmingham residents employed in the city centre rising from 33 to 42% between 1971 and 1981 (Birmingham Economic Information Centre, 1994).

The effects of the economic collapse of Birmingham's economic base, however, were not equally distributed across the city's geographical areas or its social groups. Birmingham's inner areas, which surround the city centre, and the city's black and ethnic minority communities, were particularly hard hit, experiencing the highest levels of unemployment and urban deprivation in the city during the late 1970s and early 1980s. In February 1985 the unemployment rate within Birmingham's inner city (the Birmingham Partnership Core Area) was 31.8% compared with a city and regional average of 20.8 and 15.8% respectively (Birmingham City Council, 1985).

It is within this context of Birmingham's pressing economic problems in the 1980s, and a history of municipal activism and political pragmatism, that a political consensus emerged within the city around the need to pursue an aggressive pro-growth local economic development strategy.

BIRMINGHAM'S NEW VISION 1981–1993: TRANSFORMING THE CITY

Political consensus and pragmatic local politics

Birmingham City Council's primary policy response in the early 1980s to the collapse of the city's manufacturing industry was to seek to broaden the city's economic base, through encouraging service sector investment and employment and by promoting a new and dynamic image of the city (Loftman and Nevin, 1992). Reflecting the city council's tradition of pragmatic local politics and cross-party co-operation in tackling the major urban issues facing the city, a broad consensus emerged between the city's major players in the 1980s around the need to pursue 'an aggressive pro-development strategy to manage the concurring problems of structural decline and cyclical downturn' (DiGaetano and Klemanski, 1993: 376). The basic goal of this pro-growth strategy was to promote projects that would protect the city's industrial base while facilitating the growth of its city centre office and commercial activities (DiGaetano and Klemanski, 1993).

Between 1979 and 1984 there were four changes in political control of Birmingham City Council, with the Conservative and Labour parties each enjoying two periods of city council control. This pattern of vacillating local authority political control in the 1970s and 1980s sets Birmingham apart from other major provincial cities in England (such as Manchester, Sheffield and Leeds), where Labour Party control of city government is firmly entrenched. However, despite the frequent changes in the political control of the city during this period, Birmingham's political and business leaders were able to form a close alliance around the theme of promoting service sector-orientated growth within Birmingham – in response to the city's pressing economic crisis.

For example, in the early 1970s Birmingham had made its first attempt to diversify its ailing local economy, by successfully securing national government support for the development of a National Exhibition Centre (NEC), which opened in 1976 (Birmingham City Council 1989a; Cherry, 1994; Law, 1996). The £40m. cost of developing the NEC, which is located on a greenfield site on the periphery of Birmingham, was funded by the city council, although the management of the facility was undertaken by a private limited liability company – NEC Ltd, with £10 000 of share capital owned equally by Birmingham City Council and Birmingham Chamber of Industry and Commerce. This early example of a public–private sector partnership in Birmingham was a forerunner of the philosophy which was to underpin the political coalition which supported the economic development policies of the city council through the 1980s and early 1990s (Carley, 1991). It is also argued that the development of the NEC 'marked a transitional stage in the development of Birmingham, between the construction of the post-war city and the emergence of the international business city of the 1980s' (Birmingham City Council, 1989a: 130).

Birmingham City Council's focus on tackling the economic problems facing the city continued in the early 1980s, with the establishment of an Economic Development Committee in 1980. However, the local authority's emphasis on a pro-growth strategy became most evident following the election of a Labour Party-controlled city council in May 1984, under the charismatic leadership of Sir Richard Knowles (Loftman and Nevin, 1992; DiGaetano and Klemenski, 1993; Hubbard, 1995). In contrast to more 'radical' left-wing Labour authorities such as Liverpool, Manchester and Sheffield, Birmingham City Council's ruling Labour group, under the leadership of Councillor Knowles, adopted a non-ideological and pragmatic approach to addressing the major issues facing the city, working in close collaboration with local political opponents and the private sector, simultaneously avoiding overt conflict with central government (Cheesewright, 1991). Knowles's Labour administration 'presented Birmingham as a moderate right-wing council, interested in achieving results rather than "championing slogans"' (Solomos and Back, 1995: 78). This bipartisan and pragmatic approach was neatly summed by Graham Shaylor (then Director of the council's Development Department):

> The over-riding culture of the place is that it likes to be first. Birmingham especially likes to be first, big, expensive and brash. And it won't let political dogma stand in its way. Birmingham can perhaps best be described as a city which is working class but is aspiring to be middle class (1990: 41).

By adopting a pragmatic approach, the council's Labour leadership was able to utilise its cross-party support for major urban initiatives and its extensive collaboration with the private sector, as a means of avoiding the imposition of an urban development corporation on the city by central government (Deakin and Edwards, 1993). This broad consensus between key public sector and private sector players within the city underpinned the formulation of the local authority's strategy to promote Birmingham as an international centre for service sector activity and tourism.

The new vision for Birmingham

Under the leadership of Richard Knowles, Birmingham City Council once again sought to engineer a new future for the city based on grand development projects and aggressive city promotion. Reflecting its legacy of municipal activism and powerful civic leadership during the Chamberlain era, Knowles and a small group of influential council committee chairs implemented bold and innovative development projects aimed at radically altering the physical structure and image of Birmingham:

By the close of the City's first century in 1989, great progress is being made to restore Birmingham's vitality and enterprise from the down-turn of the 1970s. The ambitious regeneration of the City in such a short period of time is remarkable when set against the economic recession of the previous decade. . . . The City Council has pitched its fortunes to the successful portrayal of Birmingham as an International City, able to attract, interest and entertain visitors who will, hopefully, help to secure the City's future prosperity (Birmingham City Council, 1989a: 154).

A key component of Birmingham City Council's vision for the economic future of the city in the 1980s, and the basis of its pro-growth local economic development strategy, was the nurturing of service sector investment, most notably business tourism, primarily through the promotion of Birmingham as a dynamic international city, as a means of broadening the city's economic base (Loftman and Nevin, 1992). A key player in the formulation and development of Birmingham City Council's new vision for the city and its pro-growth economic development strategy was Councillor Albert Bore, Chair of the local authority's Economic Development Committee (between 1984 and 1993) who was described as 'a major force in the city's pro-growth coalition' (DiGaetano and Klemenski, 1993: 377). During the 1980s the power of the council's Economic Development Committee grew considerably. In 1984 Birmingham succeeded in its application to central government for Assisted Area status, gaining access to essential European Community funds to support its economic development activities. In 1985 the city council established an Economic Development Unit which produced the council's first Economic Development Strategy (Birmingham City Council, 1985), which according to DiGaetano and Klemenski (1993) was largely written and championed by Councillor Bore. Following the abolition of the West Midlands County Council (which previously held the primary responsibility for economic development issues across the conurbation) in 1985, the city's role in local economic development and the influence of both the council's Economic Development Committee and its staff, increased significantly. Between 1980/81 and 1990/91, the Economic Development Committee's expenditure as a proportion of total (gross) revenue expenditure increased from 2.6% (£10.9m.) to 3.7% (£51.6m.) (Birmingham City Council, 1981, 1991a). When a separate city council Economic Development Department was created in 1990, it was the largest among local authorities in the UK. By March 1991, staff resources within the council dedicated to economic development functions had increased from 213 full-time equivalents in 1981 to 442 (Birmingham City Council, 1981, 1991a).

In addition to the immediate economic problems facing Birmingham, it was also deemed by the city council that Birmingham was generally perceived by city residents and outsiders (particularly potential inward investors and visitors) as having a poor image, with the city council stating that 'the public image of Birmingham is of a city with a depressed economy' (Birmingham City Council,

1985, para. 3.24). In particular, the physical environment and postwar urban design and architecture of Birmingham's city centre was consistently lambasted by numerous commentators and groups (DEWG, 1988; Hilderbrant, et al, 1988; Falk, 1989; Simms, 1989; Tibbalds et al, 1990; Lister, 1991). The scale of Birmingham's city 'image problem' was further highlighted in a survey of European cities reported in a French magazine *Le Point* (and cited in the Birmingham press), which, based on seven criteria (quality of life, culture, welfare, transport, dynamism, environment and public safety) ranked Birmingham 49th out of 50 cities, just ahead of Istanbul (Webster, 1989).

In order to address Birmingham's twin problems of economic decline and poor image, the city council sought to promote a new national and international image for Birmingham and provide an attractive climate for private investment within its city centre, which was considered to be the major asset upon which to base Birmingham's economic future:

> In order to promote urban regeneration, it is essential that the full potential of Birmingham's assets should be realised and one of the greatest assets is the City Centre. To a large degree the prosperity of the whole city will depend upon the vitality of the City Centre, which is by far the most important concentration of economic, cultural and administrative activity within the West Midlands region. It is also critical to the City Council's promotion of Birmingham as a major international city and the strengthening of its status as both the regional capital and the nation's first City outside London (Birmingham City Council, 1992c: 2).

In this context, the city council adopted a city centre-focused model of regeneration as its primary vehicle for securing the city's economic future, promoting Birmingham as an international centre for business tourism, leisure and culture, potentially attracting footloose inward private sector investment and jobs (Loftman and Nevin, 1992).

Four prestige projects, which were perceived by the city council to be building on the success of the NEC (Birmingham City Council, 1989a), provided the main focus of the city council's pro-growth strategy in the 1980s. These prestige developments, located within Birmingham's Broad Street Redevelopment Area (adjacent to the city's central business district) are:

- the £180m. International Convention Centre (ICC), opened in April 1991, with a maximum conference capacity of 3700 delegates and inclusion of a 'world class' symphony hall
- the £57m. National Indoor Arena (NIA), which was originally conceived as part of a city council bid to host the 1992 Olympics, constructed to enhance Birmingham's position as an international centre for sport, seating up to 12 000 people
- the £31m. Hyatt Hotel, built as an integral part of the ICC development

- the £250m. privately financed Brindley Place scheme (located adjacent to the ICC and NIA), which currently includes plans for the development of 79 000 sq. m of offices, 11 500 sq. m of retail space including a high-profile national aquarium and 140 units of luxury residential accommodation

The development projects within the Broad Street Redevelopment Area were supported by the creation of a new civic square (Centenary Square) at the cost of £3.4m. and a £3.3m. pedestrian footbridge which linked the ICC with the city centre.

In developing Birmingham's city-centre prestige projects, the city council drew heavily on the experience of US cities. This influence is exemplified by the fact that the original idea for the development of the ICC stemmed from a visit by Birmingham councillors and officers to Phoenix, Arizona in 1981 (Birmingham City Council, 1983). In addition, the original proposal for the construction of the Brindley Place scheme was based on Baltimore's Harborplace development, including the development of a national aquarium (Loftman, 1990). Approval for the development of the ICC, a new five-star hotel and a mixed-use development (including a national visitor attraction) was given by the council in 1983 (under the control of the Conservative Party). However, the projects were subsequently implemented by the Knowles Labour-controlled city administration.

Birmingham's investment in prestige projects has been further supported by a plethora of high-profile city council civic boosterism initiatives, which were seen as crucial in underpinning the local authority's projection of a new and positive image of an 'international city' (Birmingham City Council, 1991b). Examples of these boosterist activities include: the city's unsuccessful bid to host the 1992 and 1996 Olympic Games; the acquisition of the Sadler's Wells Royal Ballet Company and the D'Oyly Carte Opera Company from London; and the running of the Birmingham Super Prix, an annual Formula Two motor race (now defunct) held within Birmingham's city centre area. These place promotion initiatives were complemented by an aggressive city council marketing campaign portraying Birmingham as 'the Big Heart of England' and 'One of the World's Great Meeting Places' (Birmingham City Council, 1989c: 21). The implementation of these civic boosterism initiatives, however, entailed considerable city council expenditure. For example, in 1989/90 the improvement of city theatres to house the former Sadler's Wells Royal Ballet Company (now the Birmingham Royal Ballet) and the D'Oyly Carte Opera Company cost the council £2.5m., with additional annual revenue grants to its prestige cultural venues companies (including the City of Birmingham Symphony Orchestra) costing in excess of £2.7m. by the beginning of the 1990s. Furthermore, the council's bid for the 1992 Olympics cost £2.5m. and the running of the Birmingham Super Prix over a five-year period generated a financial loss of £2.5m. (Loftman and Nevin, 1992).

Engaging the private sector in Birmingham's vision

In order to finance the development of its city centre prestige projects Birmingham City Council applied its financial and organisational skills in securing private sector and European Community funds, in a bid to offset their massive construction costs. In securing finance for its prestige projects, Birmingham City Council utilised two quasi-public sector companies – Hyatt Regency Birmingham Ltd and NEC Ltd. Hyatt Regency Birmingham Ltd was established to build and operate the Hyatt Hotel development, involving three partners: the Hyatt Corporation (a US-based hotel operator), property developer Trafalgar House, and Birmingham City Council – each with a one-third stake in the venture. NEC Ltd on the other hand, acted as an agent for the city council in constructing the ICC and NIA, raising private finance for the developments (underwritten by the city council) and managing the facilities on the city's behalf. In both of these arm's-length companies, the city council secured senior elected member representation on the respective boards (Loftman and Nevin, 1996).

Over the period 1986/87–1991/92 Birmingham City Council invested £331.1m. in its city-centre prestige projects (ICC, NIA) and the NEC (see Table 6.1). The NEC Ltd played a crucial role in financing the construction costs of its major facilities, raising more than £160m. through the issue of loan stock which was subsequently guaranteed by the city council. Additionally, £114m. was transferred from the city council's capital programme to pay for construction work and £56m. was received from the European Regional Development Fund (ERDF). However, the award of the ERDF grant had a significant impact upon the council's capital programme, as prior to 1993 the Treasury insisted that the ERDF grant was offset against the local authority's permission to borrow. Thus, of the massive capital expenditure involved in Birmingham's prestige projects, over half of the total was directly subsidised by the city council, and the remaining private sector finance raised by NEC Ltd was underwritten by the local authority.

In addition to the securing of private sector assistance in financing and managing its new prestige projects, the city council also sought to engage the private sector in the formulation of policies aimed at reimaging and promoting Birmingham's city centre. In 1988 a City Centre Challenge Symposium was held at Highbury House (Joseph Chamberlain's former residence), where Birmingham's vision for the future and the development of its city centre was debated. The symposium, called the Highbury Initiative, was attended by senior city council officers and politicians (including Councillors Richard Knowles and Albert Bore), central government officials, private sector interests and a group of national and international experts in the field of urban design and regeneration (DEWG, 1988). However, the initiative was marked by the absence of any members of Birmingham's general public (Loftman and Nevin, 1992). The 1988 symposium resulted in the formulation of a strategy for

TABLE 6.1 Capital cost of major prestige projects, 1986/87–1991/92 (£m.)

	NEC	NIA	ICC	Total	ERDF
1986/87	2.7	–	7.9	10.6	–
1987/88	16.3	0.6	16.8	33.7	9.2
1988/89	39.9	0.2	29.5	69.6	–
1989/90	4.3	25.7	58.1	88.1	18.2
1990/91	5.1	24.4	45.1	74.6	27.0
1991/92	34.7	6.2	13.6	54.5	1.8
Total	103	57.1	171	331.1	56.2

Source: Loftman and Nevin (1992)

revitalising the city centre which emphasised: the need to communicate a new image for the city centre (in keeping with Birmingham's international aspirations); the downgrading of the city's Inner Ring Road; giving greater priority to the needs of city-centre pedestrians over vehicular traffic; developing a series of distinctive quarters within the city centre; and the establishment of a new association of private sector interests within the city centre (DEWG, 1988). A follow-up symposium was held in 1989 at the same venue, where the group 'united behind Birmingham's ambitious goal to become a truly international city, symbolised in the rapidly emerging International Convention Centre area' (Falk, 1989: 1).

The Highbury Initiative meetings led to two major outcomes in terms of the promotion of Birmingham's new vision and image. Firstly, the city council embarked on a major drive to improve the physical environment and urban design of the city centre in the late 1980s and early 1990s (Hubbard, 1996a), which was deemed to be crucial in promoting a positive image of the city (Hilderbrant et al, 1988; Tibbalds et al, 1990). To achieve this aim, it is estimated that almost £21m. of city council expenditure was incurred on its City Centre Enhancement programme and external infrastructure works to streets and canal sides within the city-centre area (between 1990 and 1995), with European Community grants covering almost half of the cost (Wright and Blakemore, 1995). Secondly, the Highbury Initiative led to the establishment of Birmingham's first city-centre business association in 1989. The primary aim of the association, called Birmingham City 2000, is to lobby on behalf of and promote the city as a business centre of national and international standing (Loftman, Middleton and Nevin, 1993). City 2000 is made up of 150 professional and financial services companies and its promotional literature notes that:

Together they represent one of the most powerful business groups in the region. All sectors are represented including accountants, actuaries, advertising agencies, architects, banks, building societies, consultants, finance companies, human resources, media, merchant banks, patent

attorneys, public relations, solicitors, stockbrokers, support services, surveyors and venture capitalists (Birmingham City 2000, 1992: 1).

City 2000 played an important role in facilitating the development of
Birmingham city centre during the 1990s – facilitating liaison between the city
council and the private sector and lobbying central government and the
European Community for additional resources and funds.

Opposition to Birmingham's new vision

Despite the existence of widespread support for Birmingham's investment in
prestige developments and civic promotion, among the city's political and
private sector leaders, and the local press, there was some (albeit limited)
opposition to the council's pro-growth strategy. This opposition was most
evident within Knowles's Labour ruling group itself, with a number of left-wing
councillors and the Birmingham District Labour Party in 1986 opposing the
redirection of council expenditure away from the provision of basic services
such as education, housing and social services towards prestige projects.
However, the internal split within the ruling Labour group was resolved by the
leadership disciplining rebel councillors by temporary suspension and their
removal from prominent positions within the council (Tomkins, 1988). In
taking this action, the Labour leadership effectively gagged and marginalised
opposition to its pro-growth strategy in the 1980s, with criticism limited to local
Conservative Party concerns about the spiralling costs of the prestige projects
and criticisms of the design of the council's prestige developments. Wider
public debate in Birmingham of the wider financial costs of the city council's
pro-growth economic development policies was further emasculated by
unequivocal support for the city's prestige projects from the local media, strict
financial confidentiality rules associated with council's expenditure, and the
concentration of decision-making power and information in the hands of a
select band of senior city council politicians and officials (Loftman and Nevin,
1992).

BIRMINGHAM'S PRO-GROWTH STRATEGY: THE CLAIMED ECONOMIC IMPACT

The development of prestige projects in the city centre was predicated on three
basic assumptions: first, that prestige projects will both directly and indirectly
produce substantial economic benefits to the City of Birmingham; second, that
all residents would benefit from the developments; and third, that the public
sector costs of its pro-growth strategy would be minimised by private sector and
European Community resources and outweighed by the economic benefits to
the city as a whole (Loftman and Nevin, 1992). Birmingham City Council's

massive financial investment in its prestige projects has been publicly justified by civic leaders in the following terms:

> . . . for the past seven years, the city council pursued a strategy for regenerating Birmingham which has involved attracting private sector investment into the City, which has led to a change in the City's image from a provincial manufacturing centre to that of a major European City. It has resulted for example in the development of the International Convention Centre, the Hyatt Hotel and the Birmingham National Indoor Arena as the focal points of inner city regeneration in the western part of the City Centre (Birmingham City Council, 1991c).

In terms of direct and indirect employment and income generation, the city council claimed in 1983 that the operation of the ICC alone would support around 1900 jobs through the multiplier process and would improve the city's visibility to potential investors (Birmingham City Council, 1983). These figures were subsequently updated as the 1980s progressed, and by 1990 the city council was claiming 12 000 new jobs as a result of the redevelopment of the Broad Street area (Birmingham City Council, 1990). A more recent study commissioned by the city council suggested that Birmingham's prestige projects had generated 'considerable' regional benefits in terms of expenditure and employment (KPMG Peat Marwick, 1993). The consultants estimated that between September 1992 and August 1993 the ICC and NIA generated £109m. of net expenditure within the region. However, only 41% (£45m.) of this expenditure was retained as income within the West Midlands, and only 16% (£18m.) within the City of Birmingham. According to the city council's consultants the expenditure generated by the two prestige projects, through the multiplier process, supported 4600 full-time equivalent (FTE) jobs within the West Midlands, of which only 40% (1847 FTE jobs) were estimated to be located within Birmingham (KPMG Peat Marwick, 1993).

In addition to the job creation claims attached to its prestige projects, the city council also reported that the development of the ICC had fuelled commercial activity within Birmingham's city centre, helping to attract £2bn of public and private sector investment into Birmingham (Birmingham City Council, 1992c). A boom in new office, retail and hotel development within the city centre during the late 1980s and early 1990s (such as the Pavilions shopping mall, City Plaza, and plans for the £250m. redevelopment of the Bull Ring shopping centre) was considered evidence of private sector confidence in the city council's new vision for Birmingham (Birmingham City Council, 1989a, 1992c; Carley, 1991; Smyth, 1994). However, these claims of a causal link between this private sector investment and the city council's development of prestige projects have been questioned (Loftman and Nevin, 1994). Furthermore, it has been argued that many of the jobs located at the ICC and NIA are low-skilled, temporary, part-time and low-paid (Loftman and Nevin, 1994) and that the economic benefits from the council's pro-growth strategy have failed to 'trickle down' to the most disadvantaged areas and residents within Birmingham (Loftman and Nevin, 1994, 1996).

Despite these criticisms the 'success' of Birmingham's prestige developments has been widely acclaimed by the local and national media, professional bodies (*The Planner*, 1991; *Planning*, 1991) and by some academic commentators (Carley, 1991; Martin and Pearce, 1992; Lock, 1993; Smyth, 1994), with one commentator claiming that:

> The transformation in barely a few years of Birmingham's image from cultural wasteland to England's most dynamic concentration of cultural activity outside of London is a remarkable story of local authority commitment and imagination. The achievements have put the city on the international stage (Lister, 1991: 54).

Furthermore, the city council's promotional activities have been legitimised by the local authority in terms of generating worldwide media coverage and putting the city on the international map – a view articulated by Councillor Albert Bore:

> Our bid for the Olympics not only gave the city more publicity than we could ever dream of, but also made us all realise just what was going on and what potential we had. Running a motor race through the city centre also put us on the map and it's no wonder that practically every hotel chain in the world wants to come to Birmingham (quoted in Jones, 1990: 6).

PRO-GROWTH ECONOMIC DEVELOPMENT: THE LOCAL RESOURCE DISTRIBUTION IMPACTS

Between 1981 and 1990 it is estimated that Birmingham lost £599m. in central government rate support grant (Loftman and Nevin, 1992). In such a climate of central government cuts in local authority expenditure, Birmingham City Council's significant financial investment in prestige developments resulted in the diversion of scarce public resources away from 'basic' services which the city's disadvantaged groups are particularly dependent upon. Over the period 1986/87–1991/92 the ICC and NIA prestige developments alone accounted for 18% of total Birmingham City Council capital spending (amounting to £228m.). Invariably the large-scale investment in the prestige projects, civic boosterism and general city centre refurbishment over this period, had a significant impact upon services such as housing and education. Over the period 1986/87–1991/92 the city council spent £123m. less on housing than the average performance of local authorities in England. This spending profile occurred despite an outstanding repairs bill for council housing of £1.3bn and the existence of

81 251 homes in the city which were unfit for human habitation. A similar pattern also emerged in relation to the city's education service, with the council's capital spending falling by 60% during the construction of the prestige projects (Loftman and Nevin, 1996).

However, it was the city's education revenue budget which was the most adversely affected by the cost of the city council's boosterism activities and the operational losses of the ICC and NIA. Between 1991/92 and 1995/96 the ICC and NIA accrued an accumulated operational deficit of £146m., a deficit which was exacerbated by large council expenditure on prestigious arts events, the Birmingham Super Prix and the bid for the 1992 Olympics. The effect of this revenue expenditure meant that between 1988 and 1993 the city council's revenue expenditure on education was consistently lower than that recommended by central government, and in 1990/91 the city council's £46m. revenue underspend on education accounted for nearly half of the national education budget underspend (Loftman and Nevin, 1996).

CITY COUNCIL POLICIES POST-1993: CHANGING POLITICAL PRIORITIES

The tensions within the ruling Labour group over its prioritising of the development of an 'international' city over social welfare objectives had been evident since 1987 when several prominent left-wingers on the council rebelled. However, following the publication of a critical research report (see Loftman and Nevin, 1992) which highlighted the public sector costs of pursuing the pro-growth strategy, these tensions re-emerged within the ruling group. In addition, the report's findings and the local heated debate surrounding its release led to conflict between the Labour council and the Conservative national government, culminating in the latter criticising the city council's expenditure priorities in a parliamentary debate about education (Sparkes, 1992). The fracturing of the 'consensus' in Birmingham became evident in May 1993, when Theresa Stewart (a veteran left-wing Labour councillor) became deputy leader of the council and several other left of centre colleagues were elected to chair key council committees (Smith, 1993). The new deputy leader made her views on Birmingham's prestige projects clear in a local newspaper interview the day after her election as deputy leader:

> It's been said that I'm against Birmingham's developments like the new Victoria Square, the ICC and the NIA, but it's not quite true. Now we've got them, I'm all for making them pay for themselves. But had I been in the position to determine whether we'd had them or not, then I would have left them out, preferring to go for better housing, better social services and more stable school roofs.

Now they're in place though, let's market them within strict boundaries (Messent, 1993: 14).

Councillor Stewart went on to state:

what some call 'putting Birmingham on the map' has become a priority.
I think that's wrong. The priority must be employment, housing, social services and so on (Messent, 1993: 14. Messent's emphasis).

The first significant action of the new deputy leader was to set up an independent commission to examine the quality of the education service in Birmingham. The report, published in October 1993, estimated the need to invest £200m. in the city's schools to remedy disrepair over a five-year period (Birmingham Education Commission, 1993).

Following the resignation of Richard Knowles as council leader (announced in April 1993), Theresa Stewart was elected as leader of the city council in October of the same year. The new political priorities of the Stewart administration were reflected in her first budget (1994/95) which protected housing capital expenditure (despite a decline in central government financial support) and set revenue budgets for education and social services which were £2.9m. and £9.5m. above the level recommended by central government (Stewart, 1994).

This 'back to basics' philosophy of the new council leadership led to local services such as education and social services receiving priority in council resource allocations over prestige development and civic boosterist activities. In the 1994/95 council budget the NEC, ICC and NIA were collectively allocated a cut of £2.6m. in their revenue budget. Additionally, the city council vetoed plans formulated under the Knowles administration for a bid to host the 2002 Commonwealth Games (Bell, 1993) and stated its reluctance to heavily subsidise conferences and conventions, most notably by refusing in 1995 to ratify a £2.5m. subsidy for the 1998 Lions Club Convention (considered one of the largest in the world) in the city (Howarth, 1994).

Not surprisingly, these changes in city council political priorities created disquiet among organised private sector groups, with the Chairman of City 2000 noting that: 'There is a new political climate in Birmingham which may not share the objectives of its predecessors and at the same time many of the important personalities and strong voices campaigning for Birmingham have gone' (Greyan, 1994: 9). This comment highlighted the political constraints that the new leader of the council faced, having to carefully present its new policy priorities in tandem with a commitment to a diluted form of pro-growth development. This the Stewart regime has done, showing the same pragmatic qualities as the previous Knowles regime. While civic boosterism initiatives initiated by the Knowles regimes (such as the bid for the 2002 Commonwealth Games) have been abandoned or downgraded in resource allocation terms, the council has continued to pursue the development of prestige projects, but only where external resources can be secured to finance them. This pragmatic strategy has so far prevented the total collapse of the public–private sector consensus within Birmingham, but this fragile peace is likely to be placed under considerable pressure in the future as central government has increasingly withdrawn financial resources from the city council since 1993.

Examples of Birmingham's attempt to secure external resources to finance the city's diluted pro-growth strategy (and thus minimising the impact on council resources) include its unsuccessful attempts in 1995 (via NEC Ltd) to secure National Lottery and Sports Council funding for a new £200m. National Sports Stadium (losing out to London and Manchester) and its bid to stage the prestigious £500m. Millennium Exhibition (losing out once again to the capital). However, the most significant example of Birmingham's shift in its overall local economic development strategy is the council's latest flagship project, 'Millennium Point'. Reflecting the Stewart administration's emphasis on education within the city and similar priorities identified in the council's *City Pride Prospectus* (Birmingham City Pride, 1994, 1995), Birmingham City Council, in partnership with the University of Central England (UCE) and private sector interests (the Millennium Partnership Group of Midlands Business), secured £50m. of National Lottery Funds to develop an education and technology focused complex within Birmingham city centre. The £110m. Millennium Point development is comprised of four major projects:

1. The University of the First Age: a new educational institution aimed at providing out-of-school learning in the fields of science, technology and design. It is anticipated that up to 90 000 young people within the region will benefit from the new learning opportunities generated by the university.
2. The Technology Innovation Centre: a national centre for excellence for technology and innovation designed specifically to encourage access and participation by young people, the general public and industry. The centre will also be the new home for UCE's Faculty of Engineering and Computer Technology.
3. The Discovery Centre: a major visitor attraction aimed at a regional, national and international audience – which will comprise a 'hands on' twenty-first-century science and technology museum focused on new scientific developments and the region's technological history.
4. The Hub: a major leisure and entertainment complex including an Imax cinema, conference facilities and themed restaurants, cafes and retail units.

According to the city council the Millennium Point development will generate an estimated 1600 new jobs (directly and indirectly), attract up to £500m. of private investment and generate an annual gross visitor spend of £4m. (Birmingham City Council, n.d.).

In contrast to the approach of the Knowles era, the city council under the Stewart administration has sought to utilise its entrepreneurial flair in minimising the local authority's financial burden associated with its flagship schemes. In the case of Millennium Point, in addition to the £50m. Millennium Commission National Lottery grant, the city council has sought to secure £22.5m. from the European Community (ERDF), £12.5m. from English Partnerships and approximately £19m. from the private sector. In utilising a wide range of financing sources for Millennium Point, it is anticipated that the city council's financial contribution will be limited to £5.2m. (mainly in the form of land values).

CONCLUSION

Birmingham's tradition of pragmatic local politics and close collaboration between the public and private sectors facilitated the formulation of a pro-growth local economic development strategy in response to the dramatic collapse of its manufacturing base in the 1970s and 1980s. Under the Labour Party leadership of Sir Richard Knowles, Birmingham City Council embarked on a bold policy of investing huge local authority resources in city centre prestige development projects (such as the ICC) and city promotional initiatives. This strategy was supported by the establishment of a wide range of mechanisms geared at encouraging private sector involvement in the formulation and implementation of its pro-growth strategy.

It is claimed by proponents of Birmingham City Council's pro-growth strategy (and, in particular, its investment in prestige projects) that it has led to numerous benefits for the city including the creation of a new and dynamic image for Birmingham; the physical transformation of the city centre; the generation of a significant number of new jobs; and the attraction of much needed private sector investment into the city. However, it is also argued by some commentators that the city council's strategy has resulted in a diversion of scarce city council resources away from essential services such as education and housing – particularly affecting the city's most disadvantaged communities; relatively few economic benefits for disadvantaged residents and neighbourhoods; and a reduction in public participation and involvement in the city's policy-making process.

Since 1993, under the leadership of Theresa Stewart, the city council's policies have been the subject of substantial change with a shift in the focus of the council's expenditure priorities away from prestige projects (and the city centre generally) towards 'basic services' such as education and housing. Nevertheless, the Stewart administration has continued to adopt a diluted form of entrepreneurial local economic development policies. In implementing these policies, the city council (post-1993) has continued to demonstrate a pragmatic approach to policy-making. This has minimised the local authority's financial contributions and liabilities, by focusing attention on external sources of funding – central government, European Community and private sector resources.

From the evidence presented in this chapter it is clear that the benefits and costs of Birmingham's attempted transformation from the 'manufacturing motor city' to the 'international convention and business city' have not been equally shared among city residents, or between city residents and outsiders. Looking forward to the twenty-first century, however, there remain a number of issues and questions facing Birmingham in connection with its pro-growth policies implemented in the 1980s and early 1990s. Will the city council's investment in prestige projects and civic boosterism secure its ambitious international aspirations or will further public sector investment be required to ensure that Birmingham 'keeps up' with its rival competitor cities? Will the current divide between the city's 'haves' and 'have nots' continue to widen, and if so what are the consequences for the city's international image? Will the city council's underinvestment in basic services (such as education), during the 1980s and early 1990s, serve to undermine Birmingham's attractiveness to private sector investment in the future? Finally, in a climate of shrinking resources available to local authorities, how will the current (and, indeed, any future) city council administration recoup the underinvestment in basic council services which occurred as a consequence of its pro-growth policies?

7

SUBURBAN ENTREPRENEURIALISM: REDEVELOPMENT REGIMES AND CO-ORDINATING METROPOLITAN DEVELOPMENT IN SOUTHERN CALIFORNIA

AMER ALTHUBAITY AND ANDREW E.G. JONAS

INTRODUCTION

Although local governments in the United States have been described as the last entrepreneurs (Goodman, 1979) some of the tools with which they fulfil their alleged entrepreneurial function have been available for some time now. A case in point is tax-increment financing (TIF), a mechanism employed by local redevelopment agencies to finance the redevelopment of blighted property. TIF generates a local revenue stream from the increase in property assessment over and above a base valuation following the commencement of a redevelopment project. The origins of TIF go back to the federal urban renewal programme of the 1940s and 1950s. This programme saw many states pass legislation to enable municipalities and counties to establish redevelopment authorities and raise revenues locally to repay bonds issued for redevelopment purposes. But more than simply a tool for the revitalisation of blighted property in central cities, redevelopment has become one of the few comprehensive powers which enable outer metropolitan cities and counties to acquire property, finance local economic development, capture local tax revenues, and compete for inward investment. What we shall refer to as 'suburban entre-preneurialism' would arguably be extremely limited were it not for the ability of local government in suburban areas to harness state redevelopment powers and use TIF to lever inward investment.

Despite the emerging interest in entrepreneurialism as a form of local governance in the 'post-Fordist' era (Harvey, 1989b), the actual mechanisms and instruments employed by entrepreneurial local government have received comparably little critical attention, and nor indeed have the conflicts sur-rounding their use. Yet it is extremely difficult to analyse the entrepreneurial role of US cities without acknowledging the increasingly influential role of TIF in local economic development (Clarke and Gaile, 1989, 1992; Green and

Fleischmann, 1989; Judd and Ready, 1986; Klemanski, 1990). Something amounting to a consensus has emerged in the 'new urban politics' literature suggesting that political regimes in US cities are dominated by governing coalitions organised to promote redevelopment (Cox, 1993; Cummings, 1988; Logan and Molotch, 1987; Stone and Sanders, 1987). By comparison, however, there has been relatively little critical interest in the use of TIF, especially in the redevelopment of suburban areas. Moreover, although it is well known that the political economy of postwar development in the United States has been predominantly suburban in character (Florida and Jonas, 1991), only a handful of researchers have investigated in any great depth the emergence and characteristics of redevelopment-orientated political regimes in the suburbs (DiGaetano and Klemanski, 1991; Kerstein, 1993). This chapter continues this task, simultaneously contributing to the reconstruction of urban regime perspectives on the politics of local economic development (see Lauria, 1997).

In what follows, we argue that the practices and institutions associated with the use of TIF in the redevelopment of suburban areas in southern California are not without contradictions. Drawing upon a case study of the politics of redevelopment in the Coachella Valley – a well-defined suburban metropolitan area made up of nine incorporated cities and located 160 km east of Los Angeles – we demonstrate how the use of TIF has given rise to a territorial politics. This territorial politics has in turn led to changes in local institutions of suburban governance. We consider three such changes. Firstly, local governments in the Coachella Valley have entered into agreements to restrict financially damaging redevelopment litigation. Secondly, a greater share of tax-increment revenue is redistributed to other local tax-raising authorities and affordable housing projects in the valley. Thirdly, redevelopment policy is gradually becoming co-ordinated on a metropolitan-wide basis. We suggest that such changes are consistent with a trend towards 'competitive regionalism' as an institutional framework for managing urban policy in the United States (Cisneros, 1995). However, we suggest that inter-jurisdictional co-operation in the Coachella Valley has less to do with developing a co-ordinated metropolitan response to the demands of the global economy and more to do with finding ways of managing locally the conflict between economic development and collective consumption.

Our own approach is based on the argument in Cox and Jonas (1993) about the production of new jurisdictional geographies in US metropolitan areas. It recognises that suburban redevelopment policy is mediated by struggles around issues of local economic development and collective consumption respectively. In California, these struggles are driven by the increasing dependence of local government on tax-increment revenue in the wake of the state's property tax limitation measure, Proposition 13, which was passed in 1978. From the standpoint of local jurisdictions, such dependence has focused concern on matters of fiscal equity, efficiency and economies of scale and scope in the provision of local services (concerns which have all featured strongly in struggles around suburban redevelopment). Based on this, we suggest that a reconstructed urban regime theory could develop a more convincing argument about the particular policies and projects pursued by entrepreneurial political regimes by referring to arguments in public choice theory. Public choice theory has a fairly well-developed perspective on the problem of metropolitan political fragmentation. Although somewhat sceptical of the rational choice assumptions underpinning both public choice theory and urban regime approaches, we conclude that in light of the rise of suburban entrepreneurialism in the USA, these approaches nevertheless warrant serious critical consideration.

SUBURBAN ENTREPRENEURIALISM: PUBLIC CHOICE OR POLITICAL REGIME?

The idea that cities and suburbs are engaged in competition for mobile capital has emerged as an important theme in the US literature on urban politics. For example, Paul Peterson's landmark book *City Limits* suggested that cities in the United States increasingly have to compete with other places. This is because cities, by virtue of their fixed territorial limits, are essentially dependent on local revenues. Capital, however, is mobile, and can locate almost anywhere and still make profits. Local public officials must therefore be prepared to offer incentives to the private sector in order to encourage businesses to locate within their city's limits (Peterson, 1981).

Peterson's market-based model of urban development policy subsequently attracted a lot of critical interest. It helped to situate urban entrepreneurialism in a wider economic context. This was an important development, but in retrospect it shifted the focus in the urban politics literature away from the causal role of local politics to that of economic globalisation. In the process, some potentially quite important insights into the politics and governance of cities were overlooked. We focus in particular on the contribution of public choice theory.

First-generation public choice theory[1] focused on the effects of local political boundaries on local policy outcomes (Tiebout, 1956). It began with the assumption that the metropolitan area operates as a functionally integrated public economy. Within this public economy, mobile households are presented with a choice of services provided by local governments (i.e. suburbs). Households tend to locate in those suburbs which offer a bundle of services to match their preference functions. A local government which fails to match service bundles to preferences will not be attractive to households, who vote with their feet and move to another suburb, most likely in the same metropolitan area. In the politically fragmented metropolis, the visible hand of local government – i.e. the presence of fixed local political boundaries – acts as a surrogate for the invisible hand of the market or, as Weiher (1991: 41) has more recently put it, 'The system of political boundaries in a metropolitan area facilitates the process in which persons who are guided by certain preferences form expectations about those preferences being satisfied in one place or another.' To the extent that household preferences translate into demand for new housing, then presumably public choice theory would argue that political fragmentation encourages economically efficient development policies.

Second-generation public choice theory was more concerned with issues of fiscal equity and economies of scale in the local provision of services (Bish, 1971; Bish and Ostrom, 1976; Weiher, 1991). It formed a response to the liberal reform approach which observed a correlation between patterns of socio-spatial inequality and the location of political boundaries within metropolitan areas (Danielson, 1976; Downs, 1973; Miller, 1981; Schneider, 1985). This version of public choice theory claimed that it is possible to achieve fiscal equity and exploit economies of scale in the provision of services – particularly public infrastructure – without necessarily compromising public choice (Bish and Ostrom, 1976). It harked back to the reformist tradition in American local government which identified a public interest operating at the city-wide and metropolitan levels. The goal of metropolitan reform, then, was seen as taking advantage of area-wide economies of scale. This could involve centralised systems of revenue-raising and service delivery perhaps similar to those adopted in metropolitan Los Angeles (Miller, 1981).

Third-generation public choice theory has advanced the idea of 'competitive regionalism' (Cisneros, 1995). To some extent, this latest version marks a return to the argument in first-generation public choice theory that the metropolitan area operates as a functionally integrated economy in which the exploitation of local economies of scope is possible. However, there is a new emphasis on assessing the performance of the metropolitan economy in relation to the global economy. In the global economy, economic activity tends to remain clustered within geographically discrete metropolitan areas. The United States, for example, is best 'seen as a common market of metropolitan-based local economic regions. These regions are indeed strongly interdependent, but they also compete with each other and with the rest of the world' (Cisneros, 1995: 3). The competitive potential of metropolitan areas is, however, frustrated by the political divisions and bureaucratic inefficiencies typically found within them. Mechanisms should be developed to encourage metropolitan-wide co-operation and to capitalise upon sectoral strengths and local economies of scope. This in turn involves fostering and enhancing locally incipient systems of metropolitan and regional governance.

There now seems to be a consensus within the Clinton administration that competitive regionalism offers a model framework for a new federal approach to urban policy in the USA (Cisneros, 1995). In this vein, proponents of competitive regionalism in the USA talk glowingly about the benefits of metropolitan governance but ignore potential arenas of conflict. There is, then, the matter of local interests and their role in shaping systems of governance and development policies within metropolitan areas. Here Keating (1997) suggests that arguments in urban regime theory may be helpful.

Urban regime theory begins by arguing that urban development policy is not an expression of voter (consumer) preferences but rather the outcome of a political consensus built between private and public sector interest groups (Stone, 1987, 1989). Although policy choices and outcomes do vary from one place (local government) to another, such choices and outcomes in fact depend upon some sort of compromise between powerful local interest groups. Regime theorists believe that private interest groups wield the most influence in the public policy arena because they control strategic economic resources and assets. So although there may be limited participation of consumption interest groups in land use and economic decision-making, local fiscal policies tend to be biased in favour of interests in local economic development (Piven and Friedland, 1984; Pecorella, 1987).

A mediating factor in all of this is political fragmentation. Urban regime theory makes passing reference to political fragmentation as a problem potentially frustrating consensus on development policy (Elkin, 1987; Hoxworth and Thomas, 1993). Presumably it is a problem of particular concern to those businesses 'whose revenues depend on the level of economic activity in the city *and* the metropolitan region' (Elkin, 1987: 90, our emphasis). However, regime theory does not expound upon the nature of the problem and nor does it account for its resolution. Development policies pursued at the metropolitan level must accommodate the fiscal interests of local jurisdictions. Presumably, issues of economic efficiency, fiscal equity and economies of scope and scale are salient in this regard.

To these considerations one might also add problems of malfeasance leading to mistrust among partners in development (Cox, 1997). Development policy involves building trust relations among local partners through routine negotiations and concrete actions – hence the idea of institutional embeddedness (Ramsay, 1996). Urban regime theorists mainly have in mind relations between public and private sector partners. However, it seems that problems of malfeasance and distrust are magnified in the politically fragmented metropolis. Private developers are often reluctant to divulge information about site preferences to local jurisdictions for fear that the location decision becomes politicised or important information is leaked to competitors. Indeed some level of local government co-operation seems to be a necessary precondition for inward investment at the metropolitan scale (Cox, 1997).

What also must be addressed is the latent conflict between, on the one hand, local interests in economic development and, on the other, those in collective consumption. Although the conflict may at times be suspended, there are other occasions when it will not be possible to internalise the conflict within existing local jurisdictional arrangements. This happens often because local government is by virtue of the problem of local fiscal dependence a non-neutral participant in the struggle (Cox and Mair, 1988). On such occasions, the distribution of development powers and fiscal responsibilities vertically and horizontally within the state apparatus becomes a focus of struggle, the outcome of which is indeterminable:

> Arguably there has to be a politics of consumption and accumulation. Moreover, while they may be confined to their respective institutional arenas, the contradictory unity of the two means that there also have to be links between those arenas. But how the contestation and resolution of these different issues relate to the levels of the state at which are located different powers and instrumentalities . . . is a contingent matter (Cox and Jonas, 1993: 12).

For us, the critical issue is how in the course of the struggle issues of economic efficiency, fiscal equity and economies of scope and scale become particular foci of concern. It transpires that in suburban areas of California such issues are highlighted by the growing use of redevelopment as a tool for local economic development and as a mechanism for fiscal redistribution among local jurisdictions.

THE RISE OF LOCAL REDEVELOPMENT REGIMES IN CALIFORNIA

Under the 1949 federal Housing Act, funds became available to cities for slum clearance and urban renewal. States such as California passed legislation enabling local governments – mainly the central cities – to establish local redevelopment authorities and apply for federal matching funds. Such funds could amount to as much as 90% of the cost of slum clearance and urban renewal. Local redevelopment agencies were given a wide range of powers, including eminent domain, bonding authority and revenue-raising capacity. In the bigger cities, redevelopment quickly attracted powerful pro-growth coalitions having strong ties to the national Democratic Party and promoting the commercial redevelopment of inner-urban property (Mollenkopf, 1983).

In California, redevelopment became an attractive programme for suburban municipalities after the passage in 1978 of Proposition 13, the state's property tax limitation measure. Prior to Proposition 13 property valuations would be reassessed on a regular basis, allowing property tax rates to increase broadly at the same rate as increases in service demand. This ensured a fairly predictable stream of revenues for local (county and municipal) government. However, Proposition 13 rolled back assessments to 1975 levels, permitted an annual increase in assessment of only 2% (except in case of a sale), and effectively capped property tax rates at 1% per annum. Local property tax revenues no longer rose in proportion to the rate of growth in service demand, causing severe financial problems for residential suburbs with high levels of demand.

Proposition 13 made fiscal planning far more problematic for local governments, and it had a major impact on local development policy, particularly in suburban areas. With federal funds for large-scale urban redevelopment no longer available to redevelopment agencies, cities increasingly relied upon TIF to leverage inward investment. Prior to Proposition 13 local governments were content to let the property market determine revenue levels. Subsequently they have become much more proactive in using land-use planning and economic development powers to generate new revenue sources, such as sales taxes and developer impact fees. As Fulton (1991: 209) puts it, 'since the passage of Prop 13 . . . cities and counties throughout California have become far more impatient about new development'.

Proposition 13 created what amounted to a 'rent gap' (Smith, 1979, 1982) in suburban areas; that is, a discrepancy between the actual assessed value of property and its potential assessment value resulting from a sale or redevelopment. For cash-starved suburban municipalities, redevelopment was a means of closing the rent gap and capturing the additional revenues. Redevelopment, then, played a central role in what planners such as Bill Fulton have called the process of 'land use fiscalisation' whereby municipalities and to some extent also counties have aggressively promoted redevelopment because of its local fiscal impact. These days local governments throughout California are engaged in frenetic competition with each other to attract fiscally lucrative redevelopment projects including regional shopping malls, hotels and resorts, auto malls, casinos, office parks and industrial sites. The notion of the 'serial reproduction' of land uses very much comes to mind in this context, with Harvey (1989b) suggesting that this is a central feature of the recent rise of entrepreneurial forms of local governance.

Suburban entrepreneurialism

The competition for fiscally lucrative land uses in suburban areas of California is driven by the financial interests of 'entrepreneurial' (Stone, 1989) political regimes working closely with local redevelopment agencies. In contrast to pro-growth coalitions, which cultivated support for urban renewal mainly at the federal level, suburban redevelopment regimes are more likely to nurture support at the state level. Local redevelopment powers are derived from state government which means that lobbying for the extension of, or reform to, those powers occurs at the state rather than federal level. California's Community Redevelopment Act, for example, has undergone a series of extensions and reforms over the years as a result of such lobbying. It remains a highly regarded programme among local and state representatives.

The way redevelopment works in California gives local practitioners some degree of autonomy in terms of management and decision-making. Redevelopment encourages public–private partnership activity at the local level and can be used in creative ways to leverage inward investment. Furthermore, because redevelopment involves quite complicated financial instruments such as TIF, local citizens are not always armed with sufficient knowledge to mount effective challenges to redevelopment projects promoted by local agencies. Given the ability of the programme to create jobs with limited government resources and only minimal public opposition, it is not surprising that Republican Governor Pete Wilson has championed redevelopment as California's principal local economic development programme.

Redevelopment comprises an institutional arena in which the politics of economic development intersects with that of collective consumption. This intersection arises in part because tax-increment revenue is 'passed through' to other taxing authorities, including local school and community college districts, which use the money to fund local services. In the aftermath of Proposition 13, school and community college districts have fought for a greater share of revenue from redevelopment. In 1985, on a state-wide basis 94.7% of tax-increment revenue went directly to redevelopment agencies, whereas only 5.3% was distributed among the counties, schools and other local taxing agencies. To make up for revenue shortfalls, the state assumed a greater responsibility for redistributing funds to local schools and colleges. But although public schools and colleges have built a powerful lobby at the state level, the loss of revenue to redevelopment agencies is a contentious issue for many local districts.

By law redevelopment agencies must operate a set-aside fund for affordable housing provision. This set-aside is currently set at 20% of tax-increment revenue. However, most redevelopment agencies prefer to use TIF to promote economic development rather than to meet local housing needs (Kohn, 1989). As a result, the distribution of housing set-aside revenues also tends to be a focus of struggle. In short, although redevelopment in California has become an instrument of suburban entrepreneurialism, it is also a focus of the activities of local interests in collective consumption.

REDEVELOPMENT AND TERRITORIAL COMPETITION IN THE COACHELLA VALLEY

The Coachella Valley offers an ideal laboratory for studying the practices and conflicts associated with redevelopment in a fragmented political context. Located in Riverside County, 160 km to the east of Los Angeles, the valley forms a geographically discrete metropolitan area comprised of nine incorporated cities (Figure 7.1). It originally served as an agricultural hinterland for Los Angeles, growing irrigated crops, dates and citrus for local markets. After the Second World War, the valley suburbanised, attracting mainly resort and retirement communities, and some manufacturing. The cities of Indio and Palm Springs began to use redevelopment for the traditional purpose of slum clearance and urban renewal. These initial forays into redevelopment were limited in scale and controversial, resulting in the displacement of black households from redevelopment project areas. During the 1970s and 1980s, the valley began to experience rapid growth, attracting a mixture of retail, commercial and industrial developments. Suburbanisation was encouraged by

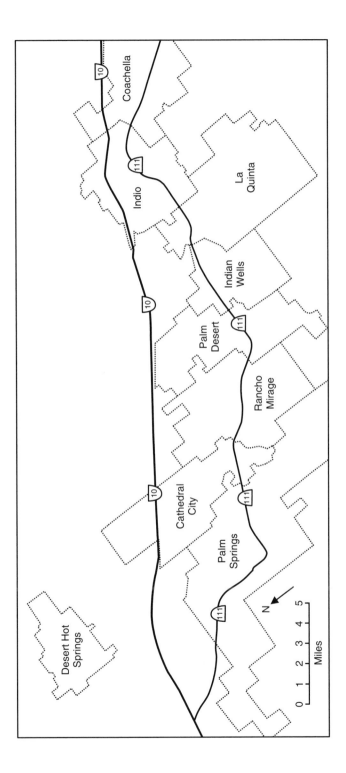

FIGURE 7.1 Cities in the Coachella Valley

the development of the I-10 freeway, making the valley more accessible to commuters. The population of the cities in the valley grew from 102 852 in 1980 to 172 421 in 1990, representing a growth rate of more than 6% per annum (Althubaity, 1995).

After Proposition 13, younger cities in the valley such as Palm Desert and Indian Wells began to get more involved in redevelopment. These cities used the programme for non-traditional purposes such as flood control, retail and resort development, and industrial site preparation. Throughout the 1980s, competition between valley cities for redevelopment projects was fierce. The cities of Palm Springs and Palm Desert competed to become the retail centre of the valley. Palm Springs used redevelopment to develop the Desert Fashion Plaza located in the downtown district, while Palm Desert developed a major regional mall. Other cities, such as Indio and Coachella, also embarked upon ambitious redevelopment projects. The region-wide collapse in the property market in the early 1990s dampened some of the enthusiasm for redevelopment. Nevertheless, most practitioners in the valley rated redevelopment as their most important tool for promoting local economic development.[2]

Most of the cities in the valley found the fiscal rewards of redevelopment substantial. Figure 7.2 shows tax-increment revenue growth for the nine valley cities between 1984 and 1992. There were significant – indeed spectacular – rates of revenue growth in the cities of La Quinta, Indian Wells, Palm Desert and Cathedral City. Revenue growth in other cities was more modest. Overall, the performance of redevelopment agencies in the valley was uneven, with those in some cities faring much better than those in others. As a result of intense redevelopment activity in the 1980s, most of the cities in the valley are financially dependent upon the programme. Some measure of this dependence is evident from a comparison of tax-increment revenues with general purpose revenues. Figure 7.3 makes this comparison for each of the nine municipalities in 1993. It shows that five cities derived more revenues from redevelopment than from general sources. In two of these cases – Indian Wells and La Quinta – tax-increment revenue was more than double the revenue from general sources. In Palm Springs and Indio, however, general revenues greatly exceeded revenues from redevelopment. Both of these cities were incorporated well before Proposition 13 and had already experienced difficulties with urban renewal. Many of the remaining cities were incorporated after 1978, suggesting a strong relationship between reliance on redevelopment and the need to confront problems of local fiscal dependence.

REDEVELOPMENT AND TERRITORIAL CONFLICT IN THE COACHELLA VALLEY

During the 1980s, inter-jurisdictional competition encouraged municipalities throughout California to over-speculate in redevelopment. Such speculation had a particularly dramatic effect on the level of indebtedness of suburban

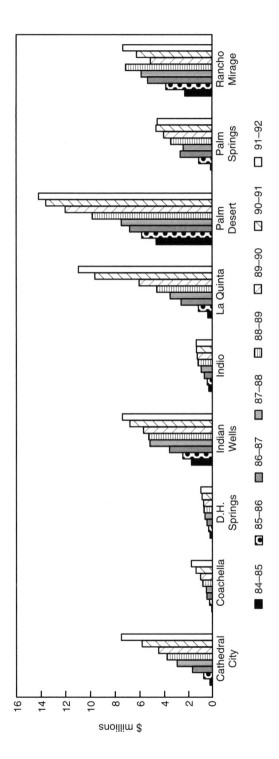

FIGURE 7.2 Tax-increment revenue to Coachella valley redevelopment agencies, 1984–92. Data source: State of California, State Controller: Annual Report of Financial Transactions Concerning Community Redevelopment Agencies of California

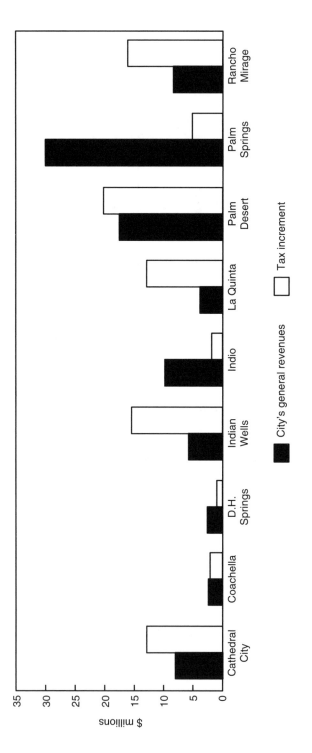

FIGURE 7.3 Tax-increment revenue compared with general revenue for Coachella Valley cities, 1993. Source as Figure 7.2

■ City's general revenues   □ Tax increment

municipalities.[3] Some jurisdictions discovered ways of subsidising redevelopment from general sources only to find that projects failed to generate sufficient tax increment to cover initial outlays. Local citizens were forced to bear the burden of indebtedness through increases in local taxation. In this context, local representatives throughout the state began to reassess the entire redevelopment programme. In the Coachella Valley, this reassessment had already begun in response to increasing territorial conflict. Such conflict highlighted issues of economic efficiency, fiscal equity and economies of scope and scale.

Economic efficiency: agreements to limit litigation on redevelopment

In California, since there is no state-level agency with regulatory authority over redevelopment, local 'abuses' of the state's redevelopment programme have proceeded with impunity. It has been left to local governments to take action against their neighbours to discourage malfeasance. More often than not this has involved litigation. At issue has been the potential loss of revenue from redevelopment projects. In the Coachella Valley, litigation activity regarding alleged misuses of redevelopment rose significantly in the 1980s. For example, in 1987 Indian Wells and Palm Springs challenged the City of Palm Desert's Redevelopment Project Area No.3. This project area comprised about 1250 ha and was expected to generate $300m. in investment and improvements over a period of 40 years. This included a $225m. resort and hotel development. The Sunrise Company, a developer involved in a rival project in Indian Wells, was also a litigant (*The Desert Sun*, 26 August 1987).

The suit filed by the City of Palm Springs contended that the redevelopment project area in question was mostly vacant property and did not meet the law's requirement that it be 'predominantly urbanised'. Meanwhile, the suit filed on behalf of the Sunrise Company claimed that the purpose of the project was not to correct conditions of blight within the project area but rather to subsidise private development in an area which was already undergoing development (*The Desert Sun*, 18 August 1987).

The City of Indian Wells itself was sued over one of its redevelopment projects. The Sunterra redevelopment project involved an investment of $1bn. The suit claimed that the project's Environmental Impact Report was inadequate because it failed to justify why the project area – which was mostly vacant – was eligible to be designated 'blighted'. Two special purpose districts, the Coachella Valley Recreation and Parks District and the Coachella Valley Mosquito Abatement District, also filed suit, claiming that the project would divert revenue from their tax rolls, thus affecting their ability to provide services (*The Desert Sun*, 17 September 1987).

A major litigant during the 1980s was the County of Riverside, which was involved in lawsuits against several valley cities. In 1982, the county challenged the validity of redevelopment project areas in the cities of Indio, Desert Hot Springs and Indian Wells. It contended that redevelopment would divert property taxes away from the county as well as other local taxing authorities. In 1984, the county – which managed its own redevelopment projects in the valley – sued the City of Rancho Mirage over an amendment to its Whitewater Redevelopment Project Area. The county argued that the amendment included properties which did not meet the criteria for being designated 'blighted' or 'predominantly urbanised'. By the end of the decade, the County of Riverside had entered into litigation with almost every city in the Coachella Valley.

Thus several local jurisdictions sued to recover revenues lost to local redevelopment agencies. But these jurisdictions found that litigation was time-consuming. It often resulted in delays to redevelopment projects, delays which increased costs. There was also the possibility that investors would pull out of projects where delays were likely. Without project investors, a redevelopment agency faced a very difficult time selling its redevelopment bonds (Fulton, 1991). Soon the longer-term costs associated with litigation began to exceed any short-term fiscal gains and, by the early 1990s, local governments in the Coachella Valley had begun to reassess the cost and benefits of litigation activity. A contributory condition was the downturn in the property market, which made it even more likely that developers would pull out of delayed redevelopment projects.

In 1993, valley cities and the County of Riverside called a truce in their litigation battles. They entered into a voluntary agreement to suspend all future litigation relating to redevelopment. The agreement called for local govern-ments to attempt to mediate and resolve disputes before filing a lawsuit. As the mayor of La Quinta put it, 'we agreed suing each other did not benefit anybody. And that it [was] about time we started working on the agreement' (*The Desert Sun*, 27 April 1993).

The agreement to limit litigation was deemed to be a more rational approach to redevelopment on fiscal grounds. Litigation caused delays to redevelopment projects and exposed project investors and redevelopment authorities to unacceptable levels of financial risk. The no-litigation agreement reached by local jurisdictions aimed to reduce financial uncertainties surrounding particular redevelopment projects. It may also have contributed to a climate of greater trust and co-operation among local government participants in redevelopment.

Fiscal equity: education and housing

The issue of fiscal equity has also featured in territorial conflicts around redevelopment in the Coachella Valley. At issue has been the distribution of tax-increment revenue among local tax-raising authorities. The principal protagonists in such conflicts have been the redevelopment agencies, local school and community college districts, and housing activists. School and community college districts have sought to claw back revenues 'captured' by local redevelopment agencies. Meanwhile, housing activists have put pressure on redevelopment agencies to spend their housing set-aside funds, albeit such spending has often occurred in other local jurisdictions, contributing to inter-jurisdictional disparities in housing provision. A latent conflict between collective consumption and economic development has thus emerged to focus attention on the inequitable distribution and spending of tax-increment revenue among the valley's local service providers.

In 1985, Coachella Valley redevelopment agencies captured 82.0% of tax-increment revenue generated locally (Althubaity, 1995). This compared to 2.8% captured by local school and community college districts. These local service districts had not anticipated the fiscal impact of Proposition 13, and were slow to realise the impact of redevelopment on their own revenue base. Since there was a widespread assumption that redevelopment would not be a major revenue-generating programme, local district officials in the Coachella Valley felt that they had much more to gain by working through the school lobby at the state level to secure additional funds. However, they soon revised this strategy.

As the first post-Proposition 13 redevelopment projects in the valley came on line, it became increasingly clear to local district officials that such projects would not only generate a lot of revenue but also that most of the revenue would be captured by local redevelopment agencies. The problem of revenue 'lost' to redevelopment agencies was compounded by the unwillingness of local voters to pass bond issues for capital projects and improvements in services. During the 1980s, in response to population growth, pressure on local districts to build new schools and to fund local facilities and staff positions increased. A consultant for the Palm Springs Unified School District put the predicament of the local districts as follows, 'Districts [were] asking for a share [of TIF revenues] because the state [had] not provided enough non-redevelopment aid [and] schools [had] nowhere else to turn for money for operation as well as capital projects' (*The Riverside Press Enterprise*, 16 December 1984).

In response to their growing fiscal predicament, local districts and other tax-raising authorities became more aggressive in their dealings with local govern-ments and the redevelopment agencies. Attention focused on pass-through agreements negotiated with local redevelopment agencies. Such agreements were allowed under California law as a means of returning revenue to local service providers. In the Coachella Valley, however, the existing agreements were not viewed as favourable to the interests of local service providers. As a member of the Riverside County Board of Supervisors put it, school districts and other tax-raising authorities became 'much tougher in what [they] negotiate[d] in a pass-through agreement. Some of the early agreements were very detrimental' (*The Desert Sun*, 12 December 1988).

As a result of the negotiation of 'tougher' agreements, a greater share of tax-increment revenue is now returned to the districts as well as other local tax-raising authorities.[4] In 1993, for instance, nearly 50% of redevelopment revenue in the valley was returned to the local districts and the county. The local school district share in 1993 was 17%, compared to 2.8% in 1985. This translated into a net increase in total annual revenues to education providers, from $577 311 in 1985–86 to $16 475 023 in 1992–93 (Althubaity, 1995).

The new pass-through agreements have provided welcome fiscal relief for local school and community college districts. It may therefore be asked: have local districts actively promoted redevelopment projects as means of generating revenue? We could find only anecdotal evidence to support the hypothesis that the increasing local fiscal dependence of districts has encouraged greater involvement in redevelopment policy-making. School district officials in the cities of Desert Hot Springs, Palm Springs, Cathedral City and Rancho Mirage did in fact approach local redevelopment agency officials and city councillors with a view to the establishment of new redevelopment project areas. Such approaches have been accompanied by requests for funds to construct, rehabilitate and/or improve school facilities. The impetus, however, has always come from local district officials rather than from parents, teachers or even students. As regards education provision, therefore, struggles around redevelopment in the valley have involved those who provide the services rather than those who consume them.

By way of contrast, the politics of consumption features much more strongly in struggles around affordable housing provision in the Coachella Valley. To recap, California's redevelopment law provides that 20% of a redevelopment agency's revenue should be set aside for low-to-moderate income housing programmes.[5] Such housing set-aside funds comprise a significant share of public funds available for affordable housing programmes in the valley. Take, for example, the City of Palm Desert. Of the $27m. available for affordable housing in the city in 1993–94, $26m. came from the local redevelopment agency alone. The remainder was made up by Section 8 housing funds provided by the federal Department of Housing and Urban Development (HUD), state funds and developer fees. Of the revenue from redevelopment, $10m. came from set-aside funds and the remainder from the sale of bonds. Palm Desert has used its housing funds for rent subsidy, purchase of property, homeless shelters, rehabilitation loans, street and neighbourhood improvements, and the construction of rental housing.

Few redevelopment agencies in the valley spend their entire set-aside fund on affordable housing projects. Several have exploited legal loopholes or simply have ignored the housing element of redevelopment.[6] Among local governments in the valley, there is a reluctance to address the issue of housing affordability due to the threat of public opposition to the construction of rental and low-to-moderate income housing units. Until relatively recently there was no state law which required redevelopment agencies to spend all of their set-aside funds on affordable housing. As a result, by 1989 redevelopment agencies in California had accumulated over $333m. in unspent housing set-aside funds (State of California, Senate Committee on Local Government, 1991).

In 1987, legislation was introduced forcing redevelopment agencies to make up for any shortages in their housing set-aside funds. Further changes introduced in 1989 encouraged those agencies with more than $500 000 in accumulated and unspent set-aside funds to spend their money within five years or turn it over to a county housing authority. This was the so-called 'use it or lose it' rule. Although this rule has encouraged agencies to take the affordable housing element of redevelopment more seriously, many still refuse to take any action on affordable housing. Agencies simply decide not to spend their housing set-aside funds and turn the accumulated revenue over to the county authority. And even if set-aside funds are spent, it is often the case that they are spent on projects outside the boundaries of the particular city in question, a practice which has been adopted by cities in the Coachella Valley.

One case concerned the City of Indian Wells. In the early 1990s, the city planned to use redevelopment to subsidise a large resort. This development created a demand for low-wage workers, but the city had made little provision to house the workers. Indeed, it resisted all attempts by local housing activists to force it to build or provide affordable housing for resort employees. Local activists sued the City of Indian Wells for its failure to spend its affordable housing funds. Eventually, the city and the housing coalition reached an agreement. The redevelopment agency agreed to subsidise the development of low-to-moderate income housing so long as such housing was constructed outside the city's limits (Althubaity, 1995). As a result of such practices, conflicts around housing provision in the valley have been increasingly portrayed as territorial conflicts which demand resolution on an inter-jurisdictional basis.

The tendency for conflict to become territorialised in such a manner is encouraged by the way in which local affordable housing needs are determined. Currently, affordable housing needs in the Coachella Valley are determined by a progressive formula based on the county median income. However, median incomes among valley cities vary greatly, which means that housing needs also vary. Based upon 1990 Census data, median incomes in the cities of Indian Wells, La Quinta, Palm Desert and Rancho Mirage exceeded the county median, whereas median income in the cities of Coachella, Desert Hot Springs and Indio fell into the low-income category. To put this differently, demand for affordable housing is concentrated in some cities but not in others. It tends to be concentrated in those cities which derive the least housing revenue from redevelopment.

In 1991, the Coachella Valley Association of Governments (CVAG) recognised a minimum need for 6000 units of affordable housing in the valley. It argued that these units should be distributed evenly among the local jurisdictions. By that time, the nine valley cities had together accumulated more than $22m. in unspent set-aside moneys (CVAG, 1991). In an attempt to address the housing disparity problem, the CVAG presented an innovative proposal to the State Senate Committee on Local Government. This proposal suggested that local jurisdictions in the valley should develop voluntary housing programmes to encourage the sharing of housing expenses and the co-ordination of spending from set-aside funds on an inter-jurisdictional basis. The idea was for local jurisdictions unwilling to build low-income housing within their city limits to donate resources towards the construction of housing in other jurisdictions. In return, '[t]he donor jurisdiction would receive credit towards its legally-mandated housing goals [but] would be required to pay for services such as fire and police for a reasonable amount of years. This plan would maximize the number of affordable units in the region' (State of California, Senate Committee on Local Government, 1991: 83).

In terms of affordable housing provision, then, there have been moves towards greater fiscal equity in the valley. Such moves have been driven by struggles resulting from the intersection of collective consumption with local economic development. Currently, such struggles hardly constitute a full-scale political movement and consequently do not present a threat to the economic development aspect of redevelopment. Redevelopment remains a lucrative economic development programme for most cities in the valley, and for this reason there is little fiscal incentive to spend housing set-aside funds within their local jurisdictions. Moves towards fiscal equity are thus limited by the dependence of local jurisdictions on redevelopment as a tool for economic development.

In search of economies of scale and scope

In the Coachella Valley, territorial competition for inward investment is driven by the 'fiscalisation of land use' resulting from Proposition 13. Cities use redevelopment first and foremost to secure a local revenue base, not only for their redevelopment agencies but also to supplement their general purpose revenue. However, the no-litigation agreement signed by local jurisdictions has called into question the economic efficiency of unrestricted territorial competition, while issues of fiscal equity have been raised in negotiations surrounding pass-through agreements and in struggles around affordable housing. A third area of concern arising from the practice of redevelopment in the valley highlights the importance of exploiting economies of scale and scope in local economic development.

In our survey of redevelopment practitioners, we found that only 25% of survey respondents rated 'high' the goal of attracting business away from neighbouring local jurisdictions. This compares to 75% who ranked competition with neighbouring cities a 'low' policy priority. However, only 5% of survey respondents felt that local jurisdictions in the valley co-operate all the time on redevelopment projects, while 35% felt that cities co-operate only on some redevelopment projects. At least 35% indicated that there is no co-operation among redevelopment agencies in the valley. Our survey results suggest, then, that the level of inter-jurisdictional co-operation around the economic development aspect of redevelopment is somewhat limited.

To determine the arenas in which greater inter-jurisdictional co-operation and co-ordination do occur, we conducted face-to-face interviews with a selective sample of redevelopment practitioners. These interviews revealed that practitioners recognise that some co-ordination and information-sharing among local agencies can contribute to economies of scale. Furthermore, economies of scope in local economic development can be realised through greater specialisation within a framework of political fragmentation.

Several redevelopment practitioners were quite prepared to share information about redevelopment policy and practice with other practitioners in the valley. The Coachella Valley currently has an informal organisation of economic development and redevelopment practitioners which meets on a monthly basis to exchange information. This organisation is apparently interested in pooling information and putting together joint incentive packages to attract new businesses into the valley. In addition, redevelopment officials regularly exchange information and knowledge about current 'best practice' in redevelopment. However, this information is usually limited to recent legislative developments or advice on how to put together a workable financial package for a redevelopment project. Currently, information is not exchanged about the specifics of particular redevelopment projects planned or already under way.

It seemed, however, that the level of inter-jurisdictional co-operation in the valley increased when it involved competition with projects outside the valley region. In fact, 29% of survey respondents indicated that local jurisdictions do not co-operate *unless* there is competition from other regions. However, not everyone felt that competition was necessarily a good thing. The local newspaper, *The Desert Sun*, addressed the issue of territorial competition in one of its editorials as follows:

> Those who believe that each valley city can forever retain its own identity are dangerously short-sighted. What affects one community eventually affects all. Like it or not, decisions made today in Palm Springs at some point will have an impact on Indio and its people. Without long-range co-operation, cities will be powerless to protect the quality of life here in the desert (*The Desert Sun*, 28 April 1993).

The interesting feature of this editorial is that it represents the opinion of a metropolitan newspaper rather than a city-based publication. City-based interests are less sympathetic to the view that decisions should be based on the interests of the valley as a whole rather than those of the individual cities. As the City Manager of Cathedral City put it, 'I don't think it's realistic that [the valley] would be one big city' (*The Desert Sun*, 27 April 1993). There seems to be little prospect that greater co-operation among valley jurisdictions is going to take place outside of the existing level of political fragmentation. Rather, what did appear to be happening is that the local jurisdictions were paying closer attention to how their local redevelopment projects fitted into broader metropolitan economic development goals. We found some evidence of increasing local specialisation within a metropolitan and regional division of labour. This specialisation is happening both in terms of the kinds of projects redevelopment agencies are willing to subsidise and also in terms of the way in which such policies are marketed on a regional basis.

On the question of financing, one practitioner began by rejecting outright the notion that his redevelopment agency was involved in luring development away from neighbouring jurisdictions, 'In our case we have not lured any type of developer from any other cities and in fact we have not provided major financial incentives to lure any developer into the city' (personal interview, 1994). Another redevelopment practitioner portrayed Rancho Mirage's redevelopment policies as follows:

> In 1989, about the time we did the redevelopment plan, we did an economic analysis of our city and measured where we were in the valley, trying to figure out . . . what is this thing called economic development and where do we fit in it. Rather than compete against everybody what do we have that is unique that we can produce, or expand, or that is not going to be in competition with all the other cities, because it's pointless to get into a bidding war for auto malls, or regional shopping centers, etc. So we decided that restaurants and furniture stores were categories that we could excel in so we didn't have to go after everybody (personal interview, 1993).

In terms of how redevelopment projects are marketed, there is a growing emphasis on the uniqueness of localities within the valley too. Thus, in promoting eight redevelopment project areas across the city, Palm Springs has tried to capitalise on its external image as the historic resort centre of the valley:

> The heart of the town has to embody and radiate the spirit of the legend. The legend has to be updated to new and current uses not well represented, or existent, in the city today to bring it up to competitive standards. The City of Palm Springs needs to find new significant uses to revitalize the entire city in addition to revitalizing the heart of the downtown area. The key is to optimize the theme, charming, eccentric village ambience that appropriately express L.A.'s own resort fantasy of Palm Springs as the playground of the rich and famous (City of Palm Springs, 1991).

Although the discourse of territorial competition features strongly, the underlying rationale is the need to take advantage of local specialisations and hence economies of scope.

Another feature of local discourse is the repositioning of the Coachella Valley in relation to other metropolitan areas. In this context, the discourse of capital mobility begins to feature more strongly. A practitioner in Palm Springs justified that city's redevelopment policies in terms of its effect on the competition with places outside the valley rather than on the competition with other cities in the valley:

> We are still in competition with a lot of places. Some of it is pirating from other areas in California. If the state business companies are going to leave Los Angeles, Orange County, or Long Beach, we would rather capture them here than [let them] go to Arizona, Utah or someplace else (personal interview, 1994).

The emphasis, then, in local discourse is on capital mobility. But the material and social roots of inter-jurisdictional co-operation clearly lie elsewhere. Valley cities are co-ordinating redevelopment policy and practice not because of global competition but because of local problems to do with economic inefficiency and fiscal inequality, and more recently the need to exploit economies of scope and scale. Underlying these developments is the latent conflict between economic development and collective consumption, a conflict which in the Coachella Valley is mediated by the dependence of local jurisdictions on tax-increment revenue.

CONCLUSION

In the Coachella Valley, the growing emphasis on exploiting economies of scope within a framework of political fragmentation appears to be consistent with arguments found in third-generation public choice theory. So-called 'competitive regionalism' talks about the need to enhance the competitive advantage of metropolitan areas in the global economy. Metropolitan areas are viewed as functionally integrated economies comprised of localised clusters of economic activity. Excessive inter-jurisdictional competition, however, inhibit the capacity of such areas to compete in the global economy. Institutional reforms are therefore required to encourage greater co-ordination of economic development policy on a metropolitan-wide or regional basis within the existing framework of metropolitan fragmentation.

If our examples of institutional reforms in the Coachella Valley are fairly representative of developments in suburban areas in other parts of the United States, the evidence that such reforms are motivated by a felt need to compete in the global economy is at best sketchy. It is true that territorial competition in the valley is underpinned by redevelopment policy and practice, and that discourses of capital mobility have begun to feature more strongly. However, institutional reforms in the valley owe their origins more to the conflict between local economic development and collective consumption than to an emergent public interest in maximising the competitive advantage of the metropolitan area *vis-à-vis* other areas in California or even, for that matter, the global economy.

We suggest that there is some benefit to be gained by situating the debate about urban entrepreneurialism in relation to the literature on metropolitan political fragmentation. In investigating the rise of entrepreneurial political regimes in suburban areas of California, we have commented on the increasing dependence of local jurisdictions on redevelopment as a tool for local economic development and revenue-raising. Territorial competition and conflicts around redevelopment practice have highlighted issues such as fiscal equity, economic efficiency and economies of scale and scope. Such issues have themselves arisen because of the conflict between local interests in collective consumption, on the one hand, and those in economic development, on the other.

Territorial conflict may be suspended by separating those institutions and jurisdictional arrangements involved in facilitating local economic development from those managing collective consumption (Cox and Jonas, 1993). It seems, however, that with respect to redevelopment in California such a separation is in practice difficult. As a result, struggles around redevelopment policy and practice have tended to focus upon mechanisms of territorial redistribution, such as the negotiation of no-litigation and pass-through agreements between local jurisdictions. These mechanisms have, however, not compromised the use of redevelopment as a revenue-generating mechanism by local governments. Since Proposition 13, local governments throughout California, but especially in suburban areas, have relied upon redevelopment to promote local economic development.

Another notable feature of redevelopment policy in the Coachella Valley is the absence of a metropolitan growth lobby, one perhaps interested in promoting the political integration of the metropolitan area for the purpose of economic development. We suggest that there are two possible explanations for this absence. The first is the political weakness of local interests in collective consumption. Local educational institutions and affordable housing groups have not sustained strong political movements locally; nor have these institutions and groups posed a sufficient threat to interests in economic development to warrant a counter-movement of the sort which has been observed in other metropolitan areas in the United States. In such areas, where social movements have highlighted intra-metropolitan inequalities, metropolitan approaches to infrastructure provision and economic development have been pursued more vigorously (Cox and Jonas, 1993).

The second possibility is the lack of a well-defined private interest operating at the metropolitan scale. Not only are local banks and utilities poorly represented in local redevelopment regimes but also they appear not to be very active at the metropolitan scale. We are unable to provide a satisfactory explanation for this other than a more general observation that throughout

California resistance to metropolitan and regional governance is deeply ingrained. This resistance goes back to the reform movement in the Progressive Era and continues today in the form of 'local control' and property rights movements which are active and influential at the local and state levels. These movements have defended the right of local government to determine local land-use patterns in California, and hence amount to *de facto* support for political fragmentation.

We further suggest that urban regime theory could benefit from revisiting the literature on metropolitan political fragmentation. Although regime theory has – in our view, correctly – emphasised that the choice of development policy is mediated by the interests of the dominant or governing coalition in a locality, it has not advanced the debate about the politics of metropolitan fragmentation very far. Public choice theory has fairly clear views on the economic rationality of political fragmentation, and yet it fails to link the pursuit of particular jurisdictional projects to specific interest groups. A key consideration for a 'reconstructed' urban regime theory is how the latent conflict between economic development and collective consumption is managed, and to what extent its resolution within a metropolitan area involves new jurisdictional projects. This consideration seems to be quite critical in light of the growing evidence that unregulated territorial competition has had redistributive consequences for both local jurisdictions and citizens residing therein.

ACKNOWLEDGEMENTS

The authors are grateful to Dr Clifford Young for his advice and input. Andrew Jonas would like to thank Kevin Cox for helping him to develop a critical perspective on urban politics and the National Science Foundation (Award no. SBR-9512033) for financial support. The usual disclaimers apply.

NOTES

1. Public choice theory does not comprise a homogeneous and unchanging body of literature. Its argument has developed over time in response both to changing conditions in metropolitan areas and to new ideas in the literature. We have identified three stages in the literature's development.
2. Three-quarters of redevelopment practitioners we surveyed in the Coachella Valley during 1994 rated redevelopment as their most important local economic development programme (see Althubaity, 1995).
3. The Los Angeles suburb of Fontana is alleged to have accumulated debts of $700m. as a result of its redevelopment policies. Davis (1990) provides a brilliant critical analysis of the use of redevelopment as a tool for Fontana's economic regeneration following the closure of the Kaiser Corporation steel mill, formerly the largest employer in the locality.
4. Most pass-through agreements are based on a progressive formula. Once a redevelopment project has begun, a redevelopment agency retains the tax increment until a specified limit is reached which has been negotiated with other local

tax-raising authorities. When revenues exceed the pre-set limit, local authorities receive a proportional share of the total revenues. If the tax increment from the same redevelopment project reaches further pre-set threshold limits, other taxing authorities receive a greater proportion of revenues. Some pass-through agreements take effect immediately and the local authorities receive a constant share throughout the life of the redevelopment project. There are also multi-jurisdictional tax-sharing agreements in those cases where the boundaries of local school districts overlap with those of two or more redevelopment agencies. The Palm Springs Unified School District, for instance, has tax-sharing agreements with agencies in Cathedral City, Desert Hot Springs, Palm Springs and Rancho Mirage.

5. To qualify as low-income housing, housing projects funded from the set-aside must be affordable to households with less than 80% of the county's median income. Moderate-income housing must be affordable for households with an income of between 80 and 120% of the county median.

6. Existing redevelopment projects were exempted from the set-aside provision when it was introduced in 1977. Furthermore, if more than 80% of a project's tax-increment revenue is applied to bond repayment, then the agency is not required to set aside the entire 20% for affordable housing. This has encouraged agencies to issue bonds exceeding the 80% threshold, thereby limiting the total contribution to affordable housing (Fulton, 1991). Clearly, however, there are financial risks attached to such a policy.

8

FROM SOCIALISM TO POST-FORDISM: THE LOCAL STATE AND ECONOMIC POLICIES IN EASTERN GERMANY

TASSILO HERRSCHEL

'Urban entrepreneurialism' has been described as a new regulatory approach in local governance, supplanting traditional managerial responses to economic restructuring by the local state (Hall and Hubbard, 1996; Mayer, 1994a, b). However, such assertions have been based entirely on the experiences of capitalist, market-based Western cities. Through this normative explanatory framework, observed changes in modes of regulation have thus been presented as a result of changes, or crises, in existing modes of production (i.e. a capitalist system) while little attention has been given to the nature of regulative local responses following complete exchanges of economic *and* governmental systems. It is this fundamental change of parameters circumscribing local state action that constitutes the attraction of investigating forms of local modes of regulation as an expression of emerging variations in *de facto* local statehood in post-socialist eastern Germany. There, the simultaneous and ubiquitous *de jure* provisions for strong local government have provided almost standardised starting conditions for local economic development. However, these provisions have not meant a *tabula rasa*, because of inherited inequalities related to varying local roles within the socialist state administration. Previously overridden by socialist principles, such inter-local differences were now permitted to resurface within the new post-socialist geography of capital accumulation (Scott and Storper, 1992; Blien, 1994), leading to crass inequalities emerging between 'cores' and 'peripheries' (Leborgne and Lipietz, 1991).

The wholesale nature of an 'overnight' change of both modes of regulation and accumulation resulted in considerable 'adjustment shock' (*Anpassungsschock*) and 'adjustment stress' (*Anpassungsstreß*) for local policy-makers who were largely unprepared and ill-equipped to respond appropriately to the 'sink or swim' situation with which they were confronted in the aftermath of *de jure* German reunification on 3 October 1990. Not surprisingly, in the absence of relevant experience and expertise of their own, and unaccustomed to the new paradigms underpinning their tasks (Wollmann, 1994; Tuchtfeld, 1993; Grabher, 1995), the newly empowered local governments sought to adopt the policy measures of their Western counterparts, or west German consultants. These were directly derived from policies developed earlier during the economic restructuring phase in western Germany in the 1980s (Heuer, 1985; Herrschel, 1995) which had a distinct 'commitment to supply-side innovation and flexibility in each of the main areas of regulation' (Jessop, 1992: 63), and eastern local policy-makers consumed these only too eagerly as a blueprint for a prosperous 'Western-style' future.

This contrasts with the observed administrative continuity in the former German Democratic Republic (GDR). Most of the local bureaucrats and government officers 'below the top rungs of the *ancien régime*' (Brabant, 1992: 87) remained in post, a situation not uncommon in post-socialist eastern European countries which adhered to established practices of administering the population and dealing with the public (Wollmann, 1994). Only the old *élite* of local government was changed substantially, being replaced by 'western imports' or 'new entries' – the latter often taken from previously oppositional factions with little governmental experience. This potentially constrained the development of the institutional ability to operate the local state, which was further limited by the initially very small size of local administrations. For example, to encourage 'continuity' and as a gesture towards local patriotism, it was attempted to match the inherited small-scale pattern of local government (47% of local authorities had fewer than 500 inhabitants; Wollmann, 1994: 21) with the new, operational tasks typical of west German local government. These inherent contradictions inevitably raise a question mark over both conditions and *de facto* local statehood in the five new *Länder*, although territorial reorganisation since 1994 has alleviated some of these problems.

Such factors have challenged the assumption that 'appropriate' modes of regulation usually follow economic processes automatically and 'miraculously' (Hirst and Zeitlin, 1992) so that policy measures would mirror the newly developing (and territorially widening) inequalities in economic scope. Hence 'effective' regulatory measures by the local state should reflect a distinct awareness of the importance of 'localness' in future economic development and policy, establishing localities as individual and differentiated nodes of regulation (cf. Stoker, 1990). Hence, the local state often attempts to develop 'sufficiently differentiated and sensitive programmes to tackle the specific problems of particular localities' (Jessop, 1994: 272). Such policies are now considered elementary responses to the imperatives of post-Fordist markets (Jessop, 1994; Mayer, 1994b), for instance, through developing sufficient flexibility and potentially acting as an 'entrepreneurial city' (Mayer, 1994b: 317). The latter may be expected to be circumscribed by a locality's size, based on varying financial possibilities, human resources and expertise – or, equally, by inherited functional roles which may translate into differential abilities to operate effectively as local states. Localities higher up in the urban hierarchy, having held specifically allocated functional roles within the previous socialist state, may be relatively better equipped for locally based decision-making and administration. They may thus be more adept at identifying and carving out a distinct economic role for themselves in a post-Fordist economy, supported by tailor-made entrepreneurial policies, than smaller 'run-of-the-mill' places. This includes the necessary identifying, rediscovering and redeveloping of local identities and responsibilities, together with the individuality and specificity of economy-relevant local location factors. Ultimately, the question may then be asked as to whether the inherently more segmented space economy under post-Fordism will raise the profile of local, and regional (*Land*), governments, in relation to the nation state (Esser and Hirsch, 1994; Jessop, 1994).

The main concern of this chapter rests with investigating the role of spatial and temporal specificity as core features of regulation theory (see Chapter 13). How far do these specificities affect, or indirectly require, the adoption of entrepreneurialism, as expressed in proactivity, initiative and civic boosterism? If the local state is an individual, and thus also potentially unique, entity of policy-making, the degree to which it embraces entrepreneurialism may vary, reflecting that individuality and specificity. In effect, different modes of regulation may emerge within the same social and economic framework, including the *régime* of accumulation in its localised version. The question is whether policies of some localities are more similar than others, suggesting that, despite expected 'individuality', common characteristics in policy responses can be identified. Reasons for this may include shared positions in the urban hierarchy, similar economic structures or past responsibilities within the state administration. These interdependencies will be investigated in four main sections. Following a brief account of the nature of the 'newly established' local state in the five new *Länder* in the east, the concept of local self-governance will be contrasted with the *status quo ante* situation in eastern Germany with the complete absence of 'local statehood' under socialism. The third section will investigate the challenges posed to the newly established local governments by the economic transformation from state Fordism to post-Fordism, with the subsequently emerging and growing spatial inequalities of economic scope. This will be succeeded by a discussion of inter-local variations in policy response as evidenced by six localities with different local features and development backgrounds (Figure 8.1).

THE LOCAL STATE UNDER THE 'WEST GERMAN MODEL' *VIS-A-VIS* THE CHALLENGES OF ECONOMIC TRANSFORMATION

Under the west German model, local government draws its considerable policy-making discretion from the institutionalised 'communal self-government' (*kommunale Selbstverwaltung*). Its two main pillars are the freedom to act on the local population's behalf and to levy locally controlled finance (cf. von Saldern, 1994). These provide for localness and locality consciousness of local policy. Both are considered to be key elements of the local state and its response to the challenges of capital interests seeking 'continually to reproduce

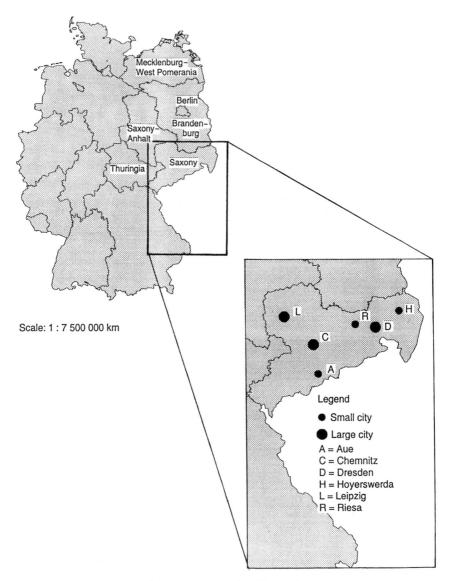

Scale: 1 : 7 500 000 km

FIGURE 8.1 Location of the six case study cities in Saxony

the conditions within which capitalist accumulation can take place' (Cockburn, 1977: 51). Although her early conceptualisation of the local state is essentially a fairly one-sided view, there is evidence from eastern Germany that local areas and government activities are shaped considerably by capital interests, especially when footloose investive capital becomes more scarce. Local uniqueness and individuality as the main characteristics of the *local* state include the development of locally specific expressions of economic restructuring and related policy responses. The latter, of course, require sufficiently local scope for identifying the need for action and for the design and implementation of policies. This 'scope' is circumscribed largely by the available *de jure* powers provided by Section 28 of the Basic Law (*Grundgesetz*); available *de facto* powers as circumscribed by 'external constraints' (e.g. central government policies, general economic trends, competing localities) and also the ability and expertise of local policy-makers to identify policy needs and define strategies to achieve these aims. In practice, therefore, local statehood may be considerably less autonomous and locally specific than it is in theory. An example is large capital projects for economic regeneration, which require substantial non-local funding. The discrepancy between *de jure* and *de facto* local policy-making autonomy, and thus, local statehood, is one that ultimately results in wide variations in governance (a tendency particularly evident in the six case studies considered subsequently).

The concern of local government with the locality's economy has two main roots: firstly, a general responsibility for local welfare as part of communal self-government, and, secondly, the direct impact of local business performance on local government finance through the locally levied *Gewerbesteuer* (business tax). Local government thus not only has a right to intervene in local economic development, but also a direct vested interest, although local welfare is the prescribed yardstick of all local policy measures. The introduction of the west German model in the east, replacing central obedience with local responsibility, thus had fundamental implications for local government, heightened by the equally radical changes in the economic environment, now driven by (previously refuted) market mechanisms. Following post-Fordist patterns, economic structures placed added emphasis on the local dimension as a locus of decision-making both in policy and business, thus raising the stakes for local policy-makers. It has been argued that changing modes of production undermine the traditional 'spatial division of labour' (Massey, 1995), especially the Taylorist separation of product development and (mass) production (Leborgne and Lipietz, 1991). In the case of eastern Germany, modes of production *and* regulation changed fundamentally, thus suggesting an equally fundamental redefinition of the spatial organisation of economic activity in its post-socialist 'differentiated spatial outcome' (Paul, 1995: 26). The new pattern appears to point towards an essential 'periphery' role for eastern Germany, depending to a considerable extent on branch plants as auxiliary 'extended production lines', with capital largely controlled by foreign and west German companies. This determines a locality's 'insertion into the [newly emerging] social and economic division of space' (Benko and Dunford, 1991: 19), while also restricting the development of external multiplier effects to support indigenous local business activity and economic development. It further contradicts the notion of post-Fordist flexibility in working practices, conditions for industrial relations, and flexible technologies seeking to respond to increasingly diverse consumer requirements (Schoenberger, 1988). One of the main tasks of economic policies may therefore be to establish indigenous growth potential, especially research and development capacities. Localities achieving that would avoid a branch plant type of existence and develop more of a post-Fordist (Western) structure.

Economic policies have thus emerged as a crucial task of local government (not least for political reasons) to meet the high expectations raised by Western politicians through promises of a 'land of milk and honey'. At the same time, local government faced the previously unknown requirements of applying proactive, locally driven policies, while having no experience in the utilisation of their new policy-making responsibilities. These include identifying and prioritising local development needs and seeking their subsequent implementation. Under the previous system, a local administration had to liaise with local production units to obtain provision of financial, material and human resources. They functioned as the actual distributors of economic resources whereas local authorities had a purely administrative control function as operative cells of the central state. Local services and improvements to physical infrastructure could only be provided in direct co-operation with local units of the state economy (usually *Kombinate*), which were the 'holders of resources' (Wollmann, 1994). These conditions were diametrically opposed to the newly established form of self-government with its emphasis on locally devolved decision-making and resource management.

Implicitly, the search for local distinctiveness and individuality encourages a more entrepreneurial and experimenting response to market interests, characterised by 'strong political responses and proactive development strategies adopted at the local level' (Jacobs, 1992: 40; Grabow and Henckel, 1994). Resulting entrepreneurial modes of governance have been broadly interpreted as essentially 'concerned with the prosperity of local economies and their ability to attract investment and jobs' in an attempt to secure the prosperity of the locality in an increasingly more spatially segmented post-Fordist market economy (Hall and Hubbard, 1996: 154). At the same time, with the local state characteristically being also part of a whole, its action and operational scope are integrated into higher-level modes of regulation (Yeung, 1994; Smith, 1995) including, in Germany, regional state (*Land*) federal government and the European Union, all with their respective policies and incentives (cf. Ridinger, 1994; Blien, 1994). These also seek to 'maintain the institutional fabric of growth in a dynamic and contradictive setting through state intervention' (Storper and Walker, 1989: 203), in this instance, through transferring the 'Western model' to the east. The effects of such intervention, here the replacement of 'plan' with 'market', are vividly displayed in eastern Germany. It is of particular interest to see how, and to what extent, suddenly 'unleashed' capitalist interests have been able to influence and shape the newly emerging local states *vis-à-vis* equally new and inexperienced local governments with their suddenly gained policy-making powers.

Consequently, there is a strong expectation that capital interests may be in a particularly influential role, because they are largely exercised by Western business with well-established experience and expertise, facing local administrations inexperienced in making evaluative judgements between general and group-specific interests. Additionally, private sector investment has been much sought after as the 'road' to Western standards of living. Given this quite imbalanced bargaining strength between local government and the private sector, as has become particularly evident in the immediate post-unification 'boom' period, a truly democratic pluralist way of operation would seem rather unlikely (cf. Dunleavy and O'Leary, 1987). Observations point towards liberal democratic processes of élitist influence by larger, generally Western investors, western German consultants (including planning bureaux), government agencies, such as the *Treuhandanstalt* and regional (*Land*) governments (Dunleavy and O'Leary, 1987: 324–5). Given the huge demand for new investment, especially to repair infrastructure, modernise buildings and restructure the economy, those non-local financiers may well be expected to exercise considerable influence. Consequently, local decisions may vary between the extremes of 'no autonomy' and 'almost full autonomy'. The first case very much reflects the situation under totalitarianism in the former GDR, whereas the latter points to the 'ideal' form of the west German model, which cannot be reached because of the inherent dependence on private sector investment. The almost diametric opposition of these two scenarios shows the long way local authorities in eastern Germany had to go literally overnight. Inevitably, local variations in the ability to adapt to those changes and satisfy the new demands will appear, magnifying any locality-specific differences which were previously overridden by a centralist system.

FROM 'LOCAL ORGAN' OF THE SOCIALIST STATE TO POLICY-MAKING AUTONOMY

The absence of a culture of empowered local *governance* in socialist East Germany, the lack of experience of strategic decision-making, together with the breathtaking speed with which familiar operating conditions disappeared, created confusion, disorientation and uncertainty among decision-makers, as the experience of the six case studies considered below illustrates. Under the system of the former GDR, they were little more than local 'organs' of the socialist government (Häußermann, 1995: 7), implementing the centrally defined socialist principles and economic plans locally. The policy-making impotence of the local administration is highlighted by the absence of local financial discretion. The local administration was completely dependent on both financial and manpower resources, which were obtained from the local industrial units (i.e. the *Kombinate* or state-owned companies – VEBs, *Volkseigene Betriebe*). The economic élite of company managers were thus more important and influential for local development schemes than the local administration. Effectively, the industrial production plant, symbol of socialist progress and development, was the *de facto* local decision-making institution, ultimately deciding on the implementation of plans designed by the local administrative *élite*. This contrasts fundamentally with the local council-centred organisation of the west German model of local government.

The introduction of the west German model of elected local government could thus not merely be a process of adjustment to 'Western principles' but demanded a completely new start for policy-making and administration (Laux, 1994). Some of the main problems faced include availability and control of local finance and administrative resources, qualification of personnel and, in particular, the small size of local government units, because it determines the operational scope of local government. If too small, financial, personnel and other resources will not permit envisaged locally defined policy-making. This was a pressing issue for the federal government after unification, with eastern Germany boasting a density of government units eight times higher than that in the west. Specifically, there were 7565 administrative units in the five new *Länder* in 1990, compared with 3438 *Gemeinden* (districts) in the 'old' Federal Republic, which accounted for 80% of the total, 'unified', population (Wollmann, 1994: 21). Not surprisingly, therefore, just under half (47%) of these had fewer than 500 inhabitants (Laux, 1994). In the regional state of Saxony, for instance, 1623 local authorities existed in 1991, compared with 396 in the twice as big and four times as populous 'old' *Land* of North Rhine-Westphalia. The whole picture is clearly one of 'atomised' local government, essentially contradicting the purpose of Germany's system of local governmental autonomy, a key element of local statehood. In response, a reorganisation of local government in 1994 reduced the number of local authority units substantially, in an attempt to create more viable entities.

For the first four years, therefore, provisions for local statehood were flawed, and certainly not helped by the lack of an inherited culture of local statehood which was compatible with the nature of a highly autocratic, centralised command system. The result has been a lack of expertise in the key areas of local policy-making – namely, developing strategic concepts and understanding the operation of the market. The challenge to local policy-making was therefore twofold: firstly, to grasp the new economic reality, with capital accumulation replacing social-political objectives as the main rationale of activities, and, secondly, to appreciate the new policy-making reality which put local policy-makers into a completely unfamiliar role as strategic decision-makers and facilitators of (capitalist) economic development. A further difficulty, with no Western policy-response blueprint, is the newly 're-created' complexity in landownership, with a flood of ownership restitution claims being made after unification, creating a sense of uncertainty in the property market and among developers. This inhibited many redevelopment schemes, especially in city centres with their particularly complex landownership structures. New hurdles also emerged from a growing awareness of their relative empowerment among the population, allowing them to use their new right of opposing or questioning proposed developments and their implementation.

The lack of experience became a distinct disadvantage for the new local governments when dealing with private sector investors, usually from the west. The latter were well accustomed to dealing with local administrations and knew how to 'play the system', for example, to obtain planning permission. In such cases, local statehood would be seriously eroded by mainly non-local, group-specific interests. Not all local states in eastern Germany found themselves in the same (inferior) position, however, because of variations in prior administrative experience. Thus, some of the larger cities had also maintained a role as regional administrative centres, or *Bezirkshauptstädte*. Dresden, Leipzig and Chemnitz possessed such regional functions, which they maintained as seats of the regional offices (*Regierungspräsidien*) of the state of Saxony. This expertise, as was made evident by the case studies discussed later, gave the respective cities something of a headstart in comparison to others. They could draw on more experience under the GDR system, particularly in strategic planning and administrative management. Also, the larger cities had a greater critical mass in resources (finance, administrative capacity, and staff expertise and qualification) than was evident in smaller places. The difference, it is argued here, was inevitably reflected in the nature of local policies and the degree to which these reflect localness. Size may thus have some influence on local policy-making and, ultimately, statehood.

LOCAL EVIDENCE OF POST-SOCIALIST ECONOMIC TRANSFORMATION

The role of the 'new' local state in eastern Germany, as both a locus of fundamental economic transformation and a maker of related local policy responses, will be demonstrated using observations of six urban localities in Saxony, one of the five new German *Länder*. The location in one *Land* is important, because the 'central government' function rests at this level, and thus constitutional provisions for local government operation and *Land* economic policies can be held constant. This is especially significant because the main focus will be on the effect of variations in the size of localities on their ability to adopt and exercise their earmarked roles as local states. Although all the localities studied hold borough status (*Stadtrecht*), and thus comparable *de jure* empowerment, they were chosen from the two opposite ends of the urban hierarchy, with the 'big' group including two large urban agglomerations of over half a million (Leipzig and the *Land* capital Dresden) and the quarter-million city of Chemnitz. By contrast, the 'small cities' group included three cities of between just over 20 000 inhabitants (Aue) to 120 000 (Hoyerswerda). The case studies thus reflect variations in typical local features, including size and related 'institutional thickness' (Amin and Thrift, 1995b), that is former functions in the socialist administration, current economic structure, degrees of government experience and expertise – all of which are expected to define scope for locally made economic policies.

Given the focus of this study, all local economies studied possessed significant, if varying, industrial heritage, thus providing the basis of major structural economic change. They were thus subjected to comparable challenges by the need to re-establish their future roles in the reconfigured space economy of eastern Germany. Different economic background, regional context, perceived economic opportunities and political–administrative experience in the six cities should be evident in the nature and contents of economic policies if localities possess sufficient scope to act as local states. Indications of the 'localness' and 'specificity' of policy measures were obtained from the very nature of policy documents, their availability, sophistication and professionalism, as well as from interviews with key actors in local economic development (senior local government officers and the directors of the respective chambers of commerce – such as *Industrie und Handelskammern*, IHK). These provided evidence highlighting different perceptions of the role, required nature and implementation of economic development policies. While these confirmed the importance of 'localness' and 'distinctiveness', some common themes could be identified, in particular policy-making constraints – for example, the possible diseconomies of territorial competition (an often misunderstood mechanism of market behaviour), the implications of regional policies and the complexities of the process of privatisation. Other factors include development potential and inherent 'dormant' determinants of statehood such as past administrative roles in the urban system of the former GDR. Under the new post-Fordist conditions, these exacerbated distinct inter-local variations in attractiveness to 'new' capital. Depending on a local area's relative attraction, it could find itself on a buyer's or seller's market, which in return will influence the degree to which local economic policies need to accommodate investors' requirements *vis-à-vis* the local community's general interests.

The impact of, and response to, economic transformation from socialism to post-Fordism was particularly obvious in the state of Saxony, because of its strong industrial history as the economic heartland of the former GDR, which makes it a good case study. In 1989, prior to unification, some 54% (3.3 million) of Saxony's workforce was employed in manufacturing (Freistaat Sachsen, 1994), decreasing to some 20% only three years later as a direct result of severe deindustrialisation and the shift from industrial to post-industrial structures. Together with steadily advancing tertiarisation, mainly in retailing and public administration, this inverted proportional shares between industry sectors: in 1989, the primary and secondary sectors combined employed some 60% of the workforce, with some 40% in services, while in 1994, the situation was reversed (BFLR, 1995b) – a situation which corresponded with conditions in western Germany. The changes were equally evident at the local level, albeit to a different extent, because observed variations include past administrative experience and 'muscle'.

The six cities studied, the 'big three', Dresden, Leipzig and Chemnitz, and their smaller counterparts, Riesa, Hoyerswerda and Aue, were chosen to exemplify localities with quite diverse economic roles under the old political–economic system, where economic and administrative 'central' functions were dictated by the central state rather than by market mechanisms. These inherited structures, it is argued, shape future economic prospects for localities, and include local economic identity, industrial infrastructure and related images of localities. Industrial monostructures, based around industrial conglomerates (i.e. *Kombinate*, Grabher, 1995), presented a particular problem, because of the immediate employment implications. Consequently, localities, if they are to be 'successful', need to be aware of *their* distinct locational features and thus development opportunities, and to define and implement relevant policies. Possibilities range from entrepreneurial localities with distinct, indigenous economic development dynamism to those with little such potential. The former allow a proactive shaping of the local (and regional) economy, thus suggesting a degree of local statehood which seeks to actively influence the future shape of the local economy, using the newly acquired local powers under the federalist German system of local government (Osterland, 1994; Häußermann, 1995). They might even wish to break free of their inherited 'socialist' economic embeddedness and seek to adopt a new role in the changing functional division of the regional space economy. Local authorities of the latter kind, those with little active impetus, are likely to be mere recipients of spin-off effects from developments and decision-making elsewhere, functioning within a wider (regional) economic framework and providing little evidence of the benefits of local statehood. These differences reflect variations and changes in the relative importance of places – i.e. whether they are 'empowered' or 'disempowered' (Amin and Thrift, 1995c) – with both conditions potentially exchangeable if 'enforced' by alterations to economic parameters.

Locally inherent development potential clearly includes the amount and range of institutional functions which may *per se* enhance the city profile. Resulting spatial differences mirror varying social, economic and adminis-trative–political factors – i.e. 'institutional thickness' (Amin and Thrift, 1995b). This would certainly encompass local economic policy-making which, under the German system of local government, is seen as a key local government task (Grabow and Henckel, 1994). The importance of local 'institutional thickness' became apparent in the six case studies where 'divergent local pathways' (to adapt Smith's 1995 concept of 'divergent regional pathways') of economic transformation were pursued in the search for a 'new "window" of territorial possibilities' (Yeung, 1994: 464). Of course, economic spaces facing the closure of old and opening of new 'windows of possibility' may not be congruent – i.e. opportunities may emerge where they were absent before and vice versa. The latter requires localities to face the fact that the old 'windows of possibility' have been closed and no new ones opened as yet, marking a situation of relative weaknesses in establishing itself in the new space economy.

New inequalities are instituted through regional policy by higher-tier government, creating additional inequalities between the two groups of localities studied. Significantly, the larger cities with the relatively highest indigenous economic potential have been excluded from support under the Regional Economic Assistance (*Regionale Wirtschaftsförderung*, RWF), whereas such support is available to the smaller, economically weaker localities, because they 'happen' to be situated in an 'Assisted Area'. Consequently, infrastructure measures and business land development through the public and/or private sector are eligible for an up to 35% capital grant in the small cities. More than half of Saxony's territory receives regional aid, comprising the peripheral mountainous region bordering the Czech Republic, and the former open-cast lignite mining areas in the north-western and north-eastern parts of the *Land*. This practice was repeatedly criticised during interviews, by local government officials and business representatives (chambers of commerce) alike as a relic of Keynesian-style inflexible 'economic equalisation policy'. Instead, they favoured support to areas with inherent development potential acting as growth poles, to gain more 'growth for money'. As might have been expected, the imposed inequality has had a clear impact on local policy-making, especially the choice of projects, as was confirmed by local policy-makers during the interviews. The reason is that RWF provides an important source of capital for local authorities to develop land for commercial use. The drawback is that grant applications must be made before the respective project commences, thus costing time, a price many investors are not willing to pay. Consequently, some local authorities (e.g. Hoyerswerda) have side-stepped this restriction, beginning the relevant project during the application period. The likely cost of 'lost opportunities' was considered higher than the risk of failing to get grant support.

It is apparent that local authorities in Saxony are facing quite unequal conditions for their policy-making, including local self-awareness as 'place', past administrative experience and central (*Land*) government regional policies. Local policy responses, therefore, might be expected to differ accordingly, when they seek to identify and maximise economic opportunities in the pursuit of their particular economic development 'pathways'. Assessment of these interrelations is still hampered by difficulties in obtaining uniform statistics or detailed local authority-based economic data – even quite basic sectoral employment figures were only available individually from local authorities and the relevant chambers of commerce. Nevertheless, using other indicators such as locality size, economic tradition, employment and accessibility, a sufficiently clear picture emerges of inter-local differences. At the same time, some of the six cities appear to be reasonably similar in many respects, with the 'big' cities characterised by higher functional centrality and degree of regional urbanisation (BFLR, 1995a), and the smaller ones by much lesser centrality. Similarly, the cities of the 'big' group show a much clearer degree of local economic individuality and specificity, which can be used to further ascertain their competitive standing, than is possible with the smaller ones. These show a more consumptive local market, a less pronounced economic identity and thus stronger dependence on existing, indigenous development potential. These two groupings thus form the basis of the following discussion.

The 'big cities' – visibly resurrected economic identity and development-facilitating individuality

Leipzig and Dresden are, after Berlin, by far the biggest and internationally most widely recognised 'names' in the former GDR's urban hierarchy. This has proved to be a vital and most effective asset in the pursuit of Western investors' capital, providing the two city governments with bargaining power not available to most other localities. This was repeatedly conceded during interviews, and evidence from elsewhere (Irmen and Blach, 1995) also showed the two cities, together with Chemnitz, as one of the few urban agglomerations with a 'very favourable' structure (and thus development prospects). This advantage translated into considerable investment interest, especially immediately after unification. All three cities possessed a long-established and well-known economic identity and specificity, albeit with varying degrees of 'relevance' to post-socialist and post-Fordist conditions. This applies in particular to Chemnitz with its domination by old manufacturing industries like textiles, whereas Leipzig and Dresden inherited more 'marketable' industrial structures, with Leipzig in particular allocated a role as the 'shop window of the GDR economy' through the annual hosting of an international trade fair, the *Leipziger Messe*. The fair is probably the single most important identity feature of the city and helped to place it on the 'mental map' of international business. Nevertheless, under the socialist system, Leipzig's economy was not allowed to utilise this local speciality and to focus on the service sector. Instead, led by the state ideology, manufacturing was promoted as the 'true socialist' economic activity, especially engineering.

Dresden's economic role within the state-controlled system was that of cultural and R&D centre, with a distinct emphasis on high-tech manufacturing products, including military equipment as part of the ex-GDR's spatial division of (military) production. This provided a potent local seedbed for new R&D-related development, with Pentacon (Practica cameras) as one of the socialist show production plants. Various technically oriented research institutions, and two universities, provide a useful potential for future R&D developments, unlike Leipzig where no such broad infrastructure exists. In both cities (as, indeed, throughout the former GDR) 'politically correct' manufacturing dominated, concentrated in the big *Kombinate* (industrial conglomerates), leaving tertiary employment on a low 21% of the workforce. In Leipzig, half of the manufacturing workforce was concentrated on 32 *Kombinate* of at least 1000 employees each, thus making the local economy dependent on a small number of key plants (Stadt Leipzig, 1992). The situation was less poignant in

Dresden with a larger base of 'survived' small and medium-sized businesses. Nevertheless, only three years after unification, manufacturing employment had collapsed to about a quarter of all jobs, similar to Leipzig (Stadt Dresden, 1994). When the *Kombinate* were broken up, much of the R&D potential disappeared, unwanted or non-viable in the absence of their functional support. Dresden's main and unique economic asset, outstripping Leipzig, is its traditional role as Saxony's historic administrative and cultural capital. This tradition was allowed to live on to a limited extent in the former GDR, and is now being resurrected to its full potential, serving as a main local attraction.

Some of the structural economic characteristics also apply to the third, if smaller, of the 'big cities', Chemnitz (renamed as Karl-Marx-Stadt during GDR times). The main difference and main source of its lesser success in developing into an investment node, are its less 'relevant', and rather disadvantaged, old-style industrial specialisms. Its economic identity as the 'Manchester of Saxony', with a long tradition in textile, engineering and commercial vehicle production, but with few internationally reputable names, has done little to facilitate the city's competitive standing in the market-place. In 1993, some 47% of firms were engaged in metal manufacturing, engineering and electrical engineering (Industrie- und Handelskammer Südwestsachsen, 1993). A potential asset are the inherited, relatively intact, small and medium-sized enterprises (alongside some large *Kombinate*) which provide considerable indigenous development potential. Nevertheless, despite some local R&D capacity in the form of a technical (engineering) university in Chemnitz and, recently, the involvement of the blue-chip research institute of Fraunhofer Gesellschaft, Chemnitz has played a much less pre-eminent 'specialist' role in its region than Dresden and Leipzig have, continuing to act as an urban and administrative focus instead. Given its much lower level of outside recognition, Chemnitz will have a more difficult task in attracting new investment than its neighbouring competitors Leipzig and Dresden with their distinct local qualities which provide extra bargaining power to local policy-makers. In the latter sense, the situation may be even less 'rosy' for the three smaller and much less well known cities. They lack outstanding local qualities appealing to outside businesses, with immediate repercussions on available policy options (or the lack of them) for the local state.

'Small cities' – lack of economic identity and limited 'utilisable' economic specificity

Low-level recognition by the outside (Western) world of business becomes a particularly important issue for the three smaller cities investigated, Hoyerswerda, Riesa and Aue, each serving as firmly embedded parts of 'their' regional economic environments. Their economic activities were largely allocated by state decree, rather than being based on genuine locational advantages. None of the smaller cities possess a specific image or local economic identity which would raise their levels of recognition above that of their regions. All three function as small to medium-sized regional centres both economically and administratively, and are thus at the lower end of the urban hierarchy in Saxony. Nevertheless, they all had their particular economic specificities, if of limited relevance under current market conditions. While Hoyerswerda's main economic purpose was to provide accommodation and urban functions for the many workers employed in the huge open-cast lignite mines in the region, Riesa was dominated by a large steel-producing *Kombinat*, located in the city for political rather than economic reasons, and employing several thousand workers. Aue, situated in peripheral hill country in southern Saxony, by contrast, largely maintained its origins in local ore mining, textile and small-scale metal manufacturing under GDR rule, supplemented by mining strategically important uranium nearby until 1990. The end of the *dirigiste* support of the three cities' economies also left relatively modern production processes of electronic equipment without a future, such as in Riesa, where the sole *raison d'être* of such a plant was to make use of female labour otherwise 'redundant' in a steel-making-dominated local economy.

This raises the pressing question of 'what else?' in all three localities. All the main businesses in Riesa and Hoyerswerda were the result of direct state intervention and directives, while in Aue the effect has been more indirect, preserving old structures which are now largely obsolete. But few new alternatives are apparent. The challenge for all three cities is now to find a new economic purpose, and develop relevant economic policies. Given the limited 'natural' appeal of these places as loci of business investment, such policies will need to produce good arguments to convince investors otherwise. This task is not helped by negative images, such as Hoyerswerda's portrayal as a 'socialist city', based on its extensive areas of 'socialist mass housing' to accommodate the region's lignite miners, and dwarfing the old town centre. The relatively narrow range of central functions in all three cities reflects the needs of their local and immediate regions' workers as judged by the state. The result is a relative weakness in indigenous development potential as a central place. Further, unfavourable geographic locations of Hoyerswerda near the Polish border and Aue just outside the region's designated new hill country Nature Park (Industrie- und Handelskammer Südwestsachsen, 1993), adds to the difficulties faced.

In summary, the effects of economic transformation on the six localities, with their diverse functional and economic structures, were found to vary considerably, responding to inter-local inequalities in the degree to which genuinely local economic advantages existed. Based on the general evidence discussed, a hierarchy of 'local economic specificity' among the six case studies can be schematically illustrated (Figure 8.2). This, in return, circum-scribes each locality's ability to identify and promote economic specificities and identities of the kind now sought by business entrepreneurs (see also

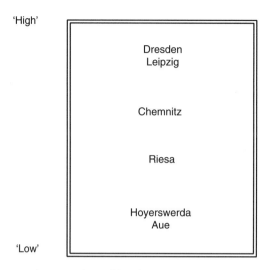

'High'

'Low'

FIGURE 8.2 Relative 'utility' of local economic specificity among the six cities

Chapter 4). Among the case studies, the situation appears to be particularly problematic for the smaller places with their less well-developed identity and poor image. Limited locational attraction, and/or presence on investors' mental maps, mark some of the main difficulties and underlying economic weakness under market conditions. The scope for locally defined policies can thus be expected to be equally limited. By contrast, the three big cities, especially Leipzig and Dresden, have maintained and further enhanced distinct local (economic) identities and qualities which appeal to business investors. Subsequently, local government in these cases not only possesses a considerably wider expertise and capacity, but can also manipulate 'useful' local economic qualities. They are thus much more likely to be sufficiently empowered to operate as local states and develop and implement locally designed economic policies, as discussed below.

IDENTIFYING AND PROMOTING LOCAL ECONOMIC SPECIFICITY

The renewed emphasis placed on inter-local variations in economic scope by the new regime of accumulation in the five new *Länder* required local states to identify their 'typical' economic strengths. Only then will they be able to respond appropriately to the increasingly more segmented and selective investors' market, as discussed earlier. Such individuality serves as a prerequisite for a local state's ability to formulate locally based 'entrepreneurial' policies. This includes the perception of economic opportunities and the nature of particular strengths available to provide a competitive edge. These opportunities are assumed to pre-empt the nature of 'responsive' local policies and, ultimately, circumscribe the degree of local statehood. The ability to develop strategic 'visions' of possible avenues of local economic specialisation may thus prove crucial for the choice of 'appropriate' policies and their success in the longer term, as illustrated by the six cities' economic policies. Post-socialist utility of local economic specificity and institutional thickness appeared as the key determinants of locally derived policy-making (and thus local statehood). Such relevant evidence of policy-inherent statehood was obtained from semi-structured interviews with key players in local economic policy-making in the six localities and from policy documents. The latter provided some background to the views expressed during the interviews. The interconnectedness between existing development potential, its local perception and the choice of 'relevant' policies seems to place the ball firmly in the court of local policy-makers and their ability to identify locally specific scope for future development and act as representatives of a local state. This 'ability' largely depends on degrees of 'utilisable' economic distinctiveness and functional inheritance (i.e. the concept of 'institutional thickness'). Forms of this interrelatedness will be reflected in inter-local variations of local policies, as highlighted below.

Strong local identity and the promotion of economic specificity

All three identity-strong localities – Dresden, Leipzig and, albeit to a somewhat lesser degree, Chemnitz – have inherited sufficient 'useful' local specificities that offered economic development opportunities and placed the three cities in a comparatively advantageous position. Utilisation of these opportunities varied between the three places, expressing their policy-making individuality as local states. In Dresden, the general appeal of the city's cultural and architectural heritage, the region's attractive landscape, its role as the historic capital of Saxony, and the relatively diverse 'entrepreneurial' business landscape with strong R&D potential and a relevantly skilled workforce, have emerged as major attractions to private (Western) investors and thus major assets in inter-local competition. The 'skill factor' has been identified by local policy-makers as a key marketable local advantage, and has subsequently been vigorously promoted as 'human capital' in its main advertising material. In fact, extensive reference is made to the city's strong cultural heritage to convey the image of skill, ability, imagination and creativity, and emphasise life style and quality of life as distinct local features. This corresponds with the efforts to attract 'matching' high-quality jobs, especially in the hi-tech sector. Similar efforts of portraying local economic specialisms as part of a distinct image are made in Leipzig, largely revolving around its fame as *Messestadt*. In fact, this specialist function helped to generate a 'boom town' image which in itself acted as a locational attraction and enhancement to its perceived economic purpose. The marketing slogan 'Leipzig means business' on local promotional material seeks to capitalise on this effect. Relocating the fairground to the edge of town next to the motorway, complemented by large retail and office developments, has thus been pivotal to policy activities. Other, if less prominent, policies aiming to draw on local specialisms seek to utilise the city's traditions in the printing and publishing industry, and to reinvent and promote the old 'printers and publishers' quarter'.

Inevitably, given the relative geographic proximity to these two high-profile local identities, the lesser known neighbouring Chemnitz feels overshadowed and relegated to the second league of contestants for corporate investment. This is not helped by the rather adverse effects of its image as a 'socialist' and 'old industrial' city, as manifested in its dominant 'socialist' architecture. The underlying uncertainty among local policy-makers about the city's economic identity and 'relevant' specificities is reflected in the initially rather low-key and vague policy outlines. They largely concentrate on publicity material emphasising general urban features and economic profile, including a rather run-of-the-mill English–German brochure *Portrayal of an Active Economic Region*, which described standard location factors. Following changes at the top of the city's administration, and the realisation that the expected flood of inward investment will not materialise, local policy-makers decided to actively promote a stronger and more self-confident image of the local state, using more aggressive, assertive and market-oriented policies. Organisationally, this change is reflected in the privatisation of the former economic development unit, now headed by a 'Western' manager. The aim is to depict a highly qualified workforce in manufacturing with a long-established entrepreneurial spirit, including technology (education) capacities and specialist manufacturing expertise, and portray the city as 'Saxony's innovation centre in manufacturing' (Stadt Chemnitz, c. 1993). The problem with these attempts is that, unlike Leipzig and Dresden, they are largely attached to old-type industries, and thus much less convincing as 'useful' location factors under today's post-industrial conditions.

In summary, the three big cities' policy-making provides clear evidence of local statehood based on their general economic identities and thus relative attraction to investment. This is particularly true of Leipzig and Dresden, whereas Chemnitz seems to be in a lower 'league' in the inter-locality competition. Both Leipzig and Dresden provide strong evidence that inherited 'relevant' economic specificities have clearly influenced the direction of development objectives, although differences in the 'how' have emerged. In Dresden, there has been a much earlier attempt at designing an integrated local development strategy within which economic development is embedded, albeit in a commanding position. In Leipzig, too, there was an immediate awareness of 'being special', as evident from the high interest from investors in the early years. However, there has not been quite the same determined and urgent attempt to develop a comprehensive, city-wide development strategy.

Instead, the city concentrated on the fairground (*Messe*) as *the* image-making project. The situation of Chemnitz appears less fortunate, because of the lower degree of 'utilisability' and thus attractiveness of its economic specificities under the new conditions, on top of the immediate competition faced from neighbouring Leipzig and Dresden. Local statehood in Chemnitz thus appears less well positioned and more subordinate to economic interests. Consequently, with such different local qualities, development strategies and policy approaches cannot simply be transferred from Dresden and/or Leipzig.

Weak local identity and the search for 'new' economic specificity

The three smaller cities, not unexpectedly, show considerably less evidence of local statehood, as indicated by the degree of local self-awareness, uncertain distinctiveness in economic policies, perceived relative economic peripherality and an absence of detailed development strategy documents, although some inter-local variations exist. The essentially passive positions of all three became most obvious in Aue where the city was judged by senior local government officers as too small to be able to generate a locally led economic regeneration, because all developments were in direct competition with neighbouring cities of similar size. Aue saw itself as an integral part of the regional economy, dependent on the region's general economic development process. The low local self-esteem in terms of comparative economic attractiveness became apparent in the confession that 'any investor is welcome' and that local plans may be adjusted to an investor's requirements, if necessary. Riesa and Hoyerswerda suggest a slightly higher awareness of 'localness' and specificity, although this has not (yet) translated into clear development strategies and local images. Enthusiasm and conviction by some local government policymakers (especially in Hoyerswerda) appear to be a substitute for essentially non-existent or, at best, fairly vague ideas about a suitable and likely economic identity. Thus, Hoyerswerda is playing with the idea of moving towards mining and recultivation-oriented technology as a possible local 'specialism', and developing the many former open-cast pits into a 'landscape of lakes'. More immediately, providing comparative cost advantages and a business-friendly and 'customer-oriented' administration are seen as locally controllable options for promoting economic development. Riesa shows the relatively highest degree of specificity, with attempts to adopt a more locally embedded approach and tailor policies to its distinct economic problems of large-scale industrial dereliction after the steel plant's collapse. 'Controlled restructuring' (i.e. closures and replacement in stages) is the slogan developed by Riesa's now privatised economic development company, which is headed by the former director of the closing steel-making *Kombinat*. His expertise and business contacts are hoped to be used to attract new manufacturing activity. Raising general awareness of Riesa as a 'place' is one of the main aims, implemented through *inter alia* a sponsorship deal with a participant in the 1996 Winter Olympics.

Overall, policy responses by localities with an unclear post-socialist economic purpose reflect this uncertainty. A less well-developed 'institutional thickness', lower 'levels of recognition' by outside investors and few utilisable inherited economic specificities have limited the scope for locally led policy-making. Most initiatives appear to be rather *ad hoc* and experimental, seeking to 'tap' any opportunity that might arise. Local confidence is much less explicit than in the bigger cities with their greater 'clout', also reflecting the less well-developed capability to act as a local state. This resulted in a relatively passive approach to policy-making. Consequently, they were less likely to have embarked on actively influencing the direction and pattern of local development. Instead, they seem to have remained hesitant, waiting for 'development pathways' to emerge on their own, possibly through regional policies. This contrasts with the local consciousness and assertiveness presented especially in Leipzig and Dresden, implying relative competitive strength, whether actual or perceived, and thus the ability to act as an effective local state. Hence, the biggest cities have carried out local economic audits to establish 'specificities' and develop related policies, produced a range of relevant documentation, and generally aimed at outside investors as part of a city marketing exercise. For instance, documents of the three larger cities are also available in English, advocating 'Leipzig Means Business', 'Human Capital' and an 'Active Economic Region'. With decreasing size of localities, such efforts became ever less explicit in their reference to specific local economic advantages.

CONCLUSION

Projected against the background of eastern Germany's transformed post-socialist modes of accumulation and regulation, this chapter has investigated evidence of re-emerging 'localness' and local 'statehood'. This 're-emergence' should be taken quite literally, because the changes for local government went from complete policy-making impotence to entitlement to autonomous policy-making. The changes also re-established 'localness' as a distinguishing factor, following the attempted deletion of local individuality in the interests of implementing socialist-based development objectives. The hidden inequalities are now re-emerging and redefining the economic development potential of subregional space economies, as well as re-establishing the basis of the operation of local states. The wholesale nature of the changes provided a unique opportunity to study the emergence of inter-local differentiation and identity, with all localities affected by the changes simultaneously. Evidence of localness was indicated in local economic policy measures, especially their individuality and 'uniqueness' in responding to specific local economic development issues. This, and growing regional disparities in the development of a new, post-industrial space economy have become apparent, confirming

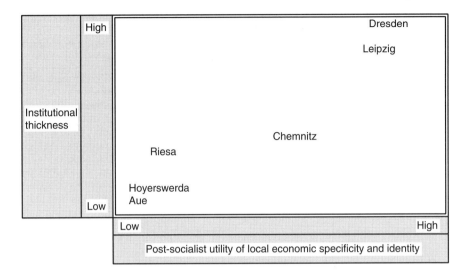

F I G U R E 8.3   The two main determinants of local specificity in policy-making among
the six cities

the notion of 'local pathways' developing in response to specific, resurrected
locally inherent economic factors.

Overall, the six cities examined provided clear evidence of two main factors
circumscribing local potential to define specific policies as a local state: firstly,
economic specificity and its utility as a locational attraction under the new
economic conditions, and, secondly, 'institutional thickness' as defined *inter
alia* by past political–administrative embeddedness and thus expertise in
strategic planning under the old system. The interdependence between the
two determinants, and their localised translation in the six cities can be
expressed graphically, illustrating the varying effects of the two factors in
simplified form (Figure 8.3). As illustrated, local statehood can become evident
if both factors provide sufficient 'specificity', or if one factor's strength
compensates for weaknesses of the other. This would mean that inventive
entrepreneurial policy-making skills could, at least partially, compensate for
less advantageous inherited economic features. Chemnitz and, to some extent,
Riesa appear to be following this path. Dresden and Leipzig excel for both
factors, thus underpinning their comparative strength as local states.
Hoyerswerda and, in particular, Aue illustrate the relatively weakest position,
possessing neither utilisable economic specificities nor particular policy-
making expertise.

This is clearly reflected in the types of policies and the varying evidence of
statehood pursued in the different cities (Table 8.1). Further case studies of a
wider range of localities, including 'average' positions, could provide a more
comprehensive picture.

TABLE 8.1 Local economic policy objectives of six cities in Saxony – evidence from interviews

Locality	Policy aims and objectives	Evidence of local statehood
Dresden	• Utilise highly skilled workforce: 'human capital' • Raise urban attractiveness • Develop Dresden as focus of regional economy • Enhance specialisation in high-tech and technology-oriented industries • Develop as centre of science, engineering, technology • Enhance function as 'gateway to the east'	• Inherited and confirmed role as 'capital city' • Early awareness of local strengths and attractiveness of its 'specificities' • Self-confidence in presenting locality • Early adoption of locally based decisions on future economic role and required policy direction • 'Playing the game' to achieve best local outcome
Leipzig	• Develop as international finance and business service centre • Use and enhance role as 'city of trade fairs' (*Messestadt Leipzig*) • Attract R&D and technology-based industries • Re-establish and enhance position as media centre	• Immediate awareness of special role and attractiveness as *Messestadt* (city of trade fairs) • Confidence and determination to establish locally led new economic role and direction • Suboptimal operationalisation through late concern with local development strategy
Chemnitz	• Advance traditional manufacturing credentials ('Saxony's Manchester') • Develop typical local identity (role), with region • Develop manufacturing R&D ('Saxony's Innovation Centre in Manufacturing)	• Hesitant adoption of new responsibilities and opportunities of 'self-government' • Uncertainty about kind of local 'uniqueness' • Privatised EDU as sign of 'buyer's market' with reduced locally based legitimacy?
Hoyerswerda	• Have always adequate sites on offer, adjust 'offer' to requests • Develop local/regional indigenous business • Develop expertise in mining/recultivation as local specialism • Utilise post-recultivation image of 'region of lakes'	• Lack of clarity about local attractiveness • Buyer's market: investor determines rules • Weak position in inter-local competition • Lack of recognisable identity • Little experience with autonomous local policy-making

continues

TABLE 8.1 (*continued*)

Locality	Policy aims and objectives	Evidence of local statehood
Riesa	• Allow flexible answers to individual business interests • Inward investment to diversify and trigger new industrialisation • Pursue 'managed restructuring'	• Lack of recognisable identity • Privatised EDU as sign of 'buyer's market' with reduced locally based legitimacy? • Little experience with autonomous local policy-making
Aue	• Attract *any* new investment • Maintain existing manufacturing • Facilitate restructuring if and where possible • Develop urban functions as mid-size urban centre	• Lack of recognisable identity • Weak position in inter-local competition • Market dictates terms of investment (if any) • Low ranking of economic policy in administrative organisation as sign of resignation?

Source: Interviews with local government officials.
EDU = Economic Development Unit.

It has become obvious, that despite an overwhelming picture of ubiquitous deindustrialisation and economic decline, locally distinct patterns of economic change emerged, based on the 'usefulness' of past or likely future economic opportunities. This acknowledgement of the importance of 'place' or 'territoriality' in general, and 'locality' in particular, provides an essential precondition of local statehood. The next important question would then be whether the necessary operative provisions have been put in place to allow the local state to operate. This includes the scope to act autonomously, as provided in principle *de jure* by statute as local self-government. Utilisation and implementation of this statutory right in response to particular local economic issues, and the subsequent design relevant policy responses, mirror 'localness' and individuality as the very characteristics of local statehood. Differences in potency of the new local states appeared to correlate with locality size, with the larger urban centres seeking to seize and build up new economic roles, while those in a weaker position (i.e. the smaller cities) were found to largely accept the roles allocated to them by market forces. Partly, this can be seen as the result of a lack of awareness about possible counteraction, as well as a function of resignation to the 'inevitable'. Thus, while the big and well-established localities appear to be in the 'driver's seat', having been able to utilise existing specificities and quickly adapt to the newly available role as local states, the situation is much less clear for the smaller cities. They appear much less aware of the implications and new possibilities of self-government, and subsequently fail to clearly recognise and actively shape their development potential and 'destiny'. They emerged as relying, whether deliberately or not, on the indigenous economic development potential of their respective regions, on which they can 'ride the tide'. This interrelationship means that in economically less attractive regions, 'development-dependent' cities (like Hoyerswerda) will show much less evidence of local statehood than those, like Riesa, benefiting from the economic spin-off effect of a nearby economic node, like Dresden. The big cities, especially the state capital Dresden, demonstrate evidence of local statehood, with a considerable degree of individuality and entrepreneurialism. They are much more diverse and entrepreneurially spirited than the 'weaker' local states, which are more likely to (and have to) be content with focusing on local issues, especially nurturing unclear development potential.

PART III

REPRESENTATION, CULTURE AND IDENTITIES

INTRODUCTION

PHIL HUBBARD

'Culture has many locations'
(Bhabha, . . . 1994: 23)

As Chapter 3 by Kim and Short argues, frenetic entrepreneurial activity, now almost ubiquitous throughout the Western world, is often based on the assumption that 'image is everything'. Fostering the 'right' city image has thus become central to entrepreneurial policy, usually based on the idea that the cultural assets of the city can be harnessed to draw in the right types of people and investment. Hence, cultural and arts industries are being vigorously promoted (and sometimes funded) by entrepreneurial city governments in their quest to be seen as innovative, attractive, *civil* places to live. Frequently, this means the promotion of 'high' culture, as city imagineers appeal to consumption practices of the emerging *nouveau riche* of the professional, managerial and service classes. Art, food, music, fashion and dance are all paraded in the city shop window as cities seek to induce economic growth through investment in arts festivals, concert halls, galleries and museums. Being host to the 'right' concerts, acquiring the most prestigious exhibitions or being designated as European City of Culture now appear as crucial to many city governors as local labour market skills or transport infrastructure in enhancing local competitiveness. Images of conspicuous consumption, of the city as a 'fun' place to live and work (if you can afford it) thus abound in the marketing hype of the city imagineers. Even Glasgow, recognised as having some of the worst social and economic problems anywhere in Europe, played this hand with some success, ostensibly reimaging itself as a pleasant cultured city, the antithesis of the Red Clydeside mythology of working-class life and labour based on hard working, hard drinking and hard men (see Chapter 2).

Yet it is not only high culture that is being harnessed by city imagineers. In recognition of the complex plurality of the contemporary (post-modern) city, often more prosaic 'low' cultures are celebrated and harnessed in the pursuit of investment and tourism. Street cultures, ethnic celebrations and working-class traditions are increasingly integrated into the narrative web of city promotion, with cities paying lip service to the notion of being a multicultural environment, tolerant of difference (within reason). Flagship projects in particular often evoke historic references and community symbolism to represent a reconciliation of diverse communities (Goss, 1997). But herein lies one of the tensions implicit in the harnessing of culture for entrepreneurial ends: within this process of appropriating and commodifying low cultures, the cultural heterogeneity of the city is lost and class, gender and racial differences elided together. Hence, many bemoan the way in which 'genuine' cultures are taken from the margins and relocated to sites (and sights) that are mere sanitised simulations of some original artistic expression (Zukin, 1995). Yet this 'symbolic framing' of culture, if successful, can of course be a powerful ideological tool harnessed by city governors in their attempts to stimulate investment:

> Whether it be the competition of growth coalitions to attract inward investment, conflict with growth coalitions elsewhere over state policy and its regionally redistributional implications, or a politics of growth organised around more developmentalist goals . . . coalitions are cemented, more often than not, by appeals of a communal nature. The cement may be of a fairly rudimentary nature based on vague notions of community welfare through trickle-down. On the other hand, the arguments propagated can also exploit more enduring symbols of local pride and solidarity as well as old rivalries (Cox, 1995: 13).

Hence, ideas of a shared city vision, an entrepreneurial city that is working for all, can be a potent discourse underlying this commodification and transformation of city culture.

But if culture is the battleground against which entrepreneurial political struggles are played out, where in the city can such cultural battles be observed? Although the entrepreneurial city is perhaps best considered a *virtual* city, one constituted through a quixotic range of images and representations (so much so that it no longer makes sense to distinguish between the myth and reality of the city), it is probably the urban landscape itself that sends out the most important messages about the nature of place. As such, the physical spaces of the city can be considered as belonging to the same set of cultural forms (brochures, videos, guidebooks, advertisements) which promote a partial and selective view of the essence of the city. The imagineers' attempt to construct a new city image is thus rarely restricted to the launching of a new advertising campaign, and goes hand in hand with the creation of new urban landscapes:

> In this competitive location game, cities and regions must market themselves: their imageability becomes the new selling point. Consequently, spatial design codes and architectural pattern languages become increasingly important in selling the look of an upmarket, upbeat environment.

In this marketing war, style of life, visualised and represented in spaces of conspicuous consumption, become important assets that cities proudly display (Boyer, 1992: 193).

Hence, entrepreneurial capital and cultural symbols often entwine in public space to create a visually seductive city centre (or, perhaps more frequently in the North American context, edge city) masking real geographies of decay and neglect.

A number of commentators have begun to examine the way these landscapes act as social representations, imaginary maps which organise desire and consumption in the name of entrepreneurial policy (e.g. Crilley, 1993b; Roberts and Schein, 1993; Hubbard, 1996b), influenced by traditions in semiology, iconography and environmental psychology respectively. Such studies have begun to draw out the way that the meanings of entrepreneurial landscapes are ideologically charged, supporting particular visions of city life. This theme forms the basis of the first chapter here by Malcolm Miles, which explores how publicly placed art and sculpture contributes to the symbolic economy of the city. Recognising the increasing success of policies aimed at supporting public art in the United Kingdom, Miles draws out the ways in which such art has become an integral part of many redevelopment schemes, contributing to a symbolic infrastructure aimed to draw in tenants as well as send out a wider message about entrepreneurial trajectories for change. Here he focuses on the tensions and contradictions facing those in the cultural industries as they seek to maintain the principles of modern, democratic, critical art in the face of the increased power wielded by entrepreneurial governors. He none the less argues that there remains potential for artists to contribute to a more democratic and emancipatory form of entrepreneurial strategy by posing important questions about the relationships between people and place.

Similar themes about the use and abuse of popular culture underpin Justin O'Connor's chapter. Drawing on the work of key cultural theorists (Pierre Bourdieu, Mike Featherstone, Sharon Zukin) he seeks to evaluate how entrepreneurial policy enhances or compromises the growth of indigenous cultural sectors. Here, it is easy to postulate a fairly straightforward relationship between economic growth and entrepreneurial strategy: by promoting and investing in cultural production, growth in the cultural industries will be enhanced. As yet though, there is a paucity of evidence that suggests direct economic benefits have accrued from cultural investment strategies (McGuigan, 1996: 106). This is, in part, because the blurred lines between production and consumption in the cultural sector makes analysis difficult, and 'traditional' notions of embeddedness, multiplier effects and intra-firm relations appear as less relevant in the new cultural industries. Considering evidence from Manchester, where vigorous place marketing has often revolved around a celebration of local street and youth cultures (as particularly manifest in the 'Madchester' rave scene born in the city's Hacienda nightclub), O'Connor begins to assess the importance of this local cultural industry in promoting job creation in specific communities. Although the chapter focuses on key cultural intermediaries, it begins to identify the gender, ethnic and sexual composition of the cultural industries, and poses questions about the potential of much vaunted 'cultural renaissance' to promote social inclusion.

In the final chapter of this section, Donald McNeill considers the problems inherent in 'writing' the cultures of the entrepreneurial city, drawing on his own research experiences in Barcelona. Clearly, in seeking to document and (re)present the nature of the entrepreneurial city, the academic writer must be wary of the ways in which their representations are not simply a mirror of the experience of the city, but ultimately become constitutive of the city, as practices of representation are exercises of discursive definition and power which define the city itself. According to Shields (1996), it is within this recursive relationship between city and text that writers must seek to escape from the extremes of representing the city solely as private or public; as objective space or subjective experience; as imagined or as lived. In short, the realisation that traditional descriptive models of the geographer, whether derived from logical empiricism or Marxism, fail to adequately convey the varied human experiences of the city, posits a fundamental challenge to the way we research and write about the entrepreneurial city.

Many contemporary geographers have thus sought to question 'objective' geographic modes of representation, with the writings of figures as diverse as Walter Benjamin, Samuel Pepys, Mike Davis, bell hooks and Helen Cixous cited as work which blurs the boundaries of practice and discourse (and Lefebvre's triadic conceptualisation of space as simultaneously experienced, perceived and imagined). Yet others have began to experiment with more innovative modes of city representation (see for example, Allan Pred's utilisation of the montage technique in his analysis of Stockholm's world expositions). While the adoption of different (post-modern) tropes of representation can sometimes seem wilfully obtuse and unnecessarily playful, McNeill argues that it often follows a theoretically informed decision based on detailed consideration of text, author and audience. By problematising his own subjective reaction to the 'new' Barcelona, and casting aside conventional expectations of what occurs in the entrepreneurial city (based especially on the North American 'growth machine' model), he argues that the trope of travel writing is one that can present as representative a story of the city as any other. In the final analysis, by posing the question as to which stories we need to recount about the entrepreneurial city, McNeill is reminding us that the academic view of the cultural diversity of city life is, of course, often a very partial one.

9

A GAME OF APPEARANCE: PUBLIC ART AND URBAN DEVELOPMENT — COMPLICITY OR SUSTAINABILITY?

MALCOLM MILES

INTRODUCTION

This chapter interrogates the policies and practices of 'public art' – permanent or temporary works of art or craft located in spaces of open public access – in entrepreneurial urban development in Britain from the late 1980s to the mid-1990s. This period of 'enterprise culture' under the Thatcher government saw a widespread adoption of public art policies by local authorities, alongside the commissioning of art in private sector developments such as Broadgate in London. The success of advocacy for public art (and consequent expansion of public arts management) largely obliterated any critical concern as to its role in development, as either complicit in the imposition of dominant conceptualisations of the city, or as a catalyst to the imagining of sustainable urban futures. Hence, the enthusiasm with which public art was promoted was accompanied by an obvious neglect of research into its reception, Sara Selwood's report for the Policy Studies Institute (Selwood, 1995) being the first structured effort to address this omission, its findings largely negative.

In this chapter it will be argued that modernist[1] sculpture located in public spaces in developments such as Battery Park City, New York, appeals only to a specialist public, and in effect lends an aesthetic mask to urban development which has consequences of gentrification which are socially divisive (Deutsche, 1991a). It is then argued that public art, when it is contemporary gallery art located in non-gallery spaces, shares with planning and architecture an abstracting perspective which suits it for this purpose. This approach to the world which constructs it as geometry on a blank (value-free) ground is characterised by Lefebvre's formulation of the 'representations of space' (Lefebvre, 1991). There is, it could be argued, an alliance between modernist art, which constructs a 'value-free' space for its reception, and development which abolishes the accumulated histories of use and habitation in the sites on which it is inscribed. Cases such as Cardiff Bay, the centre of Birmingham, and the redevelopment zone of Sunderland exhibit similarities and differences through which such a critical position can be articulated. Throughout this chapter Ernst Bloch's *The Principle of Hope* (Bloch, 1986) which links 'beauty' with social process, will be drawn on to frame discussion of the potential role of art in urban change, suggesting alternative roles for art in public spaces.

PUBLIC ART IN PRESTIGE DEVELOPMENT: BROADGATE

Advocacy for public art in British public sector development has recently been very successful, following persuasive efforts by the Arts Council in imitation of established Percent for Art policies in the USA and Europe (Arts Council, 1991). A Percent for Art policy usually entails setting aside 1% within the capital cost of a building or development for the commissioning of works of art and craft to be sited in it. In the USA, the percentage varies from 0.2 in Wisconsin to 2 in Sacramento and San Francisco; in some cases, such as Los Angeles, resources from all developments within a given zone can be combined – its Museum of Contemporary Art was built from funds pooled in this way. In Battery Park City, New York, public art is integral to the public spaces required by planning regulation, and to the public image of the site.

According to a report by the University of Westminster in 1993, 42% of local authorities in England and Wales had by then adopted a policy to encourage the provision of public art, while a further 23% were considering doing so (Roberts, Marsh and Salter, 1993: 36). Urban development corporations emerged as a significant source of patronage, with all of those surveyed implementing a public art policy of some kind, as did 74% of responding local authorities in Urban Programme areas (designated through the government's 'Action for Cities' initiative of 1988). Comments as well as figures indicated a perceived link between public art and regeneration, for example: 'Public art is considered to be an integral part of the regeneration strategy' (unattributed, Roberts, Marsh and Salter, 1993: 39). While the private sector is generally less generous in its commissioning than local authorities, some developments, notably Broadgate in London, are embellished by sculpture collections. These generally favour work by 'blue-chip' artists, such as Richard Serra, whose *Fulcrum* (1987) stands at the entrance to Broadgate (Figure 9.1). Broadgate is a major development which sets a benchmark for entrepreneurial patronage of public art in the UK, and may be influential on public sector commissioning of sculptures by artists of international status in urban development during the 1990s.

A kind of confidence is exhibited by placing five plates of partly rusted cor ten steel, each weighing 45 tonnes, amid the pink stone and tinted glass of Broadgate, though both exhibit forms of 'expensiveness'. For the developers – Stuart Lipton, a collector of contemporary art who advised on the building of the Sainsbury Wing of the National Gallery and played a role in the move to fast-track development using design-and-build contracts, and David Blackburn, his fellow Director of Broadgate Properties – it offers a way to characterise Broadgate as a unique site, and perhaps the personal satisfaction of acquiring

FIGURE 9.1 *Fulcrum* by Richard Serra, situated at the entrance to Broadgate, London. Source: Author's collection

the status of patrons of art, with attendant aura of high culture; Sharon Zukin notes the use of art patronage by business élites in the USA to demonstrate prominence in a city's symbolic economy (Zukin, 1996: 45) and Broadgate seems to follow this pattern. A *Visitors' Guide* describes the development as 'a carefully designed environment where the best architecture creates landscaped squares with sculptures' (Broadgate, nd: 1) to which *Fulcrum* offers 'a striking opposition' (Broadgate, nd: 12).

Lipton saw Serra's work at an exhibition at the Saatchi Gallery, London in 1986, when most of Broadgate remained in the planning and construction stages, following which *Fulcrum* was commissioned. Serra consulted, through his agent, with the site's architects and engineers, contributing to one of the emerging tenets of public art advocacy: that, in the words of Sandy Nairne, writing as the Arts Council's Director of Visual Arts, 'there is a natural bond between good contemporary art and craft and good contemporary architecture' (Arts Council, 1991: 9). Broadgate was a success, in that most of its space was quickly let. During summer lunch breaks its open spaces are filled with office workers, and its ambience, with generous plazas, a water feature and an arena used as an ice rink in winter, reflects corporate environmental design in the USA, following the impact of W.H. Whyte's research on the provision of 'public space' in development through the zoning regulations of New York City (Whyte, 1980) and the model of Battery Park City. Other sculptures at Broadgate include George Segal's *Rush Hour* (1983), Fernando Botero's *Venus* (1990), Jacques Lipchitz's *Bellerophon Taming Pegasus* (1966) and Barry Flanagan's *Leaping Hare* (1988), all figurative works in bronze (and all works by men). *Venus* offers an organic foil (like the proverbial architect's squiggle) to the geometry of the façade in front of which it is placed, though its representation of the feminine as a passive earth mother is problematic. The construction of the development was documented in drawings and paintings by Robert Mason (Cork, 1990). None of this art references the history of the site, as Roman burial ground, thirteenth-century Bedlam hospital or 1860s Broad Street station, nor suggests an appeal to a specific public outside the circles of enthusiasm for contemporary art, any more than the development itself seeks to be other than a new corporate enclave, its links more to other enclaves around the world than to adjacent areas of London (such as the neighbouring borough of Hackney).

A survey of Broadgate's corporate tenants in 1993 by Sara Selwood, in her report for the Policy Studies Institute, showed that the provision of high-quality public spaces was appreciated, but not directly a factor in decisions to take up a tenancy; factors which did impact that choice included location, office design and transport links (Selwood, 1995: 331), although it could be argued that the ambience provided by the open areas in which the sculpture collection is sited might give a competitive edge should Broadgate be compared to other developments of equally good location.[2] The reception of *Fulcrum* by a wider public is sometimes negative – 'You'd see something better in a scrap yard' being a comment from a construction worker (Murray, 1990: 26).

The uncompromising quality of the work and its refusal to appeal to popular tastes may, however, be a reason for its commissioning. This is less odd than it seems, for Broadgate is not a space designed for public need but a corporate enclave which includes a sculpture collection of 'blue-chip' art reflecting its intended prestige and offering the possibility of asset appreciation, as well as personal taste of the developers; it is also interesting that the controversy surrounding the proposed removal of Serra's *Tilted Arc* (1981), another work in cor-ten steel, from Federal Plaza, New York, was in progress at the time *Fulcrum* was commissioned. In 1984, William Diamond, an administrator for the General Services Administration who oversaw the installation of *Tilted Arc* in 1981, began pressing for a public hearing to determine whether the sculpture should be relocated, in response to sustained complaints from some users of the site. Among them was Edward D. Re, Chief Judge of the US Court of International Trade, who wrote:

The negative impact of this wall goes far beyond aesthetic distaste. The psychological impact on members of the community who wish to use the plaza has also been profound. Before the imposition of this rusted steel wall, the plaza served as a pleasant and humane open space (cited in Weyergraf-Serra and Buskirk, 1991: 27).

A decision to remove the piece was taken in 1985, following which, in the same year as his London exhibition, Serra brought a much-publicised lawsuit for $30m., claiming that the removal of a site-specific work constituted its destruction; Serra lost the case and appeal, and the work was removed/destroyed in 1989. This kind of controversy may not have worried Lipton, who said about the sculptures in Broadgate: 'People should like, or perhaps hate, them' (cited in Murray, 1990: 26); it may even have attracted him, since altercations about art can distract from questions of the social impact of development.

Broadgate's architecture consists of lavish façades, giving an impression of *belle époque* in detailing and architectural metalwork; it has been described as stating in the 'classical geometry of its marbled walls [and] use of heavily varnished wood in the interiors' a sense of capitalism 'as mature, prudent and authoritative' (Brighton, 1993: 47). Here, the presence of art both contributes to a sense of 'luxe' and maps on to the site the 'value-free' status of art space (as experienced in the white-walled galleries and museums of modern and contemporary art), eliding the social values of the street, affirming that the public spaces of Broadgate are not streets. Neatly inserted into the façades are the security cameras that remind visitors that Broadgate is a highly regulated, constantly cleaned and patrolled, privately owned space. The inclusion of open spaces, planting, a water feature and a performance area differentiates it from what Whyte termed 'corporate fortresses' accessed only by underground parking garages (Whyte, 1980: 87), lending the encroachment of entrepreneurial control on the public realm a humane face. These embellishments are crucial to the identity of the development; the sculptures, reminiscent of the statuary of nineteenth-century town squares, act as a mask for encroachment, while their status as high culture and location within the self-referential fields of modernist art act as subtle 'keep out' notices for those lacking cultural capital.

Much has been written (Ambrose, 1994; Sibley, 1995; Zukin, 1995; Smith, 1996) of the abjection caused by urban developments which have little regenerative impact for local communities. Art, as at Broadgate, has a capacity to be complicit in such processes, which are not confined to the private sector. Of course, to question the complicity of art in development which is not in the 'public good', or at least not for the good of diverse publics, is not to argue against aesthetic qualities, or beauty, in urban design, but to take a critical position in relation to the values of institutionalised art and urban development, to reveal the contradictions of both. This leads to a further question as to what constructions of thought engender socially divisive entrepreneurial urban development, and enable planners, architects and artists to serve it.

CONTRADICTIONS IN THE ROLE OF PUBLIC ART

As Jessop (Chapter 4) argues, discourses of entrepreneurialism produce an assumption that urban development, like public art, is a 'good thing', rightly subsidised by tax incentives and facilitated by the relaxation of planning regulations available through urban development corporations; the fall-back position is that, naturalised as 'change', it is inevitable, like wet weather. It is more accurate to say it is a consequence of layers of planning and economic decisions which are too opaque to be widely deciphered but make development a good thing for developers; this situation breeds despondency and disempowerment expressed in phrases such as 'planning blight' with its intimation of crop failure. Perhaps the opacity of the processes through which a city changes serves certain interests of power (Bernstein, 1985), though the imposition of dominant conceptualisations of the city is beginning to be challenged in the academic discourse of urban planning (Hall, 1988). But the assumption that development is 'good' is problematic not only because the narrative of progress through which such assumptions are legitimised has lost its currency, but also in that the aims, when stated, of development and the art with which it is embellished, seldom relate to the needs of identified publics. This allows entrepreneurs to claim a generalised benefit for development, often promoted through visual imagery, while consigning to invisibility development's effects of social fragmentation (Smith, 1996).

Yet, public art agencies frequently utilise the notion of a general public to mask a lack of consultation or collaboration with defined publics; a supposed inability of the 'general public' to recognise quality in art serves to consolidate control of taste in the hands of 'experts'. When public art is received negatively, this is blamed on the 'public's' lack of appreciation. Sara Selwood's report *The Benefits of Public Art* states that none of the cases studied had previously been evaluated and that the criteria by which they might have been were seldom identified (Selwood, 1995). Meanwhile, a concurrence of property and road development with the interests of the Conservative government produced a boom in construction yet homeless people beg in the margins of the South Bank Arts Centre and the advocacy of public art by the Arts Council has widened the market for art and raised the status of artists: 'Percent for Art places artists and craftspeople on the same plane as architects' (Arts Council, 1991: 11). The practice of public art, thus, led by policy and funding, and, mediated for the most part by arts managers in subsidised public art agencies and public art officers in local authorities, has become mired in questions of taste while failing to address questions of social need or benefit. Certain questions of accountability seem to arise.

Development and art depend on a separation of image from everyday life. The autonomy of modernist art, its tendency to a reductionist, self-referential evolution, counter the expectation that, when art is sited in a public space, there will be a public for it, as if awaiting its revelations. The nostalgic

FIGURE 9.2 *Bottle of Notes* by Claes Oldenburg and Coosje van Brugen, Middlesbrough. Source: Author's collection

idealism of the publicity imagery used to promote, for instance, London's Docklands, conjuring fantasies of leisure on a sparkling river, is denied by the realities of the development itself and the abjection of neighbouring publics (Bird, 1993). However, the adoption of public art policies has still been widespread, and city councils now compete for a place on an international 'culture map' by commissioning works from artists of international status. Typical of this is *Bottle of Notes* (1993) by Claes Oldenburg and Coosje van Brugen (Figure 9.2), in Middlesbrough. Although the work references the voyages of 'discovery' of local 'hero' Captain Cook, using extracts from his notebooks in its form, the relevance of the message may be as lost on some citizens as, it would appear, the reading of Cook's voyages in a post-colonial context is on the work's commissioners. *Bottle of Notes* is, primarily, an extension of the artists' continuing body of work, its derivation as much in an Edgar Alan Poe story about a message in a bottle as a response to the local context.

The Irish writer Brian McAvera coined the term 'site-general' for art in which 'the concept is so vague it will take the imposition of almost any roughly analogous situation' (McAvera, nd: 113). His object was Antony Gormley's cast-iron cruciform men on the walls of Derry, but lottery funding is likely to produce a crop of such monuments towards the end of the century. Their commonality will be a reading of 'site' as a value-free ground for art. To go beyond this uncritical position requires a renewed sense of a socially produced imagination, not to banish beauty, but align it with the 'work' of social change.

IMAGINATIVE ACTS AND URBAN CONCEPTS

Ernst Bloch writes, in *The Principle of Hope*, a massive work bringing together aspects of critical theory and psychoanalysis:

> We say of the beautiful that it gives pleasure, that it is even enjoyed. But its reward does not end there . . . it remains even after it has been enjoyed . . . hangs over into a land which is 'pictured ahead'. The wishful dream goes out here into what is indisputably better, in doing so . . . it has already become work-like, a shaped beauty. Only: is there anything more in what has been shaped in this way than a game of appearance? (Bloch, 1986: 210).

Bloch suggests that 'the beautiful', which he associates later in the paragraph with literature and, to a lesser extent, painting, articulates what is 'pre-conscious', that it brings into a form which can be communicated what is potential in a socially produced human consciousness; this consciousness, not divided between 'conscious' and 'unconscious', desires a future free from the repressions of the past. The 'work' of society thus echoes the 'work' of psychoanalysis, both recognised as negotiated processes of becoming; in a more recent text, Ernesto Laclau argues along not dissimilar lines, concluding that 'today we are at the end of emancipation and at the beginning of freedom' (Laclau, 1996: 18).[3] But Bloch's text also echoes the notion of an avant-garde ascribed to radical artists by French thinkers in the nineteenth century: the Utopian socialist Saint-Simon states that 'It is we artists who will serve you as avant-garde . . . when we wish to spread new ideas among men [sic], we inscribe them on marble or canvas' (cited in Nochlin, 1967: 5); and the Fourierist critic Laverdant that 'Art, the expression of society, manifests . . . the most advanced social tendencies' (cited in Nochlin, 1967: 6). For these thinkers, if not for bourgeois artists such as Delacroix, art and everyday life were not in opposition.[4] Bloch's concept of a 'shaped beauty' which is 'work-like' offers a frame for a critical view of art in urban change. The phrase 'game of appearance' takes on a particular colour when applied to the vistas of Battery Park City, the façades of Broadgate or the towers of Canary Wharf.

The city as freedom

Freedom is an urban concept. Both Richard Sennett and Herbert Girardet note the inscription on the gateways of the cities of the Hanseatic League: STADT LUFT MACHT FREI.[5] Urban life is free from daily subsistence labour on the land, offers the freedom to accumulate capital and construct a political sense. These freedoms were available to men of the merchant class, for whom the medieval city offered the space in which to become a class, and, in the city states of Tuscany, commission architects to realise the concept of the city thus produced (Lefebvre, 1991: 78). The freedom which began in the masculine space of the agora of Athens (Sennett, 1994) is a freedom to determine conceptually what the city is. The idea of the city as Utopia conceptually underpins Battery Park City and Canary Wharf (both developed by Olympia & York), Broadgate and the 'new' Bucharest. To set development by transglobal corporate interests beside that of centralised state power may seem strange, but there are commonalities: both kinds impose a dominant notion of the city, and both abolish a past laden with the values of human habitation and toil. The latter, as a characteristic of modernist city planning and architecture, is epitomised by Le Corbusier's proposed demolition of the centres of cities to create a zone for new design (Le Corbusier, 1987: 96). If there is a difference between the cases, it is that there is little art (though there are decorative fountains) in the new Bucharest, and that the use of force in its construction was more overt.

In the West, art affirms the dominant image of 'the city' constructed by entrepreneurial development and contributes to a symbolic economy (Zukin, 1996), while conventional histories of art and the city divert attention from the social to the aesthetic (Deutsche, 1991b). Wendy Taylor's stainless steel sculpture in the water by Canary Wharf states this relationship; it is titled *The Spirit of Free Enterprise* (Figure 9.3). A publicity brochure produced by the London Docklands Development Corporation sets out a case for this kind of art, illustrated by Taylor's sculpture photographed like a corporate logo in silhouette against the sky:

> The built and natural environments . . . are rapidly changing, with new buildings, roads and railways, alongside new open spaces, parks and landscaping schemes. Artists and crafts people can work with architects, engineers and developers to great effect, enriching and humanising the environment . . . (LDDC, nd: not paginated).

The conjunction of the 'built' and 'natural', the neutrality ascribed to change, and the 'humanising' effect of art, constitute the aesthetic reading of urban space to which Rosalyn Deutsche refers in her essay 'Alternative Space':

> All connections between art and the city drawn by aestheticist tendencies within art history are, in the end, articulated as a single relationship: timeless and spaceless works of art ultimately transcend the very urban conditions that purportedly 'influenced' them (Deutsche, 1991b: 46).

FIGURE 9.3 *The Spirit of Free Enterprise* by Wendy Taylor, Canary Wharf, London. Source: Author's collection

It is this transcendence which enables it to mask development's contradictions. Yet other histories of art, for example in the mid-nineteenth century in France, or the years immediately following the October revolution in Russia, suggest a role for artists as agents of social change, a role currently reclaimed by participants in 'new genre public art' (Lacy, 1995). New, more participatory practices, influenced by Marxism, feminism and ecology, suggest a reintegration of art in everyday life, a model of the integration of theory and practice which can also be applied to design and planning. Perhaps this is Bloch's 'shaped beauty'.

Abstract cities

Before investigating the role of art in the entrepreneurial development of Cardiff, Birmingham and Sunderland, and alternative future possibilities, it is helpful to situate conceptualisations of the city which, while proclaiming freedom, impose control in a European construction of subjectivity. This further explains the suitability of modernist art, the 'timeless and spaceless' aesthetic of which follows from the same subjectivity, for complicity in the construction of Utopias.

One aspect of the Western, urban environment in general, and modernist architecture in particular, is its uniformity and dependence on order. The geometries of glass and steel echo a view of the world which excludes much of a city's potential for diversity and appropriation. Richard Sennett sees this alienation as rooted in Puritanism:

> Impersonality, coldness, and emptiness, are essential words in the Pro-testant language of environment; they express a desire to see the outside as null, lacking value. They are words that express a certain interest in seeing; the perception of outer emptiness reinforces the value of turning within (Sennett, 1990: 46).

This inwardness supports fantasies of an ideal world in which the subject is not threatened by disorder. It is a brittle kind of world in which to live, even in suburbia. David Sibley, citing images of whiteness as signs of purity in washing powder commercials, argues that societies produce a conformity which disables them from accepting 'difference' in the forms of racial minorities or marginalised publics (Sibley, 1995). In societies which have rigid frames of conformity, difference is seen to threaten the structure of power; to neutralise the threat, spatial boundaries are strong and enforced: 'In other words, the strongly classified environment is one where abjection is most likely to be experienced' (Sibley, 1995: 80). Marginalised publics then become (as if) without value in a world of impersonality and coldness. The emptiness of this world is also in the exclusion from it of histories which denote a more diverse pattern of sociation (through which marginal publics might be reinvested with value),[6] and in the privileging of a conceptualised city over a city of experi-ences and constantly mutating forms; the retreat to abstraction assists fantasies of complete renewal and control. The whole enterprise, in turn, rests on Cartesian dualism, a distrust of sense impressions leading to the construction of an inner world of subjectivity in which external reality is reduced to its representations.

Representations of space

Urban space is configured in city plans and architectural drawings, seen from the perspective of God's eye, from a position of power. It is an abstracted reading of space simulated by a view from a tall building (de Certeau, 1988). But it is 'representations of space' (Lefebvre, 1991: 38) which enable urban planning and architecture to be distanced from everyday life. Lefebvre writes of planning that while the study of problems of circulation leads to knowledge and technical applications, to define the city as (only) a network of circulation and communication, 'is an absolute ideology . . . proceeding from a particularly arbitrary and dangerous reduction-extrapolation' (Lefebvre, 1996: 98). The professions of the built environment dwell in 'representations of space' where description becomes prescription and concept represses diversity of form. Lefebvre gives a cameo of the architect:

> the architect ensconces himself in his [sic] own space. He has a *representation of this space*, one which is bound to graphic elements – to sheets of paper, plans, elevations, sections, perspective views of façades, modules, and so on. This *conceived* space is thought by those who make use of it to be *true*, despite the fact – or perhaps because of the fact – that it is geometrical (Lefebvre, 1991: 371).

For architect we might read designer or artist – professions ensconced in spaces from which to gaze upon a world which is as value-free as the spaces of the white-walled gallery of contemporary art. The professional ideologies of those who construct the environment, including makers of conventional public art, are thus affirmative of the values of high culture – a 'beauty' which does not admit utility. Just as 'beauty' resides in 'the eye of the beholder', so the framework of values which determines 'the beautiful' is socially produced; modernism inherits and embraces a notion of beauty separate from everyday life. Development uses this to lend itself a positive image.

Public art as a representation of entrepreneurialism

In context of government policies for urban development following the 'riot' in Toxteth in 1981, Luke Rittner, as Secretary-General of the Arts Council, wrote in the Foreword to *An Urban Renaissance*:

> Urban renewal continues to be high on the national agenda. . . . The arts are making a substantial contribution to the revitalisation of our cities (Arts Council, 1989: 1).

This publication foregrounded 16 projects seen as contributing to economic regeneration through improved business confidence and upgraded environments. The text continues:

> The arts often serve as the main catalyst for redevelopment. . . . American cities are increasingly pursuing the development of city centre cultural districts, which integrate cultural and commercial development. . . . Arts activities provide a community with a focus and increase its sense of identity . . . an increased awareness of the community's needs, a determination to achieve change (Arts Council, 1989: 5–6).

It appeals to developers to commission art which will enhance the value of developments, and notes a proposed European Visual Arts Centre in Ipswich, and the integration of art in the maritime quarter of Swansea. In all, it is a happy image of art as a sign of renewed prosperity; but there is a flaw in its assertions.

The visual arts lobby, it appears, appropriated a more supportable case for the role of larger cultural industries (such as the popular music scene in Merseyside and Manchester) in the generation of employment, and applied it to visual art in development, despite the fact that modern art is produced mainly by self-employed individuals and lacks a wide public. Further, the corporate development in which public art is frequently commissioned represents global rather than local interests; Saskia Sassen writes of cities which are 'transnational spaces' for interaction between corporate and state interests using information superhighways (Sassen, 1994). Those firms and governments, financial institutions, developers and urban development corporations, currently redetermine the city, bypassing residual populations to construct enclaved corporate 'places'. One of the means they acquire to do this, as seen at Broadgate and Battery Park City, is international modern art, but this has little to do with regeneration for local publics or local economies. Investigation of the policy for art in Cardiff Bay and its commissioning in central Birmingham demonstrates how this takes place in situations in which entrepreneurial approaches are adopted by public bodies. A brief view of art in the redevelopment of Sunderland suggests the beginning of an alternative.

A contradiction between the needs of development and ecology is seen in the policy for art in the redevelopment of the dock area of Cardiff. A series of art commissions, such as sculptures on roundabouts, has followed the implementation of the *Strategy for Public Art in Cardiff Bay*, produced by a team of public art managers in 1990 (Public Art Commissions Team, 1990); the strategy takes a mechanistic, funding-led approach which locates public art within a public sector drive to encourage, through incentives, private sector investment in the redevelopment zone. Just as art lends Broadgate and Canary Wharf a cultural mask, here also it is used to convey messages of quality and access to transglobal corporate culture, in a more marginal geography.

The development includes industry, leisure and the construction of housing facing the bay, an area hitherto of mud-flats which were the breeding and feeding grounds of wading birds. To provide vistas of clear, clean water, a barrage separates the bay from tidal waters, thereby destroying the ecological balance of the mud-flats. The *Strategy* states, under the heading 'key commissions': 'Entire barrage as a work of art. Collaboration between artist, architect and engineer' (Public Art Commissions Team, 1990: 22), giving the design of South Cove in Battery Park City by Mary Miss as a comparison – difficult to sustain in that Miss did not participate in the destruction of natural habitats, simply designing a viewing platform and collaborating with landscape designers on the deployment of wooden walkways, seating, planting and a vista of boulders, while any involvement of an artist in the barrage could be no more than cosmetic. The *Strategy* typifies the emerging genre of public arts management modelled on 'enterprise culture', with its absence of moral and social concern and uncritical allegiance to development as a market for arts management. In Cardiff Bay, contemporary art becomes the sign of 'success'. So, beside the abolition of the site's history, birds (who neither vote, pay taxes nor consume commodities) are cleared out so that developers may inscribe on the site the kind of waterside vistas with which they habitually illustrate their publicity brochures.

Birmingham City Council has, since the late 1980s, integrated art and urban design in the redevelopment of the city centre. New Street, Chamberlain Square, Centenary Square and Victoria Square together form a mainly pedestrianised redefinition of that centre in which the new International Convention Centre (ICC) is the organising principle, its public subsidy justified as a means to attract further private sector investment (see Chapter 6). The city's public art programme – which includes the commissioning of several sculptures in Centenary and Victoria squares, and the decorative brick paving and street furniture of Centenary Square designed by Tess Jaray and Tom Lomax – together with some investment in Victorian-style street furniture, is central to its construction of a cultural profile, which it sees as leading to economic regeneration. While the operation of a Percent for Art policy was restricted to 1% of the initial £80m. projected cost of the ICC, and reduced by £60 000 to fund a creche, a budget for public art of £740 000 was something of a landmark in the history of public art. Leaving aside the question of value for money in the scale of public investment in the ICC – was the council setting a mackerel to catch a sprat? – and the question of access to the city's new cultural delights for publics in outer areas badly served by public transport, there remains a question as to why the city invested so heavily in design and art for its public spaces.

Here, contradictions become evident. They do so at two levels: the general level of a contradiction between the cultural (civic) image of the new city centre as epitomised by Centenary Square, and its underpinning function as a 'central business district'; and at the particular level of a contradiction between two kinds of public art in Centenary Square. Beginning with the particular, the contrast of approaches is seen at its strongest in the comparison of Tess Jaray's paving design with Raymond Mason's fibre glass, *Forward* (1991), a kind of group statue representing the 'people' of Birmingham marching to a glorious, rather Socialist Realist, future (Figure 9.4); a local paper described it in terms of contemporary television pictures of statues of Lenin being craned out of squares in eastern Europe. Mason's stereotyped images (while depicting 'types' of more than one ethnic background) are rhetorical, could not be based on individuals, and in their monumental generalisation reflect a homogeneity of urban development; Jaray's paving and street furniture seeks to provide a space for conviviality, uniting function – seating, lighting, railings, litter bins,

FIGURE 9.4 *Forward* by Raymond Mason, Centenary Square, Birmingham. Source: Author's collection

a variety of spaces and views to be appropriated – with aesthetics, and (as music exists in performance) is completed by use. Jaray is influenced by the rhythms and vocabulary of Islamic traditions of decoration and sees in them a continuity rooted in everyday life. She has since designed paving and street furniture for the precincts of Wakefield Cathedral and the General Infirmary at Leeds, but in the subsequent development of Victoria Square, the hard landscaping was taken back into the control of council officers and the emphasis placed on commissioning large pieces of sculpture. One of these, Antony Gormley's *Iron Man* (1993), a piece of 'blue-chip' art, was commissioned by the Trustee Savings Bank; it is said to reference, in its rusted surfaces, the declined metalworking industries of the West Midlands (Figure 9.5). The involvement of the private sector implies that the dressing of the development in art serves its agenda as much as that of the local authority, but then the two are closely intertwined.

FIGURE 9.5 *Iron Man* by Antony Gormley, Birmingham city centre. Source: Author's collection

It is difficult to disentangle the public and private sectors in Birmingham's central redevelopment; while most of the £180m. capital for the ICC, which attracted a European Regional Development Fund grant of £49.75m., was raised by the National Exhibition Centre (NEC), the directors of the NEC were city councillors and its debt provision underwritten by the city. The alliance of civic and commercial interests saw public art as a means to create a favourable impression on both potential investors and residents; such image manipulation serves a logic of 'social control' (Hall and Hubbard, 1996). Public art in Birmingham, then, has a key role in the manufacture of 'place' on the model of cities in the USA. As Zukin writes:

> making a place for art in the city goes along with establishing a place identity for the city as a whole. No matter how restricted the definition of

art that is implied, or how few artists are included, or how little the benefits extend to other social groups outside certain segments of the middle class, the visibility and viability of a city's symbolic economy plays an important role in the creation of place (Zukin, 1996: 45).

Tim Hall takes a similar view of the cultural centre of Birmingham:

> In establishing a series of definitional centres, the city imagined itself within certain cultural spaces, those of high culture, international culture and spectacle (Hall, 1997: 215).

The symbolic definition of place, which implies boundaries between 'here' and 'not here' which dissect the city and its patterns of sociation, boundaries fixed according to certain values, is, of course, problematic; for the advocates of conventional public art, ensconced in 'representations of space', it is seen as a physical site, blank and ready for inscription, rather than a product of sociation.

Public art in Birmingham affirms a framework of corporate values in which the ICC, as site of business conventions and symphony concerts, is central spatially and conceptually. The spaces of Centenary Square and Victoria Square are open to use and offer clear lines of sight, are public space (in public ownership), not the pseudo-public space of shopping malls or corporate enclaves – that much is not in dispute; yet the presentation of these spaces as an image of the city for distanced consumption, and their remoteness for many publics in the city as well as doubts as to the extent to which the development has created more than low-paid, part-time employment for local people, indicates a strategy not of public beneficence but of hegemony. Selwood reports that the strategy for development began with investment in the NEC, which, since its opening in 1976, has attracted new business (and businesses) to Birmingham, and is based on the model of US cities such as Baltimore (Selwood, 1995). Baltimore's Harborplace was, like New York's South Street Seaport, developed by the Rouse Company in what has been taken as a successful model of localised preservation for new consumerist purposes (Gratz, 1989), money-making dressed not with art but with history; yet Birmingham goes further, in constructing an identity which only slightly references its past and depends heavily on visual qualities. The enterprise, though it incorporates several existing nineteenth- and twentieth-century buildings, is not that different from the construction of a large corporate enclave; this may not worry tourists strolling in the squares or being photographed next to Mason's sculpture, but its sculptures perform the same work of association as those in Broadgate. It could be argued that Birmingham's civic centre, transformed into a 'central cultural district' appealing to a middle-class public, is a 'central business district' appealing to corporate interests to the exclusion of disadvantaged groups and those living in peripheral urban areas (see Chapter 6). Its spaces are produced according to decisions as to what is, or is not, visible, according to specific concepts of order and the exclusion of disorder (Zukin, 1996).

SUNDERLAND: THE BEGINNINGS OF AN ALTERNATIVE

The St Peter's Riverside Sculpture Project, in the redevelopment zone of Sunderland, offers the beginnings of an alternative, community-related model for art in urban development. Although the zone is, like Cardiff Bay, regulated by an urban development corporation, and the site, from which all physical traces of shipbuilding have been erased, represents another abolition of history, and with it the main local source of employment, its planning has incorporated mixed use to a greater extent, including a large area of housing, part of the city's university, new light industry, a marina, and provision of a riverside walkway, and its construction has provided new employment.

The art project began in 1989 with a feasibility study carried out by the Artists Agency, a local cultural organisation with a strong record of community involvement. The study found that people in Monkwearmouth and Roker saw the arts as a means to stronger community identities; a group drawn from community groups, schools and churches met with artist Colin Wilbourn and staff of the Artists Agency to further research the possibilities. While one outcome of the residency, after six years, has been a series of figurative sculptures integrated with public paths and open spaces, using stone from nearby demolitions, the social aspects of art as process are equally important here. What is not intended is a memorial to shipbuilding, the loss of which, as the sculptor was informed at an early meeting of the steering group, remained like a private grief. But perhaps there is a trace of that loss in a brick relief, one of a series made by schoolchildren in collaboration with the artist and set in a wall by the new marina – *Windows and Walls* (1995), depicting a ship breaking up in a storm. A sad face peers out of the cabin (Figure 9.6).

The sculpture project in Sunderland has received a massively positive response from local people (a public living in the redevelopment zone, across the river from the main part of the city), who clearly feel an ownership of works such as *The Red House* (1994), a red sandstone representation of a house, as if a ruin and referencing the early history of the site as housing before it became a shipyard, with details such as a clock on the mantlepiece, a book on the table, plates in the sink, a pattern carved in the carpet.[7] It may be a nostalgic game of memories, and is regarded as marginal by those who establish the canon of contemporary sculpture; but in its effective engagement of a defined public, for whom it offers recognition that they are valued through their participation in place-making, it is an alternative model of art in urban development.

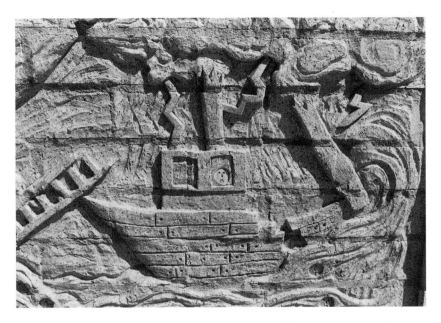

FIGURE 9.6 *Windows and Walls*, Sunderland. A collaboration between Colin Wilbourn and local schoolchildren. Source: Author's collection

CONCLUSION: IMAGINING POSSIBLE FUTURES

Returning to Bloch's 'shaped beauty' which is a 'work' of stating the pre-conscious and approaching a desire to be free from repression (in the psychoanalytic and social senses), and to an idea of art as a practice located in everyday life, the cases of art in Cardiff Bay and Birmingham, as Broadgate, seem to close rather than open such possibilities. Art's inclusion in development seems purchased by its complicity in the production of spaces of control.

Art and hegemony

To sum up the problem: conventional public art, as a veneer for urban development, is hegemonic, preserving the freedom for capital to increase and unfreedom of the majority population to determine the conceptualisation of the city. The economic interests of corporations, who finance, manage and occupy development, are advanced in ways involving both public sector subsidy, and a public presentation of development as beneficial, the latter assisted by cultural institutions dealing in aesthetic quality. The resemblance of development to art thus locates it in a domain which is outside political contention and contained in a territory of professional expertise. For Deutsche, spatial forms are social structures and art in Battery Park City 'conceals domination . . . rejects time', situating Battery Park City in a New York refigured as 'ghettoized and exclusionary' (Deutsche, 1991a: 202). The conventional, funding-led strategies for public art in the UK, looking to models such as Battery Park City, are unlikely to produce other than an art which affirms dominant 'enterprise' notions of the city. But perhaps that is a purpose for which late modernist art is well suited.

Deutsche begins from the image of homeless people in New York, their 'plight' seen by the dominant culture as an inevitable aspect of metropolitan life; she cites Lefebvre's view of space as reproducing social relations, and Manuel Castells's description of the city as a site of resistance to domination, summarised as 'the inscription of political battles in space' (Deutsche, 1991b: 161); she then argues that the divisive social policies which facilitate development justify themselves through art, as beauty:

> As a practice within the built environment, public art participates in the production of meanings, uses, and forms for the city. In this capacity, it can help secure consent to redevelopment and to the restructuring that make up the historical form of late capitalist urbanization. But like other institutions . . . it can also question and resist those operations, revealing the supposed contradictions of the urban process (Deutsche, 1991a: 164).

Acts of questioning and resistance open up other futures, and an alternative is emerging in art which is participatory, going beyond the consultation which took place in Sunderland to what might seem like a dissolution of the category 'art' yet which retains its basis in an imagination which is both political and aesthetic.

Art practice for sustainable urban futures requires a deconstruction of the division of art from everyday life, beauty from use; it supposes a reintegration of the 'representations of space' with (to use Lefebvre's other term for spatial practice) the 'representational spaces' of experience and appropriation, the spaces around the body (Lefebvre, 1991). James Donald writes:

> Rebuilding a living city – a city which jumbles together multiple and conflicting differences – therefore requires less a utopian plan than a poetics of political imagination (Donald, 1997: 182).

Perhaps this is close to Suzi Gablik's call in *The Reenchantment of Art* for a new paradigm in art, rejecting the masculine heroism of Cartesian dualism and modernism for a practice which is participatory and concerned with social and ecological healing (Gablik, 1991). Gablik sets out a 'reconstructive' alternative to deconstructive post-modernism, seeing the possibility for a reclamation of meaning and value in art and life through a recovery of a sense of the sacred. Much of the new art emerging in the USA today is participatory, informed by eco-feminism, and ephemeral. There is, then, a polarity: of conventional public art which, like architecture and planning, serves the dominant conceptualisation of the city; and art as social engagement, which seeks to imaginatively redefine the values and open up the potentials for 'beauty' of urban living.

Towards conviviality

What, then, can artists do? Perhaps, setting aside complicity, there are three possible strategies, with roots in the 1960s but taking new forms in the late 1990s, for work of the imagination in the face of current urban development: to resist; to seek out and expose the crevices of contradiction in development's argument; or to construct a new model of conviviality within the old model of control.

Resistance takes the forms of art which protests against racism, patriarchy and fascism, and of single-issue politics, as in road protest and its subculture, or the digging up of a freeway and symbolic planting of trees. It has been described as 'senseless acts of beauty' (McKay, 1996) and depends largely on direct action, performance and event.

A more subtle strategy is to make visible the contradictions of the dominant culture and power structure. Mierle Ukeles, in her long-term (unfunded) residency in the sanitation department of New York, seeks to do this in *Flow City*, creating visual access to the handling of the city's waste (Phillips, 1995). In an earlier project she shook the hands of every garbage collector, a group with whom most people do not shake (dirty) hands, but on whom they depend to keep the city 'clean'.

Most alternative models of community are located in rural areas. This does not mean there is no scope to set up models of mixed-use regeneration or permaculture in urban sites, and it is in the cultural diversity and 'edges' of the city that some of the most interesting challenges are found; groups such as Platform and The Art of Change in London (Miles, 1997), and The Power of Place in Los Angeles (Hayden, 1995), are constructing models of empowerment parallel to developments in urban planning and design, such as community-centred 'action planning'.

The work of 'beauty', in Bloch's sense, requires a new vision of urban space if it is to go beyond a game of appearances, and Lefebvre noted that the invention of linear perspective did not abolish the spaces around the body. Urban spaces are sites of constantly overlaid meaning, a palimpsest of 'disorder' (Sennett, 1996) in which artists can intervene. If there is anything more to what is shaped by art than complicity, then it is in a work of imagining a possible future in which urban dwellers occupy the place in which the form and concept of the city are produced, in which the spaces around the body are reinvested with meaning and joy.

NOTES

1. The term 'modernist' is used here to refer to a public art that is essentially placeless. As Lingwood argues: 'For much of this century, and for the whole of the modernist period, the question of place has been one of the least pressing of problems for the contemporary artist. In general, considerations of form and content have preceded and often precluded considerations of place or context' (1993: 21).

2. Similar findings in relation to other developments are reported by Roberts, Marsh and Salter (1993).

3. Laclau adds that a viable, democratic social order 'will not be a totally free society, but one which has negotiated in a specific way the duality freedom/unfreedom' (Laclau, 1996: 19).

4. The opposition of high art and everyday life is represented in Delacroix's *Liberty Leading the People* (1831); Liberty is a seductively dishevelled Greek allegory, while 'the people' are depicted in a realist language.

5. See Sennett (1994: 155). Sennett translates the inscription as 'The air of a city makes people free'; the freedom he suggests is from feudal ties of labour on the land and to enjoy new rights of property. Girardet (1992: 44) writes, romantically, of 'the "free" collaboration of merchants, priests, scholars, craftsmen [sic], and warriors that gave medieval cities their special dynamism'.

6. In this context see Hayden (1995) for a description of the work of The Power of Place, a group working with marginalised groups in Los Angeles to recover and make visible their memories of place.

7. The writer visited the site twice in the summer of 1996 and received many unsolicited appreciations from people living near by.

10

POPULAR CULTURE, CULTURAL INTERMEDIARIES AND URBAN REGENERATION

JUSTIN O'CONNOR

INTRODUCTION

The cultural industries have been increasingly seen by policy-makers and academics as a source of new employment possibilities, especially for mature industrial cities (Wynne, 1991; Lewis, 1992; Bianchini and Parkinson, 1993; Crewe and Haines, 1996). More generally, they have been characterised as at the leading edge of structural change associated with the shift from Fordist to Post-Fordist economies, where design-led, information-rich companies work within a new 'flexible' organisation of production (Hall and Jacques, 1989; Harvey, 1989a; Crook, Pakulski and Waters, 1992; Lash and Urry, 1994; Amin, 1995; Kumar, 1995). Cities are now beginning to address the problems of promoting such knowledge-intensive industrial growth in conjunction with cultural policies aimed at providing a creative milieu conducive to the attraction and retention of such knowledge or 'symbolic' specialists (Handy, 1994). Encouraging the 'creative city' is thus beginning to bring together cultural and economic policy at an ever more strategic level (Knight, 1992; Bianchini and Parkinson, 1993; Businaro, 1994; Landry and Bianchini, 1995; Mommaas and Corjan, 1995; O'Connor and Wynne, 1996a).

However, while the cultural industries are being approached as part of a wider repositioning by many cities, there has been very little research as to how these industries actually operate. Existing research has tended to focus on the larger, more established, sectors and on those that operate in ways accessible to standard economic analysis. There exists a serious lack of research among those micro and small enterprises (MSEs) which make up a large proportion of the cultural industries sector – its seedbed and innovative end. It is this MSE sector which is a major driver for innovation and creativity in the cultural industries sector, operating in complex interaction with the big cultural industry production and distribution companies (Lash and Urry, 1994). It is this sector which is most responsive to local milieu as an attractor (Clarke and Owens, 1996) and which provides the real source of a locally vibrant culture. The sector has frequently been invisible to research, either because it does not register on established indicators (Clarke and Owens, 1996; Mole, 1996) or because researchers have misrecognised its character – not 'real' jobs or simply niche employment for certain ('trendy', 'yuppie') groups (Zukin, 1991, 1995; Taylor, Evans and Fraser, 1996). Moreover, this sector is notoriously difficult to investigate (Purvis, 1996).

This situation has been mirrored in the lack of support for this sector by economic development and training agencies. There is a persistent tendency for these agencies to see the cultural industries sector as 'soft', 'volatile' and 'unbusiness-like'. Historically, this relates to a deep-seated divide between art and industry which has hampered the emergence of a design culture in traditional manufacture; but it also relates to a serious gap between orthodox models of business practice which underpin standard business education, training and support services and the way in which these small cultural businesses actually operate. This chapter will thus look at the cultural industries sector from the point of view of those actively engaged within it. However, I begin with a brief overview of the role of the cultural sector in some recent approaches to urban regeneration and examine some of the issues thrown up by the increasingly close connection between cultural producers and urban regeneration agencies. As such I examine the role of 'cultural intermediaries' in the work of Sharon Zukin and, to a lesser extent, Pierre Bourdieu.

A NEW MODEL FOR URBAN REGENERATION

In the mid-1970s, while the language of urban decline was reaching a peak in North American and European cities, there emerged a new discourse on the city – that of urban regeneration. A new valuation of city living, drawing on the lifestyles of artistic-Bohemian counter-cultures and a rediscovery of the heritage of late nineteenth- and early twentieth-century buildings and vernacular, gave rise to a new approach on behalf of urban developers. Rather than tear the old city centre down they began to see value in its preservation and 'repackaging'. The old working-class areas adjacent to the central business district (CBD), once the home of localised productive communities, are now being transformed into centres of consumption.

This transformation of the urban downtown vernacular is the focus of a famous book by Sharon Zukin, *Loft Living: Culture and Capital in Urban Change* (1982). The argument is well known, though its complexities are not often spelled out. SoHo was a downtown vernacular quarter juxtaposed to a financial district intent on expansion in alliance with political forces that saw no future for manufacturing in Manhattan. The future lay with finance. Yet the attempt at a classic 1960s style development was successfully resisted by the artist and ancillary community that had moved into the old nineteenth-century lofts, attracted by the cheapness, and space, in a New York now at the centre of the world art market. The victory, through an alliance with the growing communitarian and anti-development movement of the 1970s, led to the designation of SoHo as an artists' zone. But the end result was that manufacturing and 'down-market' retail was pushed out by this zoning, and the old vernacular became prime real estate as 'loft living' became a desirable commodity. Ultimately, many artists found it impossible to buy or rent, and any indigenous Bohemian artist ambience now became totally packaged, landscaped, for wealthy residents.

The narrative in *Loft Living* is complex. Zukin wants to show how those dealing in cultural knowledge were responsible for the transformation of SoHo, creating a new value that could be recouped by development capital. Two forces are prominent. Firstly, the historic buildings groups began to see the cast-iron frontages as aesthetic objects that should be protected rather than torn down. This represented an aestheticisation of past use which immediately devalued current industrial usage. Legitimate usage of these buildings was increasingly restricted to those who could appreciate this historic aesthetic. Secondly, the artists' community claimed for itself the central role in the revitalisation of this 'derelict' district. The economic importance of the artists to New York was stressed, but it was their cultural impact on the area that was primary. The Loft was a metonym for an artistic lifestyle which, drawing on the Bohemian and counter-cultural elements of the 1960s, would bring back a new vibrancy to the downtown. However, although this vibrancy drew on the qualities of the downtown vernacular, it was now based on a 'lifestyle' no longer linked to a productive community. It was a lifestyle that could be consumed, whether in the form of the newly fashionable lofts, or the Bohemian ambience of the restaurants, bars, galleries and shops.

Thus the aestheticisation of the vernacular achieved by cultural specialists mediated its emergence as an object of consumption. Once this cultural work had been done and the vernacular reabsorbed into the cultural landscape, the cultural specialists lost ground to those wielding economic power. In *Loft Living* the outcome is paradoxical, the victors ending up as losers. The developers quickly appreciated the importance of cultural consumption in the revalorisation of undervalued downtown areas. After SoHo they became proactive. But, as we shall see, the transposition of this model to other areas was not without its problems.

The logic of standardisation and repetition resulted in a rapid elaboration of regeneration models that could be sold to different city governments. By the late 1970s a number of large cities in North America, especially those with historic centres, began to invest in these regeneration models (Wynne, 1992; Bianchini and Parkinson, 1993). It was clear that while the 'artistic community' was often brought into these local growth coalitions, it was the developer who held the upper hand. The transformation of historical and/or waterfront areas into retail/leisure and residential developments was based around 'up-market' consumption coupled with a high cultural input. This could include cultural animation programmes, artists' residences, subsidised workshops and a public art that fitted well with a new 'post-modern' aesthetic. Such cultural input was encouraged by city governments employing 'percentage for art' programmes, and 'planning gain' initiatives. These areas had an 'up-market' ambience of speciality shopping and 'designer' restaurants and bars. They also aimed at establishing the sense of vibrancy that once attached to downtown areas, but a vibrancy now mediated by a Bohemian image represented by the presence of artists and 'artisans'. The vibrancy was one of an aestheticised nineteenth century, where the image of the downtown was reappropriated via the image of the artist-Bohemian in the guise of *flâneur*. The new-old spaces of urbanity were not the ones of the productive communities but the middle-class stroller who had the time and the cultural knowledge with which to stroll through the landscape and absorb the vernacular as aesthetic.

For Zukin, this aestheticisation of both the buildings and of the vernacular associations of downtown is a cultural work of landscaping. It is an imposition based on the cultural labour of a certain social group, though these may not be the main beneficiaries of this labour. This group Zukin calls the 'critical infrastructure', the cultural specialists who both promote and have expertise in the production and consumption of cultural goods. Zukin's work thus represents a severe indictment of the project of culturally based urban renewal, and of the role of cultural specialists as both mediators of the new consumption and as destructive of the values of place.

In *Landscapes of Power* (1991), building on her *Loft Living* (1982), Sharon Zukin attempts to analyse more closely this shift from production to consumption. For Zukin, this restructuring of the city centre is one not of the 'creative-destruction' of the built environment (Harvey, 1985a) but of the imposition of a new perspective on the city, a perspective based on cultural power. This cultural power emerges in a context of mass cultural consumption, giving rise to new mechanisms of inclusion and exclusion, and in a context where cultural consumption is increasingly abstracted from place-based production and consumption, and driven by globalised flows of information, capital and cultural goods (Harvey, 1992). This is crucial because it is precisely along these lines – the promotion of cultural production and consumption – of, and in, the city – and the attraction of cultural specialists, the creation of a critical infrastructure – that cities in Britain and western Europe have attempted to engage with the problems of the 'post-Fordist' city.

This new ersatz urban realm was initially characterised as 'post-modern' in a way that confused the debate. Both admirers and critics seemed to see this as an incarnation of the post-modern *Zeitgeist*, without inquiring as to how people used these places and to what extent, and on what basis, they were successful (Cooke, 1988; Chambers, 1991; Harvey, 1992). However, the transposition of the model of regeneration by developers is fraught with problems. If the imposition of a landscape of cultural power is to have any chance of success, even defined in narrowly economic terms, a 'critical infrastructure' is necessary. Despite Zukin's occasional functionalisms this critical infrastructure cannot just be created as required. As specialists and insiders they have a relative autonomy and a close knowledge of, and relationship to, place. It is in this context that a specific localisation involves a series of negotiations around the new emergent landscape which can be laden with meanings very different from the standardised 'post-modernity' of the development models.

ECONOMIC AND CULTURAL CAPITAL IN THE NEW URBAN REGENERATION

I have discussed some of the specifics of this attempted transposition else-where, with reference to Manchester (O'Connor and Wynne, 1996a, b). Here I simply want to flag up certain locally specific problems and broaden these out into some larger theoretical questions concerning the role of cultural intermediaries.

This model of urban regeneration development around historical–cultural urban centres was directly imported into Britain in the early 1980s. In this transposition the specificities of the local context were crucial. Firstly, there was the political context. The Thatcher government, having won a resounding second term in 1983, made 'inner cities' its target, especially after the riots in 1981 had underlined these inner cities as symbols of the 'British disease' (Robson, 1989). At this time the major British industrial cities were mainly held by the opposition Labour Party. Central government was loath to give these credit for any possible success in regeneration projects; moreover, they blamed these councils for the socialist-bureaucratic failures of the 1960s and 1970s. Urban regeneration was to be a symbol of Thatcherite Britain's escape from the cycle of postwar failure. The government wanted to use a free enterprise approach which demanded deregulation and a more flexible planning system. To this end, a whole series of legislative changes were enacted restricting local government, freeing private capital's access to public land and development contracts, and creating new semi-autonomous bodies outside the control of local government (Robson, 1989; Thornley, 1993). This in itself caused tremendous political opposition among local city élites, many of whom had looked towards the Greater London Council (GLC) model of democratic access and the redefinition of (multicultural) citizenship.

Secondly, this was a time of massive and catastrophic deindustrialisation. Apart from the social and economic consequences this was also a cultural dislocation, especially in the northern industrial towns where identity, much more than in the South, was centred on work, on manual and industrial labour (Shields, 1991; Mole, 1996; Taylor, Evans and Fraser, 1996). Urban regeneration was based on a conscious and explicit shift of the economic base from manufacturing to service industries, symbolised by the redrawing of the old historical industrial areas in terms of leisure and consumption. This generated widespread opposition and/or cynicism, which included 'cultural intermediaries'. But it also introduced a tension within the political élites in cities whose conversion to 'arts and culture'-led regeneration was never straightforward. Thus the work of urban regeneration was seen by many on the left as a symbol of Thatcherism, and despised as such. The debate around the yuppie, gentrification and 'post-modernity' in 1980s Britain cannot be divorced from this political context. This had direct impact upon the functioning of 'cultural landscaping' and the role of the 'critical infrastructure'.

Thirdly, though culture was increasingly promoted to the forefront of policy debates, the model of urban regeneration imported from North America was to be primarily driven through as an economic programme and 'arts and culture' justified in this context. This prioritisation of the economic was to set the agenda for debate around the arts throughout the 1980s, exemplified by John Meyerscough's studies. This can be interpreted as an explicitly hegemonic attempt to redraw the territories of economic and cultural capital in Bourdieu's sense. Thus 'arts and culture' were being promoted at a time when Thatcherism was engaged in an onslaught on the 'chattering classes', the liberal, intellectual, 'pinko' élites who had organised the 'culture of consensus' around a series of closely intertwined cultural institutions (Hewison, 1995). Culture-led urban regeneration was thus frequently pursued in opposition to this arts establishment who were held partly responsible for Britain's postwar social and moral decline (the sixties, permissiveness, etc.).

Fourthly, this was part of a larger problem. Cultural policy within cities had traditionally largely centred on the maintenance of the established institutions of civic culture – the library, concert hall/opera house, theatre, meeting hall and civic squares. Beyond these, 'arts and culture' usually fell under quite low-level officers – often merged with 'leisure' giving rise to the unkind stereotype of the officer responsible for the arts being an ex-public baths attendant. The increased profile of cultural policy did see a growth in the number and seniority of arts officers (O'Connor, 1991) but was it really a question of deep-seated institutional change, with city authorities revising their concepts of culture? The old 'city fathers', drawn from the industrial bourgeoisie, had a range of standard models to follow. The great town halls and warehouses of British northern cities had looked to well-codified architectural and cultural models (Briggs, 1963). The established canon of modernism, in both architecture and the arts generally, was under attack from Thatcherism, though it had arguably never been fully accepted in English culture. This coincided with the emergence of 'post-modernism', which was not so much a new style as an attack on all established canons as such. Whether legitimating the popular opposition to modernism or undermining the legitimating authority of the Academy, 'post-modernism' opened up the field to the new culture-led urban regeneration models and allowed some sharp developers to act as guides through the alien minefield of culture.

What I want to bring out here is that the relationship between cultural and economic capital is more complex than Zukin suggests, with the local context as crucial in the way in which this relationship is negotiated.

Significantly, cultural value is now related to economic value. From demand for living lofts and gentrification, large property-owners, developers, and elected local officials realised they could enhance the economic value of the centre by supplying cultural consumption (Zukin, 1991: 194).

But the initiation of culture-based urban renewal by a quasi-political body dominated by a 'free enterprise' ethos with an anti-cultural bias, and one that worked primarily with development capital using tried and trusted models for the formation of a cultural landscape, was damaging. It meant that the resultant development, while based on images of leisure and consumption and aestheticisation taken up by urban boosterists and sociologists alike (but with opposite intentions), had limited cultural resonance, and especially among those whose labour would be crucial to the transformation of the centre into cultural landscape – the cultural intermediaries. They were deeply cynical. Yet as Zukin argues:

> Gentrification received its greatest boost not from a specific subsidy, but from the state's substantive and symbolic legitimation of the cultural claim to urban space. This recognition marked cultural producers as a symbol of urban growth (Zukin, 1991: 194).

This legitimation on the part of the developers was in exclusively economic terms, where cultural production has direct economic consequences. In fact, the imposition of a model in these terms, which denied the autonomy of the cultural sphere, actually excluded cultural specialists – it refused their specific expertise. There are two points here.

Firstly, as Bourdieu (1984) makes clear, cultural capital, while related to economic capital, must also stress its distinction from it. Too obvious a connection undermines the claim of culture to be disinterested, to be 'more than' economics. While we must ask the question as to what extent this is true in the context of any post-modern cultural field, and indeed whether Bourdieu's fields themselves are not tied to an older notion of aesthetic distinction, it is certainly true that cultural value can suffer from too close a connection to the economic.

Secondly, cultural intermediaries are precisely that – intermediaries. They are able to interpret, package, transmit and manipulate symbols and knowledge in a way that produces new value. As both producers and consumers they are able to claim an expertise, a close knowledge of the inner dynamics of the cultural field (Martin, 1991). Thus in Manchester developers attempted to sell 'city centre living' in the absence of an image of city living, of a vibrant twenty-four-hour city centre outside of working hours and of a 'European' city of sociability across a range of social groups – the absence, that is, of a highly valued centrality. When this workable image did emerge it was within a cultural sphere associated with a pop music scene, specifically the rave and dance scene, which was only latterly picked up by the urban regeneration élites. The critical infrastructure thus worked independently of, or in opposition to, the developers' cultural model (O'Connor and Wynne, 1996c). Thus, although the rave and gay scenes in Manchester, for example (O'Connor and Wynne, 1996c) were annexed by parts of the regeneration élite there were many problems as regards other regulatory and legitimising authorities (police, magistrates, etc.). Thus the work of cultural producers emerged within a complex field in which the 'state's substantive and symbolic legitimation of the cultural claim to urban space' (Zukin, 1991: 194) was far from fixed, and was indeed a product of negotiation and conflict.

NEW CULTURAL INTERMEDIARIES

The term 'new cultural intermediaries' derives from Bourdieu. In *Distinction* (1984) he identifies a new middle class which breaks with the established field of the petty bourgeoisie and attempts a radical challenge to the existing hierarchies of cultural distinction. In this, their 'organic intellectuals' derive from the field of the new media and other new professions associated with lifestyle, leisure, self-exploration, etc. They articulate and guide this new middle class through the new landscape of consumer society with which they are so closely associated. This notion has been extensively adopted as an explanatory schema for 'post-modernity', most characteristically in the work of Mike Featherstone (Featherstone, 1991). A crucial characterisation of those at the vanguard of cultural change, those new cultural intermediaries who (adopting a mixture of Gramsci and Elias) would expand the values of the 'counter-culture' to a wider sphere, was that they promoted 'the aestheticisation of everyday life'.

For example, the growing popularisation of the artistic-Bohemian lifestyle was part of a much more widespread shift in cultural hierarchies and an increasingly reflexive construction of lifestyle. Consequent on the expansion of higher education and the cultural radicalisms of the 1960s, knowledge of cultural goods expanded enormously. At the same time the transgressions of the artist, the experimentation with new experiences, the desire to create the self as a work of art – all these became absorbed into a wider culture. This fed into the growing incorporation of art and culture into the design of consumer goods, and into the techniques of advertising and marketing. In *Landscapes of Power* (1991) Zukin is much more explicit in linking the operations of the new groups of cultural specialists to both the promotion of consumption and the gentrification of the city.

> . . . mediating the dialectic of power and centrality depends on a critical infrastructure for cultural production and consumption. Here I am thinking of men and women who produce and consume, and also evaluate, new market-based cultural products. Like artists, they both

comment critically on, and constitute, a new kind of market culture. Their 'inside' view opens up new spaces for consumption. They enhance market values even when they desperately want to conserve values of place (Zukin, 1991: 201–2).

This is the tragic function of the counter-culture. Ultimately, their concern with culture merely opened a new field of consumption, which, exposed to the forces of abstraction and internationalisation, destroyed the object of their desire. For Zukin, the role of these cultural specialists is functional to social distinction in an age of 'mass produced and mass distributed culture'. In the absence of 'hierarchies based on personal networks and social position', cultural specialists, 'the critical infrastructure', emerge to promote and to guide us through the new landscape of consumption.

> Today cultural consumption follows the lead of several mediators: the artist, the primary consumer, and the designer, who interpret desire and direct the consumer to equate awareness of consuming with awareness of life, and the line producer in new service industries, catering to a jaded consumer 'who yearns for homespun to ease the chintz' (Zukin, 1991: 204).

The question this opens up is one Featherstone (1991) has also raised – is this merely the jockeying for position of a new post-modern class fraction or part of a wider series of cultural shifts? Our research would indicate the latter. In doing so we would also add that the elaborate hierarchies established by Bourdieu, as different social groups compete for cultural distinction, should perhaps be seen as applicable to the era of scarcity (in Beck's (1992) notion). In an era of post-scarcity the cultural hierarchies are much more fragmented and plural. This has enormous consequences for any attempt to account for cultural change in the contemporary city.

Cultural intermediaries and cultural industries

Here I want to shift focus and look more closely at those concerned with the production of culture at the (local) city level, drawing on two research projects completed between 1992 and 1994 at the Manchester Institute for Popular Culture (MIPC): 'Metropolitan Lifestyles and Post-modern Consumption' and 'Cultural Production in the City' (O'Connor and Wynne, 1996b).

'Metropolitan Lifestyles and Post-modern Consumption' was an ESRC-funded research project (Featherstone, O'Connor and Wynne, 1994) examining new forms of cultural consumption and the construction of lifestyle in the contemporary city. These new forms were associated with a range of developments which included: a dramatic increase in the production and consumption of symbolic goods; the shift of consumption from use value to sign value; the destabilisation of established symbolic hierarchies through the articulation of alternative tastes and styles; the rise of popular and commercial cultures as alternative forms challenging established 'high culture' and the emergence of new urban spaces creating 'play spaces' for new forms of sociability. In turn, it was anticipated these would lead to new forms of display and social mixing representing a movement away from rational goal directed activity, permitting a more playful, carnivalesque exploration of emotions – a preoccupation with the aestheticisation and 'stylisation of life' as opposed to more fixed lifestyles.

This research represented a systematic examination of these processes in the context of cultural consumption in Manchester city centre and uncovered important tendencies in and the lifestyles of selected inhabitants. These included, firstly, the emergence of a 'mix and match' lifestyle among the 18–35 age group who are most prominent in the use of the cultural and leisure facilities of the city centre. This lifestyle emphasised 'anti-rationalist' values usually associated with artistic, Bohemian or counter-cultural milieux – intuition, self-expression, creativity, the exploration of subjectivity and the body, pleasure and hedonism – but is linked to a keen sense of the positional and distinction value of symbolic goods and services. Secondly, there appears to be an extension of the notion of 'cultural intermediaries' from the new middle class to a much wider range of the population, through the increased involvement of popular culture in the creation of the new city-centre sites of consumption. Thirdly, it appears that these new and extended forms of cultural consumption, characterised by rapid turnover and complex distinctions, fed directly into cultural production in order to supply these new markets. These findings form the basis of a large-scale investigation into new forms of cultural production in the city. The research indicated that for those involved:

- Making money and making culture were often one and the same activity
- There was a frequent inability and even antipathy to making a distinction between work time and leisure time
- There was a heavy reliance on informal networks for information and ideas
- There was an emphasis on intuition, emotional involvement, immersion in the field and an 'insider's' or 'enthusiast's' knowledge of the market
- There was a realised ambition to 'work for themselves' and to 'break the 9–5'

The findings of these studies pointed towards theoretical work in the social sciences which attempted to ground some of the claims of the 'post-modernity' debate in empirical research (O'Connor and Wynne, 1996c). The research also linked to the debates around 'reflexivity', which has been the subject of numerous recent conferences and papers (Beck, 1992; Beck, Giddens and Lash, 1994; Lash and Urry, 1994), arguing that large-scale social processes meant that the individual was decreasingly presented with objective social roles and had to construct her/his own identity in a situation of fluidity, anxiety and risk. The individuation of consumption thus brings an increased reflexivity, which tends to move away from a predominantly cognitive to a more aesthetic reflexivity, increasingly mediated through aesthetic objects or symbolic goods.

In summary, this research suggested: firstly, that if consumption is increasingly reflexive then so too is the production intended to satisfy that market; secondly, in targeting these forms of consumption the cultural industries sector uses different forms and circuits of knowledge, has a different conception and relationship to the consumer, and has a different approach to the very notion of 'running a business' – different, that is, from the conceptualisation of this business practice in mainstream business education and training.

Other research at MIPC conducted for Manchester City Council and North West Arts (Wynne, 1991) emphasised the divergence between cultural industries and orthodox business models, highlighting the gap between this sector and the local business training and support services. It stressed the negative experience of this education and training expressed by these businesses and the difficulties encountered by these businesses in being taken seriously by larger firms and the established business infrastructure (banks, chambers of commerce, training and enterprise councils (TECs), Enterprise Allowance, Business Link, etc.). This was confirmed by the ethnographic work among postgraduate researchers at MIPC: aside from certain technical knowledge (accountancy, grants, basic office computing) most of these small cultural businesses found the language and the theoretical models of business education disempowering, alienating and frequently useless. Enterprise Allowance (now New Business Support) and other Business Start-up schemes provided many of these businesses (very few with any formal business education) with free, compulsory (if benefits were to be received) business training courses. The language and models used were felt to have little relevance to both the way in which they worked and the motives for setting up business in the first place. There were exceptions, where courses were created by individuals active in the cultural industries sector. This notion of 'soft' business education was, however, criticised and then dropped by the local TEC (Lovatt, Milestone and O'Connor, 1994; O'Connor and Wynne, 1996a; Purvis, 1996). This criticism derived from and reflected traditional models of business theory and education. However, our initial research suggested that these producers use distinct circuits of knowledge which allow them to access these markets, relying on knowledge derived more from 'cultural' discourses than 'business' discourses.

Thus cultural businesses tend to operate in ways very different from standard models of business practice which underpin orthodox business education, training and support services. Much of this could be described as modernist; in fact, research suggests that small cultural businesses operate more as 'post-modern' organisations. This is demonstrated in Table 10.1 which pulls out the differences between cultural/traditional, modern/post-modern and Fordist/post-Fordist.

T A B L E 10.1 Differences between 'modern' business organisations and 'post-modern' cultural producers

Business area	Cultural producers, post-Fordist/ post-modern	Traditional business organisations, Fordist/modern
Market	The market is understood as subjective and volatile, linked to both mind and body, is defined by the ephemeral, the cultural and the symbolic. Cultural producers understand the market through informal networks, the 'story'. Marketing is adaptive, intuitive, reflexive, unstructured, informal and symbolic	The market is understood as objective and the consumption strategies of consumer linked to the rational and the mind, i.e. intentional. Business organisations are distinct and outside of the market and they understand it through formalised, quantitative market research methods. Marketing is strategic, objective and uses the tools of the marketing mix in a structured and formal way
Product and production	Design intensive, aesthetic, cultural and symbolic. Individualistic and embedded in the market. Production strategies demonstrate flexible specialisation to accommodate volatile markets	Formula design and linked to market research findings. Multiplicity of product linked to main design theme. Piloted and then developed. Uniformity of production strategies linked to regularised markets, e.g. seasonal fashion industry
Lifestyle and the work/leisure distinction	Cultural producers do not necessarily see the work/leisure distinction. They are often seen as cultural intermediaries who become a focus for those attempting to create identity through lifestyle	Business organisations marketing a leisure activity rather then an identity forming lifestyle option. Not a leader of change but responsive to change
Business goals and business success	Linked to lifestyle and the cultural. Business success not primarily viewed as profit but at the cutting edge of change and development in the particular cultural sphere	Profit and margins. Achievement of performance indicators. Growth and market share
People and management styles	Recruitment – informal and from same cultural milieu. Contracts – informal and fragmented. Management style – participative, stakeholder, pluralistic, decentred, empowering	Recruitment – formal and from a variety of labour markets. Contracts – formal and often short-term. Management style – hierarchical, centralised, authority and power, a unitary perspective

continues

TABLE 10.1 *continued*

Business area	Cultural producers, post-Fordist/ post-modern	Traditional business organisations, Fordist/modern
Business knowledge and business learning	Business knowledge acquired through experience and networks. The knowledge is subjective and contextual, cultural and embedded to the local. It is fluid and multidisciplinary. Business learning of cultural producers demonstrates a constructivist perspective on learning	Business knowledge acquired putting orthodox business theory into practice. Business knowledge is based on research and is objective and global. Business learning is viewed as competencies that need mastering

CONCLUSION: LOCAL CULTURES AND THE CREATIVE CITY

What does this 'post-modern' mode of cultural business imply for creative cities?

Academics have attempted to characterise the present structural change as a shift from Fordism to post-Fordism – involving the multiplication and fragmentation of markets, along with the acceleration of product turnover and volatility (or fickleness) of demand (foregrounding the marketing and design functions of firms). Flexible specialisation (Lash and Urry, 1994) means margins of competitiveness depend on the generation and exploitation of new knowledge; successful firms are R&D and innovation intensive, constantly redesigning business organisation to create the flexibility required to accommodate this. In terms of the marketing and design functions, this capacity can be defined as a cultural capacity – the ability to accumulate knowledge and manipulate symbols. This is clearest in those sectors which deal primarily with the production and distribution of symbolic goods – the cultural industries. This sector can be seen as cutting edge; 'ordinary manufacturing industry is becoming more and more like the production of culture. It is not that commodity manufacture provides the template, and culture follows, but that cultural industries themselves provided the template' (Lash and Urry, 1994: 123).

This has also been termed the 'informational economy', referring to 'a new form of economic production and management' characterised by the fact that productivity and competitiveness are increasingly based on the generation of new knowledge and on the access to, and processing of appropriate information' (Castells and Hall, 1994). Thus the transformational aspects of this information society include a new and important association between the productive elements of the economy (knowledge generation and information processing) and the cultural capacity of society – that is, its ability to accumulate knowledge and manipulate symbols (Shearman, 1995; Castells, 1994).

Cities can be seen as nodes within a global economy (Sassen, 1991) with the intersection of the global and the local becoming crucial in local economic development. While control and distribution functions may remain in global-ised (or centralised) hands, this can only be so on the basis of a sophisticated understanding of consumption patterns in specific and often very local-ised markets (Sassen, 1994). It is a knowledge of the local mediation of the global circuits of 'signs and space' that frequently defines the success of cultural industries in the local city context (Lash and Urry, 1994). This implies a knowledge of the local, but also a deep understanding for these specific forms of consumption. It is this knowledge that allows cultural industries to both innovate in the local sphere and extend their operations beyond the local.

The above points underline the new centrality of knowledge, with an increased emphasis on the cultural and symbolic aspects of this knowledge. Local economic development increasingly depends on the mobilisation of this knowledge, but the ability to do this depends on a range of historically specific social, economic, cultural and political factors (Knight, 1992; Businaro, 1994; Landry and Bianchini, 1995; Mommaas and Corjan, 1995; Mole, 1996; O'Connor and Wynne, 1996b). As a particular kind of knowledge-intensive industry, and as one especially dependent on a negotiation and articulation of a local place-based cultural milieu within a 'global space of flows', the cultural industries sector represents an important indicator of the ability of particular cities to respond to the challenge of global restructuring. As a recent work on Manchester argued:

> . . . the youth culture industry in Manchester has a more general pur-chase on the whole social and economic formation: an expression of the very rapidly changing economic circumstances of the 1980s (the 'New Times' of 'disorganised global capitalism'). . . . There is little question that this challenge is quite well understood amongst those employed in the local high-technology and 'cultural intermediary' professional classes in Manchester, particularly, we think, in the fast-moving media, popular music, leisure and communication sectors (Taylor, Evans and Fraser, 1996: 272, 303–4).

However, while a thriving cultural industries sector may indicate a level of local creativity, it is the ability to nurture this sector and link its creativity (of business and milieu) to wider economic innovation and development which is a crucial test of the adaptability of cities to this global challenge. If this ability to develop and mobilise the knowledge base of the city is (among other things) a cultural capacity, then cultural policy is due to be more closely integrated with local economic strategies – and so has been the case, with very mixed results (O'Connor and Wynne, 1992, 1996c; Bianchini and Parkinson, 1993; O'Connor, 1995).

As stated earlier, academic writing and policy are increasingly directed at this sector yet there has been no detailed research as to how it actually operates. There is hardly any research into those creative urban milieux within which cultural businesses (especially at the pop cultural end) tend to emerge. There is a need to look at how milieu, networks, districts/quarters and embeddedness may operate within this sector (Harrison, 1992; Lovatt, Milestone and O'Connor, 1994; Kumar, 1995; Crewe and Haines, 1996). There is a growing research into the city as a distinct economic generator – this is only now being linked to the question of local city cultures and the ability to change/adapt (Castells, 1994; Castells and Hall, 1994). Cultural policy previously aimed at attracting 'knowledge specialists' must also begin to promote innovation and creativity – to become 'intentional' (Businaro, 1994). This depends on linkages, networks, communication and openness that themselves cannot be divorced from the particular history of the city, its particular 'structure of feeling' (cf. Taylor, Evans and Fraser, 1996).

11

WRITING THE NEW BARCELONA

DONALD McNEILL

INTRODUCTION

Over the last couple of years, I have been endeavouring to write up doctoral research I have been doing in Barcelona. My aim has been to provide a historical interpretation of the emergence of what I call the 'New Barcelona', which I use to denote a set of discourses related to urban change. This has overlapped with the theoretical approaches developed under the umbrella of urban entrepreneurialism, which have tried to uncover the social, political and cultural processes at work in rapidly changing cities such as Barcelona. However, the representation of such processes is problematic. As the work of Walter Benjamin shows, the city is not only a text to be decoded, it is also 'a space to be written' (Gilloch, 1996: 181). It is dangerous to deny the role of the researcher or author in representing what s/he finds out. So my focus in this chapter is on the writing process, the politics of representation in the construction of an academic text. Why such an interest in writing? Within urban studies, several geographers have argued for a greater aware- ness of the politics of representation (P. Jackson, 1991; Massey, 1991; Thrift, 1993; Gregory, 1994). Writing is clearly a key issue in the construction of meaning. For writing is about more than just stylistic flair or communicative skill:

> Although we usually think about writing as a mode of 'telling' about the social world, writing is not just a mopping-up activity at the end of a research project. Writing is also a way of 'knowing' – a method of discovery and analysis. By writing in different ways, we discover new aspects of our topic and our relationship to it. Form and content are inseparable (Richardson, 1994: 516).

The way accounts are written and constructed, therefore, is deserving of more detailed analysis.

The chapter is in four parts. First, I discuss some of the particular problems faced in writing about the 'entrepreneurial city'. Second, I suggest that the academic – rather than being a detached expert – has a potentially fruitful role as a (critical) story-teller. Third, I discuss the specific problems in deciding which tales to tell, and from what perspective. Fourth, I consider the relationship between textual strategy and the purpose of the story-telling, through a discussion of theory, authorial presence, style and rhetoric.

PROBLEMS WITH THE ENTREPRENEURIAL CITY

Working within the general area of urban entrepreneurialism positioned me in a very particular way when I began my research in Barcelona. Certain problems came to the surface as I gathered data which pushed me away from interpreting Barcelona as an 'entrepreneurial city', tempting though it was.

First, 'cities' themselves are representations (King, 1996a; Shields, 1996), ascribing unity to a highly complex set of social phenomena. Describing Barcelona, Manchester or Glasgow as 'entrepreneurial cities' is problematic in that it makes a leap from being a single concept – a transition in urban governance – to a master-narrative capable of accounting for the whole set of changes going on in that discursively constructed place.

Second, and similarly, while a focus on the landscape of the 'entrepreneurial city' can be suggestive for research – '[h]ow a city looks and how its spaces are organised forms a material base upon which a range of possible sensations and social practices can be thought about, evaluated, and achieved' (Harvey, 1989a: 66–7) – the temptations involved may be too great. A focus on the changing urban landscape can help dramatise accounts of economic or political transition, but an over-reliance on the icons of urban change such as the heritage site or the waterfront development may overstate the case for transformation. Dramatic new buildings are one thing, shifts in governance or power are another.

The third problem lies in the possible obliteration of how local narratives of change differ from more general theoretical accounts (Jackson, 1991; Thrift, 1993). The case of Glasgow demonstrates that local protest was focused on the attempt to play down the city's Red Clyde heritage by the ruling Labour council (Boyle and Hughes, 1991). This was interpreted by some local groups as a case of 'selling out', rather than it being attributed directly to structural change in the Scottish economy. This raises the question of what constitutes knowledge. While academics may be confident in the superiority of their interpretation of events, the very fact that local narratives are circulating suggests a different level of reality which has to be captured.

Fourth, a focus on entrepreneurialism may divert attention from other relevant discourses. The concept seems to have emerged from some sort of mid-Atlantic theoretical and empirical convergence. Applying it to Barcelona would miss one pretty hefty local narrative: the fact that the city had thrown itself forward with such haste was closely related to its delayed or halted development under dictatorship. The transition to democracy was a process which ran through virtually all the accounts of the redevelopment of the city. So there is a question of the concept's sensitivity to local narrative.

These issues raise some difficulties for the researcher seeking to position her/his written accounts. These difficulties have been faced by other disciplines which have embraced qualitative methods, and one of the ways round the impasse which has been proposed is that of the researcher as story-teller, an approach that may be harnessed in writing the 'entrepreneurial city'.

THE RESEARCHER AS STORY-TELLER

Contrary to positivist assumptions about conducting fieldwork, the researcher is 'positioned, interconnected, and involved in the social and cultural relations under study. . . . So, rather than claiming some sort of separate Archimedean point from which the world can be critiqued, the researcher's viewpoint is largely a product of social relations both within the academy and between it and the world at large' (Cook and Crang, 1995: 7). How is this to be reflected in the text? Quite early on in my research I adopted a working title for my thesis: 'Tales from the New Barcelona'. It was taken from John van Maanen's *Tales From the Field* (1988):

> My use of the folksy term 'tales' to refer to ethnographic writing may seem somewhat curious to readers. I use the term quite self-consciously to highlight the presentational or, more properly, representational qualities of all fieldwork writing. It is a term meant to draw attention to the inherent story-like character of fieldwork accounts, as well as to the inevitable choices made by an author when composing an ethnographic work (van Maanen, 1988: 8).

This idea of the researcher as a story-teller is one that holds a great appeal. It allows positionality to be acknowledged, and it allows a break from the curse of the disembodied, male academic voice which – all too often – researchers adopt unquestioningly. Story-telling has a long track record in both sociological and anthropological ethnographies, but within urban geography there have been few attempts to write in a more personal way. Here I briefly consider three recent works which explore urban change in a way which highlights the variety of techniques which can be used to convey positionality in writing the city.

• *City of Quartz* (Davis, 1990). Thank God for the paperback version, because the hardback is not the most mobile of books. This book has influenced me enormously, not least in demonstrating that the city conceals a vast amount of fascinating stories. Davis's goal appears to be to write a radical history of Los Angeles, in contrast to a boosterist history, and through a thematic approach – the privatisation of the city, the role of religion, a history of political élites, to name a few – brings together a comprehensive account of the city's politics. I think it has two striking features of particular interest. The first is the apparent absence of a theoretical framework. Despite Davis referring the reader to one of his previous books for his political analysis, this is primarily a set of narratives with only an oblique reference to a theoretical project. This, however, does not preclude it from contributing to theoretical developments. On the contrary, Davis has managed to 'make the city come alive: to illuminate the most local of detail in such a way that it reveals a far wider canvas' (Gregory, 1994: 305). But can it be distinguished from journalism? A glance at his extensive endnotes demonstrates the breadth and depth of his reading on the city, and his account gains legitimacy – I argue – from this wealth of local detail. He thus donates to the urban studies canon an invaluable resource for those seeking to develop theory or – as in my case – to attempt similar exercises in other places. The second point is Davis's vividly rhetorical written style, a New Journalism influenced spree of freely rendered adjectives, which shows how persuasive close reference to historical records can be when combined with a powerfully argued political stance.

• *A Journey through Ruins* (Wright, 1993). What I like about this is the way Wright pursues a free-floating myth (the postwar decline of Britain) through a combination of short ethnographic 'street' pieces, longer and tenaciously pursued pieces of investigative journalism, and more historically based accounts. The result is a loose compilation of articles written over a period of time, unshackled by an over-enthusiastic attention to theory (which, as we know, has a tendency to swing in and out of fashion). Wright is inspirational in two ways: first, in his references to real places and streets which provides a sense of immediacy and a sensitivity to place (something which Davis by and large does not do); second, in his ability to pick up the thread of a promising story and pursue it through interviews, observation and – presumably – a sizeable collection of press cuttings.

• *Roissy Express* (Maspero, 1994). In this ethnographic travelogue around the suburban rail network of Paris. Maspero completely disavows pursuing any preconceived academic notion at the beginning of the book, going instead for an exploratory stroll with his photographer companion, Anaïk Frantz, to see what they could find. What I took from this was an awareness of how good travel writing can fill a place with meaning, by bringing out the political strands of everyday life gleaned from roadside or cafe conversations, from an awareness of landscape history, from local stories and anecdotes. It is as unforced as Davis's is tightly marshalled: nothing very much happens, but in the course of the pair's peregrinations and musings, a great deal of reflection on the urban experience ensues. The prose is simple but effective, written in the third person but highly personalised (recalling the emotional state of the travellers at each stage on the trip). What emerges is a destigmatisation of the unmapped towns around the periphery of Paris, giving their journey considerable political worth.

Each of these books shows different ways of representing and excavating local knowledge. Each in its way contributes something to the research and story-telling process. Each provides an 'excavation' of sorts, the culling of meaning from a huge variety of sources, be they old academic theses, gossip, or in-field insight. But, to restate the point raised at the start of this section, story-telling has another purpose too. With its fictional connotations it makes explicit the positionality of knowledge and the centrality of the academic in providing one of many possible interpretations. With this in mind, my preliminary notes on writing the New Barcelona are as follows.

WHICH STORIES TO TELL . . .?

The main problem I have had to face in constructing my text has been the sheer quantity of available data. The frightening thing was that by the time I'd spent several months in Barcelona immersed in archives and the city's social life (in the widest sense), the original research questions had been overwhelmed by a stream of new possibilities, as I turned up more and more data. Which stories to tell? And from what perspective?

Obviously, I did not turn up in Barcelona with a completely blank mind. I was there because I had certain theoretical insights which I had developed in the pre-fieldwork stage, which by and large suggested that I was looking out for a post-Fordist/entrepreneurial city. I had a fair degree of personal insight through an exposure to urban issues. And I had the benefit of a couple of books written on the city which helped to raise some of the issues peculiar to Barcelona (Hughes, 1992; Vázquez Montalbán, 1992). Following an inductive approach – allowing constant mental recoding of the data to structure the research and text – I gradually began to be aware of certain themes forming and re-forming. This could be frustratingly difficult to harness. Themes emerged within themes, new perspectives appeared with the discovery of another piece of data, and so on. I consoled myself with the thought that I could not be accused of making the facts fit a wider theoretical scheme.

Calculating that five stories were the maximum I could do justice to in the format of a doctorate, I have currently settled on the following. First, the idea of the city as an architectural Utopia, as reflected in the awesome amount of space it has received from the architectural press and the awesome amount of artistic and architectural monuments existing in the city (I include here urban design and public art artefacts). Second, the ubiquity of the mayor, Pasqual Maragall, in representations of the city's redevelopment. Third, the notion of the city's redevelopment as being the latest stage in a longer story, the heroic struggle of planners, engineers, architects and politicians to cope with the changing and expanding city (made 'real' in Eduardo Mendoza's novel *City of Marvels* (1988)). Fourth, the politics of memory. The attempts by local cynic, gastronome, communist and novelist Manuel Vázquez Montalbán to recuperate or retain the city's sense of history. Fifth, the grounding of the 1992 Olympics within Spain's wider political history, which reflects back on the status of Barcelona within the Spanish national myth.

Why did I choose the stories I did? Once theory is taken out of being an explicit guide to the research process, how research choices are made is a bit of a black box. I think I could point to six criteria which determined the selection of these themes, in no particular order of importance. First, I had to remember that I was working from a reasonably tight overall theme – the emergence of a 'New' Barcelona – and that each of the stories had to explicitly relate to some aspect of it. They could overlap, or deal with the same issues from different perspectives, but at the end of the day they had to come together to provide a collective – if partial – explanation of some of the dimensions of the New Barcelona. Second, they had to be 'thick'. There had to be scope to research them. A series of in-depth interviews with the mayor would have been very interesting, but any more than minimal access to him was impossible, so I focused on constructing a biography from his books and from archives. Third, they had to be 'balanced'. I did not want a whole load of chapters about the state. I wanted to focus on more than just landscape. I wanted to look at the past as much as the present. Basically, they needed to be varied in order to provide a greater degree of persuasiveness. Fourth, they had to be interesting. By this I mean that they had to provide a new slant on the existing theory, something which would make the final document a useful resource for other researchers in the area. Fifth, they had to reflect issues of élite power. It was obvious that some people were more important than others in creating the public discourse. The mayor of Barcelona had a greater part in the creation of the myth of the New than, say, FC Barcelona's goalkeeper. Similarly, the Olympics was a crucial event in the history of the city: it had to be given full treatment. Sixth, I wanted there to be scope in each story to express both a temporal dimension – a notion of change – and a spatial dimension, which involved the place of Barcelona as a material (and metaphorical) site.

The emergence of these stories was, therefore, a very messy process. It involved making connections between insights which would suddenly present themselves at inconvenient times and places. Rather than the coherent research diary which some people seem able to keep, my field notes consist of sheets of narrow-lined paper covered in indecipherable scrawl, half-written paragraphs which seemed brilliant at the time, scribbled Catalan verb conjugations, references, rewritten introductions which always have 'Harvey (1989)' somewhere within, and – above all – pages and pages of lists of chapter headings. I think this last point is the most significant: the agonising decision about where to put a particular incident or piece of information. The Olympics, for example: should it have a chapter on its own, or should the event be subsumed into other themes? This changed as the research went on. Initially, I began thinking about it through the lens of the literature on 'spectacle' (for example, Ley and Olds, 1988), describing the opposition of local left groups within a social control logic. Then it seemed more useful to approach it from the role Barcelona played within various political projects, of the role of place within political hegemony. Currently, I plan to write this story from the viewpoint of the recent Spanish political scene. Hence having decided which stories to convey, the little problem that remains is that of writing it, as I now describe.

. . . AND HOW TO WRITE THEM?

I am still only at the beginning of the stage commonly known as 'writing up', but there are four issues which I feel to be of particular relevance at this moment in time. They are as follows: what to do with theory, how far should I write myself into the text, what style should I use, and how persuasive should I be?

Theory, and what on earth to do with it

The extent to which theory should be used to back up an argument is open to some debate. Post-modernists argue that the linear, explanatory account tied to theory is a modernist conceit: the author tends to conceal facts which count against the particular theory. Yet there surely remains a place for a wider explanatory framework.

> There is much that cannot be understood at street level and it is a commonplace of contemporary anthropology that many ethnographies suffer from . . . a chronic failure to register the larger politico-economic systems that enter into the constitution of the localized lifeworlds that are their primary concern (Gregory, 1994: 305).

Theories of relevance to this thesis – entrepreneurial governance, the commodification of place, the internationalisation of political economy – clearly help in forming an interpretation of how Barcelona is changing. But how are they to be represented in the text? Given my unwillingness to set up a theoretical framework in advance, it is obvious that the theories have to be included in the text to some extent. But how to do this? Should it be explicitly incorporated into discussions, petitely acknowledged through Harvard referencing, or developed in parallel through the use of footnotes or endnotes (see Gregory, 1990a, b on the merits of the latter). At the moment, the footnotes are winning for the scope they give to allowing in competing interpretations or contradictory evidence to the flow of the narrative. Jacobs (1994) provides a good example of how theoretical frames can be incorporated into discussions of the empirical, meshing theoretical insights with empirical data.

Furthermore, there is an issue about how theoretical reference relates to the argument being pursued. Critics of a linear style of argument (particularly post-modernists) would suggest that both supportive and contradictory reference to theory should be included to destabilise the authority of the text, thus rendering it more open to multiple readings. I am sympathetic to this approach, and it seems that this is tightly linked to the issues of authority, style and rhetoric.

Authority

Textual authority has been under increasing scrutiny as to the tools and resources it uses to carry its argument. Calls to bring the author back into the text have been made as a corollary to the positionality of knowledge: it is an essential part of my argument in favour of a story-telling approach. However, before we all run off and write our autobiographies, there is an important point to be made, as put by Bruner (1993: 2, cited in Lincoln and Denzin, 1994: 578): 'The danger is putting the personal self so deeply back into the text that it completely dominates, so that the work becomes narcissistic and egotistical. No one is advocating ethnographic self-indulgence.'

However, there is a need to escape from the stance of detached academic when studying urban processes. When I turned up in Barcelona I almost felt duty-bound to seek out the evils of commodification, the new marinas or shopping malls. This type of landscape reading, usually undertaken through a semiotic deconstruction, can now seem somewhat lame (Duncan, 1987). As Morris (1988: 206–7) argues, in terms of a research project, the 'myths of spectacular identity-in place which characterise shopping complex management and design, are no longer particularly interesting . . . [Such] simple demythologization all too often retrieves, at the end of the process, its own untransformed basic premises now masked as surprising conclusions.' Instead, she plans to study 'only those centres where I have, or have had, some practice other than that of analyst – places I've lived near or used as a consumer, window-shopper, tourist, or as escapee from a passing mood . . .' (Morris, 1988: 207). Here she hints at another research agenda, one which avoids the tyranny of the academic viewing the city as static, and which tries to bring in the researcher's day-to-day experiences in using urban spaces.

So, the researcher's centrality to the production of knowledge justifies some degree of personal appearance in the text be it through anecdote, auto-biographical note, fieldwork confessional, or strongly held rhetorical stance (see below). His or her personal geographies of danger, of time, of paths through the city, are surely constitutive of a geographical ethnography. But they have to be interwoven with theoretical insight, reporting of facts and attention to public discourse. This is a question of style.

Style

In the last section I mentioned that hostility to a story-telling approach usually reaches its boiling point if any aesthetic considerations as to the construction of the text come to be given more than a peripheral role. Fair enough if the audience of the text is an external body demanding an easy-read set of policy conclusions. But the majority of academics are writing things for their peers, and these constraints on style are more difficult to justify here. Several commentators have argued that being interesting may be more relevant a criterion to good academic research than has hitherto been assumed.

First, van Maanen (1995: 63) makes the point that theories are more perishable than good stories. Certain ethnographies such as Whyte's *Street Corner Society* (1955) or Gans's *The Urban Villagers* (1962) 'are read today even though the functionally driven social exchange and system theory framing each work is no longer very exciting or compelling'. Good stories last a long time.

Second, Laurel Richardson has discussed how she has 'come out' to her colleagues as being highly critical of qualitative writing. A lot of it is boring, she says, and frustrating:

> Qualitative writing could be reaching wide and diverse audiences, not just devotees of the topic or the author. It seems foolish at best, and narcissistic and wholly self-absorbed at worst, to spend months or years doing research that ends up not being read and not making a difference to anything but the author's career. Can something be done? (Richardson, 1994: 517).

She goes on to recommend a wide variety of strategies by which writing could be improved, from signing up for creative writing classes to writing fieldwork situations from different subject positions.

Third, Richardson's argument would doubtless be well received by Derek Gregory, who has been very critical at the lack of experimental and evocative writing on the part of geographers: 'it may well be true that we are not trained to be painters or poets but . . . I don't think we should boast about it' (1989: 87–8). Writing, he argues, should be a key activity in the construction of geographical imaginations.

The encouragement given by these academics, along with practical experiments in style (for example, Pred, 1995), has done a lot to persuade or encourage me to make the issue of style a major preoccupation of my writing of the New Barcelona. So what styles are the most appropriate? Each story requires a different mix of styles, drawing on different genres. The chapter on the mayor would clearly draw on political biography, that on architecture could be approached through travel writing. Fictional techniques could be used to reconstruct the city's planning histories, or the unfolding of the Olympic story. But there is no rigid framework: putting together the final product involves a kind of DIY process of experimentation and deletions, the weaving of fragments of newspaper article with architectural commentary, with personal observations, and so on. My attempts to achieve the narrative of a Davis, Maspero or Pred usually fail miserably and embarrassingly, but within the wreckage there may exist a useful combination of insights or a novel perspective which can be salvaged.

Rhetoric and persuasion

One of the biggest problems facing me in the writing of the thesis is the highly politicised nature of the urban realm. It is difficult, being an urban geographer, not to have strong views about particular issues: the urban is Big Politics. This lends the poetics of the account an added relevance: how far should the author argue a persuasive line?

> The durability and pervasiveness of the political-economy approach in human geography is extraordinary. Stop a youngish and now not-so-youngish geographer on the street and more likely than not their research is informed by some question or theory or debate within political economy. It is as if a whole discipline had joined the Labour Party (Barnes, 1995: 423).

The tendency of the theoretical niceties of the political economy approach to spill over into campus-hack politics is one of the biggest problems facing writing on restructuring theory. This takes many forms, the most common being that society is basically a struggle between workers and capitalists, that shopping malls are a cunning scheme by the ruling classes to dupe the masses, that the twenty-four-hour city is for yuppies, and that economic growth is only problematic when it is iniquitously redistributed. Meta-theoretical analysis tends to reduce the political to class politics. A lot of work still derives its political analysis from the relations of production in capitalist society. This does not tell us very much about the other political struggles going on in the city over ethnicity, gender, sexuality, mobility or urban space (Massey, 1991). When translated into actual political activity, this analysis would presumably lead academics to urge a revival of the proletarian revolution, as if the world had not moved on since the 1960s.

In something as complex as a city, such a resort to proletarian whole-someness – linked to reassuring metaphors of community, vernacular and solidarity, counterposed to the inherent evils of the market, individualism and consumption – suppresses serious discussion of other forms of domination within the city, be it racist, sexist, classist or discriminatory in terms of access or age. Not that such an approach is illegitimate in itself, if it were rendered in a more openly reflexive manner. However, by invoking the full weight of Marxist restructuring theories as back-up, a political stance is pushed through the back door rather sneakily.

I came across this problem in my attempts to put together a descriptive account of Barcelona's waterfront redevelopment. When I was in Barcelona I came across a couple of exponents of fairly orthodox Trotskyism, who – not content with bemoaning (justifiably) the privatisation of waterfront space – continued with a belittling of the quality of the housing itself (which looked

OK to me) and a labelling of the residents as yuppies. This narrative is easy to repeat on the written page, as I have caught myself doing:

> Having negotiated the tourist traps of the Ramblas, you can continue on walking out into the sea along the newly christened Moll de Espanya, a Baltimoresque boardwalk leading to a multi-screen cinema, shopping and restaurant complex, artfully blended into the urban fabric by some of the city's top urban designers. Out by the water, gangs of tourists and casually dressed middle class locals are strolling past the yachts, settling down to eat in formula elegance at marine-theme restaurants, or baguette-munching at the ubiquitous Pans and Company. Or else they are inside, picking up an FC Barcelona replica shirt at the official club shop, or an over-fashioned alarm clock at the design shop. Or upstairs drinking Guinness in the Irish theme bar, all dark stained wood floors, barrels and piped fiddle music.

The message of this genre of critique is – surely – that this is commodified leisure gone wild. Look at these monied-up idlers, smugly cocooned from the dangers and dirt of the city street. It is all their fault, bloody yuppies. They do not even realise that that Irish pub is not authentic.

This tendency to side with an idealised proletariat or the socially marginalised is understandable but often seems to short-cut other avenues of research. It is a noticeable feature of *City of Quartz*:

> [Davis] clearly speaks for the underclass. We do not hear from them directly, however. In fact the only people other than Davis who we do hear from are those whom he parades before us to speak their highly edited 'confessions', and then marches out again with a resounding 'guilty'. . . . However it is clear that were these people not to be found guilty, they would not have been summoned to speak their lines. . . . While this strong narrative structure may lend illusory coherence to the plot, it may fail to produce the degree of 'reality effect' that an account more open to contradictory evidence might achieve (Duncan, 1996: 261).

This reference to creating an account which is plausible, which approximates to a version of reality, is a central criterion in judging the success of a story-telling approach. Thrift (1989b) suggests that in theoretical accounts one should consider the facts that count against a particular interpretation as well as those which support it. And as Duncan clearly illustrates, this advice would apply even to openly rhetorical approaches. Paradoxically, Davis can fail to convince through being *over*-persuasive.

So rhetorical forms of writing have to be handled with care. An over-zealous story can bully through an account which – through its very muscularity – takes too many liberties and ends up failing to convince the inquiring reader.

CONCLUSIONS

We are fortunate, now, to be working in a postmodernist climate (Richardson, 1994: 517).

Richardson is referring not to the licence given to spew out more and more books and articles based on the putatively post-modern city, but rather to the range of textual possibilities opened up by the growing protests against unexamined assertions and unwarranted closures. Post-modernist critiques of representation are important even if their preferred representational styles do not prevail. As they open up the production of academic knowledge to close scrutiny, they reflect upon the various techniques and methods by which – consciously or not – academic accounts seek to convince through rhetoric, structure or style. In particular, the use of theory has to be integral to the selection and presentation of empirical data, rather than a means of securing legitimacy or authority.

To finish, then, I suggest that the strategies I adopt to write urban change in the New Barcelona have three dimensions. The first is that I want to write a Barcelona of the street, in the sense of the material, the palpable, the everyday. Yet I also want to overlay this with narratives of structural change, expressed in the theoretical writings surrounding urban entrepreneurialism and changes in the role of the state. And third, I want to capture the dominant discourses of public life which help to naturalise these structural forces, which legitimise the changes perceptible at street level. But most of all, I want to enlist Benjamin's support to stress that writing the city – in a reflexive, experimental way – has to be as important to academics as reading it.

PART IV

POLITICS, REGIMES AND REGULATION

INTRODUCTION

PHIL HUBBARD

> The *postmetropolis* . . . signals the transition from what has conventionally
> been called the modern metropolis to something significantly different
> (Soja, 1996: 20–1).

It is tempting to draw connections between Soja's notion of the postmetropolis
and the advent of the entrepreneurial city. In the same way that Soja coins this
term to stress that there is precious little similarity between the familiar,
structured spaces of the modern industrial city and the fractured complexity of
the contemporary post-modern city (as exemplified in the ex-urban sprawl of
Los Angeles), there seems to be precious little similarity between the
managerial city governments of old and the entrepreneurial governance now
virtually ubiquitous among Western cities. This presents a number of crucial
challenges for policy, practice and theory alike, and has posed the question as
to whether established ways of analysing urban political change are still
relevant in this post-modern, postmetropolitan era. In this section, three
chapters consider the notion of entrepreneurialism from this broad perspective, thinking about what is actually new about the entrepreneurial city and
whether established packages of analytical thought can help elucidate the
relationships between urban political change, social cohesion and capital
accumulation in a late capitalist era. In doing so, they contribute to the search
for theories to explain the 'new urban politics' which go beyond the localist
(and empiricist) tendencies of a regime perspective, and relate urban politics to
more *abstract* theories (Ward, 1996).

In this sense, although some packages of Marxist political analysis appear to
be increasingly outdated and reductionist in the face of shifts in the broader
(globalised) capitalist economy, neo-Marxist ideas associated with regulation-
ism have been employed by theorists of the entrepreneurial city to generate
valuable insights about the changing role of the local state in mediating land
and labour relations. As outlined in the introduction to this volume, this holistic
perspective examines the way in which specific 'modes of regulation' play a
role in sustaining specific 'regimes of accumulation'. Inevitably, such a
perspective has recently focused on the implications of the shift from Fordism
to post-Fordism, documenting the way in which the local state has been
actively (if unwittingly) involved in forging the new social, economic and

cultural relationships conducive to this regime of flexible accumulation (Savage and Warde, 1993). This has resulted in attempts to relate trends in urban politics to crisis tendencies in the balance between production and consumption.

An important aspect of the deployment of such ideas is that they stress that capitalist processes do not resolve local tensions between labour and capital automatically, but that this regulatory capacity is *produced* through a variety of social, cultural and political processes which perpetuate particular social, moral and aesthetic values, as well as encouraging particular forms of local economic development. In this sense, when a particular set of political, social and cultural processes combine to successfully sustain capital accumulation, it can be referred to as constituting a stable mode of social regulation (or MSR). However, the exact role urban governance (as opposed to national or, increasingly, global governance) might play in a post-Fordist MSR is open to debate (Goodwin and Painter, 1996). Certainly, as Mayer (1995) argues, whether one looks at left- or right-wing local authorities in the West, the all-embracing appeal of entre-preneurial discourse (see also Chapter 4) means that all cities have sought to prioritise the flexibilisation of local labour markets at the expense of social consumption policies – but whether this is a sustainable form of urban governance is a moot point, to which we will return subsequently.

Probably the principal value of a regulationist perspective in framing debates about entrepreneurial cities is the way in which it teases out the relationships between theories of uneven (capitalist) development and the social and cultural conditions which characterise the (post-)modern city. The need to appreciate the socialisation processes which underlie the transition to entre-preneurial governance, for example, is stressed in the chapter by Joe Painter, one of the main advocates of adopting a regulationist approach to under-standing political transitions. In his chapter, Painter draws out how any understanding of the entrepreneurial city needs to start by examining what exactly it is that makes it entrepreneurial (e.g. encouraging the competitiveness of local firms and encouraging an 'enterprise' culture) and analysing the role of key agents at the local level in promoting and inculcating this entrepreneurial attitude. Here, Painter makes the point that local entrepreneurs – the 'movers and shakers' whom we often find leading local growth coalitions or on the boards of public–private partnerships (Peck and Tickell, 1995b) – are not simply 'born' with a belief in the potential of entrepreneurial policy, but are socialised and acculturated into this belief through a complex suite of social, cultural and political processes. Thus Painter also begins to pinpoint some important links between regulation and regime theory (see introduction) in suggesting that urban governance and local institutional cultures do not exist in isolation but are intimately related to wider changes in the regulation of capitalist accumulation.

The theoretical insights of regulation theory are also evident in Andrew Wood's chapter on issues of scale in entrepreneurial policy, which critically questions the conceptualisation of local economic development in an era of globalisation. Indeed, discourses of globalisation have been closely associated with the promotion of entrepreneurial policy, with 'think global, act local' as the rallying cry of those city governors who stress that cities need to adapt to changing international competition or decay and 'die' (Beauregard, 1993). Such ideas are thus prominent in the literature on the entrepreneurial city, with Swyngedouw (1989: 40) arguing that *local* regulation is crucial in 'the age of hyperspace, in which money can flow in the twinkle of an eye from one place to another as the Starship Enterprise moves at starspeed from one end of the galaxy to another'. While such ideas of capital being footloose are not necessarily incorrect, commentators like Cox (1993) stress that this mytho- logised status of capital as globalised ignores the way in which some forms of capital – in terms of economic infrastructure, productive facilities and the built environment – may be more fixed. It is this continued local fixity that Cox and Mair (1988) have postulated encourages some local firms to remain strongly committed to a specific place.

Addressing these points, Wood points out that a simplified conception of local–global relations still characterises much of the literature on entrepre- neurial governance, with a dichotomous view of local and global often implying that the city is individual, contingent and particular, while the global is abstract, social and general (Senbenberger, 1993). In arguing for a more careful examination of issues of scale and spatiality in the examination of contemporary urban politics, Wood adopts a number of important concepts again derived from regulation theory. Such ideas again show the utility of a regulation approach in elucidating links between politics, the urban arena and the Fordist mode of regulation, while warning away from the idea that it is possible to read off causal links between seemingly 'global' economic pro- cesses and 'local' responses.

Finally, in Helga Leitner and Eric Sheppard's chapter, an attempt is made to examine the efficacy of entrepreneurial policy in promoting capital accumu- lation at the local level while still attenuating the social problems which often accompany rampant entrepreneurial governance. As has been noted else- where, the evidence compiled to date documents a failure of local regulation to maintain this production/consumption nexus:

> What has been happening in many towns and cities has been the replacement of Keynesian demand-side politics by the supply-side politics of post-Fordist growth coalitions. This has been at the same time a shift from an organised-capitalist politics of legitimation to a politics of coercion. A whole section of the industrial working class has been economically marginalised by such politics (Lash and Urry, 1994: 165).

This shortfall of 'regulatory capacity' at the urban level (and the marginalisation of large sections of the community) stands then as perhaps the most obvious sign of the long-term instability of entrepreneurial governance. As Leitner and Sheppard point out (see also introduction), growth-promoting strategies might revitalise particular inner-city areas, and sometimes lead to relative economic regeneration, but they often do nothing to actually solve housing, education and health problems in the city.

Here then we encounter some of the most interesting questions about entrepreneurial governance, specifically whether it is playing a clearly defined role in a stable post-Fordist mode of regulation. The evidence presented in Leitner and Sheppard's chapter, as well as the case studies from three continents presented earlier in the book, casts doubt over this assertion. As they point out here, the overall impacts of entrepreneurial governance on the capitalist urban system might be deleterious, as long as intensive place wars are based on the sort of socially wasteful investments that contribute to, rather than ameliorate, the over-accumulation problems that lay behind the transition to flexible accumulation in the first place (see also Harvey, 1989a). Returning to Soja (1996), we find that his analysis of the postmetropolis is that it is on the cusp of a transition between the crisis-generated restructuring of the 1970s and 1980s to a current *restructuring-induced crisis* in which processes of urban governance are strongly implicated. Whether this transition is inevitable, or whether there are alternatives to an entrepreneurial mode of city governance, is a question we return to in the conclusion.

12

ENTREPRENEURS ARE MADE, NOT BORN: LEARNING AND URBAN REGIMES IN THE PRODUCTION OF ENTREPRENEURIAL CITIES

JOE PAINTER

INTRODUCTION: THE ENTREPRENEUR

They died in their hundreds with no sign to mark where
Save the brass in the pocket of the entrepreneur.
By landslide and rockblast they got buried so deep
That in death if not life they'll have peace while they sleep.
The Pogues, 'Navigator', *Rum, Sodomy and the Lash* (Stiff Records)

[Besides land, labour and capital] often a fourth factor [of production], entrepreneurship, is distinguished. The entrepreneur is the one who takes risks by introducing both new products and new ways of making old products. He organises the other factors of production and directs them along new lines (Lipsey, 1983: 51).

I have argued elsewhere (Painter, 1997a) that Stone's (1989) concept of 'urban regime' is flawed because it is based on a rational choice model of power and that a reworked urban regime theory needs to take account of the diverse knowledges and rationalities which inform urban political practice. This includes a close analysis of the ways in which the contrasting subjectivities that different actors bring to the political arena are produced through processes of political socialisation. In this chapter I want to examine how this process of socialisation depends upon specific social practices, particularly learning, and on the basis of this, to argue that entrepreneurial urban regimes must be understood as reflexively constructed political phenomena, rather than as seemingly 'natural' responses to processes of economic change.

The Pogues' elegy for the navvies who laid the foundations of Britain's industrial infrastructure is testimony to the strength of feeling provoked by the figure of the entrepreneur. For some the entrepreneur symbolises greed, oppression and exploitation; for others, excitement, innovation and wealth creation. Yet this polarisation of views is strangely muted in comparison with those generated by other related terms such as 'capitalist', 'imperialist' or, less heroically, 'yuppie'. As a hate figure the entrepreneur is unsatisfying; as a hero he or she tends towards banality. The term 'entrepreneur' was a relatively late import into the English language, catching on only from the middle of the nineteenth century. In popular discourse, and in the discourse of neo-classical economics, the concept of the entrepreneur is frequently naturalised. Entrepreneurs are viewed as those who have a natural affinity to take risks or to generate innovations. However, in opposition to these positions I want to argue that there is nothing natural about entrepreneurialism and that entrepreneurs are made rather than born. An important part of that process of making is the inculcation of particular knowledges, ways of reasoning, and self-understandings. In short, one has to learn to be an entrepreneur.

THE PERILS OF PERSONIFICATION

In the light of this, the concept of an 'entrepreneurial city' appears rather an ambiguous one. What meanings are conveyed by this kind of anthropomorphism? Even if cities are defined as bundles of social relations rather than (or as well as) physical built environments, the ambiguities remain. Much depends on the issue of agency; in other words, who is being entrepreneurial (individuals? social groups?) and what is it about their behaviour which justifies the use of the term? The following list is not exhaustive, but provides some idea of the range of meanings that the words 'entrepreneurial city' might connote.

- The city as a setting for entrepreneurial activity. In this definition, the city is seen simply as a container or location for investment and risk-taking activities on the part of private business. Therefore, if contemporary cities are more entrepreneurial than in the past, this must be simply because the nature of private business has changed (perhaps from a more monopolistic, corporate form to a form which is prepared to accept higher levels of risk for the prospect of very high returns)
- Increased entrepreneurialism among urban residents. In this case entrepreneurial cities would be those in which a large (or at least growing) proportion of residents were becoming entrepreneurs. This might be seen in the establishment of increasing numbers of small and medium-sized businesses
- A shift from public sector to private sector activity. An entrepreneurial city could be defined as a city in which an (absolutely or relatively) increasing amount of urban economic activity is undertaken by the private sector, either through direct transfers from the public to the private sector, or by competition between the two
- A shift in the values and meanings associated with urban living in favour of business. Here, an entrepreneurial city would be one in which urban life increasingly came to be associated with cultures understood to be

somehow entrepreneurial. An example is the symbolic connection which developed during the 1980s between the cores of major urban centres such as London and New York and the figure of the 'yuppie'. The transformations in the financial services sector are central to this because of the perception that they involved very high levels of both risk and potential reward

- A shift in urban politics and governance away from the management of public services and the provision of local welfare services towards the promotion of economic competitiveness, place marketing to attract inward investment and support for the development of indigenous private sector firms

Although a strong case could be made for each meaning, in this chapter I will focus on the last of these, because while the evidence for the emergence of entrepreneurial cities defined according to the first four definitions is mixed, there is little doubt that urban politics has increasingly been organised around the discourse of entrepreneurialism (see Chapter 4). Furthermore, this has often involved attempts to bring about the kinds of changes implied by the other definitions through political change and the mechanisms of urban governance.

I use the word governance (rather than government) advisedly here. Simply defining the entrepreneurial city as a political phenomenon does not solve the problem of agency to which I alluded above. Urban politics is no longer, if it ever was, a process of hierarchical government in which decisions by local politicians are translated straightforwardly by public bodies into social and economic change. Rather it involves a complex process of negotiation, coalition formation, indirect influence, multi-institution working and public–private partnership. This diffuse and multi-faceted form of rule has come to be termed 'governance'. According to Jessop (1997c) governance is associated with a particular form of rule. In contrast to the hierarchical rule provided by the (local) state and the anarchy of the market, Jessop argues that governance involves 'heterarchy' (which might be defined as 'rule through diversity'). In cities with entrepreneurial governance, therefore, political agency is not unitary or singular, but heterogeneous and complex. As a result, the emergent effects of these interactions of individual and institutional agents are likely to be partly unintended, and, moreover, beyond the control of any single individual or institution.

The definition of entrepreneurialism as political strategy was also adopted by David Harvey (1989b) in a paper that has become a key reference point for research in this area. For Harvey:

The new urban entrepreneurialism typically rests . . . on a public–private partnership focusing on investment and economic development with the speculative construction of place rather than amelioration of conditions within a particular territory as its immediate (though by no means exclusive) political and economic goal (Harvey 1989b: 8).

He goes on to identify four strategies towards which entrepreneurial governance may be directed (1989b: 8–10). They are:

- Exploiting local competitive advantages for the production of goods and services within the international division of labour
- Seeking to improve the competitive position of the urban region with respect to the spatial division of consumption
- Competition over the location of command and control functions of business, government and information-gathering and processing
- Competition over the spatial redistribution of surpluses by the state (including attracting funding for public service provision, military and defence establishments and government grants)

Harvey's survey is very helpful in fleshing out the bare bones of the definition of the entrepreneurial city that I proposed above. In this chapter, however, I am less concerned with the nature of the strategies of entrepreneurial governance than with the process of their *production*. In particular I want to consider two closely related issues in more detail. The first is the notion of a regime of entrepreneurial urban governance and the second is the role of learning and reflexivity in the constitution and operation of entrepreneurial urban regimes.

ENTREPRENEURIAL URBAN REGIMES

Urban regime theory was developed in the United States as an interpretation of urban politics that took seriously both the informal aspects of politics and the reliance of the local state and local politicians on non-governmental resources in achieving political objectives. It has some parallels with Harvey's avowedly Marxist concept of the 'regional class alliance' (1985a) but also differs from it in certain important respects. Early uses of the regime concept appeared during the mid-1980s (Fainstein and Fainstein, 1983; Elkin, 1985, 1987), but it was the publication of *Regime Politics* by Clarence Stone (1989) which provided a fully developed account.

Stone argued that the governance of Atlanta, Georgia since the Second World War could only be understood if due weight was given to the role of key individual and institutional actors outside the formal structures of city government and particularly to the informal relationships developed between such actors and the politicians. Stone's book opens with a formulation of the regime idea which is markedly similar to the concept of governance outlined above:

What makes governance in Atlanta effective is not the formal machinery of government, but rather the informal partnership between city hall and the downtown business elite. This informal partnership and the way it operates constitute the city's regime; it is the means through which major policy decisions are made (Stone 1989: 3).

Although regime theory appears to offer a useful approach to interpreting governance, it has not been without its critics. Among other things, regime theory has been criticised for its model of power, for its ethnocentrism, for a stress on continuity rather than change and for its neglect of the wider political–economic context in which regimes operate (for a review see Stoker, 1995). However, more recent work has attempted to address at least some of these shortcomings, with mixed success. (See, among others, DiGaetano and Klemanski, 1993; Harding, 1994; Horan, 1991; Orr and Stoker, 1994; Stoker and Mossberger, 1994 and especially the various contributions to Lauria, 1997. In addition Stone, 1993 has published an updated discussion of the regime concept.)

I have discussed my own misgivings about Stone's initial formulation elsewhere (Painter, 1997a) and there is space here for only a brief summary. If an urban regime is an informal coalition of political interests, then regime theory has to explain why particular actors participate in the regime while others do not. Part of the explanation relates to the unequal distribution of resources among potential regime participants. Thus business groups are more likely to be involved than some others because they control more resources and thus are both more attractive to other partners (who may need those resources to pursue their goals) and better placed to negotiate for participation in the regime. However, this part of the analysis only identifies potential regime members, it cannot explain how potential members become actual members. To explain this, Stone (1989: 186–91) invokes the concept of selective incentives. Since regime participation involves costs (of time, if nothing else) as well as benefits, there appears to be nothing to stop potential members gaining the benefits (of urban renewal or investment in downtown infrastructure, for example) without paying any of the costs, simply by waiting until others do the work. To prevent this 'free rider' problem, Stone argues that participants in the regime must acquire additional benefits exceeding those accruing to non-participants. This idea of 'selective incentives' is important in Stone's account. He argues that they are what 'holds a governing coalition together' (1989: 175).

Stone's use of the concept of selective incentives means that his explanation of regime development and survival is grounded in rational choice theory, and therefore that participation in an urban regime is the product (at least in part) of a rationalist calculation of its costs and benefits. The pros and cons of rational choice theory have been widely debated and will not be rehearsed here. Suffice it to say that the main problem with it from the point of view of my arguments in this chapter is that it is based on a particular unitary model of rational behaviour against which I wish to counterpose not *irrationality* but *multiple rationalities*.

Unlike models of regime formation based on selective incentives, my conception of an urban regime does not assume that individual and institutional actors always approach involvement in a regime through a rationalist calculation of costs and benefits. And when they do do so, the use of rationalist calculation must be seen as something to be explained, rather than itself constituting the explanation. In this view, actors take up positions in relation to a regime for a variety of reasons and motivations, some of which may be contradictory. Involvement in regimes can be motivated by emotion as well as reason and by altruism as well as self-interest and can be based on modes of rationality which vary according to the biographies and histories of individual and group actors and on imperfect, rather than complete, information and knowledge.

This approach provides the basis for an analysis that retains the many useful insights of the regime approach, without its methodological flaws. These benefits include:

- A focus on the informal, as well as the formal, structures of governance and power
- A focus on political strategies and projects, while recognising that these can vary widely from bold programmes of urban renewal to the limited goals of so-called 'maintenance' or 'caretaker' regimes
- A focus on non-governmental, as well as governmental, actors and an explicit recognition that effective governance almost always depends on the mobilisation of a range of institutional and individual actors and interests
- A recognition that a wide variety of regimes are possible and that the formation of urban regimes is a social, political and cultural process which cannot simply be derived from the dominant economic relations of the city
- A recognition that urban governance matters; that (other things being equal, and within the constraints in which all governance operates) cities with different types of urban regime experience different social and economic outcomes

The literature on urban regimes has identified numerous types and subtypes of urban regime. Stoker and Mossberger (1994), for example, identify three main types of regime and a number of subtypes (Table 12.1).

Previously I defined the entrepreneurial city as one in which urban politics and governance were increasingly focused on the promotion of economic competitiveness, place marketing to attract inward investment and support for

TABLE 12.1 Regime types and subtypes (derived from Stoker and Mossberger, 1994)

Type	Subtype	Purpose
Organic		Maintenance of status quo
	Caretaker	Low taxation; maintenance of small-town lifestyles
	Exclusive	Sustaining social cohesion through homogeneity
	Traditional	Maintenance of prestige
Instrumental		Project realisation
Symbolic		Change of image or ideology
	Progressive	'High quality' growth (e.g. environmentally sustainable, opportunity enhancing)
	Revitalisation	Attraction of investment and middle- and high-income residents

the development of indigenous private sector firms (often linked to a shift away from an earlier emphasis on welfare services for urban residents). The urban regime of such a city would not slot neatly into the typology in Table 12.1, although it seems likely that it would be partly an instrumental regime and partly a symbolic revitalisation regime. Indeed, as I have argued elsewhere (Painter, 1995), it is difficult in politics to separate the symbolic from the instrumental. Symbolic changes can themselves be instruments of urban transformation.

Following Harvey's definition of entrepreneurial urban governance, I define an entrepreneurial urban regime as a coalition of interests including the public sector and private firms which is organised through partnerships and whose goal is the enhancement of the competitiveness of the urban region with regard to (a) the location of production and consumption activities and command and control functions; and (b) the spatial redistribution of surpluses by the state and quasi-state bodies such as the European Union. There is nothing especially novel about this formulation and much work in political science, geography and urban and regional studies over the last 15 years has been directed towards assessing the impact of such strategies on particular urban regions, and relating their emergence to long-term shifts in the nature of capitalist economies (such as the supposed transition from Fordism to post-Fordism). However, much less attention has been paid to the processes through which such regimes form. Any transformation in urban governance involves significant changes in the workings of institutions and in the ways of thinking of individuals and groups. My concern in the remainder of this chapter is with how these smaller-scale (but no less important) changes are brought about. In developing an interpretation of the transition to entrepreneurial governance, I start from the assumption that such changes do not arise automatically, but are socially, politically and culturally produced.

MADE NOT BORN: INTERPRETING URBAN ENTREPRENEURIALISM

Producing entrepreneurial urban economies

Many studies of urban change treat shifts in the character of the urban economy as in some senses foundational. Economic processes are often regarded as providing a more basic level of explanation, while cultural and political change is interpreted as a dependent variable which is caused or heavily conditioned by the economy. While there is no doubt that what is conventionally understood as 'the economic' has important effects on all aspects of urban life, the view of the economy as foundational is flawed for a number of reasons. First, it is based on a false division between economic, cultural and political realms. None of these areas is independent of the others. Second, the very idea of a foundational explanation is suspect. Even if it is possible to explain some aspects of (say) political change with reference to economic processes, this does not exhaust the explanatory task, since the economic processes themselves require explaining. Third, economic changes (or, indeed, the lack of them) always have a wide range of preconditions, some of which may well be cultural and political. The emergence of mass production, for example, did not occur independently of other social changes. On the contrary it was heavily dependent on shifts in cultural norms and political institutions which in turn had themselves to be (in some cases quite actively) 'produced'.

Thus an entrepreneurial urban economy will only emerge if certain preconditions are in place. The precise specification of these preconditions is likely to vary from case to case, since it is possible that slightly different combinations of conditions could be compatible with the emergence of entrepreneurial cities. Nevertheless some broad trends (based on the British case, but with somewhat wider applicability) can be identified.

Labour markets A key precondition is the establishment of new labour market institutions, or the reform or removal of existing ones, to promote certain labour market practices, including the deregulation of all aspects of employment contracts (but particularly wage-setting) and to discourage others, including most forms of collective action. These changes are themselves legitimated through specific discourses such as the discourse of flexibility-rigidity, in which the former term is positively accented. In Britain, a range of reforms of labour market institutions have been put in place, including a long sequence of legislative measures to regulate the activities of trade unions and the replacement of corporatist institutions such as the Manpower Services Commission, with private sector dominated Training and Enterprise Councils (Local Enterprise Companies in Scotland).

Education and training In the sphere of education and training there is an increased emphasis at all levels on the provision of skills for employment. This includes attempts to develop new forms of relationships between employers and educational institutions. Again this is centrally a discursive strategy; the practical impact may be limited, but the 'education is for work' discourse promotes an understanding of the purpose of schooling in which the pressures of the labour market predominate over personal goals.

Industrial policy In the sphere of industrial policy there is a shift away from macro-economic intervention and protectionist measures in sectors of perceived national strategic importance. In their place a twofold strategy has emerged. In the small and medium enterprise (SME) sector, a range of microeconomic strategies have been advanced focusing on advice and start-up support (on a quasi-venture capital basis) for small businesses. In the large corporate sector, the strategy has been to promote new investment through targeted incentives, such as tax relief, removal of planning constraints and assistance with the provision of appropriate sites. These changes involve a range of discursive strategies including a contradictory rhetoric that stresses deregulation and improved government support simultaneously and a strongly disciplinary discourse that threatens the loss of potential future investment to 'foreign' locations unless 'competitiveness' is maintained (particularly with regard to wage rates). It is worth noting here that the 'truth' of these discourses is not directly of relevance; what matters is that (true or not) they have significant effects.

Social policy Welfare provision is now predominantly constructed discursively in Britain as a cost on private enterprise, and thus in the main at odds with the emergence of a competitive entrepreneurial economy. This is also increasingly true even in areas such as health care that have often been understood in the past as an investment in, among other things, a healthier (and therefore more productive) workforce. Institutional reform has at least three aims:

- To promote 'entrepreneurial' behaviour within state institutions (in part as symbolic encouragement to the private sector) through the introduction of new forms of management and quasi-market relationships
- To cut costs and therefore reduce the 'burden' on the 'productive' sector of the economy
- To distinguish between those deserving of public provision and those who are fit and able to work and provide for themselves and who will therefore be compelled to undertake specific tasks, such as training, employment seeking or various forms of workfare in order to prove, by doing all they can to 'help themselves', that their claim on the state is legitimate

In the latter case, there is no objective distinction between the deserving and undeserving. For example, in the past the official assumption in Britain was that unemployed people were, with very few exceptions, unemployed for reasons beyond their control. They were therefore in the 'deserving' category. More recently single parents (and specifically mothers) have been moved in official and semi-official discourse towards the less deserving end of the scale. Such discursive categorisations are highly disciplinary in their effects metaphorically and materially marginalising particular groups socially and spatially.

An active disciplinary process   The implication of these and other changes is that where entrepreneurial cities emerge, they do not do so by chance, nor are they the blind effect of global scale economic transformations. On the contrary, the outline above shows that entrepreneurial cities are produced through an active process involving a huge effort of institutional reform and discursive construction. Actors in the urban economy from schoolchildren to state officials and from business executives to welfare claimants have to learn how to be 'entrepreneurial'. In an entrepreneurial city, each actor and institution has specific roles to perform, the adoption of which is a disciplinary process. It may involve self-discipline as roles are learnt and internalised and then performed apparently freely, or it may involve a more explicit exercise of power on the part of the institutions of urban governance to compel performance.

Producing entrepreneurial urban regimes: the role of learning and knowledge

If entrepreneurial urban economies involve discipline, learning and performance, the same is true of entrepreneurial urban governance. Just as participants in the urban economy (the objects of governance) have to learn their parts, so too do participants in the urban regime. Promoting the competitiveness with other urban regions that Harvey describes, and generating the institutional and discursive transformations outlined above, involves new practices of governance that themselves have to be learnt or imposed (usually by central government). Such learning is multi-faceted. For example, in local public sector organisations (which will be among the key players in the urban regime, although not, of course, the only ones) learning to be entrepreneurial is likely to involve a wide range of new knowledges including, among other things:

- The acquisition of specific skills, such as those associated with place promotion, auditing, commercial accounting, negotiation with private sector institutions, and the preparation of funding applications
- The development of new self-understandings which may involve, for example, a subordination of the role of 'welfare provider' to that of 'business supporter', or the role of 'bureaucrat' to that of 'strategic manager'

- Acquiescence (rather than active resistance) in the face of centrally imposed requirements to shift to more entrepreneurial practices of governance
- The acceptance of change and of 'challenges' as inevitable, or even desirable, in contrast with a previous expectation of stability

In the transition from managerial to entrepreneurial governance, some of these changes may be produced by staff turnover, which may be partly natural and partly encouraged through selective redundancy and appointment practices. However, in many cases the transition and the learning associated with it will be internal to individuals who remain in post. Learning therefore takes place at the level of individual actors and at the level of the institution as a whole. In the latter case, new knowledge may become codified in manuals and policy documents or it may remain tacit in shared understandings of 'the way we do things here'.

In both cases (institutional and individual) learning does not happen automatically or through some kind of mysterious evolutionary adaptation. Rather, it involves quite specific and identifiable social practices, which inculcate new institutional norms and individual behaviours. In order to elaborate on these practices I will continue to focus by way of example on the British case and on public sector institutions. However, it is important to appreciate that learning of this sort takes place among all participants (private and public sector) in the urban regime. Indeed one of the knowledges that must be learnt is how to participate in the regime.

The social practices through which new knowledges, cultural norms and forms of behaviour are taught and learnt are very varied and involve a wide range of mechanisms. The relative importance of each will depend on the case in question, but most of them are present to a greater or lesser extent in most entrepreneurial urban regimes.

Management education   The first, but by no means necessarily the most important, is formal education, undertaken on either a full- or part-time basis in a higher education institution. Professional qualifications have long been acquired in this way by accountants, surveyors, teachers, social workers and so on. More recently, this practice has been extended to managers and bureaucrats. Of central importance here are university business schools, which have turned increasingly to the public sector as a market for management education courses. For some this amounts to little more than adapting MBA courses, but in other cases more specialised public service management courses have been developed.

Management consultancy   Second, the public sector has shown an increased willingness to use professional management consultants both for advice about organisational restructuring and a second source of management education.

The latter often involves less commitment of time than formal education in a university. There is also a growth in the supply of seminars and day courses by management consultants, marketed in a variety of ways including direct mail and inserts in trade periodicals. For example a recent day seminar on business planning in local government, aimed at local government officials in Britain, advertised a programme containing the following topics:

1. The business planning process.
2. Mission, goals and audits.
3. Techniques and models.
4. Carrying out market research.
5. Setting objectives.
6. Developing a competitive strategy.
7. Developing your operations plan.
8. Forecasts, budgets and implementation.
9. Business plan format.

Related seminars by the same organisation cover benchmarking, quality assurance and marketing.

Trade press   Most professions and occupations have one or more periodicals which deal with matters of specialist interest to the professions concerned. Within public services, the trade and practitioner press represents another potential route for the transmission of new knowledges and spreading innovative practices. In British local government, for example, the *Municipal Journal*, published weekly, includes articles on new management techniques and new strategies of urban governance. Although, as with the other mechanisms for transferring ideas it is difficult to assess directly the impact of an individual article, it is interesting that recent issues have also covered topics such as the use of focus groups in local government marketing, leadership, evaluation and performance review and the formation of partnerships.

Management 'gurus'   Management thinking is highly susceptible to fashions and fads. As Thrift has noted in the context of the private sector:

> 'Management gurus' like Peter Drucker, Charles Handy, John Kay, Theodore Levitt, Gareth Morgan, John Naisbitt, Tom Peters, Rosabeth Moss Kanter, Kenichi Ohmae, and the like, have become increasingly important as embodiments of new managerialist arguments. These gurus have been responsible for the diffusion of a whole host of the 'business fads' taught on management courses which, jointly and singly, have promoted a new managerial world view (Thrift, 1996: 18).

Rhodes (1994) and Ferlie et al (1996: 9) note a similar fashion consciousness in management ideas in the public sector.

A full account of the role of management bestsellers would need to take into account the factors affecting the supply side (such as the 'need' for management gurus continuously to generate apparently new ideas in order to create a demand for books, seminars, lectures and so on). However, it seems clear that the ideas of at least the best known and most popular gurus have filtered through in important ways to the public sector, not least because some of them are explicitly aimed at changing public service management. Tom Peters's best-selling *Thriving on Chaos*, for example, contains in many of its chapters specific sections on parallels for the public sector (Peters, 1987).

Learning within and between organisations   Learning and the transmission of new knowledges can also take place within organisations themselves. This may be formalised through mechanisms such as in-house staff training, or mentoring or it may involve the informal transmission of knowledge and the spreading of tacit knowledge. These practices can result in the maintenance of the status quo, particularly if new ways of doing things are discouraged because they do not 'fit' with the existing organisational norms, or they may produce organisational change. Similarly learning can occur directly between organisations. Sometimes this occurs through staff turnover and the recruitment of new staff with experience and ideas from other areas of the public sector, or, more rarely, from the private sector. It can also happen through sharing experiences and ideas with those working in other organisations, perhaps at professional conferences or through personal networks. New mechanisms, such as internet discussion groups are also growing in importance, although their impact to date seems limited.

Adaptive behaviour and reflexivity   The various mechanisms detailed above can, in principle, be the transmission routes for all sorts of knowledge, not just ideas relating to entrepreneurialism. Nevertheless, the development of entre-preneurial urban regimes is a good example of learning activity. In terms of their organisational structure, entrepreneurial regimes are constituted around the concept of partnerships. Unlike the more informal arrangements detailed by Stone in the Atlanta case, contemporary urban partnerships exhibit high degrees of visibility and self-consciousness. In the terminology developed by Giddens (1990), they may be termed *reflexive*.

The fourth feature of urban entrepreneurialism (competition over the redistribution of surpluses by the state) outlined by Harvey (1989b) provides a noteworthy example. In Britain, the distribution of central government urban regeneration funding (known as the Single Regeneration Budget) is now channelled to cities through a competitive bidding process. According to the regulations, bids must be submitted by partnerships involving public–private co-operation. This arrangement has resulted in a high degree of instrumentalism (partnerships being established opportunistically simply to bid for the money) and it could therefore be argued that such partnerships are not organic urban regimes. They do, however, display significant learning activity along the lines outlined above. For instance, a recent insert in the *Municipal Journal* advertised a series of seminars on the Single Regeneration Budget (SRB), sponsored by the *Journal* and provided by a firm of management consultants. The topics considered included the criteria necessary to create meaningful business partnerships, methods of project management, the roles of the partners in regeneration practice and frameworks for networking. Detailed advice was also offered on the construction of delivery plans, legal requirements, strategies for successful partnerships and so on.

Partnerships (even the instrumental ones associated with the SRB) are reflexive because they have the potential to exhibit adaptive behaviour. An unsuccessful bid can be followed by a phase of institutional learning which may lead to future success. ('Success' here must be understood in relative terms of course; the SRB does not provide British cities with more resources overall. It merely represents a new way of managing resource distribution.)

CONCLUSION

In this chapter I have concentrated on the role of knowledge and learning within public sector participants in an entrepreneurial regime. The same approach could also be applied to voluntary and non-governmental agencies and to private sector organisations. Extending the analysis in this way would, I think, reinforce the argument that urban regimes in general, and entre-preneurial regimes in particular, can never arise spontaneously. Behaving entrepreneurially, or competitively, is not something that regime participants know how to do automatically; such behaviour has to be learnt (and taught). Moreover the learning and teaching are themselves a social and cultural process embedded in other networks of supply and demand, such as the management consultancy industry, business schools, periodical publishing and so on. Such deliberate attempts to acquire the tools of entrepreneurialism might appear to contradict my earlier claim that urban regimes cannot be understood through the rational choice model. Surely, it could be argued, such apparently strategic behaviour is a vindication of the rational choice approach. In my view, precisely the opposite is true. Behaving in the strategic and rationalist way implied by the model and adopting the calculus of cost and benefits involved is itself learned, not natural, behaviour. Whatever the impacts of entrepreneurialism in cities, one thing is clear: urban entrepreneurs are made, not born.

ACKNOWLEDGEMENTS

Many of the ideas in this chapter were developed in the course of a research project entitled 'British Local Governance in the Transition from Fordism'. The project was funded by the Economic and Social Research Council (grant number L31125301101) and I am grateful for its support. I would also like to thank Mark Goodwin, who directed the project with me and the project researchers: Parminder Bakshi, Alan Southern and Michelle Wood. Responsibility for the contents of this chapter, however, rests with me.

13

QUESTIONS OF SCALE IN THE ENTREPRENEURIAL CITY

ANDREW WOOD

INTRODUCTION

A dominant theme in much social science writing over the past 15 years has been that of *globalisation* (Lipietz, 1993; Cox, 1997). This is reflected directly in the literatures on global cities, the globalisation of culture, new international divisions of labour, the globalisation of finance and investment, the emergence of transnational regulatory frameworks, the hollowing out of the nation state and so on. The issue of globalisation also looms large in recent work on the changing governance of urban areas, the development of the entrepreneurial city and the rise of a 'new urban politics' (Cochrane, Peck and Tickell, 1996; Boyle and Hughes, 1995; Harvey, 1989b; Cox, 1993; Hall and Hubbard, 1996). A central motif in much of this literature has been the 'impact' of globalisation on what are variously described as cities, communities or localities. Associated with this is a concern with the scope for meaningful 'local' action in the face of globalisation (Goetz and Clarke, 1993; Peck and Tickell, 1994; Gough, 1996; Lovering, 1995).

Definitions of globalisation are notoriously difficult to pin down and, where explicit, they vary considerably in their form. Indeed Amin suggests that 'the more we read about globalisation . . . the less clear we seem to be about what it means and what it implies' (Amin, 1997: 1). A clear reference point in many accounts, however, is the relationship between recent economic change and the regulatory power of the inter-state system. A number of authors suggest that globalisation represents a qualitative shift in the relationship between economic agents and institutions of regulation, with the global nature of economic flows and interrelationships effectively undermining extant national-based systems of regulation (see Chapter 4 on this apparent bifurcation of regulation from national to local and global levels). This is not to say that economic relationships thereby necessarily escape regulation but rather that appropriate regulatory institutions are likely to be transnational in scope (see Amin, 1997, for a useful review of these arguments).

Alternatively, various writers have suggested that globalisation represents an intensification, rather than qualitative shift, in exchange between economic units that remain essentially national in their form (Gordon, 1988; Hirst and

Thompson, 1996). These flows remain subject to inter-state regulation. Indeed the problems of globalisation, for writers such as Hirst and Thompson (1996) at least, emerge from the associated regulatory regime of neo-liberalism rather than the intensification of economic exchange or the widening geographic scope of social and economic activity *per se*. On both sides of the argument claims are made as to the appropriate scale at which regulatory mechanisms need to operate in order to manage economic change. It follows that many of the difficulties associated with recent economic change are seen to be compounded, if not indeed generated, by the absence or failure of regulatory mechanisms at the 'appropriate' scale.

This chapter is centrally concerned with these questions of scale and, in particular, the claim that globalisation has fundamentally altered the relationship between what are conventionally termed the 'local' and 'global' scales, or, more simply, the 'local' and the 'global' in the entrepreneurial city. It therefore seeks not simply to bring into question the 'local'/'global' dualism, but to argue that the need to align social processes with particular spatial scales has served to blinker the way in which we think about the entrepreneurial city and its politics in relation to globalisation. This review piece thus sets out to highlight various tensions in the literature concerning different ways of conceptualising the 'local' and the relationship between the 'local' and the 'global'. There is, for example, little consensus as to precisely what is meant by the terms themselves or indeed how we might begin to specify them. While the local is generally equated with phenomena, processes or areal units at the subnational scale, this often gets elided with more concrete phenomena, notably the city. The global is given even less attention and is generally assumed to mean spaces above the level of the nation state, although again exceptions highlight the taken-for-granted nature of the terms. This chapter seeks to bring these tensions into focus through a review of a number of works concerned explicitly or implicitly with the entrepreneurial city. It particularly argues that there are important differences (not simply of emphasis) over, for example, the capacity for local action, but also more fundamentally in the way we think about and theorise the relationship between space and social process. The chapter is thus divided into two sections. The first examines prominent attempts to specify the 'local' looking in particular at the work of David Harvey on regional class alliances and Cox and Mair's concept of local dependence. Section two examines more recent attempts to position the 'local' in relation to the 'global' and the implications of this for specifying a politics of place.

SPECIFYING THE LOCAL AND LOCAL POLITICS

The attempt to situate recent work on the 'entrepreneurial city' in context requires a brief tour through various academic literatures concerned in a more general sense with the relationship between urban change and capitalist development. In the 1970s a common argument was that urban change and urban politics were driven by economic forces external to urban arenas and thus clearly beyond the scope of city-based agents. Peterson (1981) provided one variant of this thesis while structural Marxist accounts posited a similar scenario – albeit from a very different perspective. In both cases, causality was seen to be unidirectional with more global economic changes or forces determining what goes on within cities (see Leitner, 1990, for a review). To this end there are a number of interesting parallels with variants of the globalisation thesis that argue that national economic fortunes are currently determined by processes of extra-national extent. While the relative coupling of scales may have changed, a focus on the asymmetric nature of the relationship between processes operating at different geographic scales is common to both.

Much of the work on the entrepreneurial city from within urban regime and growth coalition frameworks can be seen as a reaction to these accounts or as an attempt to rescue an autonomous urban politics in which local agency is paramount (Logan and Molotch, 1987). Those working within these schools generally counter that local politics 'matters', although the precise bases for this claim are rarely specified. Indeed much of the literature on the entrepreneurial city takes the local and local politics as given objects of study. They have a seductive taken-for-granted quality – although precisely what is meant by the 'local', 'local' politics, 'local' governance and the like is seldom investigated. The geographical specificity of the phenomena is rarely questioned.

Furthermore, while regime and coalition accounts acknowledge interaction between local agents and agents, institutions and processes extant at more spatially extensive scales, these approaches rarely interrogate the nature of these relationships or investigate how the relations that transcend the boundaries of cities might alter the constitution of urban politics. The global or 'external' context is treated as a given and concern is centred on conflict and co-operation between agents, institutions and social groups contained within the urban arena. The politics of these conflicts is principally expressed through competing demands upon the local state and the mobilisation of local state resources and powers to serve selective interests. Concern is focused upon a particular geographic space within which coalitions of interest are established and conflicts resolved. This focus on the urban arena is reflected in the dominance, in the US literature in particular, of the case study approach to the politics of entrepreneurialism. This is all the more peculiar given Stephen Elkin's original emphasis on the importance of the relationship between urban and national politics in determining city regimes (Elkin, 1987). I shall argue in this chapter, drawing on Low (1997), that this view of politics as contained within a particular arena, in this case the urban, is problematic. In short, regime and coalition approaches to the entrepreneurial city assert the autonomy of urban or local politics as a legitimate focus for study without properly theorising the basis for that politics. Urban politics is simply politics that takes place in cities rather than being a politics of the city.

Harvey's work on regional class alliances provides a more sophisticated attempt to specify the basis for an autonomous urban politics (Harvey, 1985b, 1989b). Central to Harvey's formulation is the tension between the mobility and immobility of capital. In order for production to proceed, a certain portion of capital must be immobilised in space in the form of 'fixed' physical and social infrastructures (including labour power). While this immobilisation of capital occurs across a range of spatial scales, Harvey is particularly interested in the urbanisation of capital. In the collision of capital and labour in the urban labour market, Harvey argues that the class relations in an urban region tend towards a 'structured coherence'. This coherence:

> embraces the standard of living, the qualities and style of life, work satisfactions (or lack thereof), social hierarchies (authority structures in the workplace, status symbols of consumption), and a whole set of sociological and psychological attitudes towards working, living, enjoying, entertaining and the like (Harvey, 1985b: 140).

Structured coherence is never assured, however, and Harvey points to various tendencies that serve to undermine structured coherence of the type described (Harvey, 1985b: 143). These coherences spawn urban class alliances and in the process, '(t)he confusions and instabilities of class-alliance formation create a political space in which a relatively autonomous urban politics can arise' (Harvey, 1985b: 152). Much of this politics is centred on the struggle of locally based interests to realise economic and political gain. In appropriating and reproducing the necessary means to legitimate their power and authority, locally based agents and institutions are liable to forge coalitions of interest that seek to represent a place-bound community. The conflicts around coalition building and the rewarding of certain constituencies and marginalisation of others generate an autonomous politics of urban entrepreneurialism, that is a politics that 'can point in many different directions' (Harvey, 1985b: 153).

Harvey's conceptual framework is a particularly useful one but it remains pitched at a relatively high level of abstraction. Cox and Mair (1988, 1991) have sought to extend Harvey's work thereby providing a means of specifying further the tension between mobility and immobility at the heart of Harvey's thesis. They argue that various firms, individuals and state agencies are effectively immobilised in space, giving each a defined locality of interest. As a result of their immobility these locally dependent interests are susceptible to the place-specific devaluation that results from geographically differentiated 'rhythms of accumulation' (Harvey, 1982: 427). Local dependence stems from two sources of immobility: the first is the fixity of investments in the built environment which are amortised only after lengthy periods of time; the second is the non-substitutable nature of certain exchange relations. In the former case, there are a range of firms such as the utilities, banks and building societies, landowners and property developers which cannot readily and easily avoid the threat of place-specific devaluation through relocation (Cox and Wood, 1994). In the second set of cases:

> local dependence may result from a certain non-substitutability of local exchange linkages when it is advantageous that buying and selling relationships be characterized by stability over time. The development of predictability, trust, brand loyalties and unique local knowledge all encourage stable relations with particular customers and suppliers in particular places (Cox and Mair, 1988: 308–9).

Locally dependent interests, whether through fixed assets or the specificity of exchange linkages, are thus locked into a particular set of localised social relations. In the attempt to defend existing complexes of relations, agents and institutions that possess coincident localities of interest will often collaborate with each other (Cox and Wood, 1997). It is the activities of these locally dependent interests, their forms of co-operation and their conflicts with other social interests that generate a distinctive politics of urban development (Cox, 1993). The basis for a local politics is thus rooted in the attempt of sectional but place-bound interests to defend and enhance the particular configurations of social, economic and political power on which they depend for their survival. Their activities are liable to generate conflict with other social interests within these places and with place-bound interests located elsewhere.

It is important to emphasise that both Harvey's account and that of Cox and Mair emphasise the dynamic nature of the processes generating local interests. Locally dependent interests, for example, are liable to be both geographically and historically specific in terms of their material basis and political expression. Thus there is no necessary reason as to why specific agents and institutions will be locally dependent at particular scales or indeed locally dependent in any meaningful sense. Recent changes in banking legislation and proposals for utility reform in the United States are both liable to have significant effects on the material stake of these particular firms in local and regional economic development. As the scale and degree of their dependence shift then the political strategies through which they realise their interests alter accordingly (Wood, 1996). Indeed, under certain circumstances, agents and institutions may withdraw entirely from political activity in certain arenas. Thus both schemas provide a framework for the study of the politics associated with the entrepreneurial city rather than a ready-made model of the composition of the key interests that holds across all contexts.

CONCEPTUALISING SCALE AND THE LOCAL/GLOBAL RELATIONSHIP

For both Harvey and Cox and Mair an autonomous urban politics is rooted in a local social structure expressed in the form of a ruling class alliance or locally dependent interests respectively. In both cases, there is an acknowledgement that the politics of place is positioned within a much wider field of processes and events. Indeed, it is the positioning of the locality in relation to wider divisions of labour, for example, that animates much of the work of place-bound interests. Various recent writings on place have sought to examine more closely this relationship between a place-bound or local set of interests and more global sets of relations. Rather than focusing on specifying or bounding the local, a number of writers have recently argued that the 'local' and the 'global' can only properly be seen as constituted through their relationship to one another. Massey, for example, starts out from the geographically extended nature of social relations and the fact that 'the social relations that constitute a locality increasingly stretch beyond its borders; less and less of these relations are contained within the place itself' (Massey, 1994: 162). Thus in the face of the 'deepening' of globalisation, 'geographical scales become less easy to separate – rather they constitute each other: the global, the local and vice versa' (Massey, 1994: 161). Robins takes the argument a step further arguing that:

> It is important to see the local as a relational and relative concept, which once significant in relation to the national sphere, now . . . is being recast in the context of globalization . . . as a fluid and relational space, constituted only in and through its relation to the global (Robins, in Amin and Thrift, 1995: 97).

These conceptualisations have important implications for the way we think about the entrepreneurial city and its politics, bringing into question both the search for a peculiarly local or urban politics and the counterpoising of separate 'local' and 'global' spheres of activity.

This counterpoising of the 'local' and the 'global' takes another form in the previously noted arguments about the relative importance of particular scales as sites for regulating capitalist development. There is little consensus on this issue. In one corner is an argument that globalisation has actually served to increase the salience of place or the 'local'. Swyngedouw, for example, argues that 'the locality is increasingly becoming the place of regulation and institutional organisation . . . the homogenisation of space in the face of capital, is accompanied by a growing importance of place' (Swyngedouw, 1989: 40–1). A much less sophisticated version of this argument is commonly used by academics and policy-makers to legitimate the activities of local agencies as they proactively seek to position 'their' locality within the new 'global market-place'. Yet others have argued precisely the opposite. Lovering claims that: '(r)ather than drifting down from the national to the local level, the regulation of the process of accumulation is becoming the business of an (unaccountable) international apparatus' (Lovering, 1995: 124). Peck and Tickell too suggest that local strategies or initiatives can only 'deepen the subordination of the local to the global' (Peck and Tickell, 1994: 324).

Much depends here not upon the extent to which the institutions of regulation are locally based but rather the task with which these local regulatory institutions are charged. For some, the resurgence of place as a regulatory focus opens up possibilities for new modes of local economic and political development, often of a post-Fordist bent (Mayer, 1995). The recent literature on the role of institutions and institutional networks in providing a platform for local economic development similarly claims that local institutions matter in mediating the relationship between local interests and more global processes (Amin and Thrift, 1995d; see also Wood, 1993). In short the economic success of certain locales is seen to depend, in part at least, upon the embedding of economic agents within a closely woven network of supportive formal and informal institutions and conventions. Amin and Thrift refer to this as 'institutional thickness' which they define as 'the capacity of places to develop, consolidate and transmit structures of representation, interaction and innovation' (Amin and Thrift, 1995d: 106). While this is neither 'an easy concept to grasp' nor fully specified (1995d: 101) 'processes of institutionalisation' at the local scale are deemed to be significant in seeking to 'capture' global economic flows (1995d: 92).

For others, however, any regulatory shift is seen to have a much more pernicious effect, tied to the implementation of neo-liberalism as a political project and the maintenance of local social control (Lovering, 1995). While certain institutions of regulation are locally embedded, the social power to establish and maintain a particular model of growth is seen to be centralised in the form of agents and institutions of global extent. As Peck and Tickell argue:

> Below the nation-state, local regulatory systems (particularly local states) have been conferred *responsibility without power*. . . . Above the nation-state, supra-national regulatory systems have inherited *power without responsibility* (Peck and Tickell, 1994: 324–5, original emphasis).

It is difficult to see a way out of the oppositional nature of such debates so long as they remain couched in scale, and more particularly, local/global terms. Progress would depend instead, it seems, upon harnessing together the *fluidity* and *flows* emphasised in certain formulations with the notions of coherent 'bounded' spaces developed in others. Indeed, there appears to be no necessary reason as to why a relational or fluid view should lead to an abandoning of the conceptualisation of the local as particular geographic spaces or configurations. In short, '(t)here is no logical connection between recognising the local as "in and of the global", and abandoning a sense of the local as bounded geographical space' (Amin and Thrift, 1995d: 97).

Moving in this direction may involve a thorough and much needed rethinking of the concept of globalisation in the process. Along these lines Low suggests that:

globalization is not a matter of the construction of a 'global' economic space or arena, but of the restructuring and extension of networks of flows (of money, goods, and people), and of their articulation with areal or 'regional' spaces at different scales (Low, 1997: 244).

Low argues more broadly that academic writing in political geography has tended to privilege a particular way of conceptualising politics. The dominant view is one of politics as confined within particular areal spaces, such as 'regional' or 'national' politics or, more pertinently, the local politics of the entrepreneurial city. Low argues that:

(c)onceptualizing political spaces as areal, as a set of (mutually constitutive) arenas, privileges a way of thinking about political activity as a series of confrontations between agents. These arena occupants – which may be individuals or classes, groups, movements – square off, interact, struggle, compromise, constitute each other and so on in academic writing as though mutually co-present (Low, 1997: 241).

Low's concern here is with the relationship between globalisation and representative democracy, although his arguments can be extended to the literature on the entrepreneurial city and the new urban politics. He argues further, that:

the strangely static quality of these debates (about the globalization versus localization of politics) may be attributable to the fact that arguments are embedded in a conceptual system in which areal communities at different scales are privileged by different writers, but in which the focus on areal political communities and processes is accepted by all (Low 1997: 243).

Such a view privileges a 'politics of place' in which:

the meaning and identity of political actors are referred to a particular place, a portion of areal space, whether it be a neighborhood, a city, region or national territory, and where as a result a certain degree of political closure is effected or at least reinforced (Low 1997: 255).

Low argues that while globalisation has been seen to undermine the national scale as the most appropriate regulatory space in the late twentieth century, place, or the 'local' scale, is viewed by many as a possible functional substitute. Thus one areal form is replaced by another. Low argues instead for greater emphasis on networked or non-areal conceptions of space, 'which in practice and in principle operate at cross-purposes to the areal spatial forms generally invoked by notions of political community' (Low, 1997: 244). In the context of globalisation and the entrepreneurial city, this view is important. In the first instance it challenges the need to bracket out what are seen as 'global' processes, viewing them simply as the context for political and economic changes at the urban scale. In this traditional view the entrepreneurial city is seen as principally a product of or response to globalisation rather than an integral part of its development.

An alternative conceptualisation that moves away from an exclusive focus on areal spaces and their interrelationship is important in at least two related ways. On the one hand it accommodates the view that many of the activities associated with entrepreneurial cities in turn facilitate globalisation (Leitner, 1990). Thus, rather than seeing urban entrepreneurialism as a 'product' of globalisation, changes in urban governance can be seen as constitutive of broader processes of economic and political change. This is where Harvey and Cox and Mair have the edge over many other accounts. Harvey argues, for example, that the shift to urban entrepreneurialism 'has had an important facilitative role in the transition from Fordism to flexible accumulation' (Harvey, 1989b: 12). This facilitative role has at least three dimensions which include: enhancing the geographical flexibility of multinational capital as local powers seek to 'maximise the attractiveness of the local site as a lure for capitalist development' (Harvey, 1989b: 5); the diffusion of particular forms of urban redevelopment through their serial reproduction (see also Olds, 1995); and the development of mechanisms of social control through the promotion of place-based identities. The crucial mechanism linking local developments to their more general reproduction is one of inter-urban competition (Wood, 1998). In short, what goes on in entrepreneurial cities is important not only in simply reproducing or resisting but in constituting the form of the global.

Secondly, a move away from conceptualising space in terms of bounded areas may focus more attention on the nature and dynamics of the global-isation process rather than the spatial scales privileged or undermined along the way. What matters surely is the nature of globalisation – that is to say, what precisely is being globalised – rather than its particular geometries. This is not to argue that a concern with bounded areal spaces should be displaced in the process, but rather that the articulation of linkages and spaces would direct attention to the processes underpinning the production of particular spatial configurations and their politics.

CONCLUSION

While the term 'the entrepreneurial city' is now common in the literature there has been little progress in developing our means of understanding changes in urban governance and their implications. Hall and Hubbard's recent review suggests that 'the literature on the entrepreneurial city, although sizeable, rests on theoretically and empirically impoverished grounds' (Hall and Hubbard, 1996: 154). This chapter has sought to review the work of various authors concerned to one degree or another with the entrepreneurial city, focusing in particular on the way in which scale and concepts of the 'local' and the 'global' have been mobilised. While there is a vast literature outside the scope of this chapter, I have argued that dominant academic conceptualisations concerned with boxing social processes into discrete spatial pigeon-holes can only take us so far in understanding the entrepreneurial city.

I have argued instead that we need to move away from a view that concerns itself with consigning social processes and phenomena to particular spatial scales and to adopt one that focuses on the relationships between areal spaces and networks or flows (Low, 1997). This would seem to open up a rather different window on the entrepreneurial city, not only changing the way we view the processes shaping urban areas but also recognising the constitutive role of the 'local' in shaping the broader social changes associated with globalisation.

ACKNOWLEDGEMENTS

A number of the ideas in this chapter have benefited from work undertaken as part of an ESRC-funded project entitled 'Creating Local Business Interests' with David Valler and Peter North at Sheffield University (Grant R000236566). The support of the ESRC is gratefully acknowledged.

14

ECONOMIC UNCERTAINTY, INTER-URBAN COMPETITION AND THE EFFICACY OF ENTREPRENEURIALISM

HELGA LEITNER AND ERIC SHEPPARD

INTRODUCTION

Capitalist competition, and the markets mediating it, are inherently uncertain environments. Firms can never be sure whether their product will sell, what prices their competitors will charge, or when a new product or production method will be developed that undermines their market share. The uncertainties faced by firms in turn create uncertainties for the places where they are located, which cities attempt to reduce by having as diverse a local economy as possible, and which states attempt to mitigate through regulatory regimes. Under Fordism, Keynesian and military economic policies reduced this uncertainty substantially within the Western world. Income, employment, public spending, and government procurement programmes helped secure domestic markets for manufacturing and services, dominated by large corporations which could afford to pay their workers progressively increasing wages, the costs of which could be passed on to consumers as higher prices. In this era, firms, and the cities in which they located, faced relatively little uncertainty. Even cities with highly specialised economic bases, such as the steel towns of Pittsburgh, Birmingham and Dortmund, prospered for decades relying on the same economic base, and felt little need to worry about the future or to diversify their activities. During the last 20 years, however, this has changed.

Since the early 1970s, identified by many as the time when the 'golden age' of postwar Fordism came to an end in the West, cities have experienced increasing economic uncertainty precipitated by global, national and regional economic and political restructuring. The increasing economic uncertainty faced by cities, and the rising dominance of political discourses promoting a belief in the economic and social efficiency of the 'free' market and competitiveness, have presented cities with a mix of pressures and opportunities, drawing them into more intensified competition with one another. Although a few cities, such as New York, Paris or London, are large and diverse enough to weather economic uncertainty well, many other cities have found it increasingly difficult to maintain their competitive position and have actively been seeking new investments and industries. Yet uncertainty has also created new opportunities for cities to prosper under inter-urban competition, as new niches develop and new locations become favoured.

Under pressure to take responsibility for improving the competitiveness of their city, urban policy-makers developed more active entrepreneurial strategies and created new institutional structures of urban governance, commonly referred to as urban entrepreneurialism. Urban entrepreneurialism invokes images of cities as analogous to firms, whereby the self-interested actions of cities competing for economic growth are supposed to generate benefits for all urban residents and all cities. In turn this implies the creation of a more efficient, productive and dynamic national space economy, through the operation of Adam Smith's 'hidden hand'. In this view, the widespread adoption of urban entrepreneurialism embodies the putative benefits of market-led economic development.

Arguments for the beneficial effects of urban entrepreneurialism depend, however, on two critical assumptions which we contend are unsustainable: that inter-urban competition takes place on a level playing field and that cities are like firms. Taking into account the uneven nature of the playing field and the crucial differences between cities and firms, it becomes clear that the widespread adoption of urban entrepreneurialism in an urban system can reinforce inequalities between cities, leading all too easily to a zero-sum game in which all cities feel compelled to engage in urban entrepreneurialism even if it leads to a form of inter-urban competition which becomes more destructive than it is constructive.

The first section of this chapter examines in detail the ways in which global and national processes of economic and political restructuring have generated increased economic uncertainty for cities, and the concomitant pressures and opportunities they now face. We then discuss how inter-urban competition and urban entrepreneurialism arose as a response to this, and the nature and basis of the claims that urban entrepreneurialism is beneficial. Third, we argue that the assumptions underlying these claims are questionable, and that widespread adoption of urban entrepreneurialism can be counter-productive both for individual cities, and for the society whose economic growth these cities are made responsible for. Finally, we reflect briefly on some alternative strategies for cities seeking to cope with economic uncertainty, suggesting that it is necessary to reconsider the widespread assumption that competitive entrepreneurial strategies are the only reasonable option for contemporary urban policy.

INCREASING ECONOMIC UNCERTAINTY – NEW CHALLENGES AND OPPORTUNITIES FOR CITIES AND REGIONS

Global and national processes of economic and political restructuring affecting advanced industrial economies and their cities can be characterised as having been dominated by four kinds of changes: shifts in the economic sectors driving growth, often misleadingly described as the rise of a post-industrial society; the revolution in communications technologies, catalysing reduced communications costs and increasingly flexible production, and accelerating the pace of technological change; the institutional and geographical integration of finance markets, accelerating the mobility of finance capital; and transformations in the form and content of political governance.

Sectoral shifts

Deep-seated sectoral shifts in the momentum of economic growth redefined the economic base of advanced capitalist economies in the 1970s. In North America and western Europe these shifts manifested themselves as stagnation and decline in the mass production of labour-intensive textiles, heavy manu-facturing and consumer durables, and the rise of information technology-related sectors and producer services. The growth of producer services reflects a continued tendency for command and control functions co-ordinating global production networks to locate in North America and Europe, as well as a shift to a greater degree of specialisation and customisation of services (Noyelle and Stanback, 1984). These shifts were triggered by stagnating labour productivity combined with low levels of investment in new technologies, and by inten-sified competition in traditional industries from other countries and regions with more favourable productivity and wage conditions (Aglietta, 1979; Fröbel, Heinrichs and Kreye, 1980; Armstrong, Glyn and Harrison, 1991). As a result, countries which traditionally had been confident about continued economic prosperity experienced unfamiliar uncertainty about their economic future and competitiveness in an emerging global economy (European Commission, 1994; Krugman, 1994).

These sectoral shifts had dramatic regional and urban consequences, as the industries which many cities had come to rely on for economic prosperity collapsed. Many traditional core industrial cities could no longer rely on past practices but had to cast around for new economic activities and development strategies. Pittsburgh's well-paid steel jobs practically disappeared as firms closed and residents left, before its re-emergence as a centre for producer services; and Boston underwent a similar transformation from heavy manufacturing to information technology (see Chapter 3). Others were not so fortunate, finding it difficult to replace the lost industries and employment. At the same time, new urban growth centres emerged in places able to take advantage of the different locational demands of the new growth sectors, rapidly expanding in size, prosperity and importance (the San Jose–Silicon Valley complex being the best known US example).

As David Gordon (1978) has documented, such periodic surges of economic uncertainty for cities, challenging the practices of established growth centres and providing the promise of opportunity for disadvantaged cities, have occurred on several occasions in industrial capitalism, both at the onset of the Industrial Revolution and periodically since (see also Chapter 2). In previous eras, such surges of uncertainty were followed by periods of stability, once new geographic patterns of advantage and disadvantage took shape, but as yet there is little empirical evidence that this is the case for the current restructuring. Indeed, many analysts argue that we have in fact entered a 'post-Fordist' era characterised by flexibility and change (Webber, 1991), or, as Lash and Urry (1987) describe it, 'the end of organized capitalism'. Whether or not this is the case, the high levels of uncertainty which cities are still experiencing cannot be attributed to sectoral shifts alone. A fuller explanation must take account of a variety of other closely interrelated economic and political changes continuing to fuel economic uncertainty, even as the sectoral shifts dissipate. We will examine some of the most significant of these in turn.

The communications revolution

Two broad changes in communications technologies are increasing the economic uncertainty faced by cities: a longer-term decline in the costs of transportation, and a more recent information-based communications revolution whose timing has coincided with the end of Fordism. The communications revolution in turn has stimulated wide-ranging changes in the organisation of production and production methods, particularly the rise of flexible production, with their own effects on economic uncertainty.

The declining importance of transportation costs as a component of production costs means that locational advantages stemming from accessibility to markets, resources and labour have become less important relative to other site-specific differences between cities (such as labour costs, industrial clusters and local governance systems) in affecting their attractiveness to private investors. However, differences in accessibility among regions change slowly: the locations of cities with high or low accessibility within Europe and the USA have changed little since the beginning of the century, except when political barriers such as the Iron Curtain in Europe closed off transport routes. Once reduced transportation and communications costs make differences in accessibility less important to firms, cities can no longer rely on high accessibility as a durable locational advantage that attracts economic growth. Differential advantages of accessibility have not necessarily been eliminated: it is still the case, for example, that cities located in the heart of Europe experience more rapid growth (Wegener, 1995). None the less, locationally advantaged cities are not as secure as they once were, and locationally disadvantaged cities may find it easier than before to attract investors by manipulating site-specific conditions.

Christopher Freeman and others argue that the distinctive feature of post-1973 capitalism is a technological revolution, with information technology ushering in new communications possibilities and a new Kondratieff long-wave of capitalist economic growth (cf. Freeman et al, 1982). Although this form of technological determinism may be too simple, the information revolution has certainly been one of the most significant changes of the last 25 years, and has enhanced economic uncertainty for cities (Castells, 1989, 1994). Information-based technologies have reduced communications costs in two ways, each with distinctive effects on economic uncertainty.

First, electronic communication has significantly eased the co-ordination of production between geographically distant facilities. Traditionally, the need for face-to-face communication is listed as an important factor reinforcing geographical clustering. The intra-metropolitan agglomeration of producer services has been seen as an important example of this. Electronic communication has not replaced all face-to-face communication, but has facilitated a wider range of communication needs to be taken care of at a distance. This has made it easier for firms and plants linked together through commodity or information flows, or through strategic alliances, to reduce their costs by locating different activities in different parts of the world. Multi-plant corporations, but also small firms, can participate in international production lines and assembly networks, including global sourcing and international subcontracting, which give them access to global markets and reduce their dependence on the conditions found in individual places. They can engage in national or even global searches for the most efficient locations for different production activities, selecting cities whose site conditions best meet the particular needs of each activity rather than clustering activities with different requirements within the same city.

These communications changes undermine the advantages of clustering activities together within one city (i.e. agglomeration economies) and increase the locational flexibility of firms by potentially reducing their dependence on particular cities. When corporations have production facilities in different places, it is easier for them to reduce production in one place and increase it in another if local conditions (such as labour costs, taxes or environmental regulation) seem unfavourable in a particular city. Even for firms with a single production facility, lower agglomeration economies and increased locational flexibility make it easier for a single firm to play cities off against one another in a bid to gain support from the local community, as long as they are not committed to that location by heavy prior investments in buildings and equipment (Cox and Mair, 1988).

Second, at the scale of the production line, information-based technologies such as computer-aided design and computer-aided manufacturing (CAD–CAM) are profoundly increasing the flexibility of commodity production, ushering in an era of flexible production. Such technologies not only increase the speed with which production lines can be altered from the production of one model to the production of another, but also are accelerating the overall pace of development of new products and technologies (i.e. the rate of technological change).

Increasing the flexibility of production lines effectively reduces the scale economies associated with mass production (i.e. the savings associated with the production of large quantities of the identical item), making small plants more competitive. In industries as varied as beer and steel manufacture, microbreweries and mini-mills now are able to produce nearly as cheaply as the huge production facilities that used to be dominant. This flexibility has also enabled a shift to more customised manufacture: producing a wider range of products from a single production line, in order to cater to a wider range of tastes. The effects of this are far from one-sided. Some argue that flexible production encourages a disintegration of production from large corporations to smaller businesses, which in turn cluster into industrial complexes located in and tied to the fortunes of particular cities (Scott, 1988). Others argue, however, that the smaller plants may still be owned or dominated by large corporations (Gertler, 1988), and that the enhanced need that small firms have for inter-firm linkages does not necessarily imply that they locate close to one another in intra-urban production complexes (Holmes, 1986; Schoenberger, 1988; Sayer and Walker, 1992). Yet there is agreement that flexible production technologies have reduced the fixed costs associated with production. Reductions in fixed costs mean that smaller plants can be built, which take fewer years to pay for. Thus instead of immense investments in steel plants which then operate for 40 years, supporting and providing economic inertia for the steel towns of Pennsylvania and Ohio from the 1940s to the 1970s, for example, plants can be replaced more frequently. The consequence of this for cities is that it now takes fewer years before a production facility is paid for; at which time the firm will reassess the benefits of continuing production in that city.

The increased pace of technological change for all kinds of commodities, which is also associated with the use of information technology on the production line, has tended to reduce the length of the time period in which firms must recoup their fixed capital investments. When technologies become outdated, the fixed costs invested in them become sunk costs, i.e. past investments in fixed capital which cannot easily be recuperated (Clark and Wrigley, 1995). When technological change is rapid, production facilities become out of date sooner because their economic lifetime is reduced (Sheppard and Barnes, 1990), accelerating the speed with which fixed capital investments must be paid off in order to avoid them becoming sunk costs. Firms have therefore moved to increase the rate of depreciation on their fixed investments: by raising profitability, by negotiating capital subsidies with the local state, and by seeking higher depreciation allowances on fixed capital from the national state. Currently, developers and industrialists alike seek places and conditions which allow them to pay off their investments in buildings and equipment in five years or less. When firms are successful in gaining such conditions they recoup their fixed capital investments more quickly, which in turn makes them more mobile.

Rapid technological change also poses direct challenges to cities. Cities invest in a built environment that is appropriate for technologies and economic activities of the time; investments which, if wisely made, attract particular kinds of firms. Over time, however, any built environment becomes less appropriate for new technologies and production methods and eventually can become dysfunctional. Cities then become constrained in their old built environments and infrastructures, making them relatively unattractive for subsequent investors (Harvey, 1985a). The same argument applies to other ways in which cities become committed to particular development paths whose efficacy for economic growth is subject to change. As in the case of firms, increased rates of technological change mean that a city's physical and social infrastructure becomes outdated, and needs to be remade more frequently, as firms are becoming more mobile.

To summarise, changing communications technologies are affecting the uncertainties faced by cities in four distinct ways. First, the importance of geographical accessibility between cities is declining relative to local con-ditions, as a consequence of falling transportation costs, undermining a traditionally durable source of locational advantage and disadvantage. Second, firms are becoming less dependent on particular cities, and more frequently reconsider the attractiveness of their investment in a city, and the possibility of relocation, as a consequence of enhanced ease of communication between plants and of the opportunities and pressures associated with flexible production and accelerated technological change. Third, flexible production enhances the productivity of clusters of firms, and of the cities containing those clusters, under certain conditions. Finally, cities themselves become outdated, and must reinvent themselves and replace their physical and social infrastructure more rapidly in order to remain attractive for investors.

Globalisation of finance

The economic activities discussed above are sustained by fixed capital investments: by firms purchasing buildings and equipment, and by the public sector investing in social and physical infrastructure to attract and support those firms. The capital needed to finance such fixed capital investment is often too large to be raised from profits or tax revenues, however, meaning that access to capital markets, and to institutions in those markets willing to advance the necessary credit, is a necessary prerequisite for a successful urban economy. It is important, therefore, to investigate changes in capital markets and their influence on the economic uncertainty faced by cities. We highlight three such changes: increased geographical mobility, increased complexity and flexibility of financial institutions and instruments, and the increased speed of turnover of finance capital.

First, the geographic scope of finance capital circuits has increased rapidly. It is now common for cities and their firms to seek to borrow capital from a variety of financial institutions around the world, and for financial institutions to consider lending across the globe. This global integration has been fuelled by communications technologies, making possible the instantaneous transfer of money anywhere in the world; by international negotiations, harmonising the regulations governing different national finance markets in order to make integration work; and by pressure placed on national governments, particularly by the IMF, to eliminate restrictions on international capital flows. Stocks, bonds and currencies are now traded worldwide 24 hours a day (Thrift, 1989a), and multinational corporations and wealthy individuals routinely transfer capital across international borders in response to investment needs, exchange rate fluctuations and tax law differences. Trends reinforcing the global circulation of finance capital put cities and local firms in international competition with one another to borrow money. Global integration has ostensibly made it easier for a city to attract money from elsewhere, giving cash-starved localities new opportunities in the form of a world of potential lenders; but also making it easier for locally generated deposits to flow to other cities, undermining the ability of prosperous cities to rely on local money to fuel investment in further economic growth.

Secondly, as regulatory barriers limiting the flow of money between different kinds of financial services are falling, the variety of financial instruments is increasing (as is the degree to which they are speculative in nature), and the institutional barriers between the activities of different types of financial institutions (and between financial and non-financial institutions) are dissipating. As in the case of the global integration of finance markets, this has been increasing the range of options for borrowers and lenders. Yet falling regulatory barriers have also greatly enhanced the complexity and uncertainty associated with borrowing and lending money. Potential borrowers are faced with a bewildering variety of financial instruments and institutions, each with somewhat different goals and constraints, while potential lenders seek to become familiar with a correspondingly broad range of investment opportunities with very different terms and expectations. This makes it harder for borrowers to know when they have found the best deal, or for lenders to accurately assess the risks and opportunities of a particular opportunity. Some borrowers may, by luck or good judgement, be offered loans on very good terms relative to the potential risks, from asset-rich institutions or those with a poor understanding of the risks involved, but others can only gain loans whose terms are overly restrictive relative to the risks and opportunities of the loan.

The complexity of finance markets thus enhances uncertainty about whether money can be borrowed, for what purposes and under what conditions. Furthermore, even when a successful loan agreement is negotiated on terms favourable to the local borrower, the capacity to pay off that loan depends on estimates about the anticipated prosperity of the local economy, which must generate revenues to pay back the loan. The greater the degree of economic uncertainty, the more difficult it is to make these estimates accurately. A number of countries faced exactly this problem in the early 1980s, when unexpected downturns in their national economies together with rising interest rates created a global financial crisis as they were forced to suspend payments on generous bank loans received three to five years earlier, and local economies are inherently more unpredictable than national economies. The complexity and flexibility of capital markets have even encouraged cities to raise revenues by investing in capital markets, instead of raising taxes or issuing municipal bonds. For example, the municipal funds of Orange County, in metropolitan Los Angeles, were invested in derivatives (high-risk, high-return junk bonds) in an attempt rapidly to increase revenues, creating a dramatic example of economic uncertainty. Between 1992 and 1993 the percentage of Orange County revenues generated by interest-bearing investments rose from 3 to 35%, only for the entire speculative boom to collapse overnight at the end of 1994 into a catastrophic debt exceeding US$2bn (Davis, 1995).

Thirdly, the turnover time of finance capital, i.e. the length of time that capital is loaned before the investor considers withdrawing it and moving it elsewhere, is shortening. Long-term developmental loans, to firms or cities, are generally associated with high risk because prospects of success cannot easily be judged, and require considerable commitment by the lender to the project since in the short term pay-offs are often negligible. Increasingly the stock market has become the norm against which such loans are judged. The stock market discourages long-term commitment by lenders, however, since money can be withdrawn quickly and at little cost if a stock performs below expectations. Stock market returns, averaging 15% annually in the American stock market over the last 15 years (S & P 500, 1981–96), have also set a high standard for other investments and loans to meet. When the short-term thinking characteristic of the stock market dominates the strategies of potential lenders, then firms and cities face difficulties financing long-term developmental improvements; and investors expect short-term cost-cutting measures, often to the detriment of such longer-term goals as research and development or social programmes (Hutton, 1996). This 'short-termism' (Hallsworth, 1996) is particularly widespread in Britain and the USA, but stock markets are becoming increasingly influential worldwide. As lenders' investment strategies become increasingly flexible, and as they come to know less about, and identify less with, the needs of particular creditors in particular places, the temptation to judge all loans against the stock market will increase. The speed and geographic mobility of finance capital circulation will then further accelerate, and economic uncertainty will increase.

State restructuring and geopolitical changes

Concomitant to these changing economic realities, the last two decades have seen a dramatic transformation in the forms and content of political governance which has been of great significance for cities and regions. In particular three broad trends in North America and Europe stand out. First, nation states have been adopting new modes of state intervention, reducing state spending on welfare state activities and instead channelling public resources towards the support of capital accumulation by private firms and the privatisation of public services. The reorientation of central state activities towards this supply-side philosophy has been embedded in a discourse promoting belief in the economic and social efficiency of the market, marginalising past values and goals such as social justice and social and spatial equity (Pickvance and Preteceille, 1991b: 197; see also Chapter 4). This has had profound effects on the options deemed legitimate for nations and their cities. Nation states are seen as engaged in promoting national success through economic competition, described by some analysts as a shift from geopolitics to geo-economics (Leyshon, 1992). Cities in turn are seen as the motors for national competitive success. Influential analysts have argued that the intra-national spatial clustering of economic activities encourages national competitiveness (Porter, 1990; Storper, 1992, 1995), and national governments across western Europe have increasingly come to stress the potential contribution of cities, particularly large cities, to national economic competitiveness and performance (Commission of the European Communities, 1992). For example, the Dutch national government has developed increasingly explicit national urban policies targeting key urban areas such as the Randstad as economic assets.

Second, there has been a restructuring of central–local state relations, emphasising a decentralisation of both powers and responsibilities from national to subnational levels of government. This has resulted in reduced national intervention and public expenditure in cities and regions, and a greater emphasis on local authority and management. A strong central state, with the capacity and desire to come to the aid of cities in economic distress, can limit the economic uncertainty faced by individual cities. Active and effective national urban and regional policies provided some insurance for cities, seeking to manage and reduce inter-urban inequalities in economic growth and prosperity by redistributing resources from advantaged to disadvantaged locations. This insurance has dissipated with the reduced emphasis on such policies in Europe (Cheshire, 1993) and particularly in the USA, with considerable reductions in central state funds for cities. Since the 1980s cities have increasingly been made responsible for ensuring their own economic growth and prosperity, creating new pressures and opportunities. For example, the New Federalism introduced by President Reagan during the 1980s gave US local governments greater policy discretion, but at the same time greatly reduced federal funds available for cities, thus effectively forcing them to utilise their own resources and compete aggressively for private investment. The implications were concisely stated in the President's National Urban Policy Report: 'State and local governments have primary responsibility for making their urban areas attractive to private investors' (US Department of Housing and Urban Development, 1982).

Third, the increasing influence of supranational institutions such as the EU, NAFTA, the IMF, and the associated erosion of nation states' powers to manage and control their economies, have contributed to increased economic uncertainty, as well as creating new opportunities for cities and regions. European integration has broken down many international barriers to commodity, capital and labour flows during the last decades. This has recently been reinforced by the geopolitical changes associated with the demise of the Soviet bloc, opening up the cities of western Europe to aggressive competition from former Comecon countries (see Chapter 8). One side-effect of removing international barriers can be to reduce the number of locations engaged in the same economic activity. As national markets are replaced by a supranational market there is less need for each nation state to have, for example, its own automobile industry. Production can then be concentrated in those few cities that are advantageous from a European-wide perspective, undermining the advantages held by other cities in an era of national markets. Increased supranational integration also brings higher-wage cities into more direct competition with lower-wage cities (cf. Krugman and Venables, 1990). Higher-wage cities can in principle counteract this competition by taking advantage of agglomeration economies, higher skills, accumulated expertise in particular industries and accessibility to wealthier markets. Yet in an era when technological changes are undermining the importance and prevalence of some of these factors, and with nation states less able or willing to protect their cities from global competition, low-wage competition can severely challenge the practices of established manufacturing cities and create new insecurities and uncertainties. Consider, for example, the competitive challenge currently faced by west European cities from the nearby cities of the Czech Republic, whose skilled labour force is regarded as one of the most cost effective in the world. The North American Free Trade Agreement (NAFTA) raises the prospect that Mexican cities will pose similar challenges for American cities.

INTER-URBAN COMPETITION AND URBAN ENTREPRENEURIALISM – RECONSTITUTING LOCAL ECONOMIC DEVELOPMENT POLICIES

The increased economic uncertainty faced by cities, and the economic and political changes since the early 1970s underlying this increase, have therefore created new pressures for cities to engage more explicitly in inter-urban competition to generate economic growth and prosperity, and new opportunities to do so. However, reasons for engaging in inter-urban competition vary for different cities depending on their site-specific characteristics and their situation within the broader political economic system. For some cities, economic uncertainty has undermined the reliability and success of past development practices, increasing the pressure to compete in order to reinvigorate the urban economy and retain economic prosperity. For other cities, economic uncertainty presents them with new opportunities for growth through competition and a means of overcoming unsuccessful development paths and economic stagnation. In this case, uncertainty at least suggests the possibility of a change for the better, and competition becomes the means for seeking to turn this possibility into reality.

In an attempt to improve the competitiveness of their city, urban policy-makers developed more activist, entrepreneurial strategies and created new institutional structures of urban governance, commonly referred to as urban entrepreneurialism. In turn, the adoption of urban entrepreneurialism has accelerated the intensity of inter-urban competition. As has been convincingly argued by Jessop (1996: 4; see also Chapter 4), the rise and diffusion of urban entrepreneurialism as the new dominant policy strategy have also to be seen as part and parcel of new political discourses emphasising competitiveness, enterprise, the superiority of the free market, public–private partnerships, strategic alliances, etc. The following quote from the book *The Entrepreneurial American City*, exemplifies dominant elements in this discursive construction of urban entrepreneurialism:

> The history of cities in the United States is entering a new era of public entrepreneurship. This profound change in the way cities operate may best be termed 'urban entrepreneurialism'. Cities are acting as risk-takers and active competitors in the urban economic game, and the key to each city's success is its ability to invest wisely and to market shrewdly. Urban entrepreneurship entails a new breed of municipal official, transcending the traditional local government roles of delivering services and enforcing regulations. The city entrepreneurial role includes characteristics traditionally viewed as distinctive to the private sector, such as risk-taking, inventiveness, self-reliance, profit motivation, and promotion. The bottom line for the public balance sheet is the enhanced competitiveness of the city which is critical to urban rebuilding and economic revitalization (Duckworth, Simmons and McNulty, 1986: 4–5).

This narrative constructs the entrepreneurial American city as responding to economic change and uncertainty by imitating the outlook and financial practices of the private sector, signalling a new style of urban governance for the purpose of pursuing economic growth and competitiveness under a free-market framework. Indeed, urban entrepreneurialism and inter-urban competition are so closely associated with one another that frequently they are treated as synonymous.

Urban entrepreneurialism was first championed in the United States in the late 1970s, and has since been emulated by cities across Europe, first in the

UK before diffusing to the Continent. While most of the research on urban entrepreneurialism has concentrated on larger cities, entrepreneurial strategies have been diffusing throughout the urban hierarchy to encompass economically weak and strong urban areas (Helbrecht, 1994). Notwithstanding variations between countries and among cities, and shifts in urban entrepreneurialism and discourses over time, urban entrepreneurialism in the USA and western Europe has certain common characteristics. Commonalties can be identified at the level of overall strategy and philosophy, but also in the actions pursued to implement urban entrepreneurialism.

First, public–private partnerships between local political and business élites, often including segments of organised labour but generally excluding neighbourhood movements and interests, and orchestrated by local quasi-public development agencies, have become the institutional mainstay of urban entrepreneurialism (for a detailed analysis of geographic variations in the composition and social inclusiveness of public–private partnerships see Keating, 1993). In US cities, these partnerships, often built on long-standing traditions of co-operation between business leaders and local political élites in urban development, were institutionalised within quasi-public development agencies beginning in the late 1970s. They focused on a project-oriented approach, identifying and taking advantage of opportunities for generating local economic growth, rather than a closely co-ordinated comprehensive action plan.

Second, cities act in a self-interested manner to promote economic growth within their territory, competing with one another in a manner seen as analogous to firms in the market-place. Third, local public sector resources and powers are strategically utilised to promote private sector economic growth at the expense of the traditional regulatory and social welfare functions of local governments. This signals a decline in the welfarist conception of local government and the rising influence of the market choice concept (Pickvance and Preteceille, 1991b). Fourth, despite variations in the economic base of cities, efforts to stimulate economic growth have been remarkably similar in their concentration on the retention and attraction of leading economic sectors, such as high-tech industries and associated research and development activities in science and technology parks, producer services, and the creation of a built environment attractive to professionals and tourists. Within this orientation towards new urban economic activities and consumption styles, cities do, however, develop strategic approaches which take into account their particular strengths and weaknesses (Harvey, 1985b). For example, Frankfurt 'perceives its strength in financial services and has been trying to secure the proposed European Central Bank; Stockholm builds on information-intensive activities, Birmingham attempts to offset its image as a culture-less city by building up its symphony orchestra, building a new world-class concert hall and attracting the Sadlers Wells company from London' (Cheshire and Gordon, 1993: 21; see also Chapter 6).

At the more concrete level of actions taken to implement urban entrepreneurialism, certain types of activities have taken centre stage in the entrepreneurial repertoire: these include place advertising; property-led development projects such as office, retail and recreational complexes; and promotion of knowledge-based industries such as science and technology parks and teleports. One of the most popular activities has been place advertising, designed to promote a positive place image, very often a new image replacing the old, in an effort to boost the confidence of current or potential businesses, residents and visitors in a particular city or area within a city (Kearns and Philo, 1993; Sadler, 1993). From Pittsburgh to Glasgow, Belfast to Barcelona, the collection of images being promoted in newspaper advertisements, glossy brochures, videotapes and Worldwide Web pages heralds a city's superior business climate, technical infrastructure, environmental, recreational and cultural amenities, highly educated, hard-working labour force, and superior local leadership. These attributes are considered to be important to potential investors, residents and tourists alike (Goodwin, 1993; Holcomb, 1993; Philo and Kearns, 1993; see also Chapter 3).

Property-led development projects subsidised by the public sector have been most significant in terms of the extent of public resources committed in many cities. Some focus on attracting investment in leading manufacturing and service sectors, such as science and technology parks and up-market office complexes. Others are oriented more towards providing an attractive landscape of consumption for tourists and wealthier residents, such as speciality shopping malls, concert halls, sports stadia, museums, and exhibition and conference centres. In the United States, for example, city governments ventured on a large scale into the subsidisation of private commercial real estate development in the late 1970s. Extensive public assistance packages, including tax abatements and rebates, land purchase subsidies, low-interest loans, loan guarantees, zoning bonuses and equity financing, were employed, both to promote contemporary growth sectors and consumption styles in the city centre and to improve the city's revenue base through increased property taxes – an issue of particular importance in US cities which rely on local property taxes for local public sector revenue (Clarke and Rich, 1985; Eisinger, 1988).

In an attempt to recapture some of the public funds invested in private development projects, local governments in the USA are increasingly requiring loan pay-backs from developers, are entering into land lease arrangements, and are bargaining for a share of profits from publicly assisted projects (Dowall, 1987; Frieden, 1990). In rapidly growing cities and/or cities with progressive city administrations, the provision of financial incentives has also been linked to exactions. These require developers, in return for development permits, rezoning and other public subsidies for commercial projects, to set aside a certain proportion of the project costs for the development of low-income housing, to provide employment guarantees for city residents, or to pay impact fees which are used to fund mass transit, day care and other public services. In San Francisco and Boston, for example, local authorities have had significant success with these policies (Keating, 1986; Goetz, 1988, 1990; Lassar, 1989). Property-led economic development policies have also been a dominant component in local economic development initiatives of many European cities. There is Europe-wide evidence of cities spending increased public resources for these purposes in such places as London (Goodwin, 1993), Sheffield (Cochrane, 1992), Frankfurt (Prigg and Lieser, 1992), Hamburg (Dangschat, 1992), Lyon (Müller, 1992) and Barcelona (Held, 1992).

A third set of actions common to urban entrepreneurialism is a diverse set of initiatives designed to promote knowledge-based industries. In addition to science parks, these include the development of communications infrastructure (teleports), education and training programmes, support for venture capital institutions, and promotion of co-operation and technology transfer between local universities and technical colleges, research centres and the private sector. These actions have increased in prominence in recent years, as the discourse and practice of urban entrepreneurialism have shifted from a focus on attracting external investors (i.e. an inward investment strategy) towards the promotion of local firms regarded as having a high potential to develop a competitive advantage through a synergy of rapid technological development, local networking, and skilled, high-wage employment (i.e. an endogenous development strategy, cf. Porter, 1990; Storper, 1992).

CONTESTING CLAIMS ABOUT THE BENEFITS OF URBAN ENTREPRENEURIALISM

Proponents have heralded urban entrepreneurialism as the best response to economic uncertainty, making several closely related claims about its benefits (Peterson, 1981; Duckworth, Simmons and McNulty, 1986; Frieden and Sagalyn, 1989; Porter, 1990). In the first instance, claims are made about the benefits accruing to a city and its residents, which may be summarised as the proposition that urban entrepreneurialism increases the efficiency and competitiveness of an urban economy to the benefit of all: a rising tide that lifts all boats. On the one hand, promotion of market forces is seen as allowing the hidden hand of the market to operate. In this view, efficient production maximises output at minimum costs, the market allocates goods in a Pareto optimal manner among residents according to their preferences, and local state revenues available for social programmes are also maximised (Peterson, 1981). On the other hand, under urban entrepreneurialism the economic success of a city is seen as equivalent to its capacity to generate competitive advantage, creating increasing economic returns which enable growth, good jobs at high wages, and even a desirable physical environment (Porter, 1990).

Furthermore, claims are made about the benefits of urban entrepreneurialism for society as a whole. These have received less explicit attention and often amount to little more than the presumption that if urban entrepreneurialism is good for each city taken individually it must also be good for all cities taken together. This is the logic of the hidden hand, applied to the urban system: if individuals – in this case individual cities – seek to maximise their benefits then society as a whole gains. Cities are treated as rational self-interested actors whose success or failure is determined by their entrepreneurial skill, and entrepreneurial cities are claimed to result in an efficient and competitive national economy (Porter, 1990).

A constant theme in the discourse of urban entrepreneurialism is thus the representation of cities as autonomous actors in a competition whose outcomes can only be good – enhancing efficiency, growth and social welfare. Such claims rely, however, on an analogy between inter-urban competition and perfectly competitive markets whose plausibility rests on two critical assumptions:

1. Each city, like each firm in a perfect market, is competing with a very large number of other cities on a level playing field. Each city has the same access to resources, full information and is equally situated within the market; and no city has disproportionate influence over the market.
2. Cities, as economic actors, are in all other respects analogous to firms.

Both assumptions are deeply problematic.

First, cities are not on a level playing field; they have different economic, political and cultural characteristics and histories, and are differently situated within the larger political economy. At least three dimensions of difference can be identified, each of which tilts the playing field in systematic ways which favour some cities relative to others: embeddedness, historical geographical trajectories and favouritism (Leitner and Sheppard, 1997). It is important to remember that every city is *embedded* in what has variously been termed a social system of production (Hollingsworth, 1997) or a mode of regulation (Tickell and Peck, 1992): a set of national and regional institutions, regulatory systems, traditions and norms that condition the nature and possible outcomes of local initiatives. As a consequence, identical local urban development practices function in different ways, and may have different outcomes, in different contexts. For example, EU cities are embedded in a very different social system of production from the United States (despite convergence in recent years), one where the legitimacy of state intervention remains greater, and where there is less presumption that individuals are responsible for their own success or failure. As a result, urban entrepreneurial practices in the EU differ from those in the USA in their objectives, the strategies used, the composition of public–private coalitions, and the degree of involvement of higher tiers of the state (Harding, 1991; Keating, 1993; Leitner, 1996). The outcomes of similar local initiatives may also be quite different in Europe from in North America. Within the EU, the tradition of antagonism between capital and labour in the UK is very different from the corporatist tradition in Germany or Austria, meaning, for example, that the role of labour in an urban growth coalition, and even the possibility of its successful incorporation into such a coalition, may also be very different.

Each city also has a unique *geographical trajectory* as a consequence of its historical role and location within the broader evolving political and economic system, a uniqueness that creates differences in the ability of individual cities to respond to economic and political restructuring. Restructuring, particularly when combined with high economic uncertainty, means that advantages and disadvantages on the playing field shift in unpredictable ways, differentially affecting the fortunes of cities depending on their situation on this playing field. It also means that the effectiveness of particular urban entrepreneurial strategies will vary similarly; identical strategies may have very different consequences, and different strategies may be necessary to achieve the same goals, for cities occupying different trajectories. Finally, *political favouritism* is frequently exercised by higher levels of the state favouring some cities at the expense of others, either deliberately through spatially targeted policies or as the unintentional result of sectoral policies. Markusen et al (1991) have shown, for example, how US federal defence policies, combined with the geo-strategic thinking of the US Joint Chiefs of Staff, systematically favoured cities in parts of the southern United States in the post-Second World War era relative to the Midwestern locations where defence-related manufacturing and innovation originally flourished. In an era of greatly increased federal procurement (and considerable certainty about the size and location of military spending), such policies not only favoured these cities for defence-related manufacturing, but also reinforced their momentum more generally as industrial centres, contributing significantly to the marked shift of economic momentum in the USA from 'Snowbelt' to 'Sunbelt' cities which first became evident in the 1970s.

With respect to the second assumption underlying the claims of urban entrepreneurialism, cities are of course very different from firms. The governance of cities is defined by their territoriality: they are legally fixed in place, with boundaries that can be extended only with difficulty. In contrast, firms' ties to place are contingent, depending in the final instance on considerations of profitability. Furthermore, the political structure of governance is very different. Firms are autocratic institutions governed by their owners, with a clear hierarchy of authority overlying intra-firm networks. City governance also has a hierarchical structure, but cities are complex communities and networks of public and private institutions and civil society, in which lines of authority are not dictated from above but depend in the final instance on democratic processes; the ability of governing authorities to gain legitimation in the eyes of urban residents. From this stem other important differences in goals, and in the means available to achieve these. Firms have relatively straightforward economic goals with profits often as the bottom line. Local states are not primarily responsible for making profits, but are supposed to be concerned for the welfare of their residents. Indeed the survival of local politicians depends on their success in ensuring the welfare of the citizens, not just the local state's fiscal health. In order to achieve their goal, firms have the power to hire and fire workers, and see workers' welfare as often counterposed to the firm's economic success: high wages reduce profits unless workers' productivity more than compensates for their cost. Local states cannot get rid of undesirable or excessive numbers of residents, and their prosperity is positively related to the prosperity of their residents – residents are not only a workforce but also consumers and taxpayers whose purchasing power supports local firms and local state revenues, and whose identity is closely tied with their place of residence.

ASSESSING THE IMPACT OF URBAN ENTREPRENEURIALISM

The promotion of urban entrepreneurialism as the solution to urban economic, social and fiscal problems and as furthering a city's competitiveness in an increasingly global economy, has spawned critical evaluations of the impact and effectiveness of entrepreneurial strategies. By and large, evaluations have focused on the intra-urban impact stemming from adopting a particular form of entrepreneurial strategy. By now empirical evidence has accumulated from studies of a number of cities in the USA and western Europe repeatedly suggesting that urban entrepreneurial strategies have not lived up to their promises of solving cities' economic, social and fiscal problems. While growth-promoting entrepreneurial strategies have facilitated the revitalisation of the built environment of many inner cities, and contributed to the creation of new images and economic recovery in such declining cities as Pittsburgh, Cleveland and Glasgow (Holcomb, 1993), they have not been able to redress such very real problems as a shrinking number of quality employment opportunities, housing the poor and excluded, neighbourhood decay and fiscal squeeze. Indeed in some cases they have exacerbated them (Leitner, 1990; Commission of the European Communities, 1992; Leitner and Garner, 1993). Thus although Pittsburgh is heralded in numerous reports as the success story of urban entrepreneurialism because of its vastly improved image, a revitalised city centre and restructured economic base, it nevertheless had the second highest black poverty rate among the 20 largest metropolitan areas (36.2%) in 1990, and the sixth highest male unemployment rate (12.1%) in 1993 (Glickman, Lahr and Wyly, 1996). More generally it has been shown that the search to improve competitiveness by promoting economic growth with a disregard for distributive, social and territorial equity issues, has resulted in an intensification of social and territorial inequalities within urban areas (Pickvance and Preteceille, 1991b; Commission of the European Communities, 1992).

Less attention has been paid to the importance of the inter-urban context for affecting potential costs and benefits of urban entrepreneurial strategies for individual cities, and the potential implications of urban entrepreneurialism for the larger regional and national political economy (but see Cheshire and Gordon, 1995; Leitner and Sheppard, 1997). Yet a consideration and understanding of these aspects are essential for any comprehensive assessment of the limitations and merits of urban entrepreneurialism.

Inter-urban context and the differential local effectiveness of entrepreneurialism

The likelihood that a city will benefit from entrepreneurial strategies does not just depend on the skill with which such strategies are deployed, but also on the broader inter-urban context within which cities operate. Two aspects of this context are particularly important: the number of other potential competitors employing entrepreneurial strategies, and the situation of the city on the uneven and shifting playing field where it must compete.

When fewer cities engage in competitive entrepreneurial practices, the likelihood that these will have their intended effect for an individual city is greater. For example, le Galès (1992) observed that the success of economic development strategies in the French city of Rennes during the 1980s was to a large degree attributable to the failure of such neighbouring cities as Nantes to pursue similar policies. The example of such success, and the pressure of competition – i.e. the fear that in an environment where other cities are aggressively pursuing investors and promoting local firms, any city failing to do this is bound to be disadvantaged – lead other cities to adopt similar strategies. As the number of cities engaged in entrepreneurialism increases, the potential effectiveness of any one city's efforts declines, but at the same time the disadvantages mount for any city which does not follow suit. Thus urban entrepreneurialism diffuses throughout the urban system, and at the same time cities attempt to compensate for the falling marginal benefits by offering subsidies of increased size and scope, and by devoting more effort to support the development of local firms.

Throughout this process of diffusion and declining marginal benefits, the uneven playing field establishes systematic and persistent inequalities in the effectiveness of urban entrepreneurial activities for different cities. These inequalities are related to a city's economic base and the public resources available to attract private investment and stimulate endogenous development. Cities which are already attractive to private investment, or possess clusters of technologically dynamic firms, inevitably have more financial resources for the public sector to draw on to finance entrepreneurial strategies, and also do not have to provide particularly generous subsidies to stimulate further investment. By contrast, cities already having trouble attracting private investment, or lacking highly dynamic local firms, will feel compelled to provide more generous subsidies, committing a larger proportion of a smaller pool of public resources. Thus disadvantaged cities must invest more resources, while the prospects of success are less than for advantaged cities (Rubin and Rubin,

1987; Leitner, 1990). A recent comparative study of the incentives offered by US cities found that the costs associated with attracting investors may outweigh the benefits for economically disadvantaged cities (Fisher and Peters, 1996). This study documents that cities with high levels of unemployment, presumed to be disadvantaged cities on the playing field of inter-urban competition, tendentially offer greater incentives to potential investors, but despite this do not increase their overall attractiveness for investment relative to cities with low unemployment. Even in cases where disadvantaged cities are successful in using public funds to leverage new private investors, the success comes with a greater cost and risk. The increased indebtedness is incurred on a smaller revenue base, and the chances are less that long-term improvements in economic growth, employment opportunities and local fiscal health will be great enough to pay off these debts.

The uneven playing field poses disproportionate costs and risks for disadvantaged cities, implying that universal adoption of urban entrepreneurialism is insufficient to compensate for these disadvantages. As a consequence, disparities in the economic health of cities can persist or even widen. Empirical evidence for both the European Community and the United States documents increasing regional disparities during the 1980s, at a time of growth in both economic uncertainty and the market orientation of public policies (Perrons, 1992; Suarez-Villa and Cuadrado-Roura, 1993).

The supra-urban consequences of entrepreneurialism

As the pressure of competition pushes cities to greater and greater lengths in their search for economic growth through urban entrepreneurial strategies, net benefits may diminish not only for individual cities but for the broader system as a whole. Cities engaged in strategies designed to attract inward investment with public subsidies increasingly find themselves locked into a 'buyers' market', in which firms are able to play one city off against another and demand ever more generous subsidies. It is widely acknowledged that this has forced US cities into a bidding war reaching ludicrous extremes. In 1994 the city of Amarillo, Texas, sent 1300 US companies a check for $8m., to be redeemed if the company committed to creating at least 700 new jobs in Amarillo. In the same year St Louis, Missouri, sought to attract a professional American football team at an estimated cost of $720m. to state and local taxpayers (Burstein and Rolnick, 1995). The creation of a buyers' market can have deleterious effects on both regional and national economic growth and productivity and the fiscal health of the public sector, even when some cities are able successfully to attract new investment. Bidding wars encourage firms and cities to put effort and money into relocating economic activities from one city to another, which could have been invested in job creation and product development. The increased mobility of American professional sports franchises over the last 20 years is a case in point (see also Chapter 3). In other circumstances local authorities may be able to retain a particular firm by raising their stake in the bidding war, thus subsidising the firm to stay where it is. In either case the deliberate leveraging of public funds by private investors puts undue burden on public coffers. It is very difficult for local authorities, or even firms, to know which subsidies are appropriate and which are not, particularly in a period of high economic uncertainty (enhanced by the bidding wars themselves). As the bidding wars intensify, the chance for a negative sum game (i.e. a net loss of public resources) steadily increases: inter-urban competition drives public subsidies to a level exceeding any reasonable calculation of benefits from productivity and employment increases.

No convincing evidence has been advanced to demonstrate that the increase in private sector investment in economic growth and employment has matched, let alone exceeded, public spending increases on entrepreneurial strategies. From a political economic perspective, bidding wars are reinforcing a general trend towards diverting public resources to support private capital accumulation at the expense of social expenditures; encouraging the search for short-term gains at the expense of more important longer-term investments in the health of cities and the well-being of their residents. The result is thus a net transfer of societal wealth from the public to the private sector. Even mainstream economic analysts have become vocal in their complaint that bidding wars are wasteful because they encourage firms to take actions and occupy locations which are inefficient and unproductive; in their view, an example of unwarranted state intervention in the market (Burstein and Rolnick, 1995).

Much of this discussion focuses on what we have termed inward investment types of entrepreneurial strategies. During the 1990s the discourse and practice of urban entrepreneurialism shifted to emphasise endogenous development strategies: the promotion of local firms regarded as having a high potential to develop a competitive advantage through a synergy of rapid technological development, local networking, and skilled and high-wage employment. For example, Michael Porter (1990) argues that any city, by creating and maintaining a competitive advantage, can provide high-wage jobs and improved social and environmental conditions: a 'high road' to urban development where growth and prosperity reinforce one another. This argument ignores, however, the influence of an uneven playing field on the ability of cities to pursue such a 'high road' to urban development. We contend that the presence of an uneven playing field frequently compels disadvantaged cities to lower wages in order to compensate for their disadvantage. High levels of spatial competition can then drive wages down everywhere, as the first world has learnt to its cost during the last two decades, undermining attempts to achieve prosperity through competition. Thus the problem of an unequal playing field, and its potential negative consequences for national economic growth and prosperity, is not restricted to cases of inward investment strategies, but can also apply to endogenous development strategies.

The presence of an uneven playing field means that arguments for competitive urban entrepreneurialism run afoul of what Jon Elster (1978) has dubbed the fallacy of composition: the possible beneficial consequences for an individual city, acting alone to pursue its own interests, are negated when all cities pursue the same strategy simultaneously. While it may be rational for individual cities to engage in such strategies in the short run, if all cities pursue them simultaneously the long-run consequences can be deleterious. At the same time, however, the pressures to compete are such that individual cities cannot afford to disengage from entrepreneurialism, although higher levels of the state may be able to intervene to mitigate the negative effects of competition.

CONCLUSIONS – ALTERNATIVES

One of the more seductive aspects of urban entrepreneurialism is that it sounds as if there are no alternatives; competition, local entrepreneurialism, growth and prosperity seem linked to one another in a seamless whole. Yet if there are systematic reasons undermining the ability of urban entrepreneurialism to live up to its claims, as we have argued here, it is necessary to reconsider alternatives. A full treatment of this question would require another chapter, but to give some indication of where alternatives may lie, let us briefly return to the metaphor that cities in competition are like firms in competition. Although firms are not cities, they also compete on a daily basis in an ever more uncertain environment in which the best laid plans often go awry. Firms respond to uncertainty and unintended consequences by pursuing such strategies as mergers and takeovers, strategic alliances, collusion, cheating in the market, and, when all else fails, by appealing to state regulators for special treatment or compensation.

Mergers and takeovers are, to all intents and purposes, impractical for cities, where merger can only mean territorial expansion or integration. Annexation of municipal areas does occur (see also Chapter 7), but only rarely and only for contiguous territories. Strategic alliances and collusion are forms of networks. Such networks currently are lauded as an intermediate form of interaction, between the markets that link independent firms and the organisational hierarchies of multi-plant corporations, that simultaneously engender more trust than the former and more flexibility than the latter. Cities can also engage in strategic alliances with one another, and social movements and labour unions can institutionalise inter-urban co-operation, once they can be convinced that place-based cross-class alliances may be highly problematic. Indeed groups of cities co-operating with one another may be the most effective counterweight that immobile political territories can develop in opposition to the mobility of capital. The European Union (EU) has been active in fostering such co-operative networks, although their effectiveness is not yet clear (Leitner and Sheppard, 1997).

More generally, higher-level state institutions remain the place where the costs of unmitigated competition can be alleviated through regulatory and redistributive policies. Higher tiers of the state can provide resources, regulate, and underwrite fora for new ideas, in order to mitigate the individualism associated with inter-urban competition, and supranational institutions have the additional advantage of being able to foster transnational initiatives. The EU has experimented with such practices in recent years, filling the vacuum created by the hollowing out of the nation state. Despite steadily increasing promotion of competition as the key to economic growth and prosperity, the EU is attempting to simulate a level playing field by limiting levels of state aid to private firms in different localities, through its Competition Policy. It is also providing financial resources to lower tiers of government for ameliorating social and spatial inequalities resulting from an unequal playing field, through its Structural Funds (Leitner and Sheppard, 1997). In the United States there have also been calls for greater regulation of competition and co-operation among municipalities, but with little practical impact to date.

We contend, however, that the alternatives outlined above, more direct involvement of higher tiers of the state in urban development, and inter-urban co-operation instead of inter-urban competition, are not sufficient. For example, it is critical to probe both the nature and goals of co-operation, and the inclusion of various social groups in such collaboration. If networks simply elevate inter-urban competition from the urban to the network scale, with collaboration occurring primarily either between prosperous cities or between urban élites pursuing a common growth agenda, the interests of disadvantaged cities and social groups are unlikely to be adequately addressed (Leitner and Sheppard, 1997). A more inclusive and progressive agenda for urban development must make these other voices integral to urban policy-making (Cohen and Rogers, 1993; Hirst, 1994; Amin and Thrift, 1995c). An example of such an agenda can be found in the attempts of grass-roots groups and progressive political parties in a number of United States cities (including St Paul, Minneapolis, Baltimore and Milwaukee) to make living wage initiatives integral to urban development policies. Living wage initiatives require firms to pay their workers a wage above the poverty level in return for receiving city subsidies. Local chambers of commerce and political leaders alike intensely resist such initiatives, claiming that they disadvantage cities in their competition for economic growth. An era of high economic uncertainty, underwritten by an increased mobility and global scope of capital, is thus a particularly difficult time for seeking a way out of the trap of competitive urban entrepreneurialism. Yet it is precisely at this point that the search for alternatives seems most urgent.

15

AFTERWORD: MAPPINGS OF THE ENTREPRENEURIAL CITY

TIM HALL AND PHIL HUBBARD

INTRODUCTION

The concerns and approaches of the authors in this collection are undeniably eclectic. Consequently, producing a conclusion that adequately reviews the collection with any degree of coherence, let alone producing a legitimate stand-alone argument, is difficult if not impossible. One starting point might be to explore definitions of the entrepreneurial city. It would seem legitimate to ask if at the end of a collection such as this we are able to provide any definition of *the* entrepreneurial city. This task immediately proves problematic. As Painter (Chapter 12) demonstrates, for example, the entrepreneurial city possesses many definitions, identities and interpretations. Similarly the experiences of McNeill (Chapter 11) highlight how attempts to write the entrepreneurial city are fraught with problems of methodology, selection and representation. To try and force too tight an interpretive straight-jacket around a collection such as this smacks of editorial arrogance and goes against the intentions behind the production of this book and the ways we anticipate it will be used. So, faced with these initial thoughts and a number of blank pages, what do we write?

One easy (although largely superfluous) solution would be to attempt to group together and summarise the findings of the authors collected here and to proclaim the book a definitive map of the entrepreneurial city – geographical metaphors always make good sales copy. However, as Brian Harley (1992) has demonstrated, the production of maps (and the representations therein) hide as much as they reveal and reveal as much about those who produce them as they do about the thing they purport to represent. We want to attempt to show here that maps *per se*, or rather overly cartographic metaphors, are inadequate to understand the entrepreneurial city, but that to think about the processes of mapping of the entrepreneurial city might be more revealing.

This conclusion then, if it can be called that, is to be a space of speculation – speculation born out of the ruins of attempting to write a concluding chapter that neatly summarised the preceding chapters, gave them a sheen of cohesion and hence 'defined' the entrepreneurial city. We hope that this speculation can also act as a disruption – destabilising any easy notions of what constitutes the entrepreneurial city and eschewing any easy critical positions. It would be all too easy, given the groundwork provided by a number of authors in this collection, to simply criticise the social inequity of most entrepreneurial cities and leave it at that. We wish to try and suggest that any grand statement on such an entity as *the* entrepreneurial city is prone to the dangers of abstraction and is likely to lose sight of the *geographies* of the entrepreneurial city. Our approach in this chapter is not then to attempt to pin down any definition of the entrepreneurial city but rather to highlight its differences, its contingencies and hence, we argue, its geographies. Given this, each chapter in this collection stands alone as a statement on an aspect, moment or case of entrepreneurialism, but together they amount to something more.

This chapter is organised around four themes: the production and consumption of the entrepreneurial city; the question of entrepreneurialism and the ways cities have approached the coming millennium celebrations; the relationship between entrepreneurialism and creativity in urban change and the position of the academic (within an increasing *entrepreneurial* higher education), in relation to debates about the entrepreneurial city. All of this is underlain by our belief, reflecting a number of authors in this collection, that entrepreneurialism is not an inevitable response (or process) of trends in late twentieth century urbanisation, despite its discursive representation as *the* solution to urban problems.

Given our position we hope this book will be considered a beginning, rather than an end – or, more accurately, a moment in a series of unfolding mappings rather than a definitive map. Our questioning of the inevitability of entrepreneurialism precludes such a position. If individual chapters prompt such speculations on behalf of our readers that is as good an indicator of the success of the book as any.

PRODUCTION, CONSUMPTION AND THE 'GEOGRAPHY' OF ENTREPRENEURIALISM

Highlighting what we argue to be the essentially geographical dimension of the production of the entrepreneurial city – namely that its production is not, in the widest sense, inevitable, but rather the result of processes operating and combining in and through place – points to apparently contradictory findings. While on the one hand it confirms the geographies of the production of entrepreneurial cities, the surveys contained in this collection suggest that entrepreneurialism is a deeply rooted aspect of these milieux.

If we take the case of public art, for example, highlighted by Miles (Chapter 9), it is not solely the entrepreneurialist stance or the complicity of the artist with entrepreneurialism within cities that is revealed in Miles's chapter. Miles's chapter serves to remind us, in the same way as Painter's chapter does with the case of entrepreneurs, that complicity is never given, always created.

Clearly artists are not entirely made; some inherent ability is an advantage. However, crucially they are, to some extent at least, produced – educated and socialised not only artistically but also in the sociology and political economy of the art business, of which public art has been a rapidly growing sector. It is the complicity created by the infrastructures within which artists are educated and socialised that points out both the pervasiveness of entrepreneurialism and, at the same time, its contingency. To understand the production of artists complicit in the entrepreneurialism of urban governance, and similarly those who seek to expose and highlight the contradictions of the entrepreneurial city, or who seek to resist and oppose the dominant constructions of urban space, appears, in the light of this collection, a priority for urban studies to embrace in its project to deconstruct the entrepreneurial city.

While carefully observed geographic case studies have done much to demonstrate that entrepreneurial discourse is differently articulated and produced across space, the result of complex interactions between regime players which vary from city to city, predominantly utilising the idea of regime theory (Ward, 1996), there is perhaps a tendency to overlook the way these discourses are consumed, not least by researchers (see Chapter 11). While not necessarily suggesting this as a major lacuna in the literature on the entrepreneurial city, there have been only fleeting attempts to examine how the reception of (geographically specific) entrepreneurial policies and rhetorics varies across space (and between different city communities). This issue, which we have highlighted elsewhere (Hubbard and Hall, 1996), represents a more general failure of current urban studies to engage with Lefebvre's trialectics of space as simultaneously perceived, imagined and experienced (see Soja, 1996 for an elucidation of these ideas). While not arguing that epistemological priority needs to be given to experiences of space (or Soja's *firstspace*), there has as yet been insufficient attention paid to linking representations and experiences of space, either generally (Jackson, 1993) or with reference to specific cities (Savage and Warde, 1993).

Goss (1997) has none the less recently highlighted a number of broad ways in which dominant entrepreneurial discourses are resisted or corrupted by those who invest different meanings in the entrepreneurial landscape. This may be manifest in a variety of tactics and strategies, from the formulation of alternative discourses of urban change (e.g. the racialised poor of Milwaukee articulating a vision of the city opposed to Euro-American urban culture – see Kenny, 1995) to overt forms of resistance (e.g. pickets and demonstrations in London Docklands – see Brownill, 1993). Even some of the most marginalised groups in the city may seek to impose their interpretation of the city on the official strategic vision, with Goss citing the everyday tactics of homeless people in occupying visible public space as positing a challenge to entrepreneurial developmentalist discourse (and perhaps empathetic academic studies of this population too). Here, in public space, material and metaphorical battles over the essence of 'the city' become most apparent, although the battles are often depressingly one-sided. Within the 'revanchist' city (Smith, 1996), the forces of development, wielding an idealised white, middle-class hegemonic notion of urbanity, often reclaim or gentrify marginal spaces in pursuit of entrepreneurial policy: the result is often the displacement of marginal populations, the deletion of collective memory or (more rarely) the commodification of minority ways of life.

Such examinations of how entrepreneurial culture is produced and consumed at the local level imply an important shift away from accepting a totalising, globalised notion of urban culture towards taking a fragmented view of different cultures competing for relative dominance, seeking to reify their vision of the city. This incorporation of cultural politics into the geographer's canon has been particularly espoused by P. Jackson (1991), who tempers his enthusiasm for analysis of discourse, metaphor and representation with a demand that studies of the role of culture in local economic development include more sensitivity to geographically specific cultural processes and the way that dominant (hegemonic) culture is contested and negotiated in the realms of everyday experience. The adoption of a regime perspective at the local level might begin to give some clues as to how a culture of entrepreneurialism is negotiated and produced, but offers little by way of explaining how the regime acts in response to the wider cultural context as its entrepreneurial policies are discursively and materially consumed externally and internally. In highlighting these issues relating to the very different 'geographies' of entrepreneurialism, we are seeking to challenge assumptions about the seemingly inevitable production and consumption of entrepreneurial discourses and practices implicit in many monolithic mappings of the entrepreneurial city.

IMAGINING ALTERNATIVES? MILLENNIUM CITIES

As the various chapters in this book have illustrated, entrepreneurial governance has become a stock response to the emotive discourses of urban decline that permeate the urban West (Beauregard, 1993). This is perhaps unsurprising given the way in which such a discourse externalises the problems of the city (e.g. poverty, disinvestment, environmental decline) to abstract forces (global competition and economic restructuring). As Goss (1997) argues (see also Chapter 4), the attraction of this discourse is thus that it absolves the political and economic élite from blame for these problems, and limits policy actions by suggesting that only a particular suit of externally oriented growth policies will solve these problems. Over time, such ideas become engrained as axiomatic, and questions about alternative policy directions become foreclosed. Few policy-makers question the wisdom of entrepreneurial strategy, and even when they do, they often lack the imagination to see how they might break out of what they see as ferocious bidding wars, in which they must compete or 'die' (e.g. see Chapter 6 on Birmingham City Council's changing attitudes to local economic development). Nowhere has this all-embracing commitment to the entrepreneurial ethos been more evident than in the recent fervour among UK cities to be declared as the official millennium site.

The fervour among cities for the cachet and capital available from central government funds for being declared the UK's official millennium celebration site affords us the opportunity to reflect on a number of themes associated with notions of the entrepreneurial city. The approaching millennium has invigorated the climate of competition between British cities in the last couple of years. The fiercest competition has been between two bids for national funding from Birmingham and Greenwich. This climate of competition has reinstated the importance of spectacular urban redevelopment and symbolic reimagination to British cities after a lull in the early 1990s during which the excesses of the 1980s became apparent. To readers of this book the story of the battle to become Britain's most important party site will be depressingly familiar.

The millennial celebrations, and crucially the funds that go with them, have been seen by cities as an opportunity to address persistent problems regarding the upgrading of prominent sites in their inner areas and the enhancement of their images (concerns that drove the entrepreneurialism with which much of this book is concerned). The overriding motif attached to the millennium in this context is celebration. This notion of celebration has been torn between national(ist) aspirations of central government and the local(ist) desires of the bidding coalitions (with the local authority in the co-ordinating role).

Primarily the millennium celebrations will afford cities the opportunity to transform themselves, or at least discrete spaces within themselves, into sites of spectacular display and celebration (this is in contrast to the unregulated sites of celebration associated with urban raves in the late 1980s and early 1990s; see Chapter 10 on the tensions associated with the entrepreneurial negotiations of popular culture). To be deemed appropriate these sites need to be spectacular and conspicuous. The prize for the successful city is that for a symbolically significant time (although the actual date of the dawn of the next millennium is a matter of some dispute) that city will outshine all others. Perhaps, given the significance of spatially representing this moment in time it was inevitable that the government would back the Greenwich bid.

The backing of the Greenwich bid by the UK government came during a period of intensified 'place-war' or inter-urban competition between British cities (see Chapter 14 on the consequences of this). Hence, this competition did not stop with the government's decision to support Greenwich and Birmingham's media continued to mock the (inevitable?) ongoing financial and developmental problems associated with the Greenwich project and criticised the government for once again apparently favouring London over the provinces (see Kennedy, 1996).

We mention this story of the approach of British cities to the millennium, and the construction of the millennium as an opportunity for urban development, to highlight how the perceptions of cities and governments are shaped by the prevailing climate of inter-urban competition and entrepreneurialism. However, we also highlight it to suggest that the entrepreneurial response is not necessarily inevitable. The authors in this collection have provided a number of frames through which to read the approaches of cities to the millennium. This story provided further confirmation, for example, if indeed it were needed, of the centrality of the regime to urban governance and its legitimation by central governments. For example Loftman and Nevin (Chapter 6) outline the formal and less formal participants in the regime associated with Birmingham's continuing project to celebrate the millennium. These include: the local authority, private companies, local (entrepreneurial?) educational institutions and the local media. However, regimes are never given, always produced, entrepreneurs made not born (Chapter 12).

Other authors in this collection have been concerned about the redistributional inequity produced or exacerbated by many entrepreneurial actions. Again, despite some apparent shifts in ideology, evidence would suggest that the outcomes of entrepreneurialism in the guise of millennium fever are likely to be depressingly familiar in this regard. Equitable redistribution of resources does not appear to be a grand enough, or eye-catching enough, gesture with which to welcome in the new millennium. For example, while Birmingham aims to mark the new millennium with a £100m. investment of external funding in, among other things, a spectacular, high-tech 'University of the First Age' on a derelict site near its centre, the city continues to labour under a £250m. underspend in its education budget during the years in which the £180m. International Convention Centre was constructed (Birmingham Education Commission, 1993). Is it out of the continuing contradictions of entrepreneurial cities that it now seems naïve to think that repairing every primary school roof in the city might be a more profoundly effective gesture for the future? The intensified, pervasive symbolic reconstruction of the city as a sight of carnival for the year 2000, brings with it little evidence of the material deconstruction of the city as a site of social and economic exclusion and division.

Despite feelings to the contrary, a number of authors remind us that entrepreneurialism is not an inevitable state of affairs. This suggests that, while criticising the inequitable consequences of entrepreneurialism is a valid task, we should seek to do more, and attempt to imagine alternative visions, plans and policies. This brings us to the issue of *geographies* of entrepreneurialism. We want to stress that we hope this book has helped put pay to the myth that entrepreneurialism is a grand meta-narrative – in some way inevitable beyond the realm of the social. Rather, as the chapters in this book demonstrate, entrepreneurialism is crucially *grounded*. It is produced and mediated at a variety of scales and these scales interact. Exposing this groundedness, the spatial, social, cultural and political basis of entrepreneurialism's construction confirms that, in the truest sense of the word, entrepreneurialism displays geographies of its production and also its consumption.

CREATIVITY AND THE POTENTIAL OF THE MARGINS

Much has been made recently about the supposed role of creativity as a dimension of both contemporary and historical urban change (Bianchini and Landry, 1994; Ebert, Gnad and Kunzmann, 1994; Hall, P., 1995; Landry and Bianchini, 1995). The range of examples highlighted by Landry and Bianchini (1995) confirm that it is far from inevitable that cities should approach problems confronting them and conceive solutions in narrowly entrepreneurial terms. However, we wish to examine what more fundamental challenges to entrepreneurialism or possibilities for reformulation are raised by 'creativity'. Broadly we wish to assess whether creativity is able to offer an alternative to entrepreneurialism as the dominant mode of urban imagination into the next millennium. While highlighting the narrow instrumentalism of much entrepreneurial urban government, does creativity, either exclusively or in combination with forms of entrepreneurialism, offer a way out of the malaise?

There has been no shortage of attention recently on the creative potential of cities and suggestions of creative solutions to urban problems of all sorts. As well as the works cited above, this attention includes manifestos for change such as Richard Rogers and Mark Fisher's sketching of a 'new' London (1992) and Rogers 1995 series of Reith lectures (1995a, b, c, d, e). Mark Fisher and Ursula Owen's *Whose Cities?* (1991) was an attempt to highlight some recent (and some questionable) urban success stories while recovering the importance and myth, memory and meaning to the experience of the urban landscape. Similarly the personal, social and political opportunities afforded by the city continue to provide rich subject matter for a variety of fictional genre. However, despite these expressions of interest and apparent insight, their impact to date on the issues discussed in this collection has been, at best, marginal.

Creativity has always been an important facet of urban change. However, to view creativity in this sense is to fall into the fallacy of defining creativity solely with reference to the way cities, or rather individuals, groups and institutions within them, have approached problems. Too much that has been regarded as creative in the past has formulated solutions that are judged successful in rational or instrumental terms but not on other, alternative criteria. Such a conception of creativity is too broad to provide any critical position. However, recent work has formed a broad consensus on how creativity should be defined in the urban context in the late twentieth century. There are perhaps two facets to the creativity envisaged by recent writers. Most fundamentally creativity must challenge predominant modes of thought. In the late twentieth century it should challenge modernist, rational, instrumental modes of thought. Further, the outcomes of creativity should broadly be judged on alternative criteria and should specifically aim to be sustainable and inclusive (Landry and Bianchini, 1995).

In many ways entrepreneurial strategies and modes of governance can be regarded as, at least in the broadest sense, creative. However, this judgement is fundamentally one which fails to question the essentialism of prevailing modes of thought. Adopting a more precise definition of creativity reveals the limitations of many entrepreneurialist strategies. While, for example, an individual project of place marketing might be regarded as a creative response to a particular problem, in that the blend of images and techniques is original, eye-catching and addresses the problem of image facing a particular city, by failing to question the efficacy, equity and inevitability of the entrepreneurial approach, it cannot be considered as creative in the sense envisaged by recent writers.

Landry and Bianchini have identified six areas of urban creativity which are based on the work of the Italian sociologist Alberto Melucci: 'the arts, science, advertising and communication, organisation and business management, youth sub-cultures and collective movements' (1995: 14). They argue, having stressed the importance of holistic conceptions of urban problems, solutions and outcomes, that while the creativity of urban governments remains rooted solely in advertising, communication and business organisation, then their thinking is unlikely to transcend an instrumentalist entrepreneurialism (Landry and Bianchini, 1995: 14). However, there is a considerable gap between the rhetoric of advocating creativity and the reality of a creative urban governance. O'Connor (Chapter 10), for example, illustrates the problems associated with the use and abuse of popular culture by the local authority and local cultural industries in the case of Manchester. Clearly creativity and urban governance demand some complex negotiations.

Two crucial and closely related questions concern the forms of urban governance that might emerge in the next millennium. First, what are the possibilities of urban government broadening the basis of creativity within their modes of thought and operation? Second, how might creativity, in an urban context, transcend the local and particular and affect broader processes of urban change? If creativity is becoming a more pervasive aspect of urban life, and the evidence for this is contradictory, then the reworkings and negotiations of the dialectics of creativity and entrepreneurialism, local and global, are likely to become major determinants of urban change.

Although the general awareness of the failures of entrepreneurial strategies and their iniquitous consequences has come to inform general and political, as well as academic debate, the evidence for genuinely creative reworkings of urban government in the light of these problems seems, at the moment at least, limited. Notions of sustainability, equality, progressiveness, local sensitivity and inter-urban co-operation, while prominent in the discourse of urban governments, have appeared as little more than rhetorical devices and have affected little beyond local geographies of change.

One thing that most commentators agree on, despite other differences, is that entrepreneurial cities are generally fragmented cities (Anderson, 1994). It is within the fragments that possibilities of the imagination of alternative futures are recognised. The possibilities of the marginal, the alien or the excluded, unburdened by dominant modes of conception, is a well-explored avenue of social and urban theory and imagination, a characteristic of a number of recent writings which are informed by an awareness of broader urban change. Indeed, these possibilities form much of the creative cities manifesto. Such possibilities and alternative positions have been variously termed: places on the margin (Shields, 1991) and hidden cities (Calvino, 1979).

> Throughout history, urban creativity has come from the outsiders: the resident aliens of ancient Athens, the country painters of Renaissance Florence, Picasso and his generation of starving Paris artists, the Jewish intellectuals of Vienna in 1900 and the Jewish clothiers-turned-movie moguls of Hollywood or the garage technicians of Detroit (Hall, P., 1995: 15).

> Margins, then, while a position of exclusion can also be a position of power and critique. They expose the relativity of the entrenched univer-salising values of the centre. . . . An alternative geography begins to emerge from the margins which challenges the self definition of 'centres', deconstructing cultural sovereignty and remapping the universalised and homogeneous spatialisation of Western Modernity to reveal hetero-geneous places, a cartography of fractures which emphasises the relations between differently valorised sites and spaces sutured together under masks of unity (Shields, 1991: 277–8).

> Also in Raissa, city of sadness, there runs an invisible thread that binds one living being to another for a moment, then unravels, then is stretched again between moving points as it draws new and rapid patterns so that at every second the unhappy city contains a happy city unaware of its own existence (Calvino, 1979: 116).

Creativity, while offering optimism and apparently thriving within and among the fragments of entrepreneurial cities, has, as yet, done little to demonstrate its ability to connect the fragments of these cities in new meaningful ways. This is its challenge and the broader challenge facing urban government into the next millennium.

ACADEMIA AND ENTREPRENEURIALISM

Changes in the structure and funding of education have led to institutions of higher education, indeed institutions at all levels of education, becoming increasingly entrepreneurial in recent years. This entrepreneurialism has primarily involved the pursuit of external funding, be it from restructured traditional sources such as central government or from new sources such as sponsorship from private industry. Along with this has gone a desire for greater local embeddedness in local and regional business networks. The entrepreneurialism of educational institutions has taken many forms, from the heightened importance of the primary school raffles to their annual budgets, through the emphasis placed on selecting and attracting pupils and students, to the involvement of universities as major partners in urban development regimes.

Individually, academics have come under greater pressure to justify, and safeguard, their positions through the sale of their skills to a range of external clients. Indeed it is the norm now for students, as well as other 'traditional' sources of revenue such as research assessors, to be regarded as only one among a number of external client groups (see Wernick, 1991). When viewed in this way this radically alters the roles, functions and meanings attached to institutions of higher education. The political economy of higher education and the implications for the role of the academic are relevant to academic commentary on the entrepreneurial city, as some of the major players in entrepreneurial urban regimes are the very groups being courted by entrepreneurial universities. While in one sense it is possible to envisage advantages stemming from the closer ties between academia and interests external to higher education, namely a greater understanding of these external interests, there is the clear danger that this understanding comes with the risk of the compromise of the traditional, although somewhat idealised and overstated, critical freedom and objective independence of the academic. The negotiation of the agenda within the relationship between higher education and their new clients is likely to favour the agendas of those who write the cheques rather than those who cash them.

As institutions of higher education are run more and more along the lines of businesses and become ever more closely linked with urban growth regimes (see Chapter 6) the academic community is likely to find its objectives difficult to divorce from those of its external partners. To date there is little evidence that these constraints have impinged directly on academic debates on the entrepreneurial city. However, two authors in this volume were very publicly criticised by members of their local authority following their 'gloomy' evaluation of the redistributional potential of their authority's urban regeneration strategy. As all institutions of higher education seek to forge ever more symbiotic bonds with local and regional public and private sector interests it is pertinent to wonder to what extent debate in certain media will be circumscribed by these evolving dependencies. Although a well-worn debate, the questions and problems of academic relevance are applicable to academic commentary on the entrepreneurial city and their involvement with urban growth regimes.

While this may appear a cynical conclusion, unless the existing power relations between higher education and public and private sector interests are renegotiated and questioned it seems a likely one. However, as this volume has demonstrated, entrepreneurialism and the relationships engendered by it are never given, always produced. Given this, as the relationship develops it should be interrogated and ways sought in which the critical perspective of the academic might become empowered. Despite pressure to the contrary, the academic should seek to do more than simply lend legitimacy to whatever the client wishes to say. Similarly, academics should seek ways in which their involvement with external interests might *affect* rather than simply *support* these interests. This, of course, could be regarded as an idealistic and somewhat self-evident hope as academics find the political economy of higher education changing. However, we return to the points made earlier that entrepreneurialism should not be regarded as inevitable, and positive change is more likely to come from the margins than the centre. This is a position currently occupied by academics with regard to the shaping of the entrepreneurial city and its associated policies. If academics move closer to the centre, as is possible and likely in the entrepreneurial university, it is to be hoped that the perspective of the margin is not lost. The most hope we can offer is that it is not inevitable that it should be.

CONTRIBUTORS

Amer Althubaity,
King Abdulaziz University,
Jeddah.

Kevin M. Dunn,
School of Geography,
University of New South Wales.

Tim Hall,
Department of Geography and Geology
Cheltenham and Gloucester College of Higher Education.

Tassilo Herrschel,
School of Social and Policy Sciences,
University of Westminster.

Phil Hubbard,
Geography Subject Area,
University of Coventry.

Bob Jessop,
Department of Sociology,
Lancaster University.

Andrew Jonas,
School of Geography,
University of Hull.

Yeong-Hyun Kim,
Department of Geography,
Syracuse University.

Helga Leitner,
Department of Geography,
University of Minnesota.

Patrick Loftman,
Faculty of the Built Environment,
University of Central England.

Pauline M. McGuirk,
Department of Geography,
University of Newcastle,
New South Wales.

Donald McNeill,
Department of City and Regional Planning,
University of Wales College of Cardiff.

Malcolm Miles,
School of Design,
Chelsea College of Art and Design.

Brenden Nevin,
Centre for Urban and Regional Studies,
University of Birmingham.

Justin O'Connor,
Manchester Institute for Popular Culture,
Manchester Metropolitan University.

Joe Painter,
Department of Geography,
University of Durham.

Eric Sheppard,
Department of Geography,
University of Minnesota.

John Rennie Short,
Department of Geography,
Syracuse University.

Stephen V. Ward,
School of Planning,
Oxford Brookes University.

Hilary P.M. Winchester,
Department of Geography,
University of Newcastle,
New South Wales.

Andrew Wood,
Department of Geography,
University of Sheffield.

FIGURES

2.1 Glasgow's Miles Better was the first major example of American-style municipal entrepreneurialism 32

2.2 The London Borough of Hackney's 1983 image campaign shunned the jaunty optimism of 'Glasgow's Miles Better', emphasising instead the notion of city as victim 33

2.3 The Illinois Central Railroad was one of the pioneers of place marketing, as shown in this example from the 1860s 36

2.4 Since 1879, when it secured advertising powers unique in Britain, Blackpool has dominated in the selling of the seaside. This example dates from the 1930s 40

2.5 By the 1930s, British developers had become the major sellers of suburbs, in the manner of the famous Chicago developer of the late nineteenth century, S.E. Gross 43

2.6 In 1926, the Forward Atlanta movement set new standards in industrial promotion. This shows one of many advertisements produced in the late 1920s 45

2.7 Baltimore was one of the US leaders of post-industrial reinvention, its experiences much studied by other cities throughout North America and Europe. This 1996 tourist advertisement sums up much of its image appeal 49

3.1 Atlantic City: America's favourite playground 63

3.2 St Augustine: your place in history 64

3.3 Kansas City: a place where it all works together – workforce, technology, value and location 66

3.4 Fairfax County: the twenty-first century is here 68

3.5 Jacksonville: an NFL city and expanding business city 69

3.6 Memphis: America's distribution centre 71

3.7 Milwaukee: a shining star in the Rust Belt 73

5.1 The Honeysuckle redevelopment site with proposed development precincts 108

5.2 Billboard advertising the HDC's development precincts 115

7.1 Cities in the Coachella Valley 157

7.2 Tax-increment revenue to Coachella valley redevelopment agencies, 1984–92 159

7.3 Tax-increment revenue compared with general revenue for Coachella Valley cities, 1993 160

8.1   Location of the six case study cities in Saxony   176
8.2   Relative 'utility' of local economic specificity among the six
      cities   188
8.3   The two main determinants of local specificity in policy-making
      among the six cities   193
9.1   *Fulcrum* by Richard Serra, situated at the entrance to Broadgate,
      London   205
9.2   *Bottle of Notes* by Claes Oldenburg and Coosje van Brugen,
      Middlesbrough   209
9.3   *The Spirit of Free Enterprise* by Wendy Taylor, Canary Wharf,
      London   212
9.4   *Forward* by Raymond Mason, Centenary Square, Birmingham   217
9.5   *Iron Man* by Antony Gormley, Birmingham city centre   218
9.6   *Windows and Walls*, Sunderland. A collaboration between
      Colin Wilbourn and local schoolchildren   221

TABLES

3.1   Slogans of city advertising   62
3.2   Major repertoires in city advertisements   65
6.1   Capital cost of major prestige projects, 1986/87–1991/92   140
8.1   Local economic policy objectives of six cities in Saxony –
       evidence from interviews   194–5
10.1   Differences between 'modern' business organisations and 'post-
       modern' cultural producers   236–7
12.1   Regime types and subtypes   265

ACKNOWLEDGEMENTS

We would like to thank the Urban Geography Research Group of the Royal Geographical Society (with the Institute of British Geographers) for allowing us to hold the session at their annual conference at Strathclyde University in January 1996 upon which this collection is based. We would also like to thank all those at John Wiley & Sons who have supported the project.

BIBLIOGRAPHY

Aglietta, M. (1979) *A Theory of Capitalist Regulation: The US Experience*, London: New Left Books.

Alexander, I. (1994) 'DURD revisited? Federal policy initiatives for urban and regional planning 1991–1994' *Urban Policy and Research*, **12**: 16–26.

Althubaity, A. (1995) 'The role of tax increment financing in land use change and economic development in the Coachella Valley, southern California', University of California, Riverside, unpublished PhD thesis.

Ambrose, P. (1994) *Urban Process and Power*, London: Routledge.

Amin, A. (ed.) (1995) *Post-Fordism: A Reader*, Oxford: Blackwell.

Amin, A. (1997) 'Placing globalisation', paper presented to the Institute of British Geographers/Royal Geographical Society Annual Conference, University of Exeter, January.

Amin, A. and Graham, S. (1997) 'The ordinary city', paper presented to the Institute of British Geographers/Royal Geographical Society Annual Conference, University of Exeter, January.

Amin, A. and Robins, K. (1990) 'The re-emergence of regional economies? The mythical geography of flexible accumulation', *Environment and Planning D: Society and Space*, **8**: 7–34.

Amin, A. and Thrift, N. (1992) 'Neo-marshallian nodes in global networks' *International Journal of Urban and Regional Research*, **16**: 571–87.

Amin, A. and Thrift, N. (1995a) 'Living in the global' in Amin, A. and Thrift, N. (eds.) *Globalization, Institutions, and Regional Development in Europe*, Oxford: Oxford University Press: 1–22.

Amin, A. and Thrift, N. (1995b) 'Holding down the global' in Amin, A. and Thrift, N. (eds.) *Globalization, Institutions, and Regional Development in Europe*, Oxford: Oxford University Press: 257–60.

Amin, A. and Thrift, N. (1995c) 'Institutional issues for the European regions: from markets and plans to socioeconomics and powers of association' *Economy and Society*, **24**: 41–66.

Amin, A. and Thrift, N. (1995d) 'Globalisation, institutional "thickness" and the local economy', in Healey, P., Cameron, S., Davoudi, S., Graham, S. and Madani-Pour, A. (eds.) *Managing Cities: The New Urban Context*, Chichester: John Wiley & Sons: 91–108.

Anderson, J. (1990) 'The "new right" Enterprise Zones and Urban Development Corporations' *International Journal of Urban and Regional Research*, **14**: 468–89.

Anderson, M. (1994) 'Cities within cities' *New Scientist* (The Future Supplement), 15/10/94: 15.

Armstrong, P., Glyn, A. and Harrison, J. (1991) *Capitalism since 1945*, Oxford: Blackwell.

Arts Council (1989) *An Urban Renaissance*, London: Arts Council.

Arts Council (1991) *Percent for Art: A Review*, London: Arts Council of Great Britain.

Ashworth, G.J. and Voogd, H. (1990) *Selling the City: Marketing Approaches in Public Sector Urban Planning*, London: Belhaven Press.

Auer, J. (1995) 'The mayor who preaches design' *Progressive Architecture*, May: 92–5.

Australian Bureau of Statistics (1996) *Catalogue Numbers 8731.1, 6408.D*, Canberra: AGPS.

Bachtler, J. and Clement, K. (1991) 'Inward investment in the UK and the single European market' *Regional Studies*, **24**: 173–84.

Badcock, B. (1993) 'The urban programme as an instrument of crisis management in Australia' *Urban Policy and Research*, **11**: 72–80.

Bahrami, H. and Evans, S. (1995) 'Flexible re-cycling and high-technology entrepreneurship' *California Management Review*, **37**: 62–89.

Bailey, J.T. (1989) *Marketing Cities in the 1980s and Beyond*, Chicago: American Economic Development Council.

Bailey, N., Barker, A. and McDonald, K. (1995) *Partnership Agencies in British Urban Policy*, London: UCL Press.

Barke, M. and Harrop, K. (1994) 'Selling the industrial town: identity, image and illusion' in Gold, J. R. and Ward, S. V. (eds.) *Place Promotion: The Use of Publicity and Marketing to Sell Towns and Regions*, Chichester: John Wiley & Sons: 93–114.

Barker, T.C. and Robbins, M. (1963) *A History of London Transport: Passenger Travel and the Development of the Metropolis*: Vol I: *The Nineteenth Century*, London: Allen and Unwin.

Barker, T.C. and Robbins, M. (1974) *A History of London Transport: Passenger Travel and the Development of the Metropolis*, Vol II: *The Twentieth Century to 1970*, London: Allen and Unwin.

Barnekov, T., Boyle, R. and Roch, D. (1988) *Privatism and Urban Policy in Britain and the US*, Oxford: Oxford University Press.

Barnekov, T. and Rich, D. (1989) 'Privatism and the limits of local economic development policy' *Urban Affairs Quarterly*, **25**: 212–38.

Barnes, T.J. (1995) 'Political economy I: "the culture, stupid"' *Progress in Human Geography*, **19**: 423–31.

Barnett, S. (1991) 'Selling us short? Cities, culture and economic development' in Fisher, M. and Owen, U. (eds.) *Whose Cities?*, Harmondsworth: Penguin: 161–71.

Bassett, K. (1993) 'Urban cultural strategies and urban regeneration: a case study' *Environment and Planning A*, **25**: 1773–88.

Bassett, K. (1996) 'Partnerships, business elites and urban politics: new forms of governance in an English city?' *Urban Studies*, **33**: 539–55.

Bassett, K. and Harloe, M. (1990) 'Swindon: the rise and decline of a growth coalition' in Harloe, M., Pickvance, C. and Urry, J. (eds.) *Place, Policy and Politics: Do Localities Matter?*, London: Unwin Hyman: 42–61.

Beauregard, R.B. (1988) 'In the absence of practice: locality research debates' *Antipode*, **20**: 52–9.

Beauregard, R. (1993) *Voices of Decline: The Post-war Fate of US Cities*, Cambridge, Mass.: Blackwells.

Beazley, M., Loftman, P. and Nevin, B. (1995) 'Community resistance and mega-project development: an international perspective', paper presented to British Sociological Association Annual Conference, University of Leicester.

Beck, U. (1992) *Risk Society: Towards a New Modernity*, London: Sage.

Beck, U., Giddens, A. and Lash, S. (1994) *Reflexive Modernisation*, Cambridge: Polity Press.

Belk, R. (1995) 'Studies in new consumer behaviour' in Miller, D (ed.) *Acknowledging Consumption*, London: Routledge: 46–87.

Bell, D. (1993) 'Brum backs out of Games bid' *Birmingham Evening Mail*, 2/11/93: 1.

Bell, D. (1995) 'In bed with the state: political geography and sexual politics' *Geoforum*, **25**: 445–52.

Benington, J. (1994) *Local Democracy and the European Union: The Impact of Europeanisation on Local Governance*, London: Commission for Local Democracy.

Benington, J. and Harvey, J. (1994) 'Spheres or tiers? The significance of trans-national local authority networks', in Dunleavy, P. and Stanyer, J. (eds.) *Contemporary Political Studies*, London: Political Studies Association: 943–61.

Benko, G. and Dunford, M. (1991) *Industrial Change and Regional Development: The Transformation of New Industrial Spaces*, London: Belhaven Press.

Berger, M.L. (1992) *They Built Chicago: Entrepreneurs Who Shaped A Great City's Architecture*, Chicago: Bonus.

Bernstein, R.J. (1985) *Habermas and Modernity*, Cambridge, Mass.: MIT.

Berry, M. and Huxley, M. (1992) 'Big build: property capital, the state and urban change in Australia' *International Journal of Urban and Regional Research*, **16**: 35–59.

Best, M. (1990) *The New Competition*, Cambridge: Polity.

BFLR (Bundesforschungsanstalt für Landeskunde und Raumordnung) (1995a) 'Laufende Raumbeobachtung: Aktuelle Daten zur Entwicklung der Städte, Kreise und Gemeinden' *Materialien zur Raumentwicklung*, **67**.

BFLR (1995b) 'Regionalbarometer neue Länder' *Materialien zur Raumentwicklung*, **69**.

Bhabha, H. (1994) *The Location of Culture*, London: Routledge.

Bianchini, F., Dawson, J. and Evans, R. (1992) 'Flagship projects in urban regeneration' in Healey, P., Davoudi, S., O'Toole, M., Tavsanoglu, S. and Usher, D. (eds.) *Rebuilding the City: Property-Led Urban Regeneration*, London: E. and F.N. Spon: 245–55.

Bianchini, F. and Landry, C. (1994) *Indicators of a Creative City: A Methodology for Assessing Urban Vitality and Viability*, Stroud: Comedia.

Bianchini F. and Parkinson, M. (eds.) (1993) *Cultural Policy and Urban Regeneration: The West European Experience*, Manchester: Manchester University Press.

Biddle, G. (1990) *The Railway Surveyors: The Story of Railway Property Management 1800–1990*, London: Ian Allan/British Rail Property Board.

Bird, J. (1993) 'Dystopia on the Thames', in Bird, J., Curtis, B., Putnam, T., Robertson, G. and Tickner, L. (eds.) *Mapping the Futures: Local Cultures, Global Change*, London: Routledge: 120–35.

Bird, J., Curtis, B., Putnam, T., Robertson, G. and Tickner, L. (eds.) (1993) *Mapping the Futures: Local Cultures, Global Change*, London: Routledge.

Bird, V. (1979) *Portrait of Birmingham*, London: Robert Hale.

Birmingham City 2000 (1992) *Membership Directory 1992–1993*, Birmingham: Birmingham City 2000.

Birmingham City Council (1981) *Financial Statement 1980/81*, Birmingham: Birmingham City Council.

Birmingham City Council (1983) *International Convention Centre Birmingham: Feasibility Study*, Birmingham: Birmingham City Council.

Birmingham City Council (1985) *An Economic Development Strategy for Birmingham 1985/6*, Birmingham: Birmingham City Council.

Birmingham City Council (1986) *1986 Review Economic Strategy*, Birmingham: Birmingham City Council.

Birmingham City Council (1989a) *Developing Birmingham 1889–1989*, Birmingham: Birmingham City Council.

Birmingham City Council (1989b) *Annual Report and Accounts 1988–89*, Birmingham: Birmingham City Council.

Birmingham City Council (1989c) *Birmingham City Centre Review*, Birmingham: Birmingham City Council.

Birmingham City Council (1990) *Birmingham Integrated Development Operation 1990*, Birmingham: Birmingham City Council.

Birmingham City Council (1991a) *Annual Report and Accounts 1990–1991*, Birmingham: Birmingham City Council.

Birmingham City Council (1991b) *City Strategy Report 1992/93*, Birmingham: Birmingham City Council.

Birmingham City Council (1991c) *Facing the Challenge in Birmingham: East Birmingham City Challenge*, Birmingham: Birmingham City Council.

Birmingham City Council (1992a) *Birmingham: The Case for Assisted Area Status*, Birmingham: Birmingham City Council.

Birmingham City Council (1992b) *Economic Development Strategy*, Birmingham: Birmingham City Council.

Birmingham City Council (1992c) *City Centre Strategy*, Birmingham: Birmingham City Council.

Birmingham City Council (1995) *'94–'95 Financial Review*, Birmingham: Birmingham City Council.

Birmingham City Council (n.d.) *Millennium Point: The Midlands' Project for the Year 2000 and Beyond. . .*, Birmingham: Birmingham City Council.

Birmingham City Pride (1994) *Birmingham City Pride First Prospectus: Appendices*, Birmingham: Birmingham City Pride.

Birmingham City Pride (1995) *Moving Forward Together, Birmingham's City Pride Prospectus*, Birmingham: Birmingham City Pride.

Birmingham Economic Information Centre (1994) *The Birmingham Economy: Review and Prospects*, Birmingham: Birmingham City Council.

Birmingham Education Commission (1993) *Aiming High: The Report of the Birmingham Education Commission Part 1*, Birmingham: Birmingham City Council.

Bish, R.L. (1971) *The Public Economy of Metropolitan Areas*, Chicago: Markham Publishing Co.

Bish, R.L. and Ostrom, V. (1976) 'Understanding urban government: metropolitan reform reconsidered' in Hochman, H. (ed.) *The Urban Economy*, New York: W.W. Norton: 95–114.

Bishop's Council for the Diocese of Birmingham (1988) *Faith in the City of Birmingham*, Exeter: Paternoster Press.

Blair, P. (1991) 'Trends in local autonomy and democracy' in Batley, R. and Stoker, G. (eds.) *Local Government in Europe: Trends and Developments*, London: Macmillan: 41–57.

Blien, U. (1994) 'Konvergenz oder dauerhafter Entwicklungsrückstand? Einige theoretische Überlegungen zur empirischen Regionalentwicklung in den neuen Bundesländern' *Informationen zur Raumentwicklung*, **4**: 273–87.

Bloch, E. (1986) [1959] *The Principle of Hope*, Oxford: Blackwell.

Bloomfield, E. (1983) 'Community, ethos and local initiative in urban economic growth: review of a theme in Canadian economic history' *Urban History Yearbook 1983*, Leicester: Leicester University Press: 53–72.

Boddy, T. (1992) 'Underground and overhead: building the analogous city' in Sorkin, M. (ed.) *Variations on a Theme Park: The New American City and the End of Public Space*, New York: Hill and Wang: 123–53.

Boisot, M. (1993) 'Is a diamond a region's best friend? Towards an analysis of interregional competition' in Child, J., Crozier, M., Mayntz, R. (eds) *Societal Change between Market and Organization*, Aldershot: Avebury, 163–85.

Boje, D.M., Gephart, R.P. and Thatchenkery, T.J. (1996) *Postmodern Management and Organisation Theory*, Beverly Hills: Sage.

BOMA (1993) *Newcastle; Australia's Emerging City of Opportunity*, Sydney: BOMA.

Boorstin, D. J. (1965) *The Americans: The National Experience*, New York: Vintage.

Booth, P. and Boyle, R. (1993) 'See Glasgow, see culture' in Bianchini, F. and Parkinson, M. (eds.) *Cultural Policy and Urban Regeneration: The West European Experience*, Manchester: Manchester University Press: 21–47.

Bourdieu, P. (1984) *Distinction*, London: Routledge and Kegan Paul.

Bovaird, T. (1992) 'Local economic development and the city' *Urban Studies*, **29**: 342–68.

Boyer, M.C. (1992) 'Cities for sale: merchandising history at South Street Seaport' in Sorkin, M. (ed.) *Variations on a Theme Park: The New American City and the End of Public Space*, New York: Hill and Wang: 181–204.

Boyle, M. (1995) 'Positioning the politics of place marketing in the UK – a critique of transatlanticism', paper presented to Institute of British Geographers Annual Conference, University of Northumbria, Newcastle.

Boyle, M. and Hughes, G. (1991) 'The politics of the representation of the "real": discourses from the Left on Glasgow's role as City of Culture, 1990', *Area*, **23**: 217–28.

Boyle, M. and Hughes, G. (1995) 'The politics of urban entrepreneurialism in Glasgow' *Geoforum*, **25**: 452–69.

Boyle, R. (1990) 'Regeneration in Glasgow: stability, collaboration and inequity' in Judd, D. and Parkinson, M. (eds.) *Leadership and Urban Regeneration: Cities in North America and Europe*, Urban Affairs Annual Reviews, Newbury Park: Sage: 109–32.

Brabant, J.M. (1992) *Privatizing Eastern Europe. The Role of Markets and Ownership in the Transition*, London: Kluwer Academic.

Briggs, A. (1963) [1961] *Victorian Cities*, London: Odhams.

Brighton, A. (1993) 'Is architecture or art the enemy?' in de Ville, N. and Foster, S. (eds.) *Space Invaders: Issues of Presentation, Context and Meaning in Contemporary Art*, Southampton: John Hansard Gallery: 43–53.

Broadgate (n.d.) *Broadgate Visitors' Guide*, London: Rosehaugh Stanhope Developments PLC.

Brown, M. (1995) 'Sex, scale and the "new urban politics": HIV-prevention strategies from Yaletown, Vancouver' in Bell, D. and Valentine, G. (eds.) *Mapping Desires: Geographies of Sexualities*, London: Routledge: 245–63.

Brownill, S. (1993) 'The Docklands experience: locality and community in London', in Imrie, R. and Thomas, H. (eds.) *British Urban Policy and the Urban Development Corporations*, London: PCP Press: 41–57.

Bruner, E.M. (1993) 'Introduction: the ethnographic self and the personal self', in Benson, P. (ed.) *Anthropology and Literature*, Urbana: University of Illinois Press: 1–26.

Bryson, J.R., Daniels, P.W. and Henry, N.D. (1996) 'From widgets to where?: the Birmingham economy in the 1990s' in Gerrard, A.J. and Slater, T.R. (eds.) *Managing a Conurbation: Birmingham and its Region*, Studley: Brewin: 156–68.

Burcher, G. (1992) 'Market set for solid growth' *Birmingham Post*, 27/2/92: 24.

Burgess, J.A. (1982) 'Selling places: environmental images for the executive' *Regional Studies*, **16**: 1–17.

Burgess, J. and Wood, P. (1988) 'Decoding Docklands: place advertising and the decision-making strategies of the small firm' in Eyles, J. and Smith, D.M. (eds.) *Qualitative Methods in Human Geography*, Cambridge: Polity Press: 94–117.

Burstein, M. and Rolnick, A.J. (1995) 'Congress should end the economic war among the states: Federal Reserve Bank of Minneapolis 1994 Annual Report' *The Region*, **9**: 3–20.

Businaro, U. (1994) *Technology and the Future of Cities: Responding to the Urban Malaise; an Agenda for the EU*, European Commission, DG XII, July 1994.

Business Week (1994) 'Kansas City' 26/12/94: 33–54.

Calkin and Associates (1996) *Let's Go Hunter*, Report produced for Hunter Regional Tourism Organisation, Maitland, NSW.

Calvino, I. (1979) *Invisible Cities*, London: Pan Books [trans. William Weaver].

Cappellin, R. (1992) 'Theories of local endogenous development and international cooperation', in Tykkyläinen, M. (ed.) *Development Issues and Strategies in the New Europe: Local, Regional and Interregional Perspectives*, Aldershot: Avebury, 1–20.

Carley, M. (1991) 'Business in urban regeneration partnerships: a case study of Birmingham' *Local Economy*, **6**: 100–15.

Carter, H. and Lewis, C.R. (1990) *An Urban Geography of England and Wales in the Nineteenth Century*, London: Arnold.

Castells, M. (1977) *The Urban Question: A Marxist Approach*, London: Edward Arnold.

Castells, M. (1989) *The Informational City*, Oxford: Blackwell.

Castells, M. (1994) 'European cities, the informational society and the global economy' *New Left Review*, **204**: 18–32.

Castells, M. and Hall, P. (1994) *Technopoles of the World: The Making of 21st Century Industrial Complexes*, London: Routledge.

Cerny, P.G. (1989) *The Changing Architecture of Politics: Structure, Agency and the Future of the State*, London: Sage.

Chambers, I. (1991) *Border Dialogues: Jouneys in Postmodernity*, London: Routledge.

Champion, A.G. and Townsend, A.R. (1990) *Contemporary Britain: A Geographical Perspective*, London: Edward Arnold.

Charlesworth, J. and Cochrane, A. (1994) 'Tales of the suburbs: the local politics of growth in the south east of England' *Urban Studies*, **31**: 1723–38.

Cheesewright, P. (1991) 'The inheritors of Chamberlain' *Financial Times*, 18/10/91: 22.

Cherry, G. (1994) *Birmingham: A Study in Geography, History and Planning*, Chichester: John Wiley & Sons.

Cheshire, P. (1993) *European Integration and Regional Response*, CeSAER Discussion Paper: University of Reading.

Cheshire, P. and Gordon, I. (1993) *European Integration: Territorial Competition in Theory and Practice*, CeSAER Discussion Paper: University of Reading.

Cheshire, P. and Gordon, I. (1995) 'European integration: the logic of territorial competition and Europe's urban system' in Brotchie, M., Barry, E., Blakely, E., Hall, P. and Newton, P. (eds.) *Cities in Competition: Productive and Sustainable Cities in the 21st Century*, Melbourne: Longman Australia: 108–26.

Chesnais, F. (1986) 'Science, technology and competitiveness' *STI Review*, **1**: 85–129.

Cho, M-R (1996) 'Korean development on the High-way: a regulationist perspective', mimeo.

Cisneros, H.G. (1995) *Urban Entrepreneurialism and National Economic Growth*, Washington, DC: US Department of Housing and Urban Development.

City Centre Committee (1993) *Operating Plan*, Newcastle: City Centre Committee.

City of Palm Springs (1991) *Palm Springs: Draft General Plan Text*, Palm Springs, Calif.: City of Palm Springs.

Clark, E. and Ashley, P. (1992) 'The merchant prince of Cornville' *Chicago History*, **XXI**, 3: 4–19.

Clark, G. and Wrigley, N. (1995) 'Sunk costs: a framework for economic geography' *Transactions of the Institute of British Geographers* N.S., **20**: 204–23.

Clarke, D. and Owens, P. (1996) *Transaction Tracking – a Research Project in the Economic Lives of Practioners in the Cultural Sector*, Cardiff: Chaper Ltd.

Clarke, M. and Steward, J. (1994) 'The local authority and the new community governance' *Regional Studies*, **28**: 201–19.

Clarke, S. (1993) 'The new localism: local politics in a global era' in Goetz, E. and

Clarke, S. (eds.) *The New Localism: Comparative Urban Politics in a Global Era*, London: Sage: 1–22.

Clarke, S. and Gaile, G. (1989) 'Moving toward entrepreneurial economic development policies: opportunities and barriers' *Policy Studies Journal*, **17**: 575–98.

Clarke, S. and Gaile, G. (1992) 'The next wave: postfederal local economic development strategies' *Economic Development Quarterly*, **6**: 187–98.

Clarke, S. and Rich, M.J. (1985) 'Making money work: the new urban policy arena' *Research in Urban Policy*, **1**: 101–15.

Clavel, P. (1985) *The Progressive City*, New Brunswick, NJ: Rutgers University Press.

Clegg, S.R. (1990) *Modern Organisations: Organisation Studies in the Postmodern World*, London: Sage.

Cobb, J.C. (1984) *Industrialization and Southern Society 1877–1984*, Lexington, Ky: University Press of Kentucky.

Cobb, J.C. (1993) *The Selling of the South: The Southern Crusade for Industrial Development 1936–1990*, 2nd edition, Urbana/Chicago: University of Illinois Press.

Cochrane, A. (1992) 'Das veränderte Gesicht städtischer Politik in Sheffield: vom "municipal liberalism" zu "public–private Partnership"' in Heinelt, H. and Mayer, M. (eds.) *Politik in europäischen Städten: Fallstudien zur Bedeutung lokaler Politik*, Berlin: Birkhäuser Verlag: 119–36.

Cochrane, A. (1993) *Whatever Happened to Local Government?*, Milton Keynes: Open University Press.

Cochrane, A., Peck, T. and Tickell, J. (1996) 'Manchester plays games: exploring the local politics of globalisation' *Urban Studies*, **33**: 1319–36.

Cockburn, C. (1977) *The Local State: Management of Cities and People*, London: Pluto Press.

Cohen, J. and Rogers, J. (1993) 'Associative democracy' in Bardhan, P. and Roemer, J. (eds.) *Market Socialism: The Current Debate*, Oxford: Oxford University Press: 236–52.

Cole, B. and Durnack, R. (1990) *Happy as a Sandboy*, London: HMSO.

Cole, B. and Durnack, R. (1992) *Railway Posters 1923–1947 from the Collection of the National Railway Museum, York*, London: Lawrence King.

Colenutt, B. (1991) 'The London Docklands Development Corporation: has the community benefited?' in Keith, M. and Rogers, A. (eds.) *Hollow Promises? Rhetoric and Reality in the Inner City*, London: Mansell: 31–41.

Collinge, C.J. (1996) *Spatial Articulation of the State: Reworking Social Relations and Social Regulation Theory*, Birmingham: Centre for Urban and Regional Studies, University of Birmingham.

Collinge, C.J. and Hall, S. (1995) 'Hegemony and regime in urban governance: towards a theory of local policy networks and partnerships', paper presented to British Sociological Association, Leicester University, 10–14 April, 1995.

Collis, C. and Noon, D. (1994) 'Foreign direct investment in the U.K. regions: recent trends and policy issues' *Regional Studies*, **28**: 849–58.

Commission of the European Communities (1992) *Urbanisation and the Functions of Cities in the European Community*, Luxembourg: Office for Official Publications of the European Communities.

Cook, I. and Crang, M. (1995) *Doing Ethnographies*, Concepts and Techniques in Modern Geography series, 58. Published by the Quantitative Methods Study Group of the Institute of British Geographers.

Cooke, P. (1988) 'Modernity, postmodernity and the city' *Theory, Culture and Society*, **5**: 472–92.

Cooke, P. (1989) 'Locality, economic restructuring and world development' in Cooke, P. (ed.) *Localities: The Changing Face of Urban Britain*, London: Unwin Hyman: 1–44.

Cooke, P. (1990) 'Modern urban theory in question' *Transactions, Institute of British Geographers* N.S., **15**: 331–43.

Cork, R. (1990) 'Artist at work', *The Independent*, magazine section, 8/9/90: 34–9.

Cowen, H., McNab, A. Harrison, S., Howes, L. and Jerrard, B. (1989) 'Affluence amidst recession: Cheltenham' in Cooke, P. (ed.) *Localities: The Changing Face of Urban Britain*, London: Unwin Hyman: 86–128.

Cox, K.R. (1991) 'Questions of abstraction in studies in the new urban politics' *Journal of Urban Affairs*, **13**: 267–80.

Cox, K.R. (1993) 'The local and the global in the new urban politics: a critical view' *Environment and Planning D: Society and Space*, **11**: 433–48.

Cox, K.R. (1995) 'Globalisation, competition and the politics of local economic development' *Urban Studies*, **32**: 213–25.

Cox, K.R. (ed.) (1997) *Spaces of Globalization: Reasserting the Power of the Local*, New York: Guilford.

Cox, K.R. and Jonas, A.E.G. (1993) 'Urban development, collective consumption and the politics of metropolitan fragmentation' *Political Geography*, **12**: 8–37.

Cox, K.R. and Mair, A. (1988) 'Locality and community in the politics of local economic development' *Annals of the Association of American Geographers*, **78**: 307–25.

Cox, K.R. and Mair, A. (1989) 'Book review essay: urban growth machine and the politics of local economic development' *International Journal of Urban and Regional Research*, **13**: 137–46.

Cox, K.R. and Mair, A. (1991) 'From localised social structures to localities as agents' *Environment and Planning A*, **23**: 197–213.

Cox, K.R. and Wood, A. (1994) 'Local government and local economic development in the US' *Regional Studies*, **23**: 640–5.

Cox, K.R. and Wood, A. (1997) 'Competition and co-operation in mediating the global: the case of local economic development' *Competition and Change*, **2**: 65–94.

Crewe, L. and Haines, L. (1996) *Building a Civilised and Competitive City: The Lace Market as a Cultural Quarter*, Report to Nottingham City Council, February 1996.

Crilley, D. (1993a) 'Architecture as advertising: constructing the image of redevelopment' in Kearns, G. and Philo, C. (eds.) *Selling Places: The City as Cultural Capital, Past and Present*, Oxford: Pergamon Press: 231–52.

Crilley, D. (1993b) 'Megastructures and urban change: aesthetics, ideology and design' in Knox, P. (ed.) *The Restless Urban Landscape*, Englewood Cliffs, NJ: Prentice-Hall: 127–64.

Crook, S., Pakulski, J. and Waters, M. (1992) *Postmodernisation*, London: Sage.

Cruikshank, J. and Korza, P. (1988) *Going Public*, Amherst, Mass.: University of Massachusetts.

Cullen, M. (1991) 'The Honeysuckle research process' in *The Honeysuckle Development*, Proceedings of a symposium held on the 9/11/91, Department of Sociology and Anthropology, in association with the Departments of Geography and Social Work and the Division of Leisure Studies, University of Newcastle: 54–64.

Cummings, S. (ed.) (1988) *Business Elites and Urban Development: Case Studies and Critical Perspectives*, Albany, NY: State University of New York Press.

Cusick, J. (1990) 'Refuseniks attack "facsimile city"' *The Independent*, 31/12/90: 5.

CVAG (Coachella Valley Association of Governments) (1991) *Regional Housing Needs Analysis*, Palm Desert: CVAG.

Dabinett, C. and Ramsden, P. (1993) 'An urban policy for people: lessons from Sheffield' in Imrie, R. and Thomas, H. (eds.) *British Urban Policy and the Urban Development Corporations*, London: PCP Press: 123–35.

Dangschat, J. (1992) 'Konzeption, Realität und Funktion "neuer Standortpolitik" – am Beispiel des "Unternehmens Hamburg"' in Heinelt, H. and Mayer, M. (eds.) *Politik in*

Europäischen Städten: Fallstudien zur Bedeutung Lokaler Politik, Berlin: Birkhäuser Verlag: 29–48.

Danielson, M.N. (1976) *The Politics of Exclusion*, New York: Columbia University Press.

Darby, H.C. (ed.) (1973) *A New Historical Geography of England*, Cambridge University Press.

Daunton, M.J. (1990) 'American cities' in Daunton, M.J. (ed.) *Housing the Workers: A Comparative History, 1850–1914*, Leicester: Leicester University Press: 249–86.

Davis, M. (1990) *City of Quartz: Excavating the Future in Los Angeles*, London: Verso.

Davis, M. (1995) 'Bankruptcy on the backs of the poor' *The Nation*, **260**: 121–2.

De Certeau, M. (1988) *The Practice of Everyday Life*, Berkeley, Calif.: University of California Press.

De Ville, N. and Foster, S. (eds.) *Space Invaders: Issues of Presentation, Context and Meaning in Contemporary Art*, Southampton: John Hansard Gallery.

Deakin, N. and Edwards, J. (1993) *The Enterprise Culture and the Inner City*, London: Routledge.

Dear, M. (1995) 'Prolegomena to a postmodern urbanism' in Healey, P., Cameron, S., Davoudi, S., Graham, S. and Madani-Pour, A. (eds.) *Managing Cities: The New Urban Context*, Chichester: John Wiley: 27–44.

Deutsche, R. (1991a) 'Uneven development', in Ghirardo, D. (ed.) (1991) *Out of Site*, Seattle, Wash.: Bay Press: 157–219.

Deutsche, R. (1991b) 'Alternative space', in Wallis, B. (ed.) *If You Lived Here*, Seattle, Wash.: Bay Press: 45–66.

DEWG (1988) *The Highbury Initiative: Proceedings of the Birmingham City Centre Challenge Symposium 25th–27th March 1988*, London: DEWG.

Dicken, P. and Tickell, A. (1992) 'Competitors or collaborators? Inward investment promotion in Northern England' *Regional Studies*, **26**: 99–106.

DiGaetano, A. and Klemanski, J. (1991) 'Restructuring the suburbs: political economy of economic development in Auburn Hills, Michigan' *Journal of Urban Affairs*, **13**: 137–58.

DiGaetano, A. and Klemanski, J. (1993) 'Urban regimes in comparative perspective: the politics of urban development in Britain' *Urban Affairs Quarterly*, **29**: 54–83.

Donald, J. (1997) 'Imagining the modern city', in Westwood, S. and Williams, J. (eds.) *Imagining Cities: Scripts, Signs and Memories*, London: Routledge: 181–201.

Doro, S. (1992) *Blue Collar Goodbyes*, Watsonville: Papier-Mache Press.

Dowall, D. (1987) 'Public land development in the United States' *Journal of Real Estate Development*, **2**: 19–28.

Downs, A. (1973) *Opening up the Suburbs*, New Haven: Yale University Press.

Duckworth, R., Simmons, J.M. and McNulty, R.H. (1986) *The Entrepreneurial American City*, Washington DC: Partners for Livable Places.

Duffy, H. (1995) *Competitive Cities: Succeeding in the Global Economy*, London: Spon.

Dumke, G. S. (1944) *The Boom of the 'Eighties in Southern California*, San Marino, Calif.: Huntington Library.

Duncan, J.S. (1987) 'Review of urban imagery: urban semiotics' *Urban Geography*, **8**: 473–83.

Duncan, J.S. (1996) 'Me(trope)olis: or Hayden White among the urbanists' in A.D. King (ed.) *Re-Presenting the City: Ethnicity, Capital and Culture in the 21st-century Metropolis*, Basingstoke: Macmillan: 253–68.

Duncan, S. and Goodwin, M. (1982) 'The local state and restructuring social relations' *International Journal of Urban and Regional Research*, **6**: 157–85.

Duncan, S. and Goodwin, M. (1988) *The Local State and Uneven Development*, Cambridge: Polity Press.

Duncan, S., Goodwin, M. and Halford, S. (1988) 'Policy variations in local states: uneven development and local social relations' *International Journal of Urban and Regional Research*, **12**: 107–28.

Dunford, M. (1990) 'Theories of regulation' *Environment and Planning D: Society and Space*, **8**: 297–322.

Dunleavy, P. and O'Leary, B. (1987) *Theories of the State: The Politics of Liberal Democracy*, Basingstoke: Macmillan Education.

Dunn, K.M., McGuirk, P.M. and Winchester, H.P.M. (1995) 'Place-making: the social construction of Newcastle' *Australian Geographical Studies*, **33**: 149–66.

Dunn, P. and Leeson, L. (1993) 'The art of change in Docklands' in Bird, J., Curtis, B., Putnam, T., Robertson, G. and Tickner, L. (eds.) *Mapping the Futures: Local Cultures, Global Change*, London: Routledge: 136–49.

Dunning, J. (1994) 'Prospects for foreign direct investments' in Buckley, P.J. and Ghauri, P.N. (eds.) *The Economics of Change in Eastern and Central Europe – Its Impact on International Business*, London: Academic Press: 373–88.

Ebert, R., Gnad, F. and Kunzmann, K. (1994) *The Creative City: Concepts and Preconditions*, Stroud: Comedia.

Eggers, W.D. (1993) 'America's boldest mayors' *Policy Review*, Summer: 67–74.

Eisenschitz, A. and Gough, J. (1993) *The Politics of Local Economic Development*, London: Macmillan.

Eisenschitz, A. and Gough, J. (1996) 'The conditions of neo-Keynesian local economic strategy' *Review of International Political Economy*, **3**: 434–59.

Eisinger, P. (1988) *The Rise of the Entrepreneurial State*, Madison, Wis.: University of Wisconsin Press.

Elkin, S. (1985) 'Twentieth century urban regimes' *Journal of Urban Affairs*, **5**: 11–27.

Elkin, S. (1987) *City and Regime in the American Republic*, Chicago, Ill.: University of Chicago Press.

Elster, J. (1978) *Logic and Society: Contradictions and Possible Worlds*, Chichester: John Wiley & Sons.

Elton and Associates (1996) *Social Impact Assessment and Social Infrastructure Strategy*, Newcastle: Newcastle City Council.

Esser, J. and Hirsch, J. (1994) 'The crisis of Fordism and the dimensions of a post-Fordist regional and urban structure' in Amin, A. (ed.) *Post-Fordism: A Reader*, Oxford: Blackwell: 71–99.

Esser, K., Hillebrand, W., Messner, D., and Meyer-Stamer, J. (1996) 'Systemic competitiveness: a new challenge for firms and for government' *Cepal Review*, **59**: 39–53.

Ettlinger, N. (1994) 'The localization of development in comparative perspective' *Economic Geography*, **70**: 144–66.

European Commission (1994) *White Paper on Growth, Competitiveness and Employment*, Brussels–Luxembourg: ECSC–EC–EAEC.

Evatt Foundation (1996) *The State of Australia*, Sydney: Evatt Foundation.

Eyles, J. and Peace, W. (1990) 'Signs and symbols in Hamilton: an iconography of Steeltown' *Geografiska Annaler* **72 B**: 73–88.

Fagan, R. and Le Heron, R. (1994) 'Reinterpreting the geography of accumulation: the global shift and local restructuring' *Environment and Planning D: Society and Space*, **13**: 265–87.

Fagan, R. and Webber, M. (1994) *Global Restructuring: The Australian Experience*, Melbourne: Oxford University Press.

Fainstein, N. and Fainstein, S.S. (1983) 'Regime strategies, communal resistance and economic forces' in Fainstein, S.S. and Fainstein, N. (eds.) *Restructuring the City*, New York, NY: Longman: 245–82.

Fainstein, N. and Fainstein, S. (1996) 'Urban regimes and black citizens: the economic and social impacts of black political incorporation in US cities' *International Journal of Urban and Regional Research*, **20**: 22–38.

Fainstein, S.S. (1991) 'Promoting economic development: urban planning in the United States and Great Britain' *Journal of the American Planning Association*, **57**: 22–33.

Fainstein, S.S. (1994) *The City Builders: Property and Planning in London and New York*, Oxford: Blackwell.

Fainstein, S. (1995) 'Urban redevelopment and public policy in London and New York' in Healey, P., Cameron, S., Davoudi, S., Graham, S. and Madani-Pour, A. (eds.) *Managing Cities: The New Urban Context*, Chichester: John Wiley: 127–43.

Fainstein, S. and Fainstein, N. (1985) 'Economic restructuring and the rise of urban social movements' *Urban Affairs Quarterly*, **21**: 187–206.

Falk, N. (1986) 'Baltimore and Lowell: two American approaches' *Built Environment*, **12**: 145–52.

Falk, N. (1989) *The Highbury Initiative: City Centre Challenge Symposium 1989. Report of Proceedings*, London: URBED.

Featherstone, M. (1991) *Consumer Culture and Postmodernism*, London: Sage.

Featherstone, M., O'Connor, J. and Wynne, D. (1994) *ESRC Grant Award, Final Report*, Ref R000233075.

Felshin, N. (ed.) (1995) *But is it Art?*, Seattle, Wash.: Bay Press.

Ferlie, E., Pettigrew, A., Ashburner, L. and Fitzgerald, L. (1996) *The New Public Management in Action*, Oxford: Oxford University Press.

Filmer, R. and Dao, D. (1994) *Economic Effects of Microeconomic Reform*, Background paper 38, Canberra: Economic Planning and Advisory Council.

Financial World (1993) 'Memphis: target practice' 2/3/93: 51.

Financial World (1994) 'Fairfax County' 24/05/94: 51–4.

Fisher, M. and Owen, U. (eds.) (1991) *Whose Cities?*, London: Penguin.

Fisher, P.S. and Peters, H.A. (1996) 'Taxes, incentives and competition for investment' *The Region*, **10**: 52–7.

Fitte, G.C. (1966) *The Farmer's Frontier 1865–1900*, New York: Holt, Rinehart and Winston.

Fitzgerald, F., Ely, J. and Cox, K. (1990) 'Urban economic development strategies in the USA' *Local Economy*, **7**: 278–89.

Fleming, D. and Roth, R. (1991) 'Place in advertising' *Geographical Review*, **81**: 281–91.

Florida, R.L. and Jonas, A. (1991) 'US urban policy: the postwar state and capitalist regulation' *Antipode*, **23**: 349–84.

Flynn, A. and Marsden, T. (1995) 'Rural change, regulation and sustainability' *Environment and Planning A*, **27**: 1180–92.

Fogarty, M.P. (1947) *Plan Your Own Industries: A Study of Local and Regional Development Organizations*, Oxford: Blackwell.

Foley, P. (1992) 'Local economic policy and job creation: a review of evaluation studies' *Urban Studies*, **29**: 565–98.

Fosler, R.S. (ed.) (1988) *The New Economic Role of American States*, New York: Oxford University Press.

Fox-Przeworski, J. (1986) 'Changing intergovernmental relations and urban economic development' *Environment and Planning C*, **4**: 423–38.

Freeman, G., Clark, J.A. and Soete, L. (1982) *Unemployment and Technical Innovation: A Study of Long Waves and Economic Development*, London: Pinter.

Freistaat Sachsen (1994) *Wirtschaft und Arbeit in Sachsen 1994: Bericht zur wirtschaftlichen Lage im Freistaat Sachsen*. Dresden: Sächsisches Ministerium für Wirtschaft und Arbeit.

Freistaat Sachsen (1995) *Regionale Wirtschaftsförderung für die gewerbliche Wirtschaft des Freistaates Sachsen*, Dresden: Staatsministerium für Wirtschaft und Arbeit.

Freshman, P. (ed.) (1992) *Public Address: Krzysztof Wodiczko*, Minneapolis, Minn.: Walker Art Gallery.

Fretter, A.D. (1993) 'Place marketing: a local authority perspective' in Kearns, G. and Philo, C. (eds.) *Selling Places: The City as Cultural Capital, Past and Present*, Oxford: Pergamon Press: 163–74.

Frieden, B. (1990) 'Deal making goes public: learning from Columbus Center' in Lassar, T.J. (ed.) *City Deal Making*, Washington, DC: The Urban Land Institute: 45–56.

Frieden, B. and Sagalyn, L.J. (1989) *Downtown, Inc. – How America Rebuilds Cities*, Cambridge, Mass.: The MIT Press.

Fröbel, F., Heinrichs, J. and Kreye, O. (1980) *The New International Division of Labour*, Cambridge: Cambridge University Press.

Frostick, E. and Harland, L. (1993) *Take Heart: People, History and Change in Birmingham's Heartlands*, Birmingham: Hutton Press.

Fulton, W. (1991) *Guide to California Planning*, Point Arena: Solano Press Books.

Funnell, C.E. (1975) *By the Beautiful Sea: The Rise and High Times of that Great American Resort, Atlantic City*, New York: Knopf.

Gablik, S. (1991) *The Reenchantment of Art*, London: Thames and Hudson.

Gaffikin, F. and Warf, B. (1993) 'Urban policy and the post-Keynesian state in the United Kingdom and the United States' *International Journal of Urban and Regional Research*, **17**: 67–84.

Galligan, B., Lim, B. and Lovegrove, K. (eds.) (1993) *Managing Microeconomic Reform*, Canberra: Federalism Research Centre, Australian National University.

Galster, G.C. (1992) 'A cumulative causation model of the underclass: implications for urban economic development policy' in Galster, G.C. and Hill, E.W. (eds.) *The Metropolis in Black and White*, New Brunswick, NJ: The State University of New Jersey, Center for Urban Policy Research: 190–215.

Gans, H.J. (1962) *The Urban Villagers: Group and Class in the Life of Italian-Americans*, New York: Free Press of Glencoe/Macmillan.

Gates, P.W. (1934) *The Illinois Central Railroad and Its Colonization Work*, Cambridge, Mass.: Harvard University Press.

Georgia (1773) *[By his Excellency Sir James Wright, Baronet, Captain General, Governor and Commander in Chief of his Majesty's said Province, Chancellor, Vice-Admiral and Ordinary of the same] A PROCLAMATION, Land Secured by Treaty from Indians for Settlement*, Washington: Library of Congress, Portfolio 14, no. 12.

Gertler, M. (1988) 'The limits to flexibility: comments on the post-Fordist vision of production and its geography' *Transactions, Institute of British Geographers* N.S., **13**: 419–32.

Ghaussy, A. and Schäfer, W. (1993) *The Economics of German Unification*, London: Routledge.

Ghirardo, D. (ed.) (1991) *Out of Site*, Seattle, Wash.: Bay Press.

Giddens, A. (1990) *The Consequences of Modernity*, Stanford, Calif.: Stanford University Press.

Gilloch, G. (1996) *Myth and Metropolis: Walter Benjamin and the City*, Cambridge: Polity.

Girardet, H. (1992) *The Gaia Atlas of Cities*, London: Gaia.

Glickman, N., Lahr, M. and Wyly, E. (1996) *The State of the Nation's Cities*, Database and machine readable file documentation, version 1.5A. New Brunswick, NJ: Centre for Urban Policy Research, Rutgers University.

Goetz, E. (1988) 'Office–housing linkage programs: a review of the issues' *Economic Development Quarterly*, **2**: 182–96.

Goetz, E. (1990) 'Type II policy and mandated benefits in economic development' *Urban Affairs Quarterly*, **26**: 170–90.

Goetz, E.G. and Clarke, S.E. (1993) *The New Localism: Comparative Politics in a Global Era*, London: Sage.

Gold, J.R. (1994) 'Locating the message: place promotion as image communication' in Gold, J.R. and Ward, S.V. (eds.) *Place Promotion: The Use of Publicity and Marketing to Sell Towns and Regions*, Chichester: John Wiley & Sons: 19–38.

Gold, J.R. and Gold, M. M. (1990) '"A Place of Delightful Prospects": promotional imagery and the selling of suburbia' in Zonn, L. (ed.) *Place Images in Media: Portrayal, Experience and Meaning*, Savage, Md.: Rowman and Littlefield: 159–82.

Gold, J.R. and Gold, M.M. (1994) '"Home at Last!": building societies, home ownership and the imagery of English suburban promotion in the interwar years' in Gold, J. R. and Ward, S. V. (eds.) *Place Promotion: The Use of Publicity and Marketing to Sell Towns and Regions*, Chichester: John Wiley & Sons: 75–92.

Gold, J.R. and Ward, S.V. (eds.) (1994) *Place Promotion: The Use of Publicity and Marketing to Sell Towns and Regions*, Chichester: John Wiley & Sons.

Goodman, R. (1979) *The Last Entrepreneurs*, New York: Simon and Schuster.

Goodwin, M. (1992) 'The changing local state' in Cloke, P. (ed.) *Policy and Change in Thatcher's Britain*, Oxford: Pergamon.

Goodwin, M. (1993) 'The city as commodity: the contested spaces of urban development' in Kearns, G. and Philo, C. (eds.) *Selling Places: The City as Cultural Capital, Past and Present*, Oxford: Pergamon Press: 145–62.

Goodwin, M. (1995) 'Governing the spaces of difference: regulation and globalisation in London', paper to 10th Urban Change and Conflict Conference, Royal Holloway University of London.

Goodwin, M., Duncan, S. and Halford, S. (1993) 'Regulation theory, the local state, and the transition of urban politics' *Environment and Planning D: Society and Space*, **11**: 67–88.

Goodwin, M. and Painter, J. (1996) 'Local governance, the crisis of Fordism and the changing geographies of regulation' *Transactions of the Institute of British Geographers*, **21**: 635–48.

Gordon, D. (1988) 'The global economy: new edifice or crumbling foundations' *New Left Review*, **168**: 24–65.

Gordon, D.M. (1978) 'Capitalist development and the history of American cities' in Tabb, W. and Sawers, L. (eds.) *Marxism and the Metropolis: New Perspectives in Urban Political Economy*, New York: Oxford University Press: 25–63.

Gornig, M. and Häußermann, H. (1994) 'Regionen im Süd/Nord und West/Ost-Gefälle' in Roth, R. and Wollmann, H. (eds.) *Kommunalpolitik. Politisches Handeln in den Gemeinden*, Opladen: Leske+Budrich: 155–75.

Goss, J.D. (1993) 'Placing the market and marketing place: tourist advertising of the Hawaiian Islands, 1972–92' *Environment and Planning D: Society and Space*, **11**: 663–88.

Goss, J. (1997) 'Representing and re-presenting the contemporary city' *Urban Geography* **18**: 180–8.

Gottdiener, M. (1986) *Cities in Stress: A New Look at the Urban Crisis*, Beverly Hills: Sage.

Gottdiener, M. (1987) *The Decline in Urban Politics*, Beverly Hills: Sage.

Gough, J. (1996) 'Neoliberalism and localism: comments on Peck and Tickell' *Area*, **28**: 392–8.

Gough, J. and Eisenschitz, A. (1996) 'The modernisation of Britain and local economic policy: promise and contradictions' *Environment and Planning D: Society and Space*, **14**: 203–19.

Grabher, G. (1995) 'The disembedded regional economy: the transformation of East German industrial complexes into Western enclaves' in Amin, A. and Thrift, N. (eds.)

Globalization, Institutions, and Regional Development in Europe, Oxford: Oxford University Press: 177–95.

Grabow, B. and Henckel, D. (1994) 'Kommunale Wirtschaftspolitik' in Roth, R. and Wollmann, H. (eds.) *Kommunalpolitik. Politisches Handeln in den Gemeinden*, Opladen: Leske+Budrich: 424–39.

Graham, S. (1995) 'The city economy' in Healey, P., Cameron, S., Davoudi, S., Graham, S. and Madani-Pour, A. (eds.) *Managing Cities: The New Urban Context*, Chichester: John Wiley: 83–91.

Graham, S. and Marvin, S. (1996) *Telecommunications and the City: Electronic Spaces, Urban Places*, London: Routledge.

Gramsci, A. (1971) *Selections from the Prison Notebooks*, London: Lawrence and Wishart.

Gratz, R. (1989) *The Living City*, New York: Simon and Schuster.

Green, G. and Fleischman, A. (1989) 'Analyzing local strategies for promoting economic development' *Policy Studies Journal*, **17**: 557–73.

Gregory, D. (1989) 'Areal differentiation and post-modern human geography', in Gregory, D. and Walford, R. (eds.) *Horizons in Human Geography*, Basingstoke: Macmillan: 67–96.

Gregory, D. (1990a) 'Gregory, D. (1990)' *Environment and Planning D: Society and Space*, **8**: 1–3.

Gregory, D. (1990b) '(1)' *Environment and Planning D: Society and Space*, **8**: 4–6.

Gregory, D. (1994) *Geographical Imaginations*, Cambridge, Mass.: Blackwell.

Greyan, P. (1994) 'City 2000 chief warns of dangers in council policies' *Birmingham Post*, 12/4/94: 9.

Guiskind, R. (1987) 'Bringing Madison Avenue to Main Street' *Planning* Feb.: 4–10.

Hackney LBC (London Borough Council) (1983) *The Case for Hackney: Britain's Poorest Borough*, Hackney: London Borough of Hackney Council.

Haider, D. (1992) 'Place wars: new realities of the 1990s' *Economic Development Quarterly*, **6**: 127–34.

Hall, P. (1988) *Cities of Tomorrow: An Intellectual History of Urban Planning*, Oxford: Blackwell.

Hall, P. (1995) 'Urban stress, creative tension' *The Independent*, 21/2/95: 15.

Hall, S. and Jacques, M. (1989) *New Times*, London: Lawrence and Wishart.

Hall, T. (1992) 'Art and image: public art as symbol in urban regeneration', School of Geography, University of Birmingham: working paper no. 61.

Hall, T. (1994) 'Urban regeneration and cultural geography: the International Convention Centre, Birmingham', School of Geography, University of Birmingham: unpublished PhD thesis.

Hall, T. (1995) '"The second industrial revolution": cultural reconstructions of industrial regions' *Landscape Research*, **20**: 112–23.

Hall, T. (1997) '(Re)placing the city: cultural relocation and the city as centre' in Westwood, S. and Williams, J. (eds.) *Imagining Cities: Scripts, Signs and Memories*, London: Routledge: 202–18.

Hall, T. and Hubbard, P. (1996) 'The entrepreneurial city: new urban politics, new urban geographies?', *Progress in Human Geography*, **20**: 153–74.

Hallsworth, A. (1996) 'Short-termism and economic restructuring in Britain' *Economic Geography*, **72**, 23–37.

Hambleton, R. (1990) *Urban Government in the 1990s: Lessons from the USA*, Bristol: School of Advanced Urban Studies.

Hambleton, R. (1991) 'American dreams, urban realities' *The Planner*, **77**: 6–9.

Handy, C. (1994) *The Empty Raincoat*, London: Arrow Business.

Harding, A. (1991) 'The rise of urban growth coalitions, UK-style?' *Environment and Planning C: Government and Policy*, **9**: 295–317.

Harding, A. (1992) 'Property interests and urban growth coalitions in the UK: a brief encounter' in Healey, P., Davoudi, S., O'Toole, M., Tavsanoglu, S. and Usher, D. (eds.) *Rebuilding the City: Property-led Urban Regeneration*, London: Spon Ltd: 223–32.

Harding, A. (1994) 'Urban regimes and growth machines: toward a cross-national research agenda' *Urban Affairs Quarterly*, **29**: 356–82.

Harding, A. (1995) 'European city regimes? Inter-urban competition in the new Europe', paper to the ESRC Local Governance Conference, Exeter, 19–20 September 1995.

Harding, A. and Garside, P. (1995) 'Urban and economic development', in John Stewart and Gerry Stoker (eds.) *Local Government in the 1990s*, Basingstoke: Macmillan: 166–87.

Harley, J.B. (1992) 'Deconstructing the map' in Barnes, T.J. and Duncan, J.S. (eds.) *Writing Worlds: Discourse, Text and Metaphor in the Representation of Landscape*, London: Routledge: 231–47.

Harris, R. and Hamnett, C. (1987) 'The myth of the promised land: the social diffusion of home ownership in Britain and North America' *Annals of the Association of American Geographers*, **77**: 173–90.

Harrison, B. (1992) 'Industrial districts: old wine in new bottles?' *Regional Studies*, **26**(5): 469–483.

Hartman, C. (1984) *The Transformation of San Francisco*, San Francisco, Calif.: Rowan and Allanheld Publications.

Harvey, D. (1982) *The Limits to Capital*, Oxford: Basil Blackwell.

Harvey, D. (1985a) 'The geopolitics of capitalism' in Gregory, D. and Urry, J. (eds.) *Social Relations and Spatial Structures*, Basingstoke: Macmillan: 128–63.

Harvey, D. (1985b) *The Urbanization of Capital*, Oxford: Blackwell.

Harvey, D. (1987) 'Flexible accumulation through urbanisation: some reflections on "post-modernism" in the American city' *Antipode*, **19**: 260–86.

Harvey, D. (1988) 'Voodoo cities' *New Statesman and Society*, 30/9/88: 33–5.

Harvey, D. (1989a) *The Condition of Postmodernity: An Enquiry into the Origins of Cultural Change*, Oxford: Blackwell.

Harvey, D. (1989b) 'From managerialism to entrepreneurialism: the transformation of governance in late capitalism' *Geografiska Annaler*, **71B**: 3–17.

Harvey, D. (1992) 'Social justice, postmodernism and the city' *International Journal of Urban and Regional Research*, **16**: 588–601.

Harvey, D. (1993) 'From space to place and back again: reflections on the condition of postmodernity' in Bird, J., Curtis, B., Putnam, T., Robertson, G. and Tickner, L. (eds.) *Mapping the Futures: Local Cultures, Global Change*, London: Routledge: 3–29.

Harvey, D. (1994) 'The invisible political economy of architectural production' in Bouman, O. and van Toorn, R. (eds.) *The Invisible in Architecture*, London: Academy Editions: 420–7.

Häußermann, H. (1995) 'Von der "sozialistischen" zur "kapitalistischen" Stadt' *Aus Politik und Zeitgeschehen*, **12**: 17/03/95: 3–15.

Hay, C. (1994) 'Moving and shaking to the rhythm of local economic development? Towards a local Schumpeterian workfare state?', Lancaster Working Papers in Political Economy, no. 49.

Hay, C. (1995) 'Re-stating the problem of regulation and re-regulating the local state' *Economy and Society*, **24**: 387–407.

Hay, C. and Jessop, B. (1995) 'The governance of local economic development and the development of local economic governance: a strategic–relational aproach', paper presented to the Annual Conference of American Political Science Association, Chicago, 29 August–1 September 1995.

Hayden, D. (1995) *The Power of Place*, Cambridge, Mass.: MIT.

HDC (Honeysuckle Development Corporation) (1995) *Inner City Renewal: An Update*, BC Newsletter for Honeysuckle and Environs.

HDC (n.d.) *A Partnership for the Future*, Newcastle: HDC.

Healey, P. (1995) 'The institutional challenge for sustainable urban regeneration' *Cities*, **12**: 221–31.

Healey, P., Davoudi, S., O'Toole, M., Tavsanoglu, S. and Usher, D. (eds.) (1992) *Rebuilding the City: Property-led Urban Regeneration*, London: Spon.

HEDC (Hunter Economic Development Council) (1991) *Hunter Economic Development Council Development Strategy*, Newcastle: HEDC.

HEDC (n.d.) *The Hunter: Aim for the Best*, Newcastle: HEDC.

Helbrecht, I. (1994) *Stadtmarketing: Konturen einer kommunikativen Stadtentwicklungspolitik*, Berlin: Birkhäuser Verlag.

Held, G. (1992) 'Barcelona 2000 – Lokale Politik als internationale Strategie?' in Heinelt, H. and Mayer, M. (eds.) *Politik in europäischen Städten: Fallstudien zur Bedeutung lokaler Politik*. Berlin: Birkhäuser Verlag: 187–212.

Herrschel, T. (1995) 'Local policy restructuring: a comparative assessment of policy responses in England and Germany' *Area*, **27**: 228–41.

Hess, T. and Ashbery, J. (eds.) (1967) *Avant Garde Art*, London: Collier-Macmillan.

Heuer, H. (1985) *Instrumente kommunaler Gewerbepolitik, Ergebnisse empirischer Erhebungen*, Stuttgart: Kohlhammer.

Hewison, R. (1995) *The Culture of Consensus*, London: Methuen.

Hilderbrant, D., Lewis, G., Mereschak, A., Macomish, N., Cleaveley, T., Montoya, C., Amos, M. and Chichester, K. (1988) *Pedestrian Movement and Open Space Framework*, London: LDR/HLN Consultancy.

Hilmer, F. (1993) *National Competition Policy*, Report of the Independent Commission of Inquiry into Competition Policy in Australia, Canberra: AGPS.

Hirsch, J., Esser, J. and Fach, W. (1991) *Modernisierungspolitik Heute: die Deregulationspolitiken von Regierungen und Parteien*, Frankfurt: Materialis Verlag.

Hirst, P. (1994) *Associative Democracy: New Forms of Economic and Social Governance*, Cambridge: Polity Press.

Hirst, P. and Thompson, G. (1996) *Globalization in Question: The International Economy and the Possibilities of Governance*, Cambridge: Polity.

Hirst, P. and Zeitlin, J. (1992) 'Flexible specialization versus post-Fordism: theory, evidence, and policy implications' in Storper, M. and Scott, A.J. (eds.) *Pathways to Industrialization and Regional Development*, London: Routledge: 70–115.

Hirst Consulting Services Pty Ltd (1995) *Newcastle Commercial Centres Study*, Report for Newcastle City Council, Sydney: Hirst Consulting Services Pty Ltd.

Hoggart, K. (1989) 'Politics, society and urban problems: a theoretical introduction' in Herbert, D.T. and Smith, D.M. (eds.) *Social Problems and the City*, Oxford: Oxford University Press: 48–59.

Hoggart, K. (1991) *People, Power and Place: Perspectives on Anglo-American Politics*, London: Routledge.

Holcomb, B. (1993) 'Revisioning place: de- and re-constructing the image of the industrial city' in Kearns, G. and Philo, C. (eds.) *Selling Places: The City as Cultural Capital, Past and Present*, Oxford: Pergamon Press: 133–43.

Holcomb, B. (1994) 'City make-overs: marketing the post-industrial city' in Gold, J.R. and Ward, S.V. (eds.) *Place Promotion: The Use of Publicity and Marketing to Sell Towns and Regions*, Chichester: John Wiley & Sons: 115–32.

Hollingsworth, J.R. (1997) 'Continuities and changes in social systems of production: the cases of Japan, Germany and the United States' in Hollingsworth, J.R. and Boyer, R. (eds.) *Contemporary Capitalism*, Cambridge: Cambridge University Press: 276–310.

Holmes, J. (1986) 'The organization and locational structure of production subcontracting' in Scott, A.J. and Storper, M. (eds.) *Production, Work, Territory*, London: Allen & Unwin: 80–106.

Horan, C. (1991) 'Beyond governing coalitions: analysing urban regimes in the 1990s' *Journal of Urban Affairs*, **13**: 119–35.

Howarth, J. (1994) 'Cash row could chase lions away' *Birmingham Post*, 2/11/94: 3.

Howitt, R. (1993) 'The world in a grain of sand: towards a reconceptualisation of geographical scale' *Australian Geographer*, **42**: 33–45.

Hoxworth, D. and Thomas, J. (1993) 'Economic development decision-making in a fragmented polity: convention center expansion in Kansas City' *Journal of Urban Affairs*, **15**: 275–92.

Hoyle, B.S., Pinder, D.A. and Hussain, M.S. (eds.) (1988) *Revitalising the Waterfront: International Dimensions of Dockland Redevelopment*, London: Belhaven Press.

Hubbard, P. (1995) 'Urban design and local economic development: a case study in Birmingham' *Cities*, **12**: 243–51.

Hubbard, P. (1996a) 'Re-imaging the city: the transformation of Birmingham's urban landscape' *Geography*, **81**: 26–36.

Hubbard, P. (1996b) 'Urban design and city regeneration: social representations of entrepreneurial landscapes' *Urban Studies*, **33**: 1441–61.

Hughes, R. (1992) *Barcelona*, London: Collins Harvill.

Hula, R. (1990) 'The two Baltimores' in Judd, D. and Parkinson, M. (eds.) *Leadership and Urban Regeneration: Cities in North America and Europe*, Vol. 37: Urban Affairs Annual Reviews, Newbury Park: Sage: 191–215.

Hunter Valley Research Foundation (1995) *The Economic Impacts of the Honeysuckle Redevelopment on the Hunter Region. 1992/3–1994/5*, Newcastle: Hunter Valley Research Foundation.

Hutton, W. (1996) *The State We're In*, London: Vintage.

Imrie, R. and Thomas, H. (eds.) (1993a) *British Urban Policy and the Urban Development Corporations*, London: Paul Chapman.

Imrie, R. and Thomas, H. (1993b) 'The limits of property-led regeneration' *Environment and Planning C: Government and Policy*, **11**: 87–102.

Imrie, R. and Thomas, H. (1995) 'Changes in local governance and their implications for urban policy evaluation' in Hambleton, R. and Thomas, H. (eds.) *Urban Policy Evaluation: Challenge and Change*, London: Paul Chapman: 123–37.

Imrie, R., Thomas, H. and Marshall, T. (1995) 'Business organisation, local dependence and the politics of urban renewal in Britain' *Urban Studies*, **32**: 31–47.

Industrie- und Handelskammer Dresden (1995) 'Konjunkturbericht zur wirtschaftlichen Situation im Kammerbezirk Dresden zur Jahreswende 1994/95', unpublished.

Industrie- und Handelskammer Südwestsachsen (1993) 'Zahlen, Fakten Übersichten', Chemnitz, IHK: unpublished.

Industrie- und Handelskammer zu Leipzig (1995) 'Statistische Informationen', unpublished.

Industry Commission (1993) *Impediments to Regional Industry Adjustment*, Canberra: AGPS.

Irmen, E. and Blach, A. (1995) 'Infrastrukturdefizite in den neuen Bundesländern' *Materialien zur Raumentwicklung*, **69**: 105–13.

Jack, I. (1984) 'The repackaging of Glasgow' *Sunday Times Magazine*, 2 December: 37–45.

Jackson, A.A. (1986) *London's Metropolitan Railway*, Newton Abbot: David and Charles.

Jackson, A.A. (1991) *Semi-Detached London: Suburban Development, Life and Transport 1900–39*, 2nd edition, Didcot: Wild Swan.

Jackson, K.T. (1985) *Crabgrass Fronter: The Suburbanization of the United States*, New York: Oxford University Press.

Jackson, P. (1991) 'Mapping meanings: a cultural critique of locality studies' *Environment and Planning A*, **23**: 215–28.

Jackson, P. (1993) 'Toward a cultural politics of consumption' in Bird, J., Curtis, B., Putnam, T., Robertson, G. and Tickner, L. (eds.) *Mapping the Futures: Local Cultures, Global Change*, London: Routledge: 207–28.

Jacobs, B.D. (1992) *Fractured Cities: Capitalism, Community and Empowerment in Britain and America*, London: Routledge.

Jacobs, J.M. (1994) 'Negotiating the heart: heritage, development and identity in postimperial London' *Environment and Planning D: Society and Space*, **12**: 751–72.

Jameson, F. (1984) 'Postmodernism, or the cultural logic of late capitalism' *New Left Review*, **146**: 53–92.

Jessop, B. (1982) *The Capitalist State: Marxist Theory and Methods*, Oxford: Blackwell.

Jessop, B. (1990) 'Regulation theory in retrospect and prospect' *Economy and Society*, **19**: 153–216.

Jessop, B. (1992) 'Fordism and post-Fordism: critique and reformulation' in Scott, A.J. and Storper, M.J. (eds.) *Pathways to Regionalism and Industrial Development*, London: Routledge: 43–65.

Jessop, B. (1993) 'Towards a Schumpeterian workfare state? Preliminary remarks on post-Fordist political economy', *Studies in Political Economy*, **40**: 7–39.

Jessop, B. (1994) 'Post-Fordism and the state' in Amin, A. (ed.) *Post-Fordism: A Reader*, Oxford: Blackwell: 251–80.

Jessop, B. (1995) 'The entrepreneurial city; re-imaging localities, re-designing economic governance or re-structuring capital?' Paper presented to the Tenth Urban Change and Conflict Conference, Royal Holloway University of London.

Jessop, B. (1996) 'The entrepreneurial city: re-imaging localities, re-designing economic governance or re-structuring capital'. Paper presented to the Annual Conference of the Institute of British Geographers, University of Strathclyde.

Jessop, B. (1997a) 'A neo-Gramscian approach to the regulation of urban regimes', in Lauria, M. (ed.) *Reconstructing Urban Regime Theory*, London: Sage: 51–73.

Jessop, B. (1997b) 'The entrepreneurial city: re-imaging localities, redesigning economic governance, or restructuring capital?', in Jewson, N. and MacGregor, S. (eds.) *Realising Cities: New Spatial Divisions and Social Transformation*, London: Routledge (in press).

Jessop, B. (1997c) 'The governance of complexity and the complexity of governance: preliminary remarks on some problems and limits of economic guidance', in Amin, A. and Hausner, J. (eds.) *Beyond Markets and Hierarchy: Third Way Approaches to Transformation*, Aldershot: Edward Elgar: 111–47.

Jessop, B., Nielsen, K., and Pedersen, O.K. (1993) 'Structural competitiveness and strategic capacities: the cases of Britain, Denmark, and Sweden', in Sjöstrand, S-E (ed.) *Institutional Change: Theory and Empirical Findings*, New York: M.E. Sharpe: 227–62.

Jones, B. (1990) 'All set for take off, Business City of the 1990s' *Birmingham Post/ Evening Mail*, 16/1/90: 6.

Judd, D. and Parkinson, M. (eds.) (1990a) *Leadership and Urban Regeneration: Cities in North America and Europe*, Vol. 37: Urban Affairs Annual Reviews, Newbury Park: Sage.

Judd, D. and Parkinson, M. (1990b) 'Urban leadership and regeneration' in Parkinson, M. and Judd, D. (eds.) *Leadership and Urban Regeneration*, London: Sage: 13–30.

Judd, D. and Ready, R.L. (1986) 'Entrepreneurial cities and the new politics of economic development' in Peterson, G.E. and Lewis, C.W. (eds.) *Reagan and the Cities*, Washington DC, Urban Institute Press: 209–47.

Kearns, G. (1988) 'History, geography and world systems theories' *Journal of Historical Geography*, **14**: 281–92.

Kearns, G. and Philo, C. (eds.) (1993) *Selling Places: The City as Cultural Capital, Past and Present*, Oxford: Pergamon Press.

Keating, M. (1988) *The City that Refused to Die – Glasgow: The Politics of Urban Regeneration*, Aberdeen: Aberdeen University Press.

Keating, M. (1991) *Comparative Urban Politics, Power and the City in the US, Canada, Britain and France*, Aldershot: Edward Elgar.

Keating, M. (1993) 'The politics of economic development: political change and local development policies in the United States, Britain and France' *Urban Affairs Quarterly*, **28**: 373–98.

Keating, M. (1997) 'The political economy of regionalism' in Keating, M. and Loughlin, J. (eds.) *The Political Economy of Regionalism*, London: Frank Cass: 17–40.

Keating, W.D. (1986) 'Linking downtown development to broader community goals: an analysis of linkage policy in three cities' *Journal of the American Planning Association*, **52**: 133–41.

Keith, M. and Cross, M. (1993) 'Racism and the postmodern city' in Keith, M. and Cross, M. (eds.) *Racism, the City and the State*, London: Routledge: 1–31.

Keith, M. and Pile, S. (1994) *Place and the Politics of Identity*, London: Routledge.

Kelty, W. (1993) *Developing Australia: A Regional Perspective*, A report to the federal government by the Task Force on Regional Development, 2 volumes, Canberra: AGPS.

Kennedy, M. (1996) 'Greenwich wins Millennium battle' *The Guardian*, 24/2/96: 2.

Kenny, J.T. (1995) 'Making Milwaukee famous: cultural capital, urban image and the politics of place' *Urban Geography*, **16**: 440–58.

Kerstein, R. (1993) 'Suburban growth politics in Hillsborough County: growth management and political regimes' *Social Science Quarterly*, **74**: 614–30.

King, A.D. (1996a) 'Introduction: cities, texts and paradigms', in King, A.D. (ed.) *Re-Presenting the City: Ethnicity, Capital and Culture in the 21st-Century Metropolis*, Basingstoke: Macmillan: 1–19.

King, A. (ed.) (1996b) *Re-Presenting the City: Ethnicity, Culture and Capital in the 21st-Century Metropolis*, Basingstoke: Macmillan.

Kirlin, J.J. and Marshall, D.R. (1988) 'Urban governance and the new politics of entrepreneurship' in McGeary, M. and Lynn, L. (eds.) *Urban Change and Poverty*, Washington DC: National Academic Press: 348–73.

Kirwan, R. (1986) 'Local fiscal policy and inner city economic development' in Hausner, V. (ed.) *Critical Issues in Urban Economic Development*, Vol. I, Oxford: Clarendon Press: 200–28.

Klemanski, J. (1990) 'Using tax-increment financing for urban redevelopment projects' *National Civic Review*, **79**: 179–86.

Knight, R. (1992) *The Future of European Cities, Part 4: Cities as Loci of Knowledge-Based Development*, Report for the FAST Programme, European Commission, DG V.

Knights, D. (1995) 'Organisation theory in the age of deconstruction: dualism, gender, and postmodernism revisited', paper for *Workshop on Action, Structure and Organisations, EESEC IMD*, Paris, May.

Knights, D. and Raffo, C. (1990) 'Milkround professionalism in personnel recruitment: myth or reality' *Personnel Review*, **19**: 28–37.

Knights, D., Sturdy, A. and Morgan, G. (1994) 'The consumer rules? An examination of rhetoric and "reality" in financial services' *European Journal of Marketing*, **28**: 42–54.

Knopp, L. (1994) 'Social justice, sexuality and the city' *Urban Geography*, **15**: 644–61.

Knox, P.L. (1991) 'The restless urban landscape: economic and socio-cultural change and the transformation of Washington D.C.' *Annals, Association of American Geographers*, **81**: 181–209.

Kohn, C. (1989) 'California redevelopment agencies; urban renewal for business, not housing' *California Journal*, **20**(6): 265–67.

Kotler, P., Haider, D.H. and Rein, I. (1993) *Marketing Places: Attracting Investment, Industry, and Tourism to Cities, States, and Nations*, New York: Free Press.

KPMG Peat Marwick (1993) *The Economic Impact of the International Convention Centre, the National Indoor Arena, Symphony Hall, and the National Exhibition Centre on Birmingham and the West Midlands. Main Report*, Birmingham: KPMG Peat Marwick.

Krätke, S. (1995) *Stadt, Raum, Ökonomie: Einführung in aktuelle Problemfelder der Stadtökonomie und Wirtschaftsgeographie*, Basle: Birkhäuser Verlag.

Krugman, P. (1994) 'Competitiveness: a dangerous obsession' *Council on Foreign Relations*, **73**: 28–44.

Krugman, P. and Venables, A. (1990) 'Integration and the competitiveness of peripheral industry' in Bliss, C. and Braga de Macedo, J. (eds.) *Unity with Diversity in the European Community*, Cambridge: Cambridge University Press: 56–75.

Kumar, K. (1995) *From Post-Industrial to Post-Modern Society*, Oxford: Blackwell.

Laclau, E. (1996) *Emancipation(s)*, London: Verso.

Lacy, S. (ed.) (1995) *Mapping the Terrain*, Seattle, Wash.: Bay Press.

Landry, C. and Bianchini, F. (1995) *The Creative City*, London: Demos/Comedia.

Lash, S. (1990) *The Sociology of Postmodernism*, London: Routledge.

Lash, S. and Urry, J. (1987) *The End of Organized Capitalism*, Cambridge: Polity Press.

Lash, S. and Urry, J. (1994) *Economies and Signs and Space*, London: Sage.

Lassar, T.J. (1989) *Carrots and Sticks: New Zoning Downtown*, Washington, DC: The Urban Land Institute.

Lauria, M. (ed.) (1997) *Reconstructing Urban Regime Theory: Regulating Urban Politics in a Global Economy*, Thousand Oaks, Calif.: Sage.

Laux, E. (1994) 'Erfahrungen und Perspektiven der kommunalen Gebiets- und Funktionalreformen' in Roth, R. and Wollmann, H. (eds.) *Kommunalpolitik:Politisches Handeln in den Gemeinden*, Opladen: Leske and Budrich: 136–54.

Law, C.M. (1992) 'Urban tourism and its contribution to economic regeneration' *Urban Studies*, **29**: 599–618.

Law, C. M. (1993) *Urban Tourism: Attracting Visitors to Large Cities*, London: Mansell.

Law, C.M. (1996) *Tourism in Major Cities*, London: International Thompson Business Press.

Lawless, P. (1994) 'Partnership in urban regeneration in the U.K.: the Sheffield central area study' *Urban Studies*, **31**: 1303–24.

Laws, G. (1995) 'Social justice and urban politics' *Urban Geography*, **15**: 603–12.

LDDC (n.d.) *London Docklands Development Corporation Arts Action Programme*, London: LDDC (not paginated).

Leborgne, D. and Lipietz, A. (1991) 'Two social strategies in the production of new industrial spaces' in Benko, G. and Dunford, M. (eds.) *Industrial Change and Regional Development: The Transformation of New Industrial Spaces*, London: Belhaven Press: 27–50.

Le Corbusier (1987) [1929] *The City of Tomorrow and its Planning*, New York: Dover.

Le Galès, P. (1992) 'Rennes – lokal gesteuerte Entwicklung in Frankreich' in Heinelt, H. and Mayer, M. (eds.) *Politik in europäischen Städten: Fallstudien zur Bedeutung lokaler Politik*, Berlin: Birkhäuser Verlag: 137–66.

Lefebvre, H. (1974) 'La production de l'espace' *Homme et la Société*, **31/32**: 15–32.

Lefebvre, H. (1991) [1974] *The Production of Space*, Oxford: Blackwell.

Lefebvre, H. (1996) *Writings on Cities*, Oxford: Blackwell.

Leitner, H. (1990) 'Cities in pursuit of economic growth: the local state as entrepreneur' *Political Geography Quarterly*, **9**: 146–70.

Leitner, H. (1992) 'Urban geography: responding to new challenges' *Progress in Human Geography*, **16**: 105–18.

Leitner, H. (1996) 'European variants of urban entrepreneurialism', unpublished manuscript.

Leitner, H. and Garner, M. (1993) 'The limits of local initiatives: a reassessment of urban entrepreneurialism for urban development' *Urban Geography*, **14**: 57–77.

Leitner, H. and Sheppard, E. (1997) 'Transcending urban individualism: conceptual issues, and policy alternatives in the European Union' in Wilson, D. and Jonas, A. (eds.) *The Growth Machine Twenty Years After*, Albany, NY: State University of New York Press: (forthcoming)

Lewis, J. (1992) *Art, Culture and Enterprise*, London: Routledge.

Lewis, J.R. (1994) 'City Challenge: involving the community in UK urban policy?' in Braun, G.O. (ed.) *Managing and Marketing of Urban Development and Urban Life*, Berlin: Dietrich Reimer Verlag: 367–78.

Ley, D. and Mills, C. (1993) 'Can there be a postmodernism of resistance in the urban landscape?' in Knox, P. (ed.) *The Restless Urban Landscape*, Englewood Cliffs, NJ: Prentice-Hall: 255–78.

Ley, D. and Olds, K. (1988) 'Landscape as spectacle: World's Fairs and the culture of heroic consumption' *Environment and Planning D: Society and Space*, **6**: 191–212.

Leyshon, A. (1992) 'The transformation of regulatory order: regulating the global economy and environment' *Geoforum*, **23**: 249–67.

Lim, C.Y. (1990) 'The Schumpeterian road to affluence and communism', *Malaysian Journal of Economic Studies*, **27**: 213–23.

Lincoln, Y.S. and Denzin, N.K. (1994) 'The fifth moment' in Denzin, N.K. and Lincoln, Y.S. (eds.) *Handbook of Qualitative Research*, Thousand Oaks: Sage: 575–86.

Lingwood, J. (1993) 'Place' in de Ville, N. and Foster, S. (eds.) *Space Invaders: Issues of Presentation, Context and Meaning in Contemporary Art*, Southampton: John Hansard Gallery: 21–7.

Lipietz, A. (1993) 'The local and the global: regional individuality or interregionalism?' *Transactions Institute of British Geographers* NS, **18**: 8–18.

Lipietz, A. (1994a) 'The national and the regional: their autonomy vis-à-vis the capitalist world crisis', in Palan, R.P. and Gills, B. (eds.) *Transcending the State–Global Divide: A Neostructuralist Agenda in International Relations*, Boulder: Lynne Rienner: 23–43.

Lipietz, A. (1994b) 'Post-Fordism and democracy' in Amin, A. (ed.) *Post-Fordism: A Reader*, Oxford: Blackwell: 338–57.

Lipsey, R.G. (1983) *An Introduction to Positive Economics*, London: Weidenfeld and Nicolson.

Lister, D. (1991) 'The transformation of a city: Birmingham' in Fisher, M. and Owens, U. (eds.) *Whose Cities?*, Harmondsworth: Penguin: 53–61.

Lloyd, M.G. and Newlands, D.A. (1988) 'The growth coalition and urban economic development' *Local Economy*, **3**: 31–9.

Lock, D. (1993) 'Birmingham's path to self-confident splendor' *Town and Country Planning*, **62**: 320.

Loftman, P. (1990) *A Tale of Two Cities: Birmingham the Convention and Unequal City. The International Convention centre and Disadvantaged Groups*, Faculty of the Built Environment Research Paper No. 6. Birmingham: University of Central England in Birmingham.

Loftman, P., Middleton, A.and Nevin, B. (1993) 'Council agenda hidden under growth coalition?' *Planning*, **1030**: 6–7.

Loftman, P. and Nevin, B. (1992) *Urban Regeneration and Social Equity: A Case Study of Birmingham 1986–1992*. Faculty of the Built Environment Research Paper No. 8. Birmingham: University of Central England in Birmingham.

Loftman, P. and Nevin, B. (1994) 'Prestige project development: economic renaissance or economic myth? A case study of Birmingham' *Local Economy*, **8**: 307–25.

Loftman, P. and Nevin, B. (1995) 'Prestige projects and urban regeneration in the 1980s and 1990s: a review of benefits and limitations' *Planning Practice and Research*, **3**: 299–317.

Loftman, P. and Nevin, B. (1996) 'Going for growth: prestige projects in three British cities' *Urban Studies*, **33**: 991–1019.

Loftman, P. and Nevin, B. (1997) 'Evaluation for whom?: The politics of evaluation research' *Regional Studies*, forthcoming.

Logan, J.R. and Molotch, H.L. (1987) *Urban Fortunes: The Political Economy of Place*, Berkeley: University of California Press.

Lovatt, A. (ed.) (1994) *Towards the 24 Hour City*, Manchester: MIPC Publication.

Lovatt, A. and O'Connor, J. (1995) 'Cities and the night time economy' *Planning Practice and Research*, **10**: 127–33.

Lovatt, A., Milestone, K. and O'Connor, J. (1994) 'Culture and the northern quarter' *MIPC Working Papers*, Series II.

Lovering, J. (1995) 'Creating discourses rather than jobs' in Healey, P., Cameron, S., Davoudi, S., Graham, S. and Madani-Pour, A. (eds.) *Managing Cities: The New Urban Context*, Chichester: John Wiley: 109–26.

Low, M. (1997) 'Representation unbound: globalization and democracy' in Cox, K. (ed.) *Spaces of Globalization: Reasserting the Power of the Local*, New York: Guilford: 240–80.

Lowe, M. (1993) 'Local hero! An examination of the role of the regional entrepreneur in the regeneration of Britain's regions' in Kearns, G. and Philo, C. (eds.) *Selling Places: The City as Cultural Capital, Past and Present*, Oxford: Pergamon Press: 211–30.

Lyall, K. (1982) 'A bicycle built-for-two: public–private partnership in Baltimore' in Fosler, R.S. and Berger, R.A. (eds.), *Public–Private Partnership in American Cities*, Lexington, Mass.: Heath: 17–58.

McAvera, B. (n.d.) *Art, Politics and Ireland*, Dublin: Open Air.

McConville, D.J. (1993) 'Making it in Memphis' *Distribution*, November: 50–8.

McGuigan, J. (1996) *Culture and the Public Sphere*, London: Routledge.

McGuirk, P.M. (1994) 'Economic restructuring and the realignment of the urban planning system: the case of Dublin' *Urban Studies*, **31**: 287–309.

McGuirk, P.M. (1997) 'Multiscaled interpretation of urban change: the federal, the state and the local in the Western Area Strategy of Adelaide' *Environment and Planning D: Society and Space*, **15**: (in press).

McKay, G. (1996) *Senseless Acts of Beauty*, London: Verso.

McKelvey, B. (1963) *The Urbanization of America*, New Brunswick, NJ: Rutgers University Press.

McKinsey and Company (1994) 'Business investment and regional prosperity: the challenge of rejuvenation', discussion paper.

Maillot, D. (1990) 'Transborder regions between members of the European Community and non-member countries', *Built Environment*, **16**: 25–37.

Malpass, P. (1994) 'Policy making and local governance: how Bristol failed to secure City Challenge funding (twice)', *Policy and Politics*, **22**: 301–17.

Maretzke, S. (1995a) 'Beschäftigung und Arbeitslosigkeit' *Materialien zur Raumentwicklung*, **69**: 41–66.

Maretzke, S. (1995b) 'Wandel ostdeutscher Industriestrukturen' *Materialien zur Raumentwicklung*, **69**: 66–80.

Markusen, A. (1987) *Regions: The Economics and Politics of Territory*, Totowa, NJ.: Rowman and Littlefield.

Markusen, A. and Gwiasda, V. (1994) 'Multipolarity and the layering of functions in world cities: New York's struggle to stay on top' *International Journal of Urban and Regional Research*, **18**: 128–44.

Markusen, A., Hall, P., Campbell, S. and Dietrick. S. (1991) *The Rise of the Gun Belt: The Military Remapping of Industrial America*, New York: Oxford University Press.

Martin, S. (1995) 'From workshop to meeting place? The Birmingham economy in transition', in Turner, R. (ed.) *The British Economy in Transition: From the Old to the New*, London: Routledge.

Martin, S. and Pearce, G. (1992) 'The internationalization of local authority economic development strategies: Birmingham in the 1980s' *Regional Studies*, **26**: 499–509.

Maspero, F. (1994) *Roissy Express: A Journey through the Paris Suburbs*, London: Verso.

Massey, D. (1978) 'Regionalism: some current issues' *Capital and Class*, **6**: 106–25.

Massey, D. (1984) *Spatial Divisions of Labour: Social Structures and the Geography of Production*, London: Macmillan.

Massey, D. (1991) 'Flexible sexism' *Environment and Planning D: Society and Space*, **9**: 31–57.

Massey, D. (1994) *Space, Place and Gender*, Cambridge: Polity Press.

Massey, D. (1995) *Spatial Divisions of Labour: Social Structures and the Geography of Production* (second edition), London: Macmillan.

Mayer, M. (1991) 'Politics in the post-Fordist city' *Socialist Review*, **21**: 105–24.

Mayer, M. (1992) 'The shifting local political system in European cities' in Dunford, M. and Kafkalas, G. (eds.) *Cities and Regions in the New Europe*, London: Belhaven: 255–274.

Mayer, M. (1994a) 'Public–private Partnership – eine neue Option und Chance für kommunale Wirtschaftspolitik?' in Roth, R. and Wollmann, H. (eds.) *Kommunalpolitik: Politisches Handeln in den Gemeinden*, Opladen: Leske and Budrich: 440–50.

Mayer, M. (1994b) 'Post-Fordist city politics' in Amin, A. (ed.) *Post-Fordism: A Reader*, Oxford: Blackwell: 316–37.

Mayer, M. (1995) 'Urban governance in post-Fordist cities' in Healey, P., Cameron, S., Davoudi, S., Graham, S. and Madani-Pour, A. (eds.) *Managing Cities: The New Urban Context*, Chichester: John Wiley: 231–49.

Meegan, R. (1993) 'Urban Development Corporations, urban entrepreneurialism and locality' in Imrie, R. and Thomas, H. (eds.) *British Urban Policy and the Urban Development Corporations*, London: PCP Press: 58–73.

Mendoza, E. (1988) *City of Marvels*, London: Collins Harvill (published in Spain as *La Ciudad de los Prodigios*, 1986. Barcelona: Seix Barral).

Merrifield, A. and Swyngedouw, E. (1996) 'Social justice and the urban experience' in Merrifield, A. and Swyngedouw, E. (eds.) *The Urbanisation of Injustice*, London: Lawrence and Wishart: 1–17.

Messent, M. (1993) 'The sensible socialist' *Birmingham Evening Mail*, 12/5/93: 14.

Messner, D. (1996) *Die Netzwerkgesellschaft: Wirtschaftliche Entwicklung und internationale Wettbewerbsfähigkeit als Probleme gesellschaftlicher Steuerung*, Cologne: Weltforum Verlag.

Metcalfe, A.W. and Bern, J. (1994) 'Stories of crisis: restructuring Australian industry and rewriting the past' *International Jounal of Urban and Regional Research*, **18**: 658–73.

Miles, M. (1997) *Art, Space and the City*, London: Routledge.

Milestone, K. (1996) 'Regional variations: northernness and the new urban economies of hedonism' in O'Connor, J. and Wynne, D. (eds.) *From the Margin to the Centre: Cultural Production and Consumption in the Post-Industrial City*, Ashgate: Arena: 91–116.

Miller, G. (1981) *Cities by Contract: The Politics of Municipal Incorporation*, Cambridge, Mass.: MIT Press.

Mole, P. (1996) 'Fordism, post-Fordism and the contemporary city' in O'Connor, J. and Wynne, D. (eds.) *From the Margin to the Centre: Cultural Production and Consumption in the Post-Industrial City*, Ashgate: Arena: 15–48.

Mollenkopf, J.H. (1983) *The Contested City*, Princeton, NJ: Princeton University Press.

Mollenkopf, J.H. and Castells, M. (1991) *Dual City: Restructuring New York*, New York, NY: Sage.

Molotch, H. (1976) 'The city as a growth machine: toward a political economy of place' *American Journal of Sociology*, **82**: 309–32.

Molotch, H. (1988) 'Strategies and constraints of growth elites' in Cummings, S. (ed.) *Business Elites and Urban Development*, Albany: State University of New York Press: 25–48.

Molotch, H. and Logan, J. (1987) *Urban Fortunes*, Berkeley, Calif.: UCLA Press.

Mommaas, H. and Corjan, E. (1995) *Cultural Policy in Europe*, Report to Cultural Committee, Eurocities.

Morris, M. (1988) 'Things to do with shopping centres', in Sheridan, S. (ed.) *Grafts: Feminist Cultural Criticism*, London: Verso: 193–225.

Morris, R.J. (1989) 'The reproduction of capital and labour: British and Canadian cities during industrialization' *Urban History Review*, **18**: 48–63.

Muligan, G. (1995) *Freedom's Children*, London: Demos.

Müller, S. (1992) 'Lyon: Moderation der Modernisierung mit der Idee des Metropolitanen' in Heinelt, H. and Mayer, M. (eds.) *Politik in europäischen Städten: Fallstudien zur Bedeutung lokaler Politik*, Berlin: Birkhäuser Verlag: 167–86.

Murray, C. (1990) 'The art of development', *Architects Journal*, 24/10/90: 26–8.

Naylor, R.T. (1975) *The History of Canadian Business 1867–1914* II: *Industrial Development*, Toronto: James Lorimer.

NCC (Newcastle City Council) (1988) *CBD Business Plan*, Newcastle: Newcastle City Council.

NCC (1992) *Central Area Strategy*, Newcastle: Newcastle City Council.

Neill, W.J.V., Fitzsimons, D.S. and Murtagh, B. (1995) *Reimaging the Pariah City: Urban Development in Belfast and Detroit*, Aldershot: Avebury.

Neilson, L. and Spiller, M. (1992) 'Managing the cities for national economic development: the role of the Building Better Cities Programme', paper presented to the Biennial Congress of the Royal Australian Planning Institute, Canberra, 26–30 April 1992.

Newcastle Herald (1992a) 'City plan stuck in mire of politics', 3/4/92: 8.

Newcastle Herald (1992b) 'City plan: 19,000 jobs', 24/7/92: 1.

Newcastle Herald (1992c) 'Honeysuckle back on track as Council toes State line', 25/7/92: 4.

Newcastle Herald (1992d) 'Newcastle awaits State reply on Civic', 28/7/92: 3.

Newcastle Herald (1992e) 'Fahey offers Newcastle $30m icebreaker', 5/8/92: 1.

Newcastle Herald (1994a) 'Marine housing envisaged for Throsby Creek', 7/5/94: 1.

Newcastle Herald (1994b) 'Delayed rail cut study had image problem', 19/8/94: 1.

Newcastle Herald (1994c) 'Poll shows support to maintain rail line', 21/9/94: 1.

Newcastle Herald (1995) 'Designs on Civic scales down by big risks', 31/3/95: 3.

Newcastle Times (1994) Advertisement, 19/8/94: 12.

Nochlin, L. (1967) 'The invention of the avant garde' in Hess, T. and Ashbery, J. (eds.) *Avant Garde Art*, London: Collier-Macmillan: 3–24.

Nolte, D. and Ziegler, A. (1994) 'Neue Wege einer regional- und sektoralorientierten Strukturpolitik in den neuen Ländern zur Diskussion um den Erhalt industrieller Kerne' *Informationen zur Raumentwicklung*, **4**: 255–67.

Noyelle, T.J. and Stanback, T.M. (1984) *The Economic Transformation of American Cities*, Totowa, NJ: Rowman and Allanheld.

O'Connor, J. (1991) 'Local government and cultural policy' in Wynne, D. (ed.) *The Culture Industry*, Aldershot: Avebury: 56–69.

O'Connor, J. (1993) 'Manchester and the Millennium: whose city, whose civilisation' *Regenerating Cities*, **1–2**: 17–19.

O'Connor, J. (1995) 'The regeneration buisness: Cities '95' *Cities*, **1–2**: 48–52.

O'Connor, J. and Wynne, D. (1992) 'The uses and abuses of popular culture: cultural policy and popular culture' *Loisir et Société*, **14**: 465–83.

O'Connor, J. and Wynne, D. (1996a) 'From the margins to the centre: cultural production and consumption in the post-industrial city' in Holmwood, J., Radner, H., Schulze, G. and Sulkunen, P. (eds.) *Constructing the New Consumer Society*, Oxford: Macmillan: 152–72.

O'Connor, J. and Wynne, D. (eds.) (1996b) *From the Margin to the Centre: Cultural Production and Consumption in the Post-Industrial City*, Ashgate: Arena.

O'Connor, J. and Wynne, D. (1996c) 'Left loafing' in O'Connor, J. and Wynne, D. (eds.) *From the Margin to the Centre: Cultural Production and Consumption in the Post-Industrial City*, Ashgate: Arena: 49–90.

O'Connor, T.H. (1993) *Building a New Boston: Politics and Urban Renewal 1950–1970*, Boston: Northeastern University Press.

Ohmae, K-I. (1995) *The End of the Nation State: The Rise of Regional Economies*, New York: HarperCollins.

O'Neill, P. (1991) 'The Hunter regional economy: a place for Honeysuckle' in *The Honeysuckle Development*, Proceedings of a symposium held on 9/11/91, Department of Sociology and Anthropology, in association with the Departments of Geography and Social Work and the Division of Leisure Studies, University of Newcastle: 31–8.

Olds, K. (1995) 'Globalization and the production of new urban spaces: Pacific Rim megaprojects in the late twentieth century' *Environment and Planning A*, **27**: 1713–43.

Orr, M. and Stoker, G. (1994) 'Urban regimes and leadership in Detroit' *Urban Affairs Quarterly*, **30**: 48–73.

Orum, A. M. (1995) *City Building in America*, Boulder: Westview Press.

Osterland, M. (1994) 'Coping with democracy: the re-institution of local-self government in Eastern Germany' *European Urban and Regional Studies*, **1**: 5–18.

Paddison, R. (1993) 'City marketing, image reconstruction and urban regeneration' *Urban Studies*, **30**: 339–50.

Page, S. (1995) *Urban Tourism*, London: Routledge.

Painter, J. (1991) 'Regulation theory and local government' *Local Government Studies*, **17**: 23–44.

Painter, J. (1995) *Politics, Geography and Political Geography: A Critical Perspective*, London: Arnold.

Painter, J. (1997a) 'Regulation, regime and practice in urban politics' in Lauria, M. (ed.) *Reconstructing Urban Regime Theory: Regulating Urban Politics in a Global Economy*, Thousand Oaks, Calif.: Sage: 122–43.

Painter, J. (1997b) 'Local politics, anti-essentialism and economic geography' in Lee, R. and Wills, J. (eds.) *Geographies of Economics*, London: Arnold (in press).

Painter, J. and Goodwin, M. (1995) 'Local governance and concrete research:

investigating the uneven development of regulation' *Economy and Society*, **24**: 334–56.

Parisi, P. and Holcomb, B. (1994) 'Symbolising place: journalistic narratives of the city' *Urban Geography*, **15**: 376–94.

Parkinson, M. and Bianchini, F. (1993) 'Liverpool: a tale of missed opportunities' in Bianchini F. and Parkinson, M. (eds.) *Cultural Policy and Urban Regeneration: The West European Experience*, Manchester University Press: 155–77.

Parkinson, M. and Harding, A. (1995) 'European cities toward 2000: entrepreneurialism, competition and social exclusion', in Rhodes, M. (ed.) *The Regions and the New Europe: Patterns in Core and Periphery Development*, Manchester: Manchester University Press: 53–77.

Paul, L. (1995) 'Regional development in central and eastern Europe: the role of inherited structures, external forces and local initiatives' *European Spatial Research and Policy*, **2**(2): 19–41.

Peck, J. (1995) 'Moving and shaking: business elites, state localism and urban privatism' *Progress in Human Geography*, **19**: 16–46.

Peck, J. and Tickell, A. (1994) 'Jungle law breaks out: neoliberalism and global-local disorder' *Area*, **26**: 317–26.

Peck, J. and Tickell, A. (1995a) 'Business goes local: dissecting the "business agenda" in Manchester' *International Journal of Urban and Regional Research*, **19**: 79–95.

Peck, J. and Tickell, A. (1995b) 'The social regulation of uneven development: regulatory deficit, England's South east and the collapse of Thatcherism' *Environment and Planning A*, **27**: 15–40.

Pecorella, R.F. (1987) 'Fiscal crisis and regime change: a contextual approach' in Stone, C.N. and Saunders, H.T. (eds) *The Politics of Urban Development*, Lawrence, Kan.: University of Kansas Press: 52–72.

Perrons, D. (1992) 'The regions and the single market' in Dunford, M. and Kafkalas, G. (eds.) *Cities and Regions in the New Europe: The Global–Local Interplay and Spatial Development Practices*, London: Belhaven: 170–94.

Peters, T. (1987) *Thriving on Chaos: Handbook for Management Revolution*, New York, NY: Alfred A. Knopf.

Peterson, P.E. (1981) *City Limits*, Chicago: University of Chicago Press.

Petzold, S. (1994) 'Zur Entwicklung und Funktion der kommunalen Selbstverwaltung in den neuen Bundesländern' in Roth, R. and Wollmann, H. (eds.) *Kommunalpolitik: Politisches Handeln in den Gemeinden*, Opladen: Leske and Budrich: 34–51.

Phillips, P. (1995) 'Maintenance activity' in Felshin, N. (ed.) *But is it Art?*, Seattle, Wash.: Bay Press: 165–93.

Philo, C. and Kearns, G. (1993) 'Culture, history, capital: a critical introduction to the selling of places' in Kearns, G. and Philo, C. (eds.) *Selling Places: The City as Cultural Capital, Past and Present*, Oxford: Pergamon: 1–32.

Pickvance, C. and Preteceille, E. (1991) *State Restructuring and Local Power: A Comparative Perspective*, London: Pinter.

Pinch, P. (1995) 'Governing urban finance: changing budgetary strategies in British local government' *Environment and Planning A*, **27**: 965–83.

Pinch, S. (1985) *Cities and Services: The Geography of Collective Consumption*, London: Routledge and Kegan Paul.

Piven, F.F. and Friedland, R. (1984) 'Public choice and private power: a theory of the urban fiscal crisis' in Kirby, A., Knox, P. and Pinch, S. (eds.) *Public Service Provision and Urban Development*, New York: Croom Helm/St Martins: 390–420.

Planning (1991) 'Birmingham takes broader view in regeneration drive' *Planning*, **948**: 11.

Pooley, S. (1991) 'The state rules OK? The continuing political economy of nation-states' *Capital and Class*, **43**: 65–82.

Porter, M.E. (1990) *The Competitive Advantage of Nations*, Basingstoke: Macmillan.

Porter, M.E. (1995) 'The competitive advantage of the inner city', *Harvard Business Review*, May–June: 55–71.

Pred, A. (1995) *Recognizing European Modernities: A Montage of the Present*, London: Routledge.

Preston, P. and Simpson-Housley, P. (eds.) (1994) *Writing the City: Eden, Babylon, and the New Jerusalem*, London: Routledge.

Preteceille, E. (1990) 'Political paradoxes of urban restructuring: globalization of the economy and localization of politics?', in Logan, J.R. and Swanstrom, T. (eds.) *Beyond the City Limits*, Philadelphia: Temple University Press: 27–59.

Prigg, W. and Lieser, P. (1992) 'Keine Metro, aber Polarisierung. Lokale Politik zwischen Stadt und Land' in Heinelt, H. and Mayer, M. (eds.) *Politik in europäischen Städten: Fallstudien zur Bedeutung lokaler Politik*, Berlin: Birkhäuser Verlag: 49–70.

Probert, B. (1994) 'Globalisation, economic restructuring and the state' in Bell, S. and Head, B. (eds.) *State Economy and Public Policy in Australia*, Melbourne: Oxford University Press: 98–117.

Property Services Group (n.d.) *Honeysuckle Concept Masterplan*, Sydney: PSG.

Przeworski, J.F. (1986) 'Changing intergovernmental relations and urban economic development', *Environment and Planning C: Government and Policy*, **4**: 423–38.

Public Art Commissions Team (1990) *The Strategy for Public Art in Cardiff Bay*, Cardiff: Cardiff Bay Development Corporation.

Purvis, S. (1996) 'The interchangeable roles of the producer, consumer and cultural intermediary: the new pop fashion designers' in O'Connor, J. and Wynne, D. (eds.) *From the Margin to the Centre: Cultural Production and Consumption in the Post-Industrial City*, Ashgate: Arena: 117–40.

Pusey, M. (1991) *Economic Rationalism in Canberra: A Nation-Building State Changes its Mind*, Melbourne: Cambridge University Press.

Quiett, G.C. (1934) *They Built the West: An Epic of Rails and Cities*, New York: Appleton-Century.

Quilley, S. (1996) 'Manchester's gay village', unpublished paper.

Ramsay, M. (1996) *Community, Culture and Economic Development: The Social Roots of Local Action* Albany, New York: State University of New York Press.

Randall, S. (1995) 'City Pride – from "municipal socialism" to "municipal capitalism"', *Critical Social Policy*, **43**: 40–59.

Rea, K.J. (1985) *The Prosperous Years: The Economic History of Ontario 1939–1975*, Toronto: University Press.

Reed, C. (1987) 'Developers fight back against US voter power' *Age*, 10/06/87: 19.

Reps, J. (1965) *The Making of Urban America*, Princeton, NJ: Princeton University Press.

Rhodes, R. (1994) 'Reinventing excellence: or how the best seller thwarts the search for lessons to transform the public sector' *Public Administration*, **72**: 281–9.

Richardson, L. (1994) 'Writing: a method of inquiry' in Denzin, N.K. and Lincoln, Y.S. (eds.) *Handbook of Qualitative Research*, Thousand Oaks: Sage: 516–29.

Ridinger, R. (1994) 'Einsatz regionalpolitischer Instrumente in den neuen Ländern' *Informationen zur Raumentwicklung*, no. 4: 267–73.

Roberts, M., Marsh, C. and Salter, M. (1993) *Public Art in Private Places*, London: University of Westminster.

Roberts, S. and Schein, R. (1993) 'The entrepreneurial city: fabricating urban development in Syracuse, New York' *The Professional Geographer*, **45**: 21–33.

Robins, K. (1991) 'Tradition and translation: national culture in its global context' in

Corner, J. and Harvey, S. (eds.) *Enterprise and Heritage: Cross-Currents in National Culture*, London: Routledge: 21–44.

Robinson, F. and Shaw, K. (1991) 'Urban regeneration and community involvement' *Local Economy*, **6**: 61–71.

Robson, B. (1989) 'Social and economic futures for larger cities' in Herbert, D.T. and Smith, D.M. (eds.) *Social Problems and the City*, Oxford: Oxford University Press: 17–31.

Rofe, M. (1996) 'Gentrification as an indicator of social change within Newcastle', unpublished Honours thesis submitted to the Department of Geography, University of Newcastle, Callaghan, NSW.

Rogers, R. (1995a) 'Learning to live with the city' *The Independent*, 13/2/95: 17.

Rogers, R. (1995b) 'Looking forward to compact city' *The Independent*, 20/2/95: 18.

Rogers, R. (1995c) 'The imperfect form of the new' *The Independent*, 27/2/95: 18.

Rogers, R. (1995d) 'Let London live again for all our sakes' *The Independent*, 6/3/95: 18.

Rogers, R. (1995e) 'Building cities to move the spirit' *The Independent*, 13/3/95: 18.

Rogers, R. and Fisher, M. (1992) *A New London*, Penguin, Harmondsworth.

Rosa, P. (1992) 'Entrepreneurial training in the UK: past confusion and future promise?', Sterling: University of Sterling – Scottish Enterprise Foundation.

Rose, G. (1992) 'Local resistance to the LDDC: community attitudes and action' in Ogden, P. (ed.) *London Docklands: The Challenge of Development*, London: Cambridge University Press: 32–42.

Ross, P. (1991) 'Honeysuckle and the established CBD' in *The Honeysuckle Development*, Proceedings of a symposium held on 9/11/91, Department of Sociology and Anthropology, in association with the Departments of Geography and Social Work and the Division of Leisure Studies, University of Newcastle: 39–46.

Rothblatt, D.N. and Sancton, A. (1993) *Metropolitan Governance: Intergovernmental Perspectives*, Berkeley: Regents.

Rubin, I.S. and Rubin, H.J. (1987) 'Economic development incentives – the poor (cities) pay more' *Urban Affairs Quarterly*, **23**: 37–62.

Rubinstein, W.D. (1983) 'Entrepreneurial effort and entrepreneurial success: peak wealth-holding in three societies, 1850–1939', *Business History*, **25**: 11–29.

Runte, A. (1991) 'Promoting the Golden West: advertising and the railroad' *California History*, **70**: 62–75.

Runte, A. (1992) 'Promoting Wonderland: Western Railroads and the evolution of National Park advertising' *Journal of the West*, **31**: 43–8.

Runte, A. (1994) *Trains of Discovery: Western Railroads and the National Parks*, collector's edition, Niwot, Colo.: Roberts Rinehart.

Russell, J.M. (1988) *Atlanta 1847–1890*, Baton Rouge: Louisiana State University Press.

Rutheiser, C. (1996) *Imagineering Atlanta: The Politics of Place in the City of Dreams*, London: Verso.

Ryan, K.B. (1990) 'The official image of Australia' in Zonn, L. (ed.) *Place Images in Media: Portrayal, Experience and Meaning*, Savage, Md: Rowman and Littlefield: 135–58.

Sadler, D. (1992) *The Global Region: Production, State Policies and Uneven Development*, Oxford: Pergamon Press.

Sadler, D. (1993) 'Place-marketing, competitive places and the construction of hegemony in Britain in the 1980s' in Kearns, G. and Philo, C. (eds.) *Selling Places: The City as Cultural Capital, Past and Present*, Oxford: Pergamon Press: 175–92.

Saldern, A. von (1994) 'Geschichte der kommunalen Selbstverwaltung in Deutschland' in Roth, R. and Wollmann, H. (eds.) *Kommunalpolitik. Politisches Handeln in den Gemeinden*, Opladen: Leske and Budrich: 2–19.

Salomon, A. (1995) 'Memphis distributes word on its benefits' *Advertising Age*, 2/10/95: 14.

Sassen. S. (1991) *The Global City: New York, London, Tokyo*, Princeton: Princeton University Press.

Sassen, S. (1994) *Cities in a World Economy*, Thousand Oaks, Calif.: Pine Forge Press.

Saunders, P. (1981) 'Community power, urban managerialism and the local state' in Harloe, M. (ed.) *New Perspectives in Urban Change and Conflict*, Heinemann: London: 27–49.

Saunders, P. (1986) *Social Theory and the Urban Question*, London: Hutchinson.

Saunders, H.T. and Stone, C.N. (1987) 'Development politics reconsidered' *Urban Affairs Quarterly*, **22**: 521–39.

Savage, M. and Warde, A. (1993) *Urban Sociology, Capitalism and Modernity*, Basingstoke: Macmillan.

Savitch, H.V. and Kantor, P. (1995) 'City business: an international perspective on marketplace politics' *International Journal of Urban and Regional Studies*, **19**: 495–512.

Sayer, A. (1992) *Method in Social Science: A Realist Approach*, London: Routledge.

Sayer, A. and Walker, R. (1992) *The New Social Economy: Reworking the Division of Labour*, Oxford: Blackwell.

Schäfer, D. (1982) *Zentralisation und Dezentralisation: Eine verwaltungswissenschaftliche Studie zur Kompetenzverteilung im Politisch-Administrativen System der Bundesrepublik Deutschland, empirisch illustriert am Beispiel der Funktionalreform in Nordrhein-Westfalen*, Berlin: Duncker and Humblot.

Schneider, M. (1985) 'Suburban fiscal disparities and the location decisions of firms' *American Journal of Political Science*, **29**: 587–605.

Schneider, M. and Teske, P. (1993) 'The progrowth entrepreneur in local government' *Urban Affairs Quarterly*, **29**: 316–27.

Schoenberger, E. (1988) 'From Fordism to flexible accumulation: technology, competitive strategies and international location' *Environment and Planning D: Society and Space*, **6**: 245–62.

Schumpeter, J.A. (1934) *Theory of Economic Development: An Inquiry into Profits, Capital, Credit, Interest and the Business Cycle*, Cambridge: Harvard University Press.

Schumpeter, J.A. (1943) *Capitalism, Socialism and Democracy*, London: Unwin.

Scott, A. (1988) *New Industrial Spaces*, London: Pion.

Scott, A. and Storper, M. (1990) 'Regional development reconsidered' Lewis Centre for Regional Policy Studies UCLA, Working paper no. 1.

Scott, A.J. and Storper, M. (1992) 'Industrialization and regional development' in Storper, M. and Scott, A.J. (eds.) *Pathways to Industrialization and Regional Development*, London: Routledge: 3–20.

Selwood, S. (1995) *The Benefits of Public Art: The Polemics of Permanent Art in Public Places*, London: Policy Studies Institute.

Senbenberger, W. (1993) 'Local development and international economic competition' *International Labour Review*, **132**: 313–29.

Sennett, R. (1990) *The Conscience of the Eye*, New York: Norton.

Sennett, R. (1994) *Flesh and Stone*, London: Faber.

Sennett, R. (1996) [1970] *The Uses of Disorder*, London: Faber.

Seyd, P. (1990) 'Radical Sheffield – from socialism to entrepreneurialism' *Political Studies*, **38**: 325–44.

Shaylor, G. (1990) 'Planning in the West Midlands' *The Planner*, **76**(49): 41–3.

Sheppard, E. and Barnes, T.J. (1990) *The Capitalist Space Economy: Geographical Analysis after Ricardo, Marx and Sraffa*, London: Unwin and Hyman.

Shearman, B. (1995) 'Communities, networks, creativity and culture: insights into localisation within globalisation' in Farrand, C., Falaley, T. and Toze, R. (eds.) *Technology, Wealth and Power in the New Global Political Economy*, London: Routledge: 35–56.

Shields, R. (1991) *Places on the Margin: Alternative Geographies of Modernity*, London: Routledge.

Shields, R. (1996) 'A guide to urban representation and what to do about it: alternative traditions of urban theory' in A.D. King (ed.) *Re-Presenting the City: Ethnicity, Capital and Culture in the 21st-Century Metropolis*, Basingstoke: Macmillan: 227–52.

Short, J. (1989) *The Humane City: Cities as if People Matter*, Oxford: Blackwell.

Short, J.R. (1996) *The Urban Order*, Oxford: Blackwell.

Short, J.R. (1998) 'Urban imagineers: boosterism and the representation of cities' in Jonas, A. and Wilson, D. (eds.) *The Urban Growth Machine*, Albany: SUNY Press.

Short, J.R., Benton, L.M., Luce, W.B. and Walton, J. (1993) 'Reconstructing the image of an industrial city' *Annals of the Association of American Geographers*, **83**: 207–24.

Sibley, D. (1995) *Geographies of Exclusion: Society and Difference in the West*, London: Routledge.

Simms, M. (1989) *The Highbury Initiative Birmingham City Centre Challenge 1989. The New Birmingham – Remaking a City*, Birmingham: Action for Cities/City of Birmingham/Birmingham Polytechnic.

Sinclair, M. and Page, S. (1993) 'The Euroregion: a new framework for tourism and regional development', *Regional Studies*, **27**: 475–83.

Smith, A. (1995) 'Regulation theory, strategies of enterprise integration and the political economy of regional economic restructuring in central and eastern Europe: the case of Slovakia' *Regional Studies*, **29**: 761–72.

Smith, D.M. (1994) *Geography and Social Justice*, Oxford: Blackwell.

Smith, N. (1979) 'Toward a theory of gentrification: a back to the city movement by capital not people' *Journal of the American Planning Association*, **45**: 538–48.

Smith, N. (1982) 'Gentrification and uneven development' *Economic Geography*, **58**: 139–155.

Smith, N. (1996) *The New Urban Frontier: Gentrification and the Revanchist City*, London: Routledge.

Smith, P. (1993) 'Labour's civilised revolution' *Birmingham Post*, 12/5/93: 13.

Smith, S.J. (1990) 'Society, space and citizenship: human geography for the new times?' *Transactions, Institute of British Geographers* (N.S.), **14**: 144–56.

Smith, S.J. (1994) 'Urban geography in a changing world' in Gregory, D., Martin, R. and Smith, G. (eds.) *Human Geography: Society, Space and Social Science*, London: Macmillan: 232–51.

Smyth, H. (1994) *Marketing the City: Flagship Developments in Urban Regeneration*, London: E and FN Spon.

Soja, E. (1980) 'The sociospatial dialectic' *Annals of the Association of American Geographers*, **70**: 207–25.

Soja, E. (1989) *Postmodern Geographies: The Reassertion of Space in Critical Social Theory*, London: Verso.

Soja, E. (1996) *Thirdspace: Journeys to Los Angeles and other Real-and-Imagined Places*, Oxford: Blackwell.

Soja, E. (1997) 'Six discourses on the postmetropolis' in Westwood, S. and Williams, J. (eds.) *Imagining Cities: Scripts, Signs and Memories*, London: Routledge: 19–30.

Solomos, J. and Back, L. (1995) *Race, Politics and Social Change*, London: Routledge.

Sparkes, S. (1992) 'Patten clashes on Brum schools' *Birmingham Evening Mail*, 28/10/92: 5.

Spencer, K., Taylor, A., Smith, B., Mawson, J., Flynn, N. and Batley, R. (1986) *Crisis in the Industrial Heartland: A Study of the West Midlands*, Oxford: Clarendon Press.

Squires, G. (1991) 'Partnership in the pursuit of the private city' in Gottdiener, M. and Pickvance, C. (eds.) *Urban Life in Transition,* London: Sage: 196–221.

Stadt Chemnitz (c. 1993) 'Portrait einer aktiven Wirtschaftsregion – Portrayal of an active economic region', Chemnitz: unpublished.

Stadt Dresden (1992) 'Dresden's Wirtschaft in Zahlen', 1st quarter 1992. Dresden: unpublished.

Stadt Dresden (1994) 'Wirtschaft und kommunale Wirtschaftsförderung', Dresden: unpublished.

Stadt Dresden (c. 1993) 'Konzeption zur Förderung des Wissenschaft- Forschungs- und Technologiestandortes Dresden', Dresden: unpublished.

Stadt Leipzig (1992) 'Wirtschaftsstandort Leipzig – Leipzig means business', Leipzig: unpublished.

Standing Committee on State Development (1994) *Achieving Sustainable Growth: Regional Business Development in NSW,* 2 vols, Parliament of NSW, Legislative Council.

State of California, Senate Committee on Local Government (1991) *Redevelopment Agencies' Housing Programs,* Sacramento, Calif.: State of California.

Steinle, W.J. (1992) 'Regional competitiveness and the Single Market', *Regional Studies,* **26**: 307–18.

Stenton, F. (1947) *Anglo-Saxon England,* second edition, Oxford: Clarendon.

Stephenson, D. (1993) 'Honeysuckle, Newcastle: reimagining the city in the post-Fordist era', unpublished PhD Thesis, Department of Sociology and Anthropology, University of Newcastle, NSW.

Stewart, J. and Stoker, G. (eds.) (1989) *Local Government in Europe: Trends and Developments,* London: Macmillan.

Stewart, T. (1994) *Leader's Press Statement on the City Council Budget 1994/95,* Birmingham: Birmingham City Council.

Stilwell, F. (1993) 'State and capital in urban and regional development' in Head, B. (ed.) *State Economy in Australia,* Melbourne: Oxford University Press: 199–218.

Stöhr, W. (1989) 'Regional policy at the cross-roads: an overview', in Albrechts, L., Moulaert, F., Roberts, P. and Swyngedouw, E. (eds.) *Regional Policy at the Cross-Roads: European Perspectives,* London: Jessica Kingsley: 191–7.

Stöhr, W. (ed.) (1990) *Global Challenge and Local Response: Initiatives for Economic Regeneration in Contemporary Europe,* New York: Mansell for The United Nations University.

Stoker, G. (1990) 'Regulation theory, local government and the transition from Fordism' in King, D.S. and Pierre, J. (eds.) *Challenges to Local Government,* Newbury Park, Calif.: Sage: 242–64.

Stoker, G. (1995) 'Regime theory and urban politics' in Judge, D., Stoker, G. and Wolman, H. (eds.) *Theories of Urban Politics,* London: Sage: 54–71.

Stoker, G. and Mossberger, K. (1994) 'Urban regime theory in comparative perspective' *Government and Policy,* **12**: 195–212.

Stone, C.N. (1987) 'Summing up: urban regimes, development policy, and political arrangements' in Stone, C.N. and Saunders, H.T. (eds.) *The Politics of Urban Development,* Lawrence, Kan.: University of Kansas Press: 269–90.

Stone, C.N. (1989) *Regime Politics: Governing Atlanta 1946–1988,* Lawrence, Kan.: University of Kansas Press.

Stone, C.N. (1993) 'Urban regimes and the capacity to govern: a political economy approach' *Journal of Urban Affairs,* **15**: 1–28.

Stone, C.N. and Saunders, H.T. (1987) *The Politics of Urban Development,* Lawrence, Kan.: University of Kansas Press.

Storper, M. (1992) 'The limits to globalization: technology districts and international trade' *Economic Geography*, **68**: 60–93.

Storper, M. (1995) 'Competitiveness policy options: the technology-regions connection' *Growth and Change*, **26**: 285–308.

Storper, M. (1997) 'The city: centre of economic reflexivity' *Service Industries Journal*, **17**: 1–27.

Storper, M. and Scott, A.J. (1995) 'The wealth of regions: market forces and policy imperatives in local and global context', *Futures*, **27**: 505–26.

Storper, M. and Walker, R. (1989) *The Capitalist Imperative: Territory, Technology, and Industrial Growth*, Oxford: Blackwell.

Strange, S. (1988) *State and Markets*, London: Pinter.

Struthers, J. (1986) *Glasgow's Miles Better: 'They said it' About Glasgow*, Glasgow: Struthers.

Suarez-Villa, L. and Cuadrado-Roura, J.L. (1993) 'Regional economic integration and the evolution of disparities' *Papers in Regional Science*, **72**: 369–87.

Sutcliffe, A. and Smith, R. (1974) *Birmingham 1939–1970*, London: Oxford University Press.

Sutton, J. (1991) 'Community concerns' in *The Honeysuckle Development*, Proceedings of a symposium held on 9/11/91, Department of Sociology and Anthropology, in association with the Departments of Geography and Social Work and the Division of Leisure Studies, University of Newcastle: 73–9.

Swyngedouw, E. (1989) 'The heart of the place: the resurrection of locality in an age of hyperspace' *Geografiska Annaler*, **71**(B): 31–42.

Swyngedouw, E. (1992) 'The Mammon quest: glocalization, interspatial competition and the monetary order' in Dunford, M. and Kafkalas, G. (eds.) *Cities and Regions in the New Europe*, London: Belhaven: 36–67.

Taylor, I., Evans, K. and Fraser, P. (1996) *A Tale of Two Cities: Global Change, Local Feeling and Everyday Life in the North of England*, London: Routledge.

Taylor, P. (1993) *Political Geography: World-Economy, Nation-State and Locality*, London: Longman.

The Economist (1995) 'The brave marketeer of Milwaukee' 17/6/95: 34.

The Planner (1991) 'Award for planning achievement 1991' *The Planner*, **77**(40): v–vi.

Thomas, G., Stirling, T., Brownill, S. and Razzaque, K. (1996) 'Locality, urban governance and contested meanings of place' *Area*, **28**: 186–98.

Thomas, H. (1994) 'The local press and urban renewal: a South Wales case study' *International Journal of Urban and Regional Studies* **18**(2): 315—33.

Thornley, A. (1993) [1991] *Urban Planning under Thatcherism: The Challenge of the Market*, London: Routledge.

Thrift, N. (1989a) 'The geography of international economic disorder' in Johnston, R.J. and Taylor, P.J. (eds.) *A World in Crisis*, London: Blackwell: 12–62.

Thrift, N.J. (1989b) 'New times and spaces? the perils of transition models' *Environment and Planning D: Society and Space*, **7**: 127–30.

Thrift, N.J. (1993) 'An urban impasse?' *Theory, Culture and Society*, **10**: 229–38.

Thrift, N.J. (1996) '"Not a straight line but a curve", or cities are not mirrors of modernity', paper presented to conference on Shaping Places, University of Newcastle upon Tyne, Oct.

Tibbalds, F., Stewart, I., Alcock, C., Chapman, D. and Rangsi, S. (1990) *City Centre Design Strategy*, Birmingham: Tibbalds/Colbourne/Karski/Williams.

Tickell, A. and Peck, J.A. (1992) 'Accumulation, regulation and the geographies of post-Fordism: missing links in regulationist research' *Progress in Human Geography*, **16**: 190–218.

Tiebout, C.M. (1956) 'A pure theory of local expenditures' *Journal of Political Economy*, **64**: 416–24.

Tomkins, R. (1988) 'Council split' *Financial Times* Survey, 1/12/88: 1.

Travis McEwen Group Pty Ltd and Brian Elton and Associates (1993) *Inner Newcastle Housing Strategy*, Sydney: BBC.

Tuchtfeld, E. (1993) 'The transformation of economic systems: the German example' in Ghaussy, A. and Schäfer, W. (eds.) *The Economics of German Unification*, London: Routledge: 18–25.

Turok, I. (1992) 'Property-led urban regeneration – panacea or placebo' *Environment and Planning A*, **24**: 361–81.

US Department of Housing and Urban Development (1982) *The President's National Urban Policy Report*, Washington, DC: US Government Printing Office.

USA Today (1995) 'Monet is Chicago's stroke of fortune' 7/12/95: A3.

Van Maanen, J. (1988) *Tales of the Field: On Writing Ethnography*, Chicago: University of Chicago Press.

Van Maanen, J. (1995) 'Trade secrets: on writing ethnography' in Brown, R.H. (ed.) *Postmodern Representations: Truth, Power and Mimesis in the Human Sciences and Public Culture*, Urbana: University of Illinois Press: 60–79.

Vázquez Montalbán, M. (1992) *Barcelonas*. (Translated by Andy Robinson). London: Verso.

Veltz, P. (1996) *Mondialisation Villes et Territoires: L'Economie Archipel*, Paris: Presses Universitaires de France.

Vicari, S. and Molotch, H. (1990) 'Building Milan: alternative machines of growth' *International Journal of Urban and Regional Research*, **14**: 602–24.

Wallis, B. (ed.) (1991) *If You Lived Here*, Seattle, Wash.: Bay Press.

Walton, J.K. (1983) *The English Seaside Resort: A Social History 1750–1914*, Leicester: Leicester University Press.

Ward, C. (1989) 'Selling places: the rise of an economic development profession', unpublished manuscript.

Ward, K. (1996) 'Rereading urban regime theory: a sympathetic critique' *Geoforum*, **27**: 427–38.

Ward, S.V. (1988) 'Promoting holiday resorts: a review of early history to 1921' *Planning History*, **10**(2): 7–11.

Ward, S.V. (1990) 'Local industrial promotion and development policies 1899–1940' *Local Economy*, **5**: 100–18.

Ward, S.V. (1991) 'Municipal policies and the industrialization of Ontario 1870–1939: the example of Oshawa' *Canadian Studies Research Award End of Grant Report*, CSRA 90/36.

Ward, S.V. (1994) 'Time and place: key themes in place promotion in the USA, Canada and Britain since 1870' in Gold, J.R. and Ward, S.V. (eds.) *Place Promotion: The Use of Publicity and Marketing to Sell Towns and Regions*, Chichester: John Wiley & Sons: 53–74.

Ward, S.V. (1998) *Selling Places: The Marketing and Promotion of Towns and Cities 1850–2000*, London: Spon.

Ward, S.V. and Gold, J.R. (1994) 'Introduction' in Gold, J.R. and Ward, S.V. (eds.) *Place Promotion: The Use of Publicity and Marketing to Sell Towns and Regions*, Chichester: John Wiley & Sons: 1–18.

Warr, P.G. (1994) 'Comparative and competitive advantage', *Asia-Pacific Economic Literature*, **8**: 1–15.

Watson, S. (1991) 'Gilding the smokestacks: the new symbolic representations of deindustrialised regions' *Environment and Planning D: Society and Space*, **9**: 59–70.

Webber, M. (1991) 'The contemporary transition' *Environment and Planning D: Society and Space*, **9**: 165–82.

Webster, P. (1989) 'Birmingham the ill-loved city' *Guardian*, 15/6/89: 20.

Wegener, M. (1995) 'The changing urban hierarchy of Europe' in Brotchie, M., Barry, E., Blakely, E., Hall, P. and Newton, P. (eds.) *Cities in Competition: Productive and Sustainable Cities in the 21st Century*, London: Longman: 139–60.

Weiher, G.R. (1991) *The Fractured Metropolis: Political Fragmentation and Metropolitan Segregation*, Albany, NY: State University of New York Press.

Wernick, A. (1991) *Promotional Culture: Advertising, Ideology and Symbolic Expression*, London: Sage.

Westwood, S. and Williams, J. (eds.) (1997) *Imagining Cities: Scripts, Signs and Memories*, London: Routledge.

Weyergraf-Serra, C. and Buskirk, M. (eds.) (1991) *The Destruction of Tilted Arc*, Cambridge, Mass.: MIT.

Whitelock, D. (1972) *The Beginnings of English Society*, revised edition, Harmondsworth: Penguin.

Whittle, S. (1994) *The Margins of the City: Gay Men's Urban Lives*, Ashgate: Arena.

Whyte, W.F. (1955) *Street Corner Society: the Social Structure of an Italian Slum*, 2nd edition. Chicago: University of Chicago Press.

Whyte, W.H. (1980) *The Social Life of Small Urban Spaces*, Washington, DC: The Conservation Foundation.

Williams, R. (1965) *The Long Revolution*, London: Penguin.

Williams, R. (1980) 'Advertising: magic system' in Williams, R. *Problems in Materialism and Culture*, London: Verso: 170–95.

Willke, H. (1992) *Ironie des Staates: Grundlinien einer Staatstheorie polyzentrischer Gesellschaft*, Frankfurt: Suhrkamp.

Willke, H. (1997) *Supervision des Staates*, Frankfurt: Suhrkamp.

Wilson, D. (1996) 'Metaphors, growth coalition discourses and black poverty neighbourhoods in a US city' *Antipode*, **18**: 72–96.

Wilson, P.A. (1995) 'Embracing locality in local economic development', *Urban Studies*, **32**(4–5): 645–58.

Wilson, W.H. (1989) *The City Beautiful Movement*, Baltimore: Johns Hopkins University Press.

Winchester, H.P.M. (1991) 'Redevelopment, gentrification, displacement' in *The Honeysuckle Development*, Proceedings of a symposium held on 9/11/91, Department of Sociology and Anthropology, in association with the Departments of Geography and Social Work and the Division of Leisure Studies, University of Newcastle.

Winchester, H.P.M. and Costello, L. (1995) 'Living on the street: social organisation and gender relations of Australian street kids' *Environment and Planning D: Society and Space*, **13**: 329–48.

Winter, I. and Brook, T. (1993) 'Urban planning and the entrepreneurial state: the view from Victoria, Australia' *Environment and Planning C*, **11**: 263–78.

Wishart, D. (1987) 'Settling the Great Plains 1850–1930: prospects and problems' in Mitchell, R.D. and Groves, P.A. (eds.) *North America: The Historical Geography of a Changing Continent*, London: Hutchinson: 225–78.

Wishart, R. (1991) 'Fashioning the future: Glasgow' in Fisher, M. and Owen, U. (eds.) *Whose Cities?* Harmondsworth: Penguin: 43–52.

Wollmann, H. (1994) 'Kommunalpolitik und -verwaltung in Ostdeutschland im Umbruch' in Roth, R. and Wollmann, H. (eds.) *Kommunalpolitik. Politisches Handeln in den Gemeinden* Opladen: Leske and Budrich: 20–33.

Wolman, H. and Goldsmith, M. (1992) *Urban Politics and Policy: A Comparative Approach*, Oxford: Blackwell.

Wolman, H.L., Ford, C.C. and Hill, E. (1994) 'Evaluating the success of urban success stories' *Urban Studies*, **13**: 835–50.

Wood, A. (1993) 'Organising for local economic development: local economic development networks and prospecting for industry' *Environment and Planning A*, **25**: 1649–61.

Wood, A. (1996) 'Analysing the politics of local economic development: making sense of cross-national convergence' *Urban Studies*, **33**: 1281–95.

Wood, A. (1997) 'Making sense of urban entrepreneurialism' *Scottish Geographical Magazine* (forthcoming).

Wright, G. and Blakemore, J. (1995) 'Victoria Square, Birmingham' *Urban Design*, **54**: 21–4.

Wright, P. (1993) *A Journey through Ruins: A Keyhole Portrait of British Postwar Life and Culture*, London: Flamingo.

Wulf, S. (1995) 'Bad bounces for the N.F.L.' *Time*, 11/12/95: 64–5.

Wynne, D. (ed.) (1992) *The Culture Industry*, Aldershot: Avebury.

Yeung, H. (1994) 'Critical reviews of geographical perspectives on business organizations and the organization of production: towards a network approach' *Progress in Human Geography*, **18**: 460–90.

Young, I.M. (1990) *Justice and the Politics of Difference*, Princeton, NJ: Princeton University Press.

Zelenko, L. (1992) 'Mid-size cities blitz N.F.L. for new franchise' *American Demographics*, **14**: 9–10.

Zukin, S. (1988) [1982] *Loft Living: Culture and Capital in Urban Change*, London: Radius.

Zukin, S. (1991) *Landscape of Power: From Detroit to Disneyworld*, Berkeley, Calif.: UCLA Press.

Zukin, S. (1995) *The Cultures of Cities*, Oxford: Blackwell.

Zukin, S. (1996) 'Space and symbols in an age of decline', in King, A. (ed.) *Re-Presenting the City: Ethnicity, Culture and Capital in the 21st-Century Metropolis*, Basingstoke: Macmillan: 43–59.

Zullo, R. (1991) 'Honeysuckle, Newcastle: a partnership for the future' in *The Honeysuckle Development*, Proceedings of a symposium held on 9/11/91, Department of Sociology and Anthropology, in association with the Departments of Geography and Social Work and the Division of Leisure Studies, University of Newcastle.

INDEX

accumulation, *see* capital accumulation
adjustment stress/shock, 174
administrative capacity, 181
advertisments, 6–7
Allan Poe, E., 209
alliances, *see* public–private partnership, urban coalition
Althubaity, A., 23, 149–172
Amarillo, 304
Amin, A., 281
architecture, 7, 38, 55, 189, 200, 203, 230, *see also* built form
Arizona, 169
art, 199–202, 203–225, *see also* public art
Artists Agency, 220
Arts Council, 204–205
Ashton-under-Lyne, 38
Athens, 211, 317
Atlanta, 3, 7, 12, 18, 45, 52, 262–263
Atlantic City, 39, 67
Atlantic Fordism, 79, 90, *see also* Fordism
Aue, 181–196
Australia, 11, 14, 60, 104–105, 107–128
Austria, 301

Baltimore, 11, 18, 34, 41, 47, 49, 105, 139, 219, 307
Barrow-in-Furnace, 38
Barcelona, 7, 96, 202, 241–252, 298
Barke, M., 74
Battery Park, 204, 206, 210–211, 221
Belfast, 298
Benjamin, W., 202, 252
Bianchini, F., 315–317
Birmingham, 21–22, 48, 103–104, 129–148, 203, 212, 215–221, 297, 313–314
Birmingham Chamber of Commerce, 134
Birmingham City Council, 129–148, 216, 312
Birmingham City 2000, 140–141, 145
Birmingham Super Prix, 138
Blackburn, D., 204

Blackpool, 39–40, 52
Bloch, E., 204, 210, 221, 223
Boisot, M., 90
boosterism, *see* civic boosterism
Bore, A., 136, 140
Boston, 34, 47–48, 61, 67, 125, 287, 299
Botero, F., 206
Bourdieu, P., 201, 226, 232–233
Brindley Place, 138
Britain, 3, 13, 31–54, 92–96, 104, 260, 271–272
Broadgate, 203–207, 210–211, 219
Bruner, E., 248
Bucharest, 211
built form, 55, 228, 250, *see also* architecture
Bull Ring shopping centre, 132

California, 154–156, 171, *see also* Southern California
Canada, 29, 31–53
Canary Wharf, 210–211
capital, 109–110, 127–128
capital accumulation, 2, 15–16, 79–80, 89, 173, 278, *see also* Fordism, post-Fordism, flexible accumulation
capital mobility, 5–6, 16–17, 51, 56, 81–82, 90–92, 124–125, 151, 257, 278, 290–291
capitalism, 6, 12–18, 79, 207, *see also* capital accumulation, urban political economy
Cardiff, 212, 221
Cardiff Bay, 203, 215–221
Castells, M., 222
Catalonia, 246
Cathedral City, 158–162, 167
Centenary Square, 216–217
Chamberlain, J., 131–132
Charlestown Square, 113
Cheltenham, 6
Chemnitz, 181–196
Chicago, 41–43, 63, 67

Chicago School, 1
City Challenge, 139
city economy, 131–132
city image, 7, 27, 58–61, 72–74, 104, 111, 123–124, 140, 231, 302, *see also* place marketing
civic boosterism, 6–7, 21, 34, 82, 95, 131–132, 145, 148, 175
Cixous, H., 202
class, 9, 58, 126, 200, 226
class alliance, *see* regional class alliance
Cleethorpes, 41
Cleveland, 5, 34, 47, 72, 302
Clinton, W., 152
Coachella, 158–162
Coachella Valley, 150, 156–171
Coachella Valley Association of Governments, 165
coalition, *see* growth coalition
collective consumption, 13, 153, 156, 170
Commonwealth Games, 145
community, 3, 18, 21, 77, 107
comparative advantage, 81–82
competition, *see* inter-urban competition, City Challenge
competitive advantage, 67, 79, 81–82, 110, 261, 305
competitive regionalism, 150
consumption, 14–15, 111, 164, 199, 227, 285, 310–312
Conservative Party, 77, 144, 208
counter-culture, 232, 234, *see also* opposition
Cox, K., 16, 19 79, 87, 150, 257, 276, 278–279
creativity, 315–317
culture, 3, 12, 21–22, 37, 89, 109, 117, 185, 199–202, 225–240
cultural capital, 231
cultural intermediaries, 225–240
cultural power, 228
Czech republic, 295

Davis, M., 202, 243–244, 249
de-industrialisation, 2, 46
Democratic Party, 154
dependency, 1, *see also* welfare
Derby, 95
Derry, 210
Desert Fashion Plaza, 158
Detroit, 5, 11, 18

Deutsche, R., 211, 221
development corporations, 9, 47, 57, 111, 135
Disney, Walt, 7
discourse, 2, 84–85, 107, 110, 122, 68–169, 200, 208, 261, 285, 300, 311–312, *see also* entrepreneurial discourse
division of labour, *see* spatial division of labour
Docklands, 12, 21, 61, 209, 211, *see also* Canary Wharf
D'Oyly Carte Opera, 138
Dresden, 181–196
Dublin, 96
Duncan, J., 251
Dunn, K.M., 23, 107–128

East Asia, 95
East Germany, 173
Economic and Social Research Council, 233
economic development, 2, *see also* local economic development
economic equalisation policy, 184
economic growth, 5, 13
economic policy, 134–135, 173–198
economic sustainability, *see* sustainability
economic uncertainty, 285–309
economies of scale, 152
edge city, 1, 201
education, 145, 148, 162–163, 170, 267, 314
Elkin, S., 277
Elster, J., 306
embeddedness, *see* local embeddedness
England, 131, 134, 204
English Partnerships, 147
enterprise, 77–100
entrepreneurs, 11, 17, 82–84, 87, 149, 256, 259–274, 310
entrepreneurial discourse, 2, 77–100, 256, *see also* narrative
entrepreneurialism, *see* urban entrepreneurialism
ethnicity, 29, 72, 88, 133, 199–200, 250
ethnography, 243, 247
Europe, 77–78, 85, 92–96, 142, 204, 226, 288, 294
European Central Bank, 297
European City of Culture, 7, 199

European Community, 133, 139, 141, 302, *see also* European Union
European Regional Development Fund, 139, 147, 218
European Union, 92–96, 295, 306–307, *see also* European Community
Evans, K., 21
exclusion, 219, 317, *see also* marginalisation
Exeter, 38

Fahey, J., 122
Fairfax, 67–68
fallacy of composition, 306
Featherstone, M., 201, 232
federal state, 114–115, 178
Ferlie, E., 271
Fisher, M., 315
flagship development, *see* prestige development
Flanagan, B., 206
flâneur, 228
flexible accumulation, 89, 174, 225, 256, 283
flexible specialisation, 237
Florence, 317
footloose investment capital, 176, *see also* capital mobility
Fordism, 15, 79, 225, 235–237, 283, 285
foreign direct investment, 95, 176, 289
Fraunhofer Gesellschaft, 186
France, 212
Frankfurt, 297, 299
Frantz, A., 244
Fraser, P., 21
Freeman, C., 288
Fulton, W., 155

Gablik, S., 222
Gans, H., 249
gender, 18, 88, 129, 200, 250, *see also* sexuality
gentrification, 1, 119, 203, 231
Georgia, 262–263
German reunification, 173
Germany, 103–105, 173–196, 301
Giddens, T., 271
Giradet, H., 211, 213
Glasgow, 5, 10, 31–34, 47, 52–53, 199, 242, 298, 302
global cities, *see* world cities
global economy, 238, 256

globalism, 16, 275–284
globalisation, 6, 16–17, 57, 90–92, 107, 116, 126, 151, 257, 275–284, 291–293, 312
glocalisation, 109
Goodwin, M., 19
Gordon, D., 287
Gormley, A., 210, 217
Goss, J., 311–312
Gough, J., 6
governance, *see* urban governance
Gramsci, A., 9
Greater London Council, 229
Gregory, D., 249
Greenwich, 313–314
growth coalition, 5–6, 155, 202, 318, *see also* urban coalition
growth machine, *see* growth coalition

Hacienda, 201
Hackney, 31–34, 47, 206
Hall, T., 1–24, 27–30, 103–106, 219, 283, 309–320
Hamburg, 299
Hanseatic League, 211
Harding, A., 77, 80
Harley, B., 309
Harvey, D., 8, 14, 16–19, 87, 246, 261–262, 265, 271, 276, 278–279, 283
hegemony, 9, 89, 110, 221–223
heritage, 1, 18, 29, 61, 95, 117, 126, 189, 227, 242
Herrschel, T., 23, 173–196
high-tech industry, 5, 60, 63–65, 67, 112
Highbury Initiative, 139
higher education, 317–318
Hoggart, K., 3
Holcomb, B., 28, 59–60, 67
homelessness, 311, *see also* housing
Honeysuckle development, 107–108, 113–128
hooks, b., 202
housing, 94, 114, 118–119, 143, 152, 154, 163, 165, 170, 187, 302
Hoyerswerda, 181–196
Hubbard, P., 1–24, 199–202, 255–258, 283, 309–320
Hyatt Regency, 137, 139–141
hypermobility, 110, *see also* capital mobility

identity, 3, 16, 29, 128, 189–192
imagineering, 7, 199, *see also* place
    marketing, city image
income redistribution, 14, 74, 110, 314,
    318
Indian Wells, 156–162
Indio, 155, 156–158, 167
industrial city, 59, 190, 225
industrial decline, 112–118, 132–133
industrialisation, 44–46, 288
informational economy, 237, 289
inner city, 90, 133, 229, 258
International Convention Centre, 137–142,
    218, 314
International Monetary Fund, 292, 295
institutional embeddedness, 88
institutional thickness, 181, 183, 193
inter-urban competition, 29, 77, 86, 110,
    190, 283, 285–308, 314
Iowa, 35
Ipswich, 215

Jackson, P., 312
Jacksonville, 68
Jacobs, J.M., 247
Jaray, T., 216
Jessop, B., 2, 29, 77–100, 208, 261, 296
Jonas, A., 23, 149–172

Kansas City, 61, 65–66
Karl Marx Stadt, 186
Keating, M., 153
Keynesian welfare state, 108, 184, 257,
    285, *see also* welfare state
Kim, Y.H., 22, 29, 55–76
Knowles, R. 130, 136, 145
Kondratieff, N., 289
Kratke, S., 86

La Quinta, 158–162
labour market, 266
Labour Party, 130, 134, 144, 229, 250, *see
    also* New Labour
Laclau, E., 210
Landry, C., 315–317
landscape, 21, 29–30, 103, 110–111, 200,
    229, 233, 242, *see also* architecture
Lash, S., 288
Le Corbusier, 211
Le Galès, 303
Leeds, 134, 217
Lefebvre, H., 21, 201–202, 223, 311

Leipzig, 181–196
Leitner, H., 20, 23, 258, 285–308
Lipchitz, J, 206
Lipietz, A., 89
Lipton, S., 204
litigation, 161–162
Liverpool, 5, 48, 135
local accountability, 119–123
local authorities, 28, 46, 92, 128, 143, 203,
    318
local dependence, *see* local
    embeddedness
local economic development, 2–8, 13, 60,
    77–78, 90–96, 153
local economic specificity, 187–194
local embeddedness, 5, 57, 88, 201, 239,
    279, 300
local entrepreneurs, *see* entrepreneurs
local government, 51–52, *see also* urban
    governance
local media, *see* media
local state, 15, 17, 88, 173, *see also* state
localism, 17, 107–128, 275–284
locality, 2, 17, 20, 79, 87, 126, 174, 177,
    183, 280
Loftman, P., 23, 129–148, 314
Logan, J., 19, 57–58
Lomax, T., 216
London, 3, 6–7, 12, 19, 21, 31, 38, 42–43,
    52, 61, 137, 203–207, 223, 261, 285,
    297, *see also* Docklands
Long Beach, 169
Los Angeles, 3, 150, 152, 156, 168–169,
    204, 223, 243–244, 255
Low, M., 277, 281–282
Luton, 44

McGuirk, P.M., 23, 107–128
McNeill, D., 23, 202, 241–252, 310
Mair, A., 87, 257, 276, 278–279
managerialism, *see* urban managerialism
Manchester, 10, 21, 134–135, 201, 215,
    229–239, 242, 316
Manchester City Council, 235
Manchester Institute of Popular Culture,
    233
Manpower Services Commission, 266
manufacturing, 132–133
Manzoni, H., 132
mapping, 309–310
Margall, P., 245
marginalisation, 74, 213, 268, 312, 317

Markusen, A., 301
Marseilles, 5
Marxism, 255, *see also* urban political
    economy
Mason, R., 216–217
Maspero, F., 244, 249
Massey, D., 16
Mayer, M., 256
media, 9, 61–74, 122–123, 137, 143, 167,
    200, 298
mega-events, 8, *see also* Olympic Games,
    World Expos
mega-projects, *see* prestige developments
Melucci, A., 316
Memphis, 29, 67–72
Mendoza, E., 245
mental map, 185
Merseyside, 215
metropolitan development, 149–172
micro enterprises, 225
Middlesbrough, 38, 209
Milan, 5
Miles, M., 23, 202, 203–224
Millennium projects, 145, 312–314
Milwaukee, 41, 61, 67–72, 307, 311
Minneapolis-St. Paul, 307
mixed-use development, 1, 18
mode of accumulation, *see* capital
    accumulation
mode of production, 15
mode of regulation, *see* regulation
Modernism, 201, 315, 317
Molotch, H., 19, 57–58
Monkwearmouth, 220
Montalbán, M.V., 245
Montpellier, 5
Montreal, 37
Mopyfish, 240
multiculturalism, 84
multiple rationality, 264
multiplier effects, 117–119, 201
municipal socialism, 77–78

Nairne, S., 205
narrative, 33, 77–100, 296, *see also*
    discourse
Nashville, 60
National Exhibition Centre, 134, 218
National Indoor Arena, 137, 139, 142
neo-liberalism, 6, 77, 96, 109, 117, 120,
    276, 281
Nevin, B., 23, 129–148, 314

New Journalism, 244
New Labour, 77, 80, 96
New Street, 216
new urban politics, 1–24, 107, 150, 255,
    275, 294
New York, 3, 6–7, 31, 34, 47, 67, 203–204,
    206, 219, 226–229, 261, 285
Newcastle, NSW, 103–105, 112–128
Norquist, J., 72
North America, 10, 31–54, 92, 149–172,
    201, 226, 287, *see also* United States,
    Canada
North American Free Trade Agreement,
    295
North Rhine, 180
North West Arts, 235
Norwich, 38

O'Connor, J., 23, 201, 225–240
office development, 12, 142
Ohio, 290
Ohmae, K. 90
Oldenburg, C., 209
Olympia and York, 12, 211
Olympic Games, 7–8, 10, 12, 56, 105,
    137–138, 144, 245–247
Ontario, 44
opposition, 141, 311–312
Orange County, 169, 293
outward orientation, 1, 13
Owen, U., 315

Paddison, Ronan, 58
Painter, J., 23, 256, 259–274, 310
Palm Desert, 158–162
Palm Springs, 155, 156–164, 168
Pareto optimum, 299
Paris, 7, 244, 285, 317
Parkinson, M., 77, 80
partnership, *see* public–private
    partnership
Peck, J., 58, 151, 280–281
Pennsylvania, 290
Pentacon, 185
Pepys, S., 202
Percent for Art, 216
Peter, T., 271
Peterson, P., 57, 277
Philadelphia, 39, 61, 72
Phoenix, 138
Pittsburgh, 287, 298, 302
place, 184, *see also* locality

place marketing, 6, 28–30, 31–54, 55–76, 77–100, 189–192, 298, *see also* city image, media
place promotion, *see* place marketing
planners, 2, 207
planning, 28, 121, 143, 203
polarisation, *see* social polarisation
Policy Study Institute, 203, 206
political science, 3
Porter, M., 90, 305
post-colonial, 209
post-Fordism, 15, 17, 105, 149–150, 174–175, 178, 225, 235–237, 245, 281
post-industrial (city), 1, 67
post-metropolis, 255
Post-modernism, 1, 20, 60, 67, 126, 199, 202, 227–228, 230, 232, 247, 252
Post-modernity, 234, *see also* Post-modernism
poverty, 1
Pred, A., 202, 249
prestige development, 7, 18, 57, 105, 129–148, 199–200, 298
production, 14–15
pro-growth coalition, *see* growth coalition, growth machine
promotion, 2, *see also* place marketing
property developers, 9, 18, 140–141, 161, 278
protest, 21, *see also* opposition
Proposition Thirteen, 104, 150, 154
psychoanalysis, 210
psychology, 22, 201
public art, 7, 201, 203–223, 310–311
public choice theory, 151–152
public–private partnership, 2, 8–9, 11, 57, 77, 88, 110, 116, 153, 256, 297

quality of life, 55–76, 137
Quebec, 44

race, 18, 311, *see also* ethnicity
Raissa, 317
Ramblas, 252
Rancho Mirage, 168
Reaganomics, 57, 294
reflexivity, 234, 252, 262, 271
regime theory, 9–10, 20, 151, 153–155, 171, 256, *see also* urban regime
regional class alliance, 14, 276, 278
Regional Economic Assistance, 183

regulation, 15, 17, 103, 108–109, 161 173–175, 255–256, 275, 281–282, 300
regulatory capacity, 17
Rennes, 303
rent gap, 155
representation, 21, 55–75, 199–202, 213–214, 281, 311
Republican Party, 155
research and development, 185–186, 189, 237
resistance, 222, *see also* opposition
resorts, 3, 9–41
retailing 113, 142, 156, 228, 248, 298
Rhodes, R., 271
Richardson, L., 249, 252
Riesa, 181–196
risk society, 85
Ritner, L., 213
Riverside City, 156, 162
Robins, K., 280
Rochester, 67
Rogers, R., 315
Roker, 220
Rouse Corporation, 219
Russia, 212
Rutheiser, C., 8, 12
Ryan, C., 60

St. Louis, 304
St. Peter's Riverside Sculpture Project, 220
Saatchi Gallery, 205
Sacremento, 204
Sadler, D., 60
Sadler's Wells, 138, 297
San Francisco, 125, 204, 299
Sassen, S., 215
Saunders, P., 13
Sayer, A., 3
Saxony, 176–179
scale, 3, 90–92, 97, 124–125, 257, 275–284
Schaefer, W., 105
Schumpeter, J.A., 78–79, 82–84, 86
Schumpeterian workfare state, 78, 108
Scotland, 31–32, 94
Segal, G., 206
sectoral shift, 287
selective incentive, 263
Selwood, S., 203, 206
Sennett, R., 211, 213
Serra, R., 204, 209
services, 134, 136
Seville, 5

sexuality, 1, 18, 85, 232, 250
Sheffield, 18, 21, 134–135, 299
Sheppard, E., 23, 258, 285–308
Shields, R., 202
shopping, *see* retailing
Short, J.R., 23, 29, 55–76
Sibley, D., 213
Silicon Valley, 287
Single Regeneration Budget, 105, 271
slogans, 61–62, 138, 192
Smith, A., 286
Smith, N., 183
Smith, S., 19
social control, 72–74, 218, 246
social equity, 124
social justice, 19
social polarisation, 2, 29, 148
socialism, 175
SoHo, 226–227
Soja, E., 255, 258
South Bank Arts Centre, 208
Southern California, 103–104, 149–172
Soviet bloc, 295
Spain, 246
spatial division of labour, 16, 80, 177, 275
spectacle, 20, 55, 92, 246
state, 13–14, 17, 22, 88, 108–110,
    122–124, 174, *see also* welfare state
state socialism, 105, 173–198
Stewart, T., 130, 144–145, 147
Stockholm, 297
Stoker, G., 20
Stone, C., 9, 262–263, 271
suburban entrepreneurialism, 149–171,
    see also suburbs
suburbs, 41–44, 50, 95
Sunderland, 95, 203, 212, 215–221
Sunrise Company, 161
Sunterra, 161
sustainability, 116, 125–126, 203–224, 316
Swansea, 215
Sweden, 34
Swindon, 6
Swyngedouw, E., 257, 280
Sydney, 7, 113, 125
symbolic goods, 233–234

Taylor, Ian, 21
Taylor, W., 211
Taylorism, 177
Tax Increment Financing, 140–150, 156,
    159–161

text, 202, 247
Thatcher, M., 203
Thatcherism, 34, 57, 77, 229–230
thick description, 246
Third Italy, 89
Thrift, N., 251, 270, 281
Tickell, A., 58, 280–281
time–space compression, 16
territory, 3
territorial alliance,
territorial competition, 168–169, *see also*
    inter-urban competition
Tokyo, 6
Toronto, 11, 37
Toxteth, 214
tourism, 112–113, 136
Training Enterprise Councils, 235
transport, 35–37, 40–44, 121, 132, 137,
    288
trickle-down theory, 19–20, 118, 200
Tuscany, 211
Trustee Savings Bank, 217

Ukeles, M., 223
underclass, 19, 251
United Kingdom, 301
United States, 9, 11, 19, 28–29, 31–54,
    55–75, 149–151, 170, 204, 294,
    296–299, 304
University of Central England, 146
University of the First Age, 146, 314
University of Westminster, 204
urban boosterism, *see* civic boosterism
urban coalitions, 9–12, 48, 88, 200, *see*
    also urban regime
urban decline, 107–128
urban design, 7–8, 140, *see also*
    landscape, architecture
urban entrepreneurialism, *see* urban
    governance, new urban politics
urban governance, 8–18, 149, 179, 255,
    261, 293–295, 316
urban hierarchy, 38, 85, 111, 174, 297
urban managerialism, 14, 129, 173, 269,
    see also urban governance
urban political economy, 22, 55, 255
urban politics, *see* governance, new urban
    politics
Urban Programme, 204
urban regime, 9–12, 16, 57, 111, 150, 255,
    259–274, 277, 297, 311
urban renewal, 149

urban representation, *see* representation
urbanisation, 12, 28, 87
urbanism, 106
Urry, J., 288
Utah, 169
utopia, 211, 213, 245

van Brugen, C., 209
van Maanen, J., 243, 249
Vancouver, 7, 11, 105
Veltz, P., 84
Victoria Square, 144, 216
videos, 7, 200, 298
Vienna, 317

Wakefield, 217
Wales, 31, 94, 204
Ward, S., 23, 29, 31–54
waterfront development, 1, 18, 86,
    112–114, 125, 227, 242, 248
welfare, 6, 11, 13, 15, 19, 72, 297
welfare state, 14–15, *see also* Keynesian
    welfare state

Wernick, A., 61
West Germany, 175–179
West Midlands, 95, 131–132, 142, 217
Westphalia, 180
Whitewater Redevelopment Project Area,
    161
Whyte, W.H., 206, 249
Wilbourne, C., 220
Williams, R., 61
Wilson, P., 156
Winchester, H.P.M., 107–128
Wisconsin, 35, 204
women, *see* gender
Wood, A., 257, 275–284
world cities, 67, 86
World Expos, 8, 105
World Wide Web, 298
Wright, P., 244
writing, 72–73, 202, 241–252

zero-sum game, 286
Zukin, S., 201, 205, 218, 226–230, 231,
    233